This is the back of the boo

You're looking at the last page of the book, not the first one.

PERSONA 4 is a comic series originally published in Japan. Japanese co (known as "manga") are traditionally read from right to left, the rever most English comics.

In this English edition, the Japanese format has been left intact. Check example below to see how to read the word balloons in the proper ord

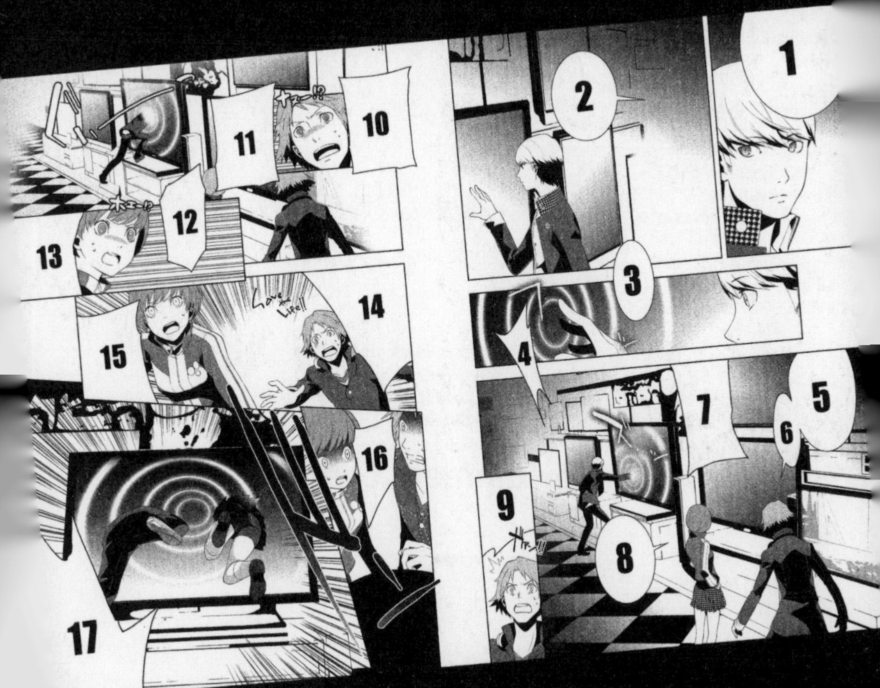
1
2
3
4
5
6
7
8
9
10
11
12
13
14
15
16
17

book and enjoy PERSONA 4!

Persona 4

*Vol.2: Shuji SOGABE /ATLUS

ENGLISH EDITION
Translation: M. KIRIE HAYASHI
Lettering: MARSHALL DILLON

UDON STAFF
Chief of Operations: ERIK KO
Director of Publishing: MATT MOYLAN
Senior Editor: ASH PAULSEN
VP of Sales: JOHN SHABLESKI
Senior Producer: LONG VO
Marketing Manager: JENNY MYUNG
Production Manager: JANICE LEUNG
Japanese Liaison: STEVEN CUMMINGS

PERSONA 4 Volume 2
©ATLUS ©SEGA All Rights Reserved.
©Shuji SOGABE 2010
Edited by ASCII MEDIA WORKS
First published in 2010 by KADOKAWA CORPORATION, Tokyo.
English translation rights arranged with KADOKAWA CORPORATION, Tokyo.

English language version published by UDON Entertainment Inc.
118 Tower Hill Road, C1, PO Box 20008
Richmond Hill, Ontario, L4K 0K0 CANADA

www.UDONentertainment.com

BISAC:
CGN004100 *COMICS & GRAPHIC NOVELS / Manga / Crime & Mystery*
CGN004160 *COMICS & GRAPHIC NOVELS / Manga / Media Tie-In*
GAM013000 *GAMES / Video & Electronic*

First Printing: February 2016
ISBN-13: 978-1-927925-66-9
ISBN-10: 1-927925-66-5

Printed in the United States

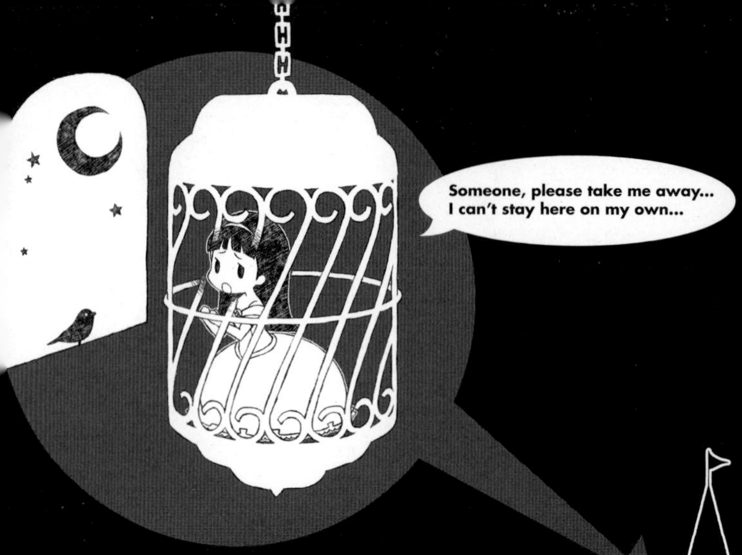
Someone, please take me away...
I can't stay here on my own...

II Persona4

#Vol.2: Shuji SOGABE / ATLUS

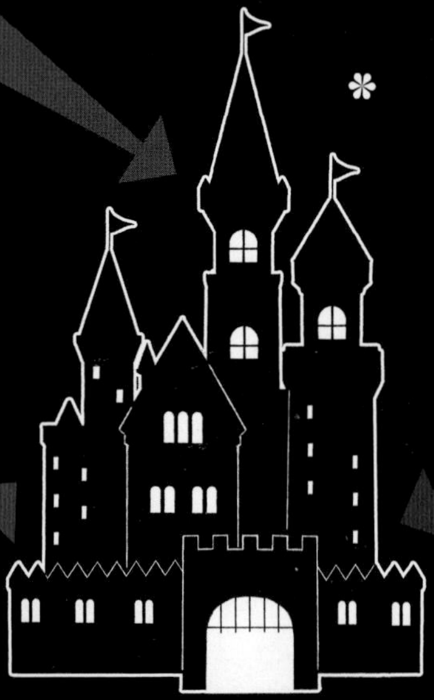

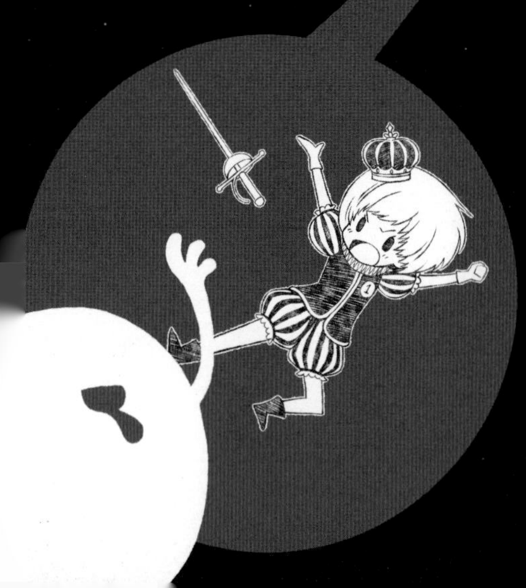

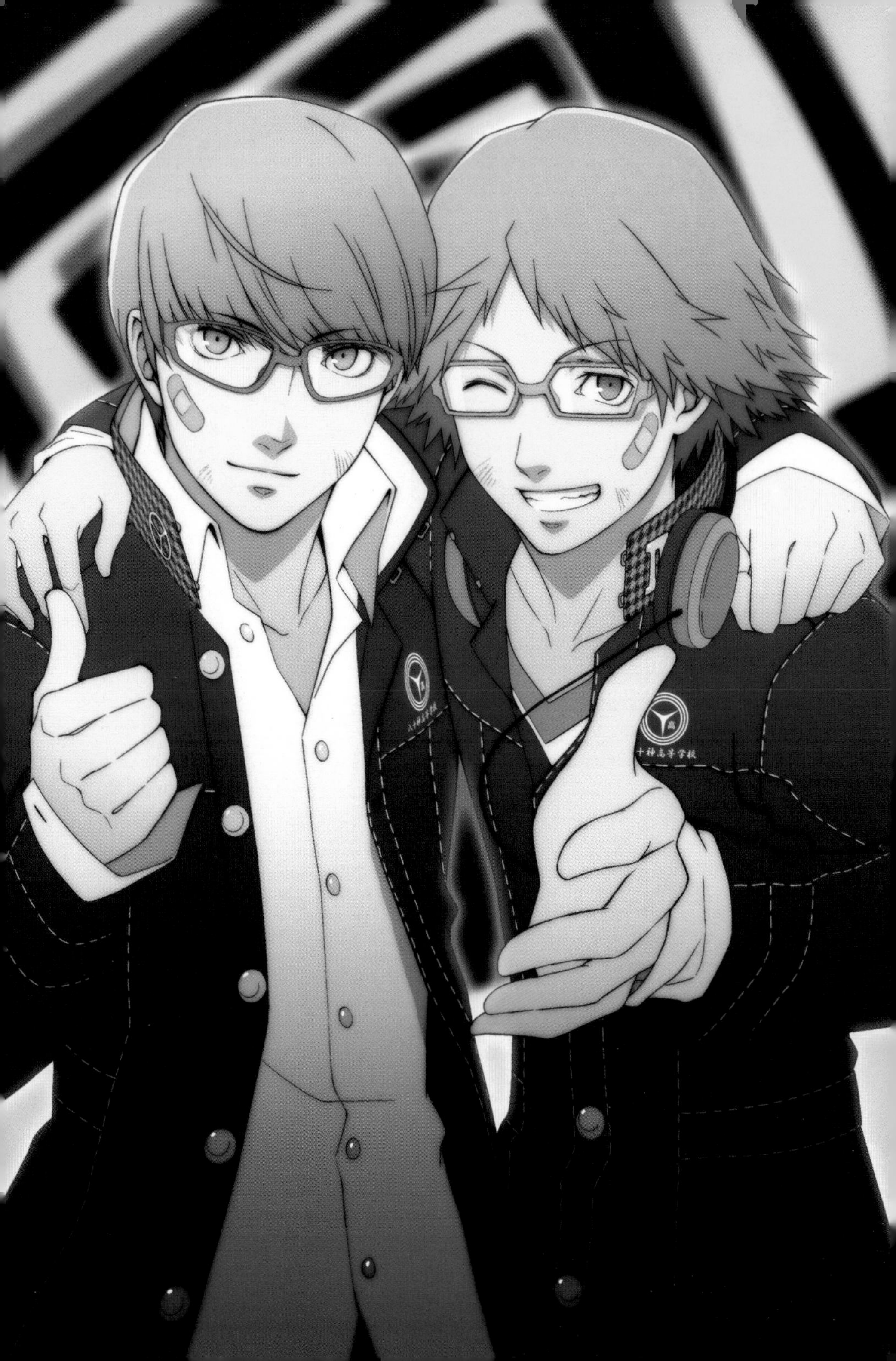

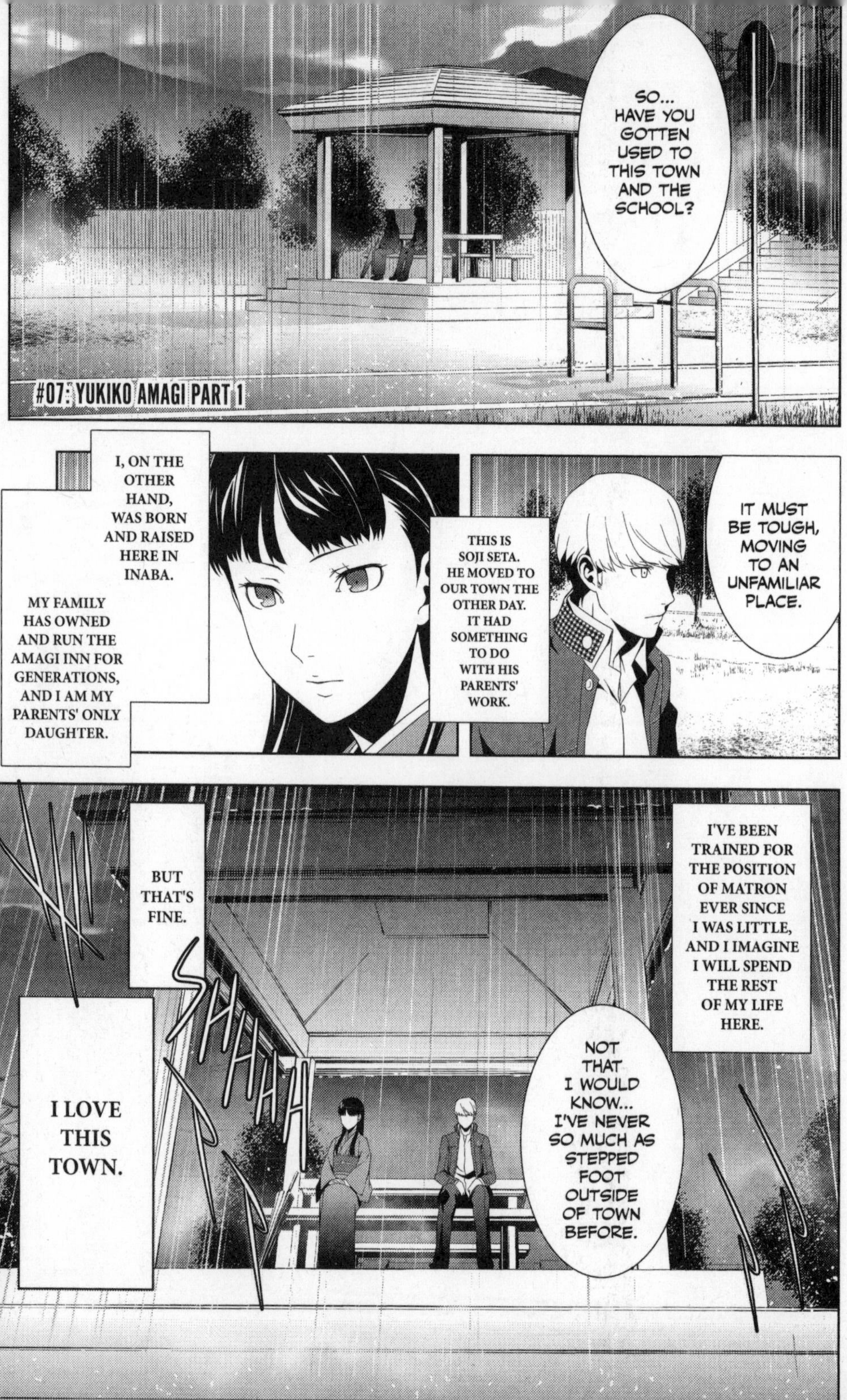
SO... HAVE YOU GOTTEN USED TO THIS TOWN AND THE SCHOOL?
#07: YUKIKO AMAGI PART 1
IT MUST BE TOUGH, MOVING TO AN UNFAMILIAR PLACE.
THIS IS SOJI SETA. HE MOVED TO OUR TOWN THE OTHER DAY. IT HAD SOMETHING TO DO WITH HIS PARENTS' WORK.
I, ON THE OTHER HAND, WAS BORN AND RAISED HERE IN INABA.
MY FAMILY HAS OWNED AND RUN THE AMAGI INN FOR GENERATIONS, AND I AM MY PARENTS' ONLY DAUGHTER.
I'VE BEEN TRAINED FOR THE POSITION OF MATRON EVER SINCE I WAS LITTLE, AND I IMAGINE I WILL SPEND THE REST OF MY LIFE HERE.
NOT THAT I WOULD KNOW... I'VE NEVER SO MUCH AS STEPPED FOOT OUTSIDE OF TOWN BEFORE.
BUT THAT'S FINE.
I LOVE THIS TOWN.

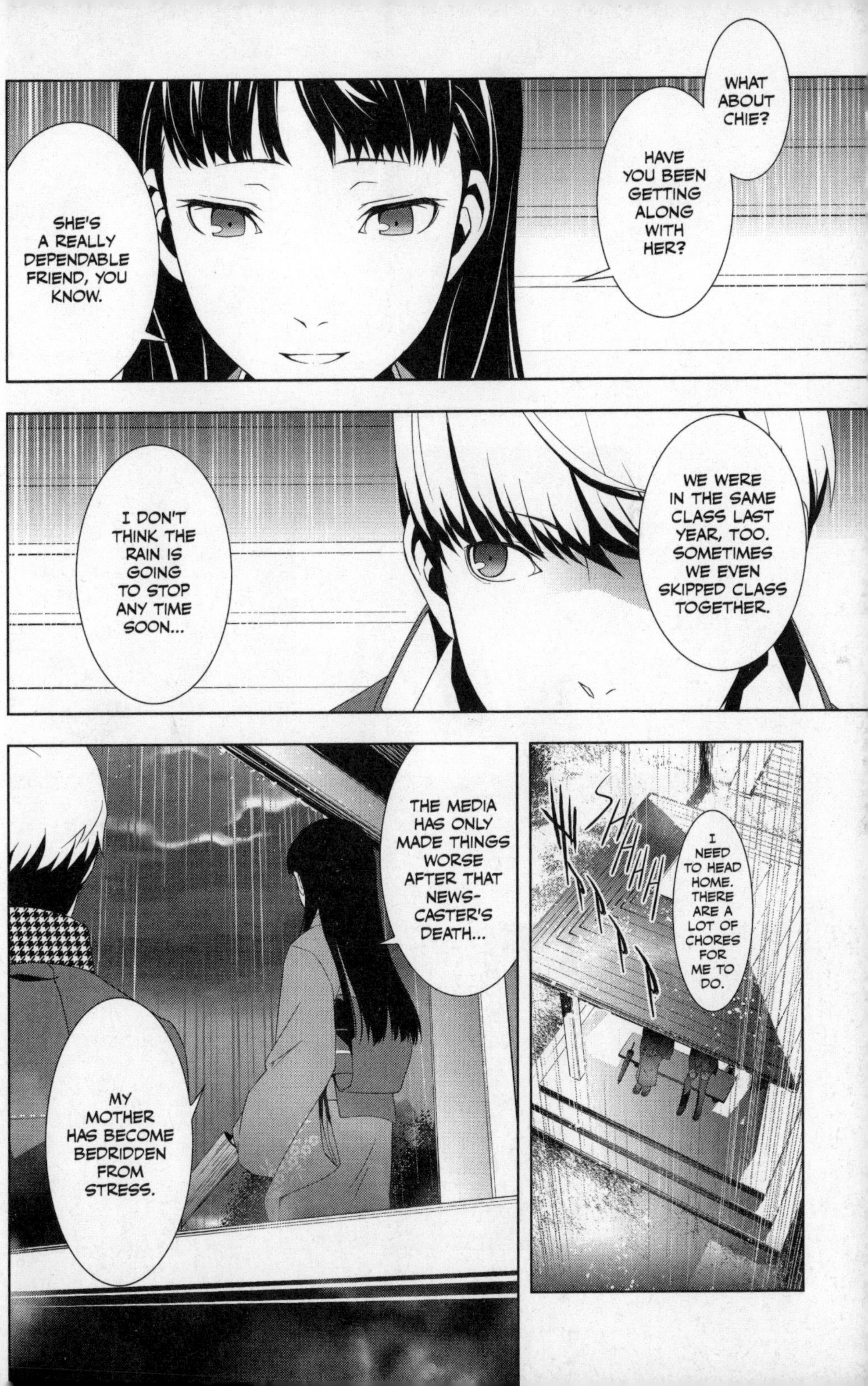
WHAT ABOUT CHIE?
HAVE YOU BEEN GETTING ALONG WITH HER?
SHE'S A REALLY DEPENDABLE FRIEND, YOU KNOW.
WE WERE IN THE SAME CLASS LAST YEAR, TOO. SOMETIMES WE EVEN SKIPPED CLASS TOGETHER.
I DON'T THINK THE RAIN IS GOING TO STOP ANY TIME SOON...
SHHHH
I NEED TO HEAD HOME. THERE ARE A LOT OF CHORES FOR ME TO DO.
THE MEDIA HAS ONLY MADE THINGS WORSE AFTER THAT NEWS-CASTER'S DEATH...
MY MOTHER HAS BECOME BEDRIDDEN FROM STRESS.

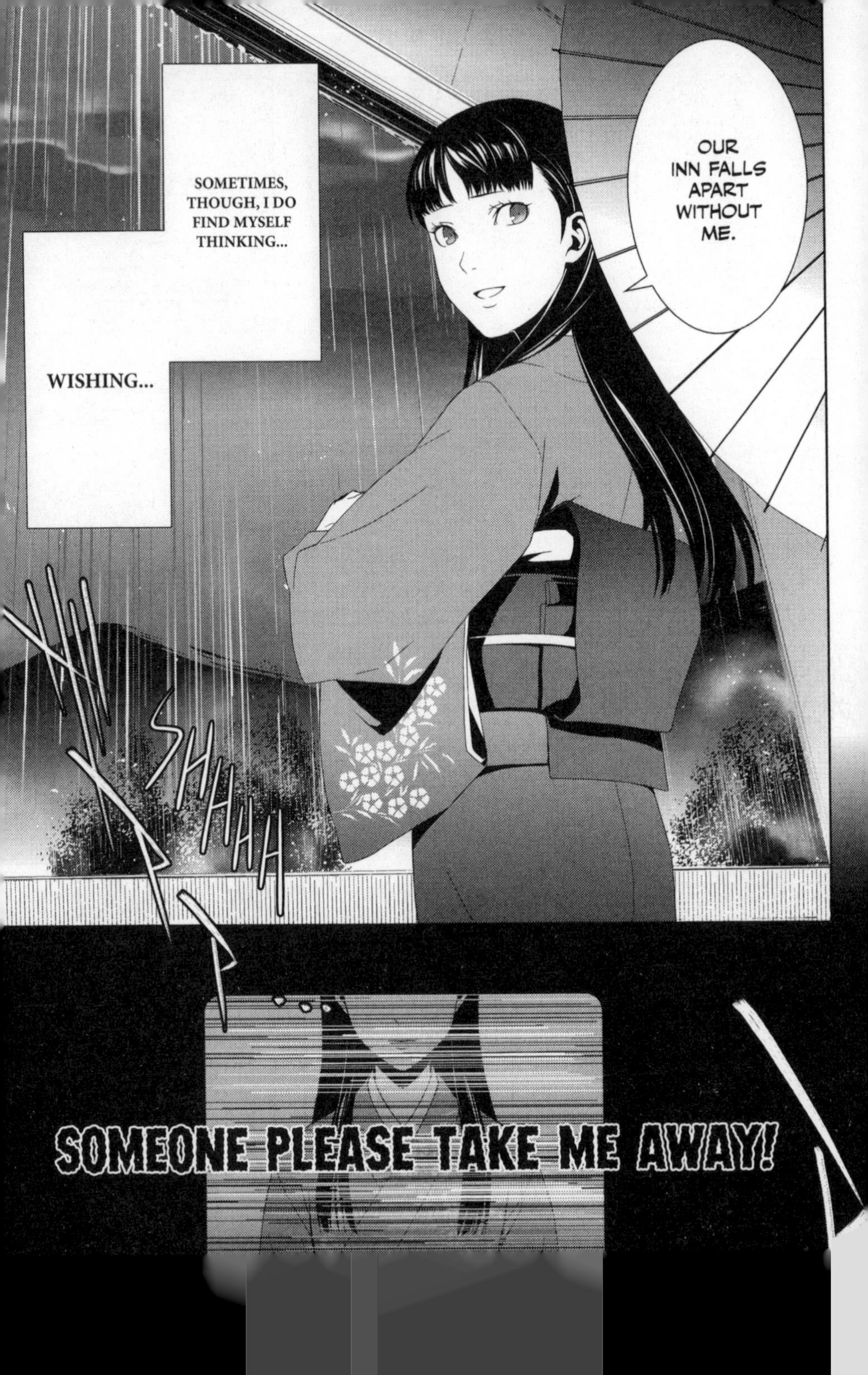
OUR INN FALLS APART WITHOUT ME.
SOMETIMES, THOUGH, I DO FIND MYSELF THINKING...
WISHING...
SHHHHH
SOMEONE PLEASE TAKE ME AWAY!

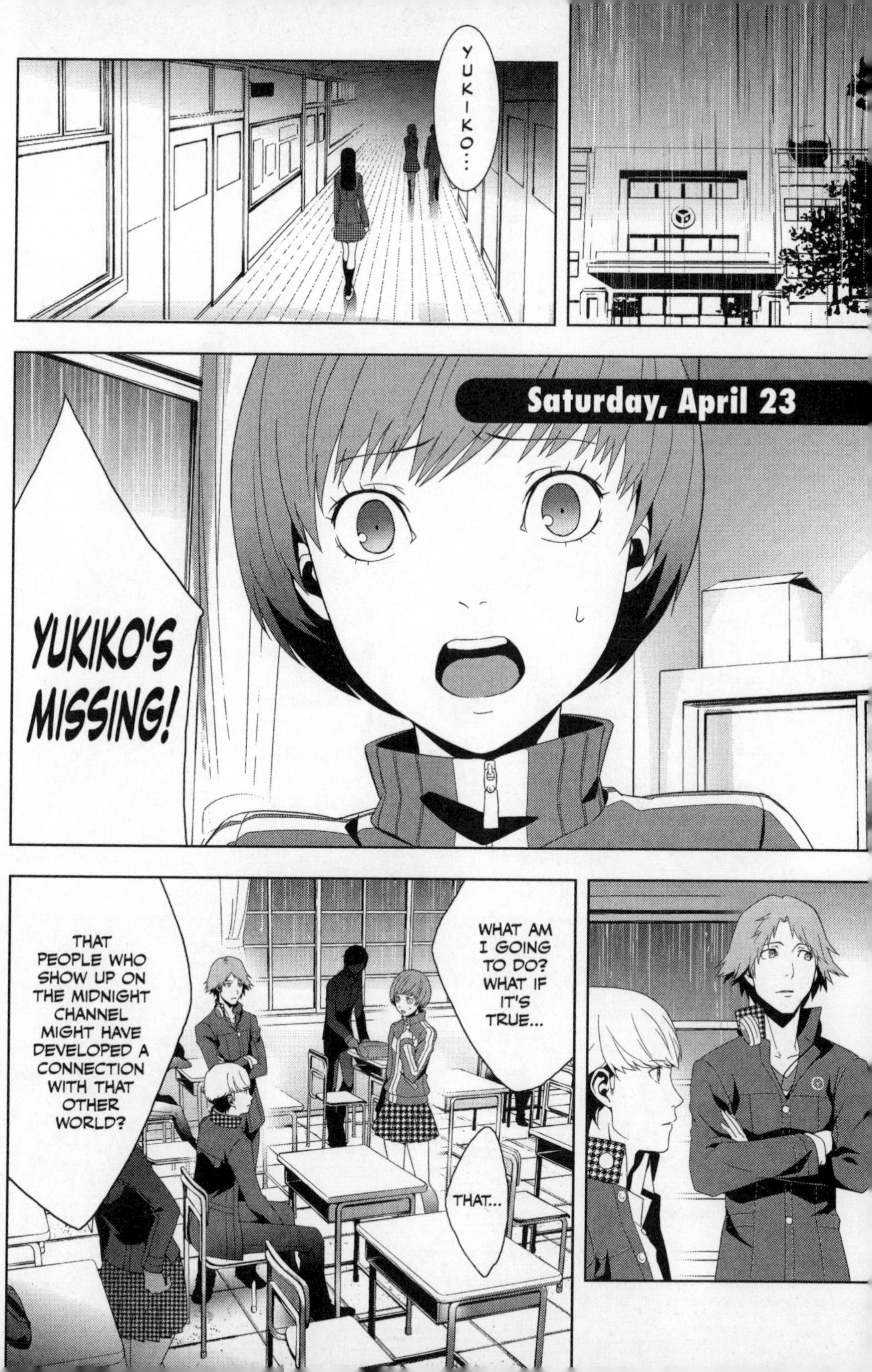
YUKIKO...
Saturday, April 23
YUKIKO'S MISSING!
WHAT AM I GOING TO DO? WHAT IF IT'S TRUE...
THAT PEOPLE WHO SHOW UP ON THE MIDNIGHT CHANNEL MIGHT HAVE DEVELOPED A CONNECTION WITH THAT OTHER WORLD?
THAT...

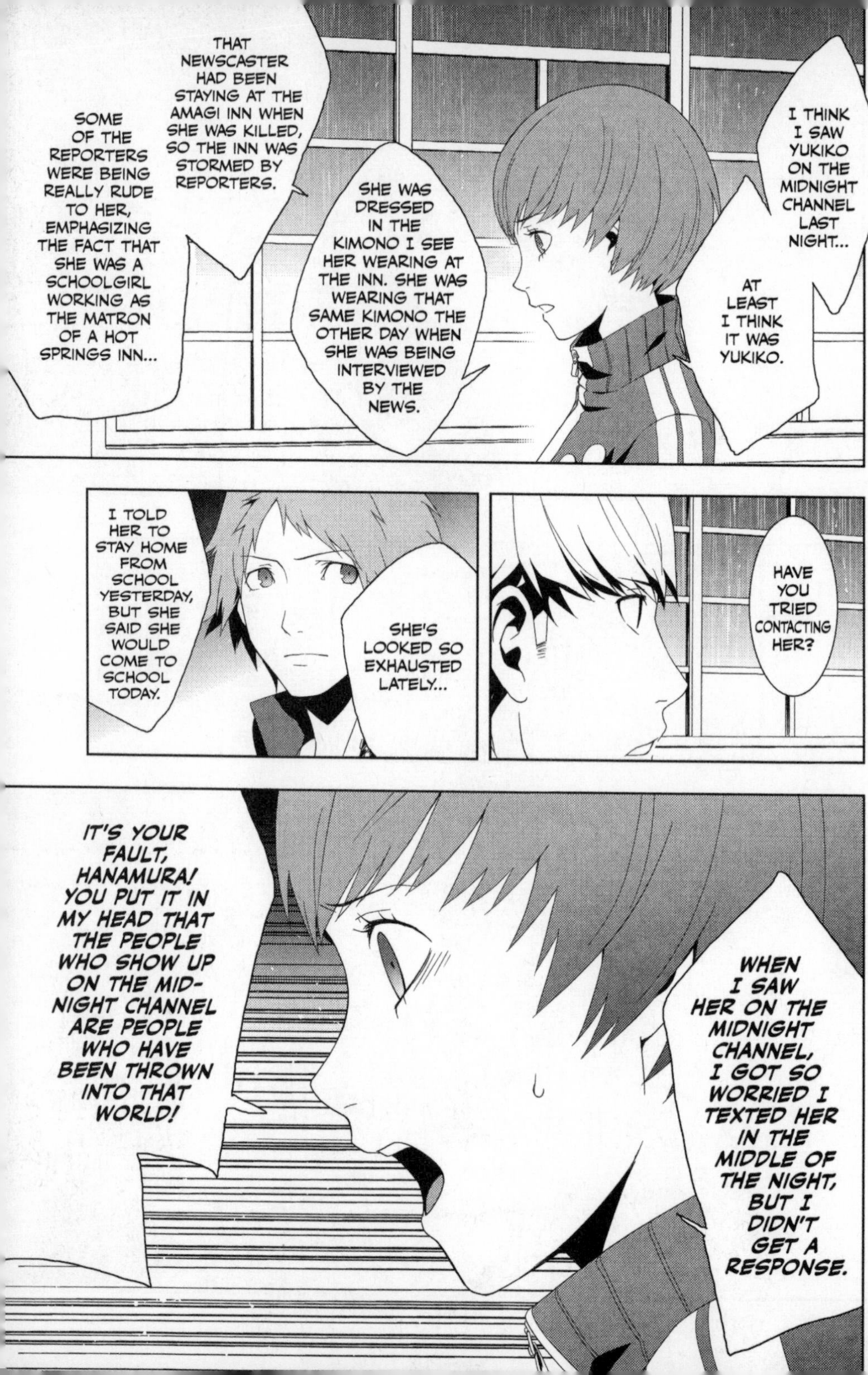
I THINK I SAW YUKIKO ON THE MIDNIGHT CHANNEL LAST NIGHT...
AT LEAST I THINK IT WAS YUKIKO.
SHE WAS DRESSED IN THE KIMONO I SEE HER WEARING AT THE INN. SHE WAS WEARING THAT SAME KIMONO THE OTHER DAY WHEN SHE WAS BEING INTERVIEWED BY THE NEWS.
THAT NEWSCASTER HAD BEEN STAYING AT THE AMAGI INN WHEN SHE WAS KILLED, SO THE INN WAS STORMED BY REPORTERS.
SOME OF THE REPORTERS WERE BEING REALLY RUDE TO HER, EMPHASIZING THE FACT THAT SHE WAS A SCHOOLGIRL WORKING AS THE MATRON OF A HOT SPRINGS INN...
HAVE YOU TRIED CONTACTING HER?
SHE'S LOOKED SO EXHAUSTED LATELY...
I TOLD HER TO STAY HOME FROM SCHOOL YESTERDAY, BUT SHE SAID SHE WOULD COME TO SCHOOL TODAY.
WHEN I SAW HER ON THE MIDNIGHT CHANNEL, I GOT SO WORRIED I TEXTED HER IN THE MIDDLE OF THE NIGHT, BUT I DIDN'T GET A RESPONSE.
IT'S YOUR FAULT, HANAMURA! YOU PUT IT IN MY HEAD THAT THE PEOPLE WHO SHOW UP ON THE MID-NIGHT CHANNEL ARE PEOPLE WHO HAVE BEEN THROWN INTO THAT WORLD!

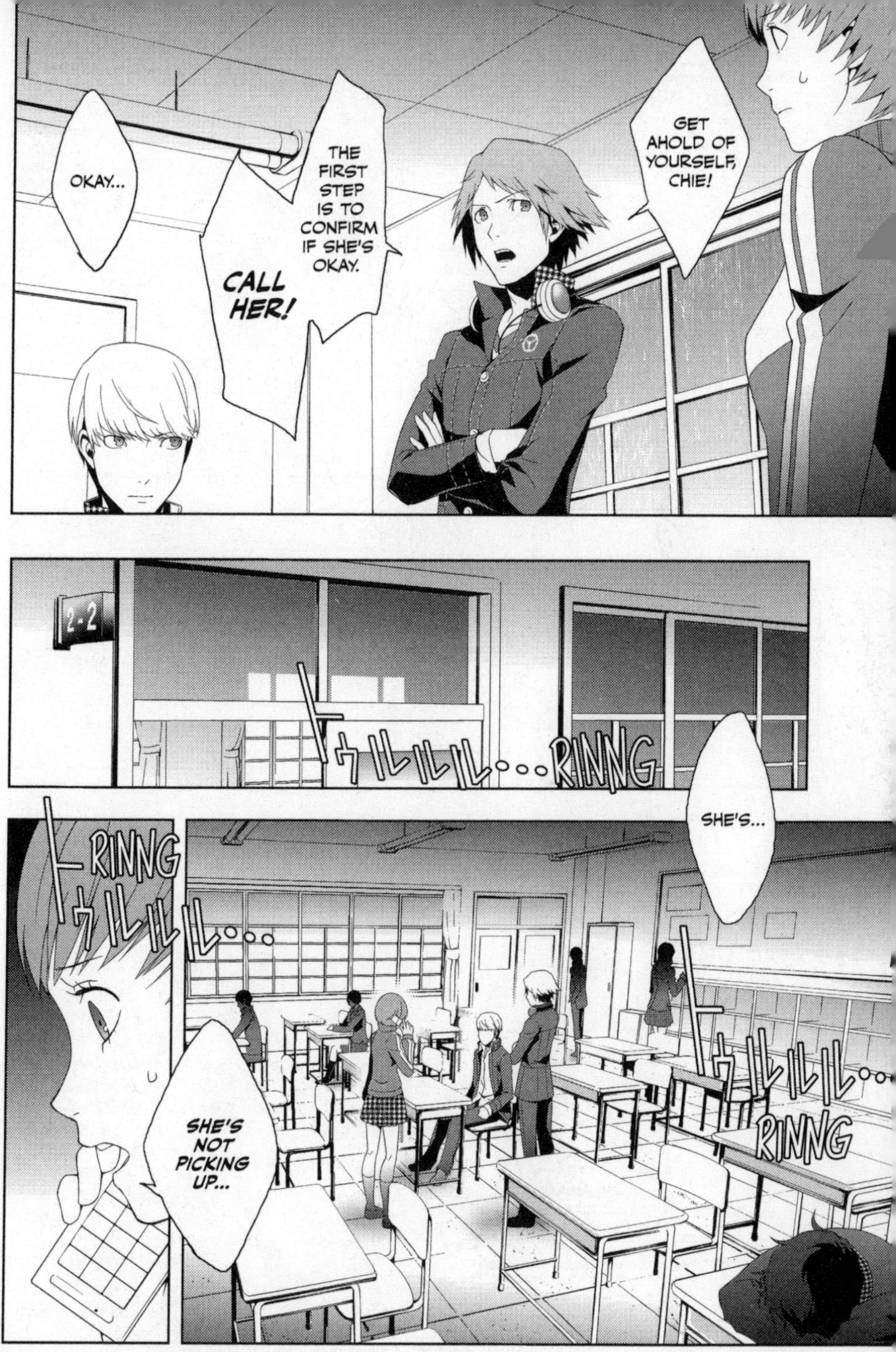
GET AHOLD OF YOURSELF, CHIE!
THE FIRST STEP IS TO CONFIRM IF SHE'S OKAY.
CALL HER!
OKAY...
トゥルルル…RINNG
SHE'S...
トゥルルル…RINNG
トゥルルル…RINNG
SHE'S NOT PICKING UP...

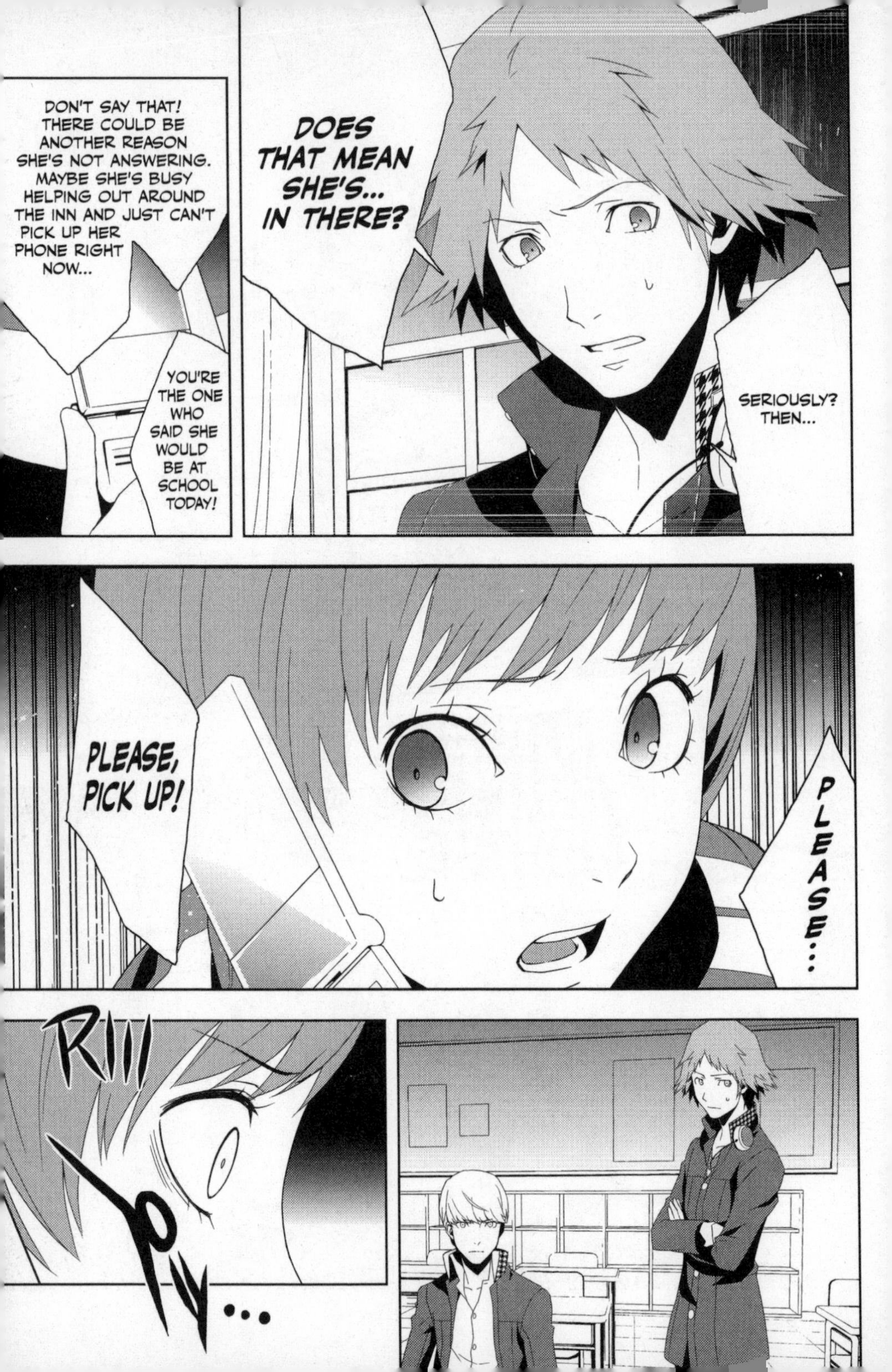
SERIOUSLY? THEN...
DOES THAT MEAN SHE'S... IN THERE?
DON'T SAY THAT! THERE COULD BE ANOTHER REASON SHE'S NOT ANSWERING. MAYBE SHE'S BUSY HELPING OUT AROUND THE INN AND JUST CAN'T PICK UP HER PHONE RIGHT NOW...
YOU'RE THE ONE WHO SAID SHE WOULD BE AT SCHOOL TODAY!
PLEASE...
PLEASE, PICK UP!
RIII PY...

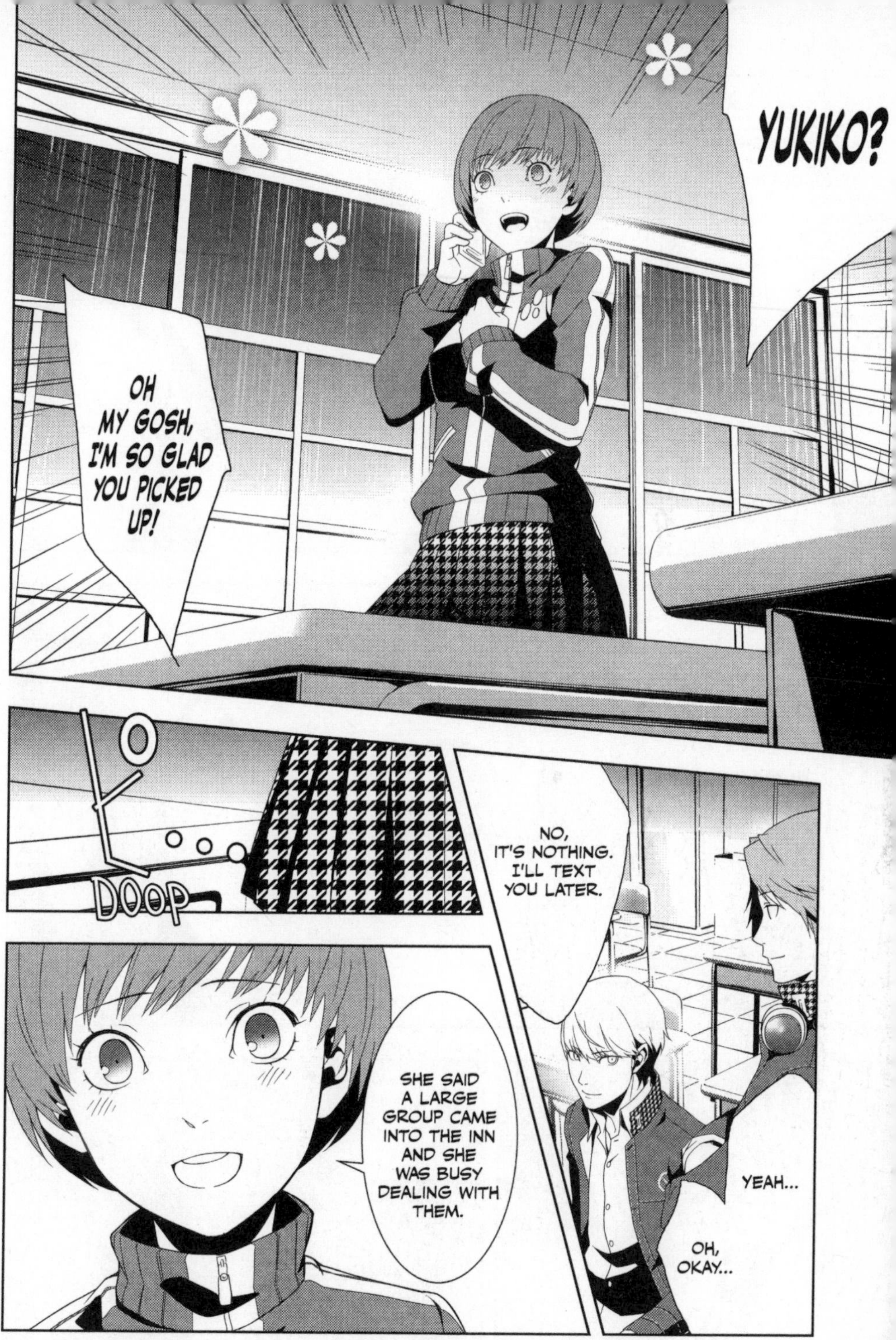
YUKIKO?
OH MY GOSH, I'M SO GLAD YOU PICKED UP!
NO, IT'S NOTHING. I'LL TEXT YOU LATER.
YEAH...
OH, OKAY...
DOOP
SHE SAID A LARGE GROUP CAME INTO THE INN AND SHE WAS BUSY DEALING WITH THEM.

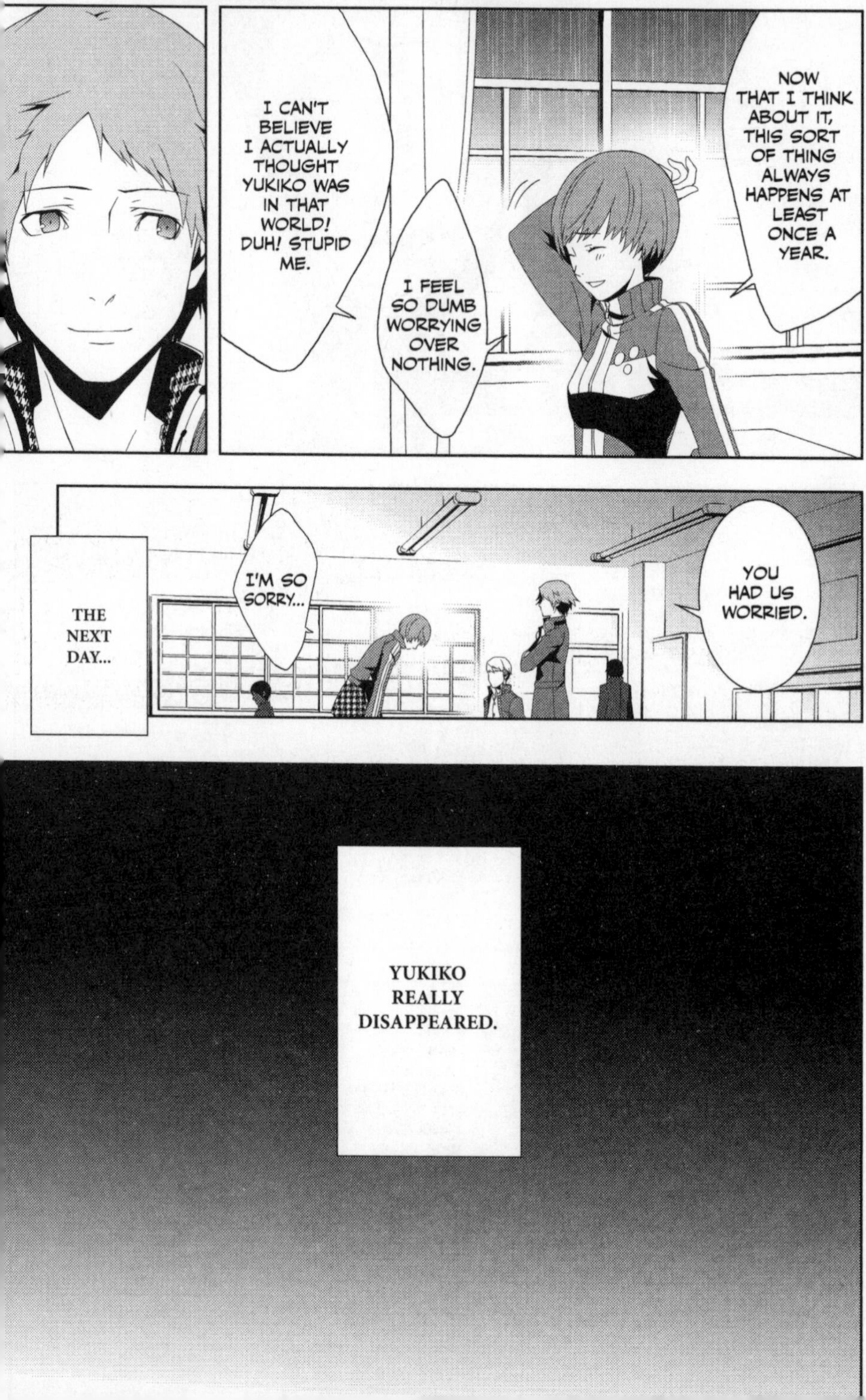
NOW THAT I THINK ABOUT IT, THIS SORT OF THING ALWAYS HAPPENS AT LEAST ONCE A YEAR.
I FEEL SO DUMB WORRYING OVER NOTHING.
I CAN'T BELIEVE I ACTUALLY THOUGHT YUKIKO WAS IN THAT WORLD! DUH! STUPID ME.
YOU HAD US WORRIED.
I'M SO SORRY...
THE NEXT DAY...
YUKIKO REALLY DISAPPEARED.

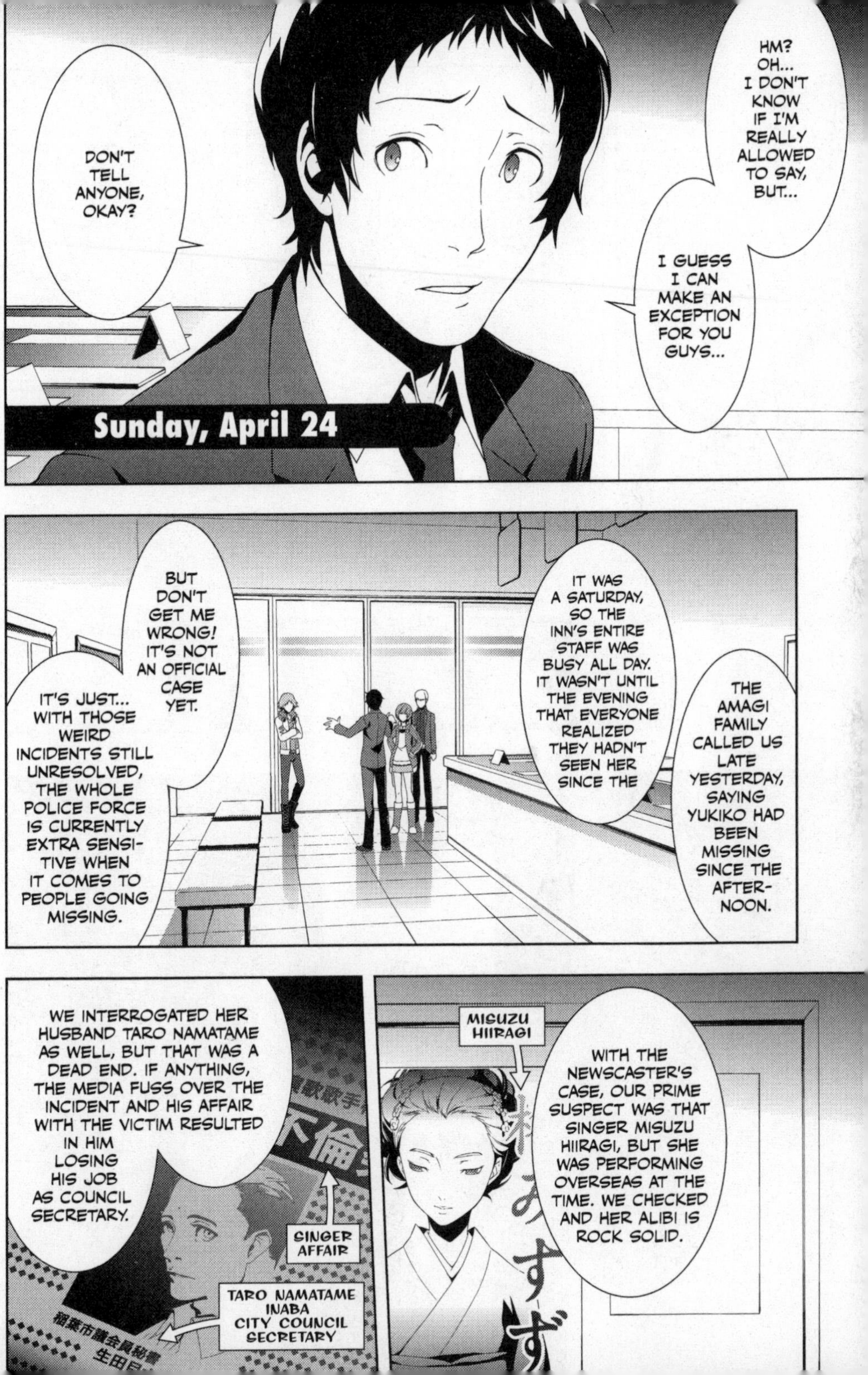
HM? OH... I DON'T KNOW IF I'M REALLY ALLOWED TO SAY, BUT...
I GUESS I CAN MAKE AN EXCEPTION FOR YOU GUYS...
DON'T TELL ANYONE, OKAY?
Sunday, April 24
THE AMAGI FAMILY CALLED US LATE YESTERDAY, SAYING YUKIKO HAD BEEN MISSING SINCE THE AFTER-NOON.
IT WAS A SATURDAY, SO THE INN'S ENTIRE STAFF WAS BUSY ALL DAY. IT WASN'T UNTIL THE EVENING THAT EVERYONE REALIZED THEY HADN'T SEEN HER SINCE THE
BUT DON'T GET ME WRONG! IT'S NOT AN OFFICIAL CASE YET.
IT'S JUST... WITH THOSE WEIRD INCIDENTS STILL UNRESOLVED, THE WHOLE POLICE FORCE IS CURRENTLY EXTRA SENSI-TIVE WHEN IT COMES TO PEOPLE GOING MISSING.
MISUZU HIIRAGI
WITH THE NEWSCASTER'S CASE, OUR PRIME SUSPECT WAS THAT SINGER MISUZU HIIRAGI, BUT SHE WAS PERFORMING OVERSEAS AT THE TIME. WE CHECKED AND HER ALIBI IS ROCK SOLID.
WE INTERROGATED HER HUSBAND TARO NAMATAME AS WELL, BUT THAT WAS A DEAD END. IF ANYTHING, THE MEDIA FUSS OVER THE INCIDENT AND HIS AFFAIR WITH THE VICTIM RESULTED IN HIM LOSING HIS JOB AS COUNCIL SECRETARY.
SINGER AFFAIR
TARO NAMATAME INABA CITY COUNCIL SECRETARY

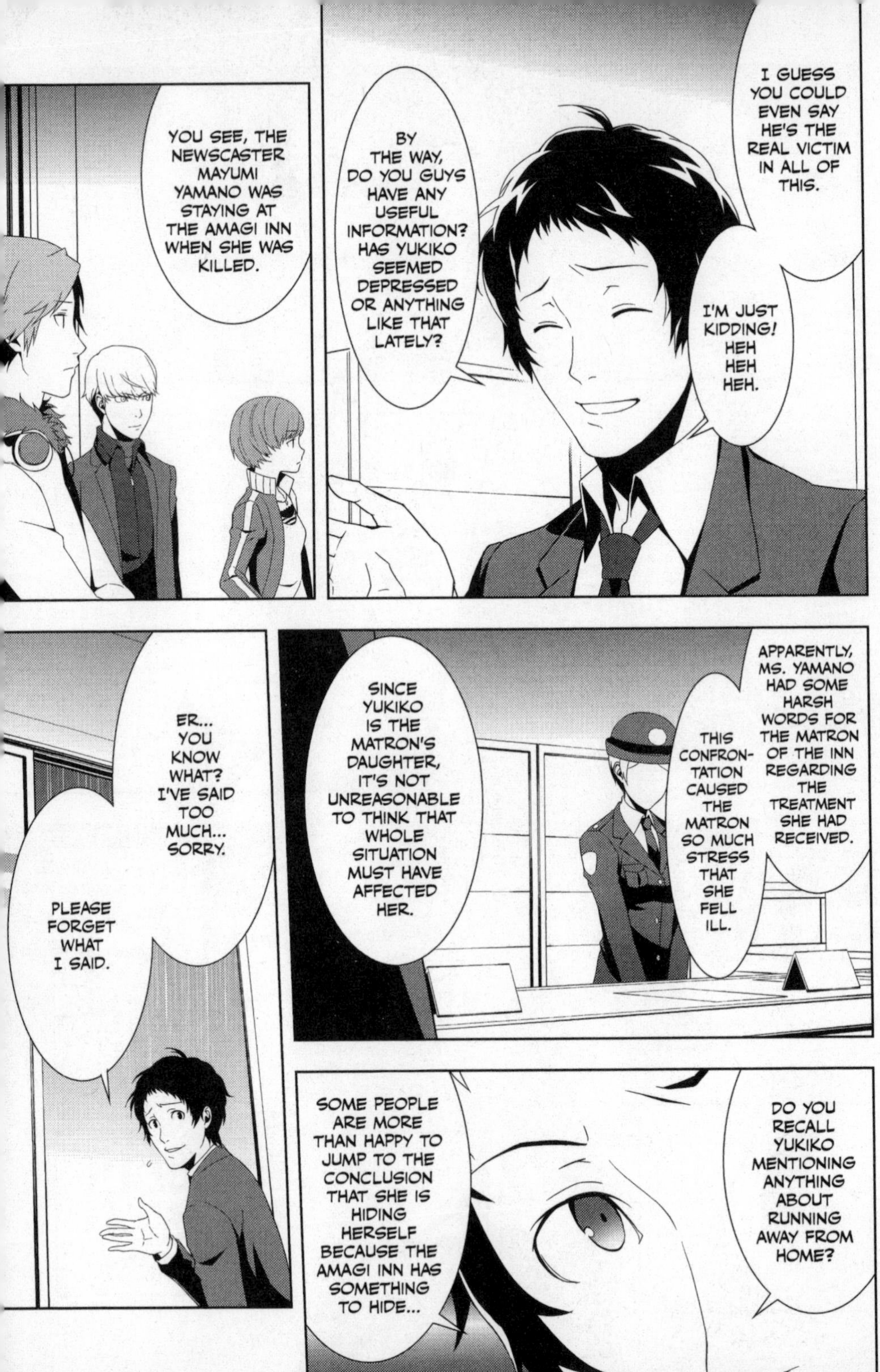
I GUESS YOU COULD EVEN SAY HE'S THE REAL VICTIM IN ALL OF THIS.
I'M JUST KIDDING! HEH HEH HEH.
BY THE WAY, DO YOU GUYS HAVE ANY USEFUL INFORMATION? HAS YUKIKO SEEMED DEPRESSED OR ANYTHING LIKE THAT LATELY?
YOU SEE, THE NEWSCASTER MAYUMI YAMANO WAS STAYING AT THE AMAGI INN WHEN SHE WAS KILLED.
APPARENTLY, MS. YAMANO HAD SOME HARSH WORDS FOR THE MATRON OF THE INN REGARDING THE TREATMENT SHE HAD RECEIVED.
THIS CONFRONTATION CAUSED THE MATRON SO MUCH STRESS THAT SHE FELL ILL.
SINCE YUKIKO IS THE MATRON'S DAUGHTER, IT'S NOT UNREASONABLE TO THINK THAT WHOLE SITUATION MUST HAVE AFFECTED HER.
DO YOU RECALL YUKIKO MENTIONING ANYTHING ABOUT RUNNING AWAY FROM HOME?
SOME PEOPLE ARE MORE THAN HAPPY TO JUMP TO THE CONCLUSION THAT SHE IS HIDING HERSELF BECAUSE THE AMAGI INN HAS SOMETHING TO HIDE...
ER... YOU KNOW WHAT? I'VE SAID TOO MUCH... SORRY.
PLEASE FORGET WHAT I SAID.

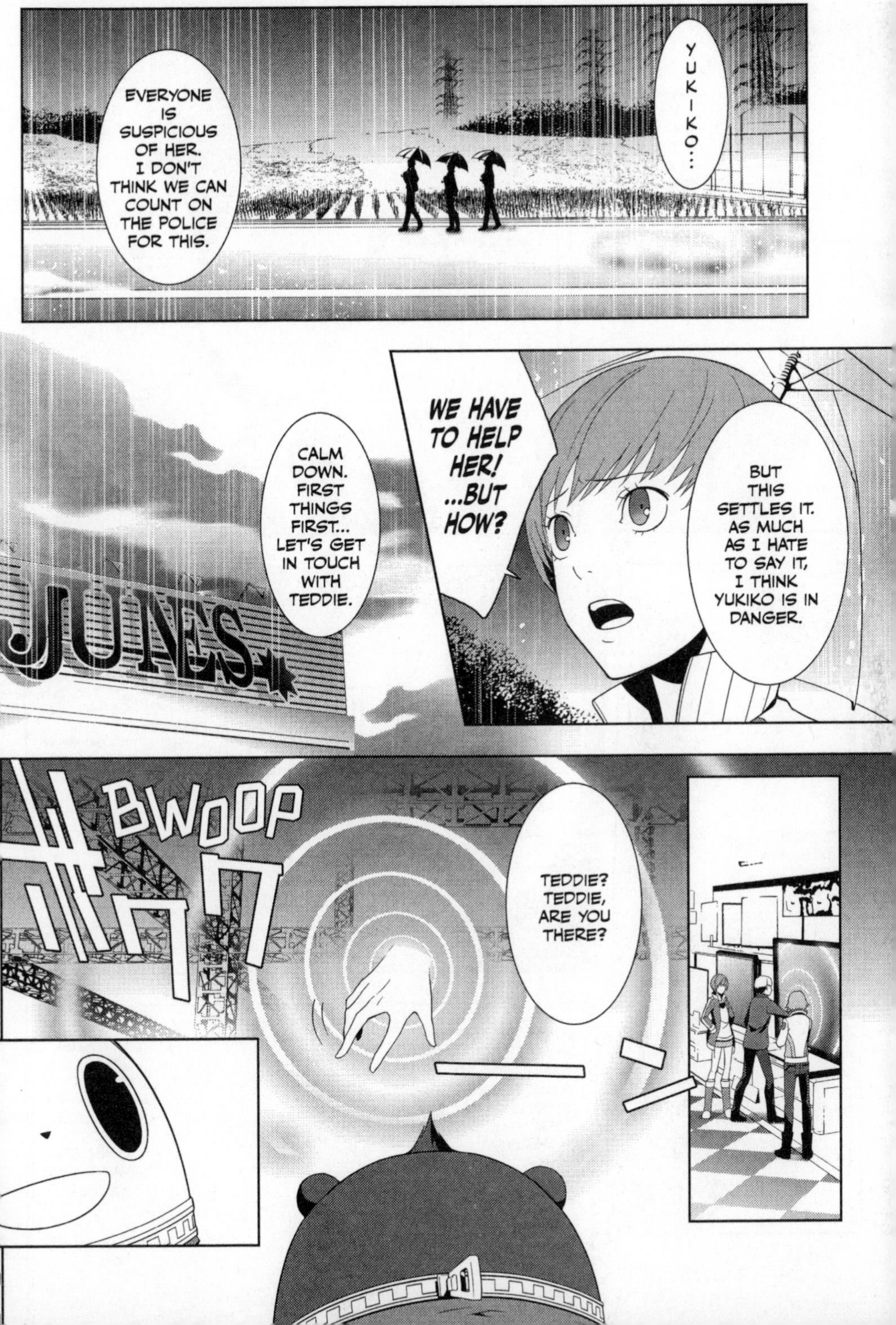
YUKIKO...
EVERYONE IS SUSPICIOUS OF HER. I DON'T THINK WE CAN COUNT ON THE POLICE FOR THIS.
JUNES
BUT THIS SETTLES IT. AS MUCH AS I HATE TO SAY IT, I THINK YUKIKO IS IN DANGER.
WE HAVE TO HELP HER! ...BUT HOW?
CALM DOWN. FIRST THINGS FIRST... LET'S GET IN TOUCH WITH TEDDIE.
TEDDIE? TEDDIE, ARE YOU THERE?
BWOOP

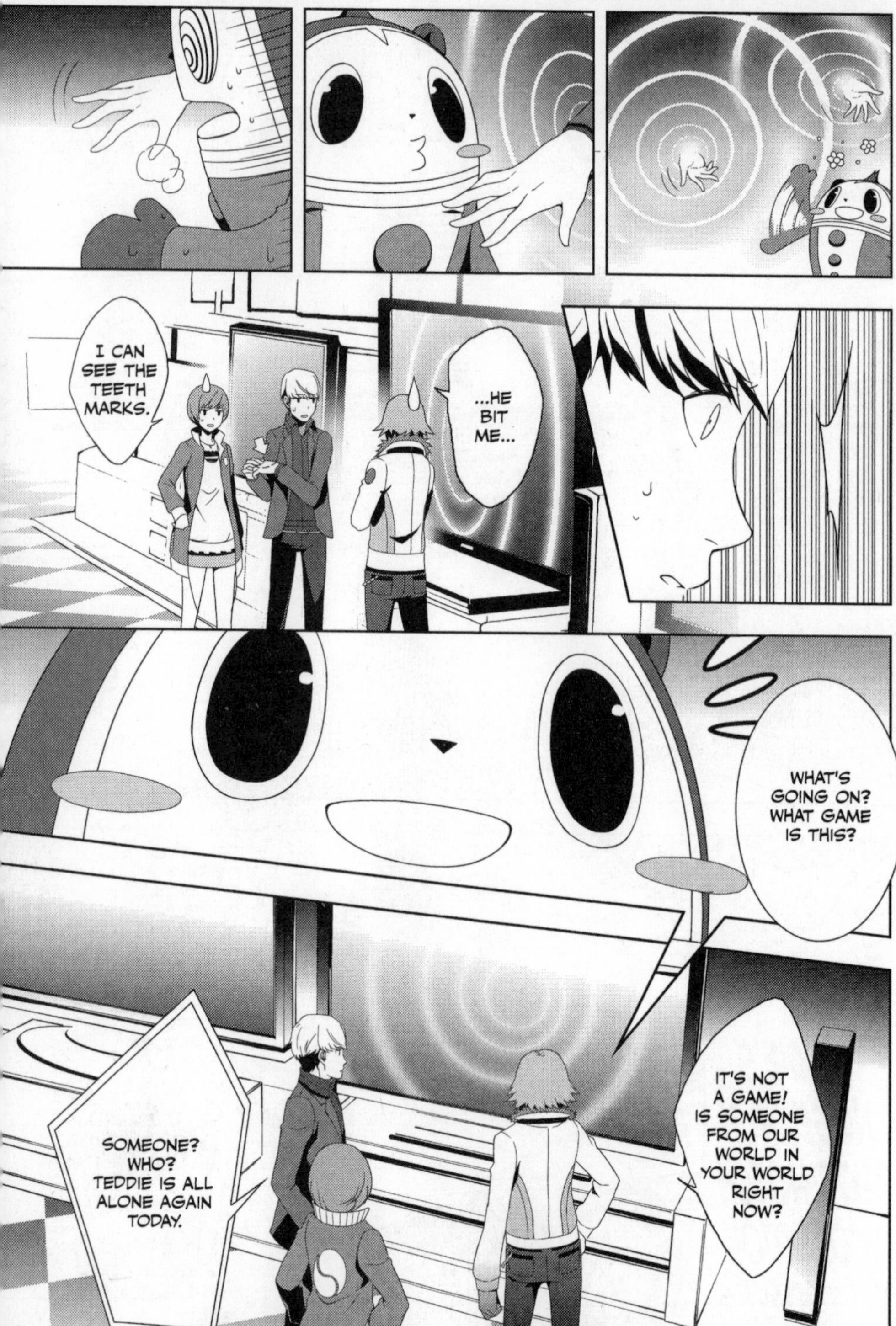
...HE BIT ME...
I CAN SEE THE TEETH MARKS.
WHAT'S GOING ON? WHAT GAME IS THIS?
IT'S NOT A GAME! IS SOMEONE FROM OUR WORLD IN YOUR WORLD RIGHT NOW?
SOMEONE? WHO? TEDDIE IS ALL ALONE AGAIN TODAY.

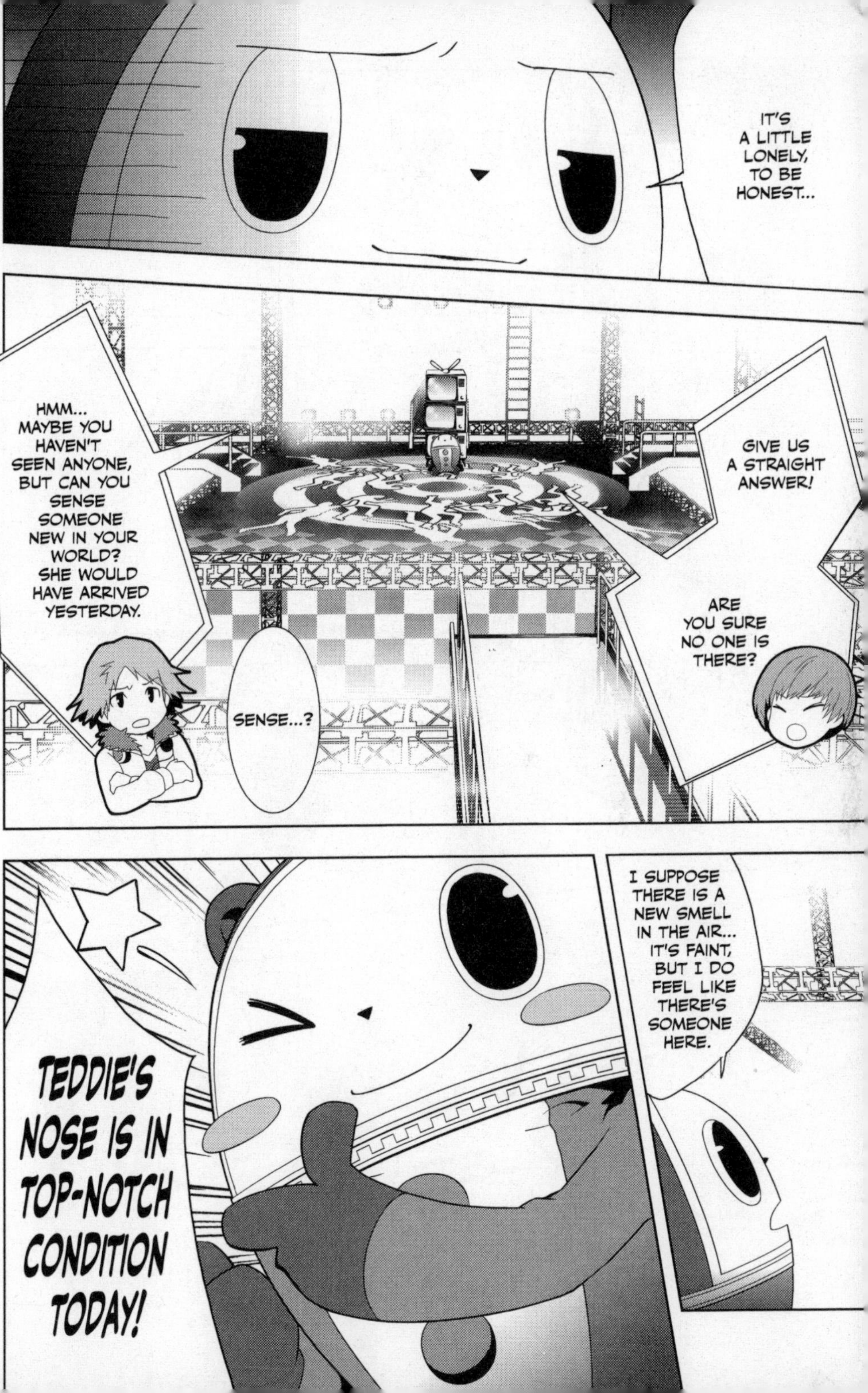
IT'S A LITTLE LONELY, TO BE HONEST...
GIVE US A STRAIGHT ANSWER!
ARE YOU SURE NO ONE IS THERE?
HMM... MAYBE YOU HAVEN'T SEEN ANYONE, BUT CAN YOU SENSE SOMEONE NEW IN YOUR WORLD? SHE WOULD HAVE ARRIVED YESTERDAY.
SENSE...?
I SUPPOSE THERE IS A NEW SMELL IN THE AIR... IT'S FAINT, BUT I DO FEEL LIKE THERE'S SOMEONE HERE.
TEDDIE'S NOSE IS IN TOP-NOTCH CONDITION TODAY!

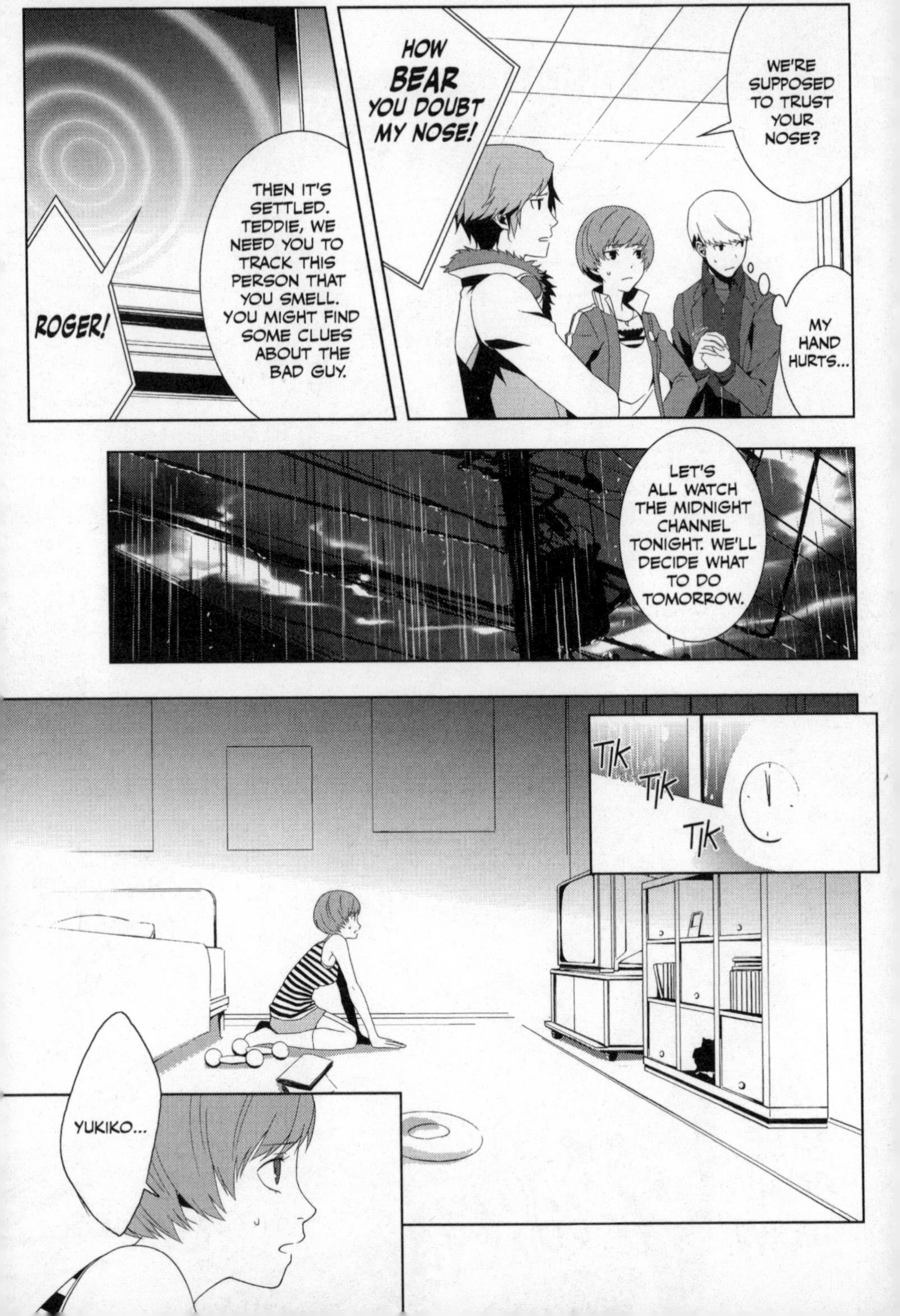

WE'RE SUPPOSED TO TRUST YOUR NOSE?
HOW **BEAR** YOU DOUBT MY NOSE!
MY HAND HURTS...
THEN IT'S SETTLED. TEDDIE, WE NEED YOU TO TRACK THIS PERSON THAT YOU SMELL. YOU MIGHT FIND SOME CLUES ABOUT THE BAD GUY.
ROGER!
LET'S ALL WATCH THE MIDNIGHT CHANNEL TONIGHT. WE'LL DECIDE WHAT TO DO TOMORROW.
TIK
TIK
TIK
YUKIKO...

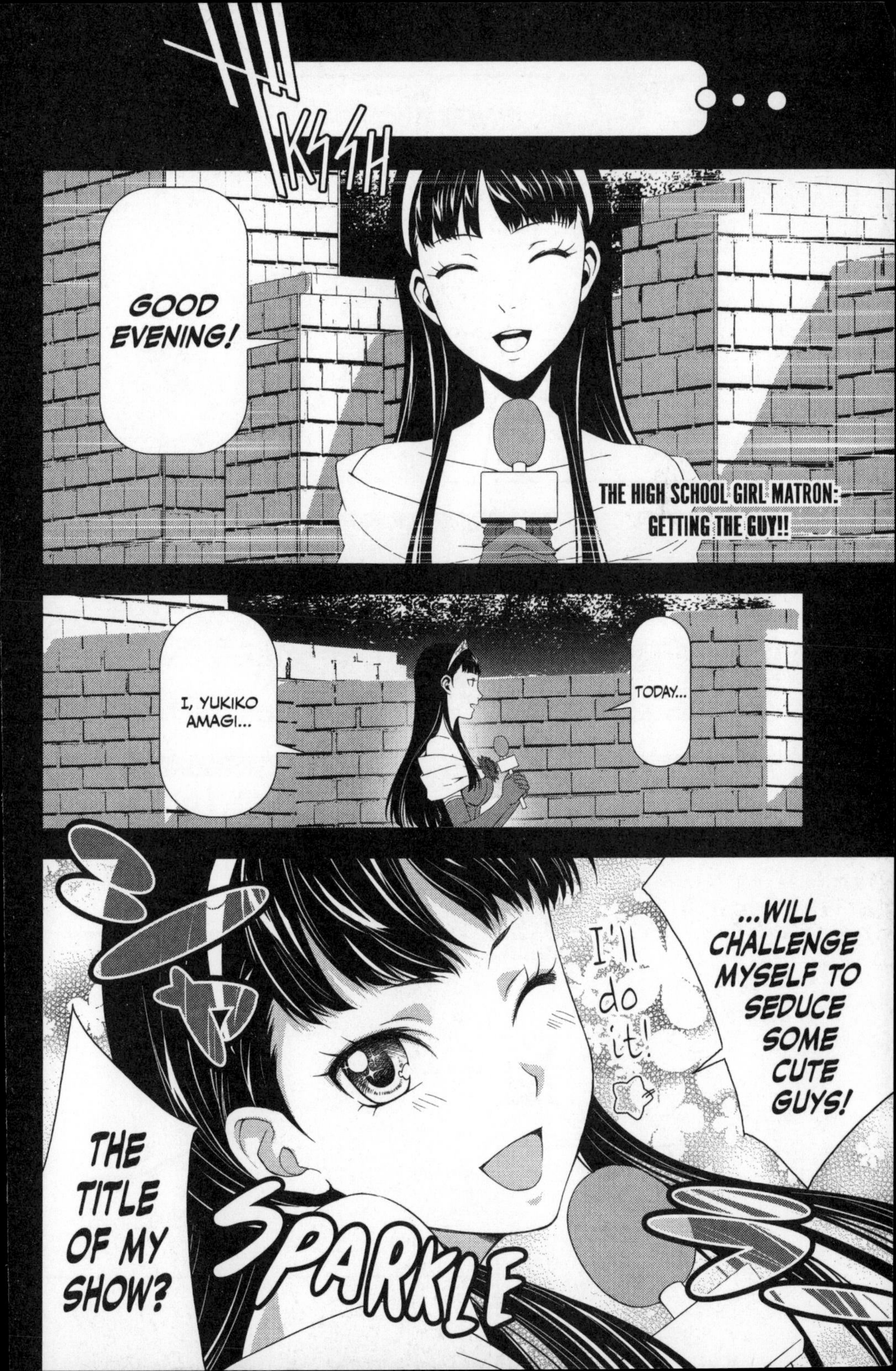
...
KSSH
GOOD EVENING!
THE HIGH SCHOOL GIRL MATRON: GETTING THE GUY!!
TODAY...
I, YUKIKO AMAGI...
...WILL CHALLENGE MYSELF TO SEDUCE SOME CUTE GUYS!
I'll do it!
SPARKLE
THE TITLE OF MY SHOW?

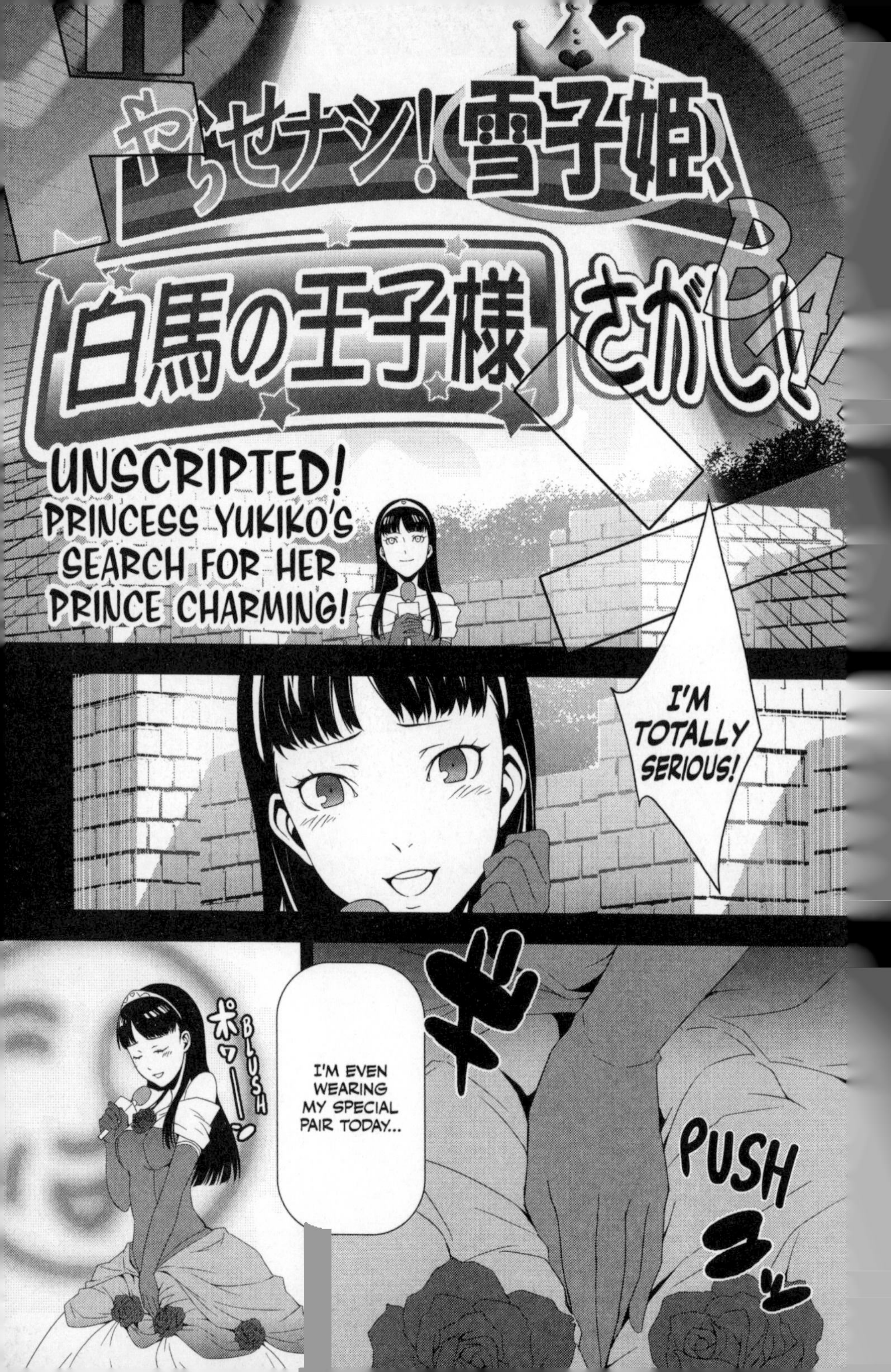

やらせナシ！雪子姫、白馬の王子様さがし！
UNSCRIPTED! PRINCESS YUKIKO'S SEARCH FOR HER PRINCE CHARMING!
I'M TOTALLY SERIOUS!
ギュッ
PUSH
I'M EVEN WEARING MY SPECIAL PAIR TODAY...
ポワー
BLUSH

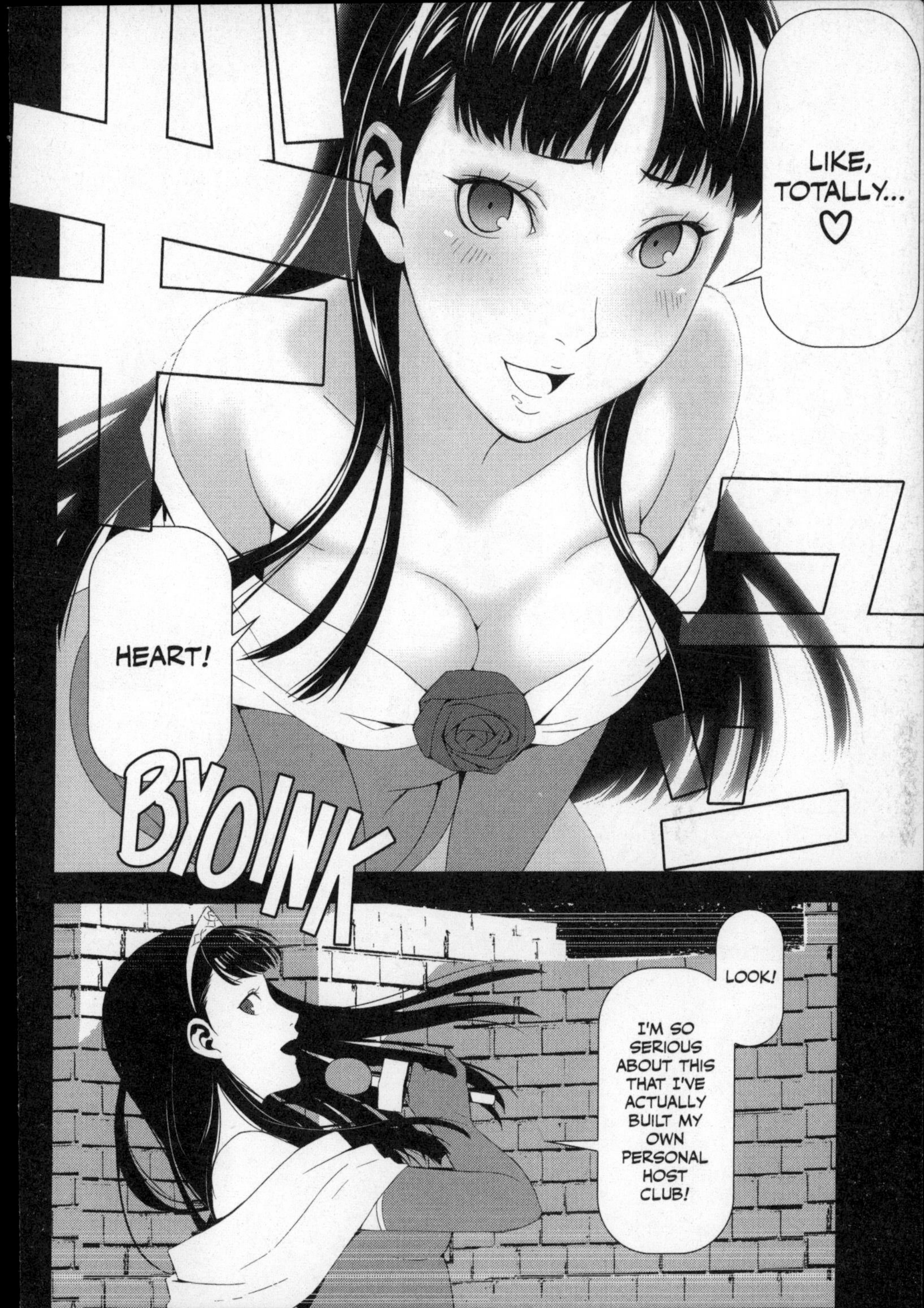
LIKE, TOTALLY... ♥
HEART!
BYOINK
LOOK!
I'M SO SERIOUS ABOUT THIS THAT I'VE ACTUALLY BUILT MY OWN PERSONAL HOST CLUB!

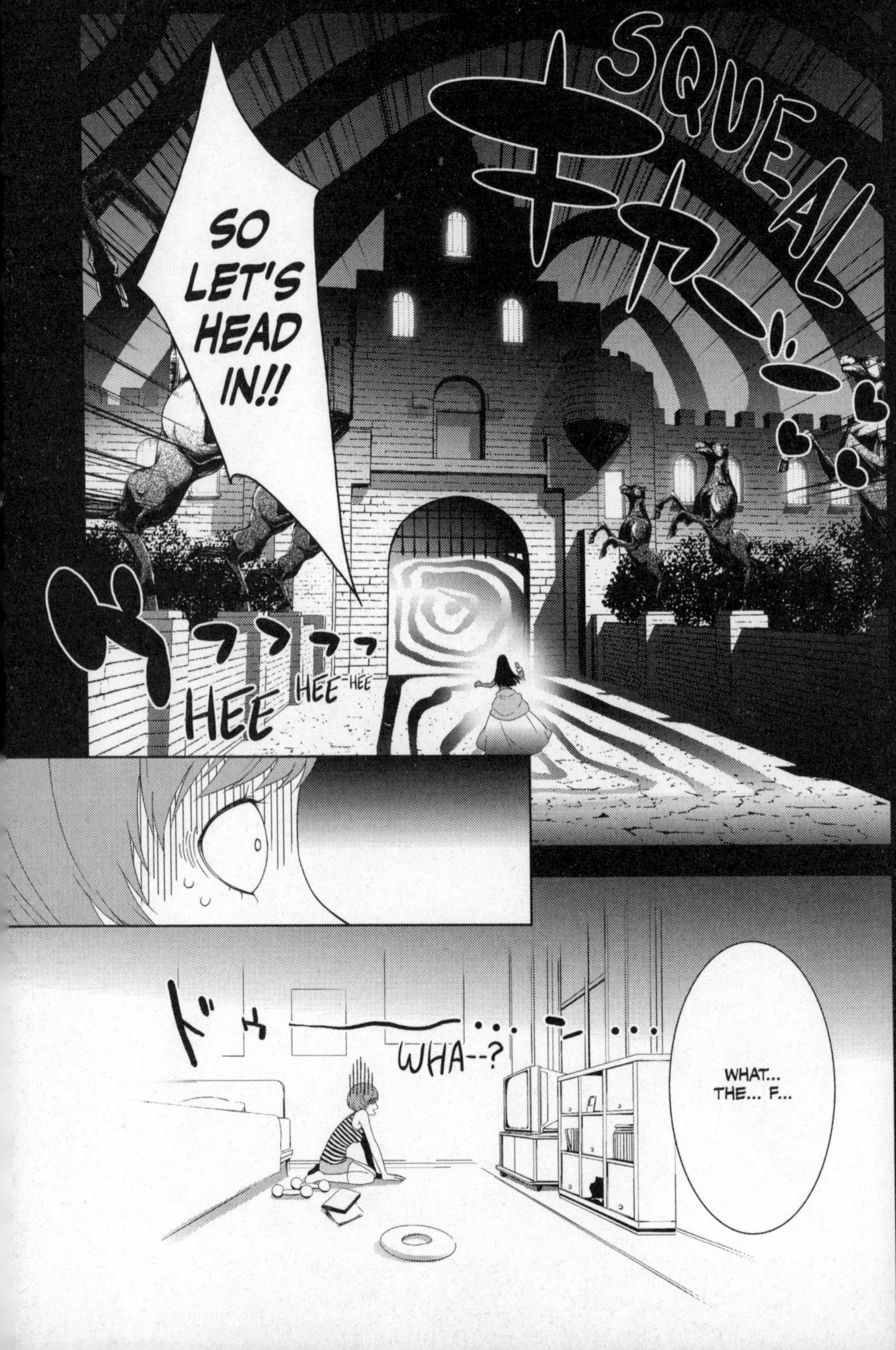
SQUEAL
SO LET'S HEAD IN!!
HEE HEE HEE
WHAT... THE... F...
WHA--?

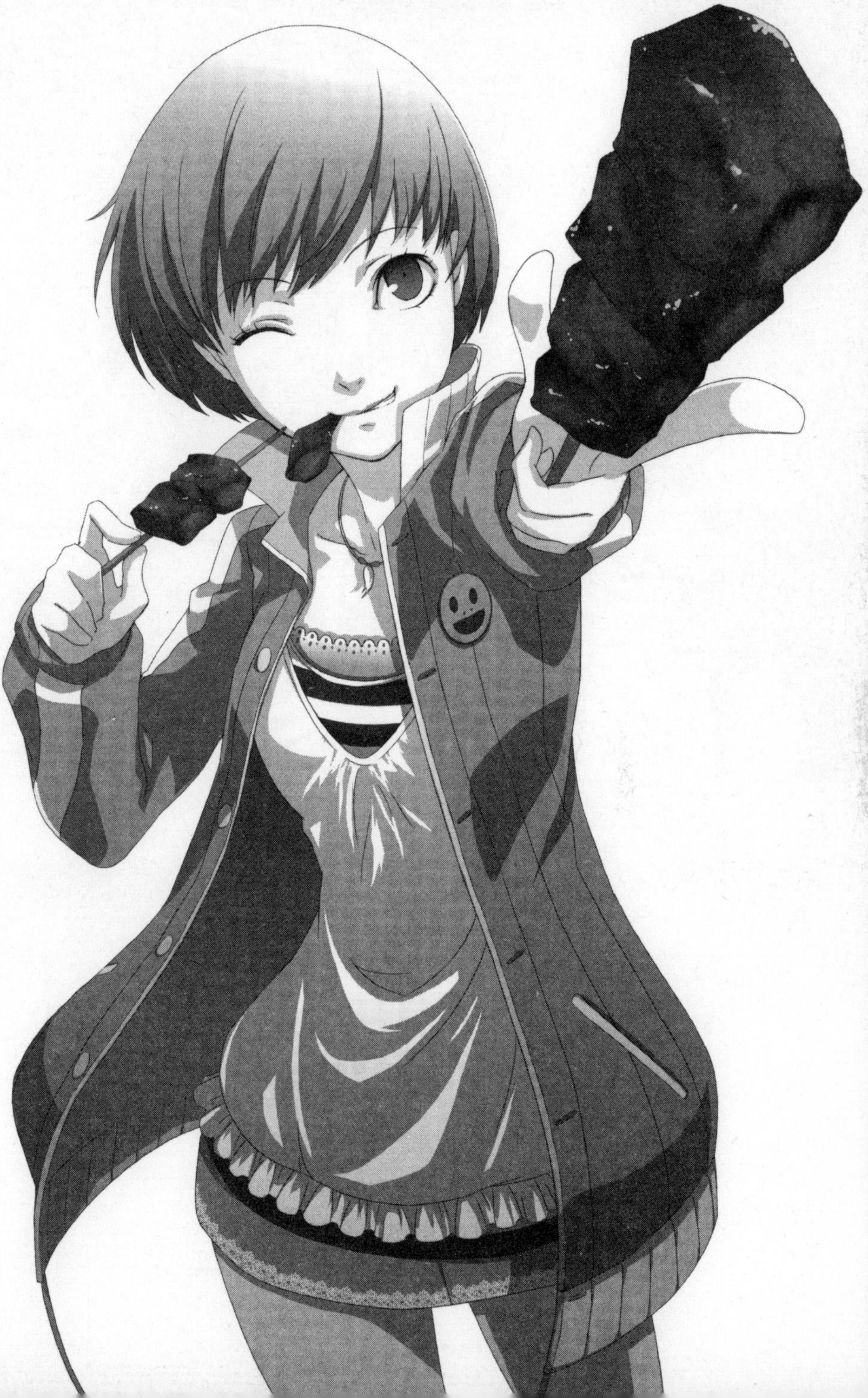

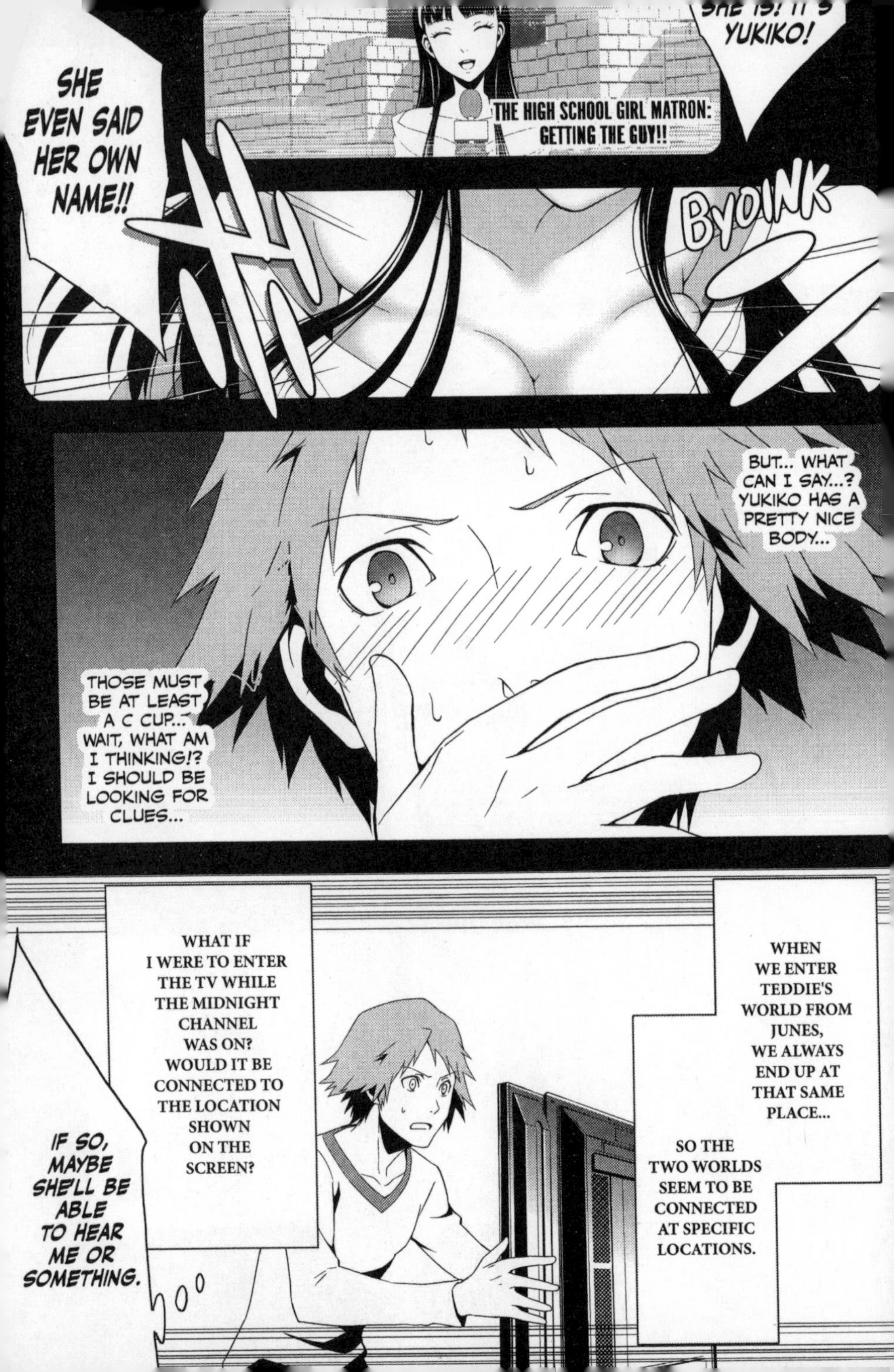
SHE IS! IT'S YUKIKO!
THE HIGH SCHOOL GIRL MATRON: GETTING THE GUY!!
SHE EVEN SAID HER OWN NAME!!
BYOINK
BUT... WHAT CAN I SAY...? YUKIKO HAS A PRETTY NICE BODY...
THOSE MUST BE AT LEAST A C CUP... WAIT, WHAT AM I THINKING!? I SHOULD BE LOOKING FOR CLUES...
WHEN WE ENTER TEDDIE'S WORLD FROM JUNES, WE ALWAYS END UP AT THAT SAME PLACE...
SO THE TWO WORLDS SEEM TO BE CONNECTED AT SPECIFIC LOCATIONS.
WHAT IF I WERE TO ENTER THE TV WHILE THE MIDNIGHT CHANNEL WAS ON? WOULD IT BE CONNECTED TO THE LOCATION SHOWN ON THE SCREEN?
IF SO, MAYBE SHE'LL BE ABLE TO HEAR ME OR SOMETHING.

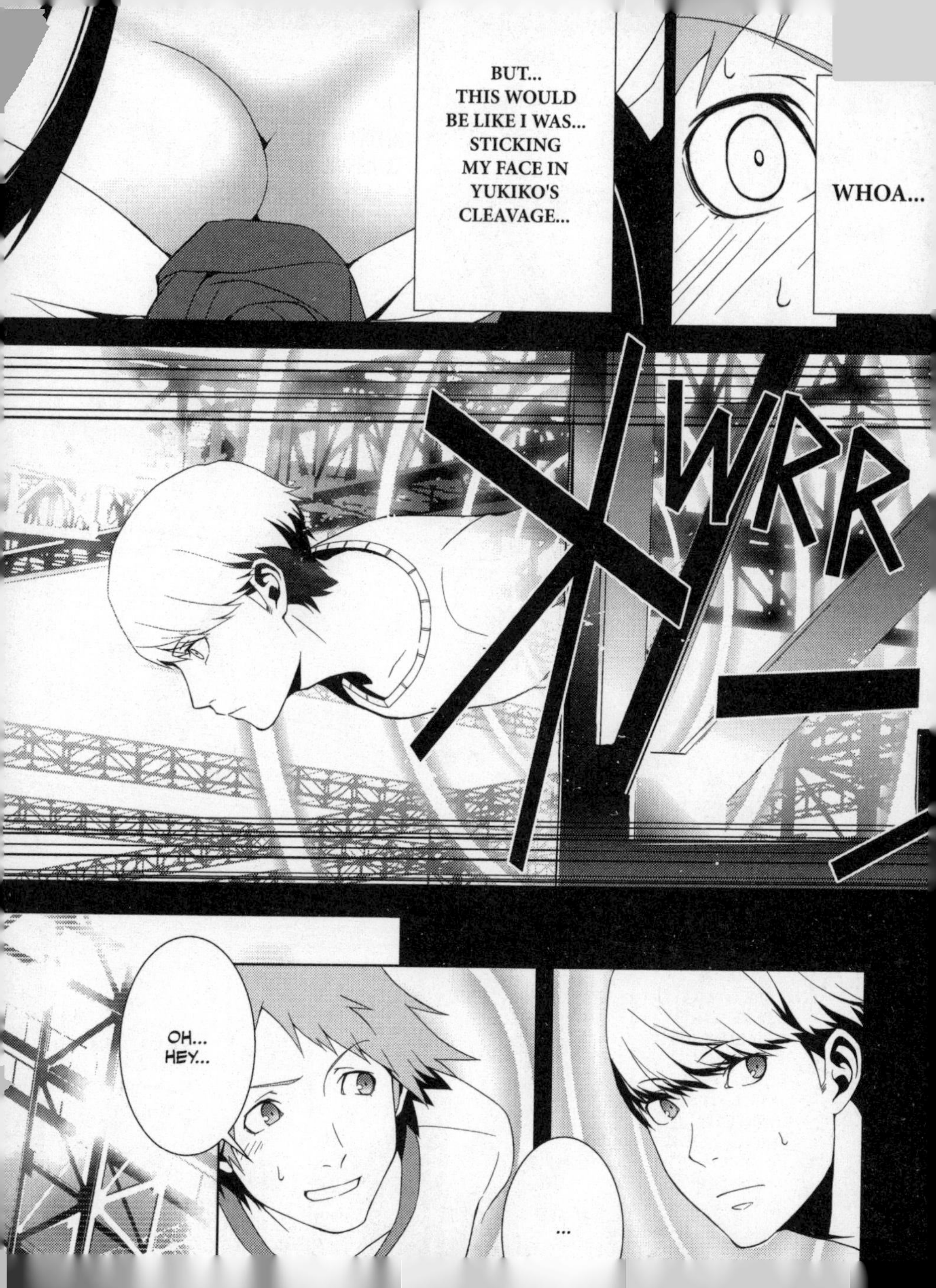
WHOA...
BUT... THIS WOULD BE LIKE I WAS... STICKING MY FACE IN YUKIKO'S CLEAVAGE...
WRR
...
OH... HEY...

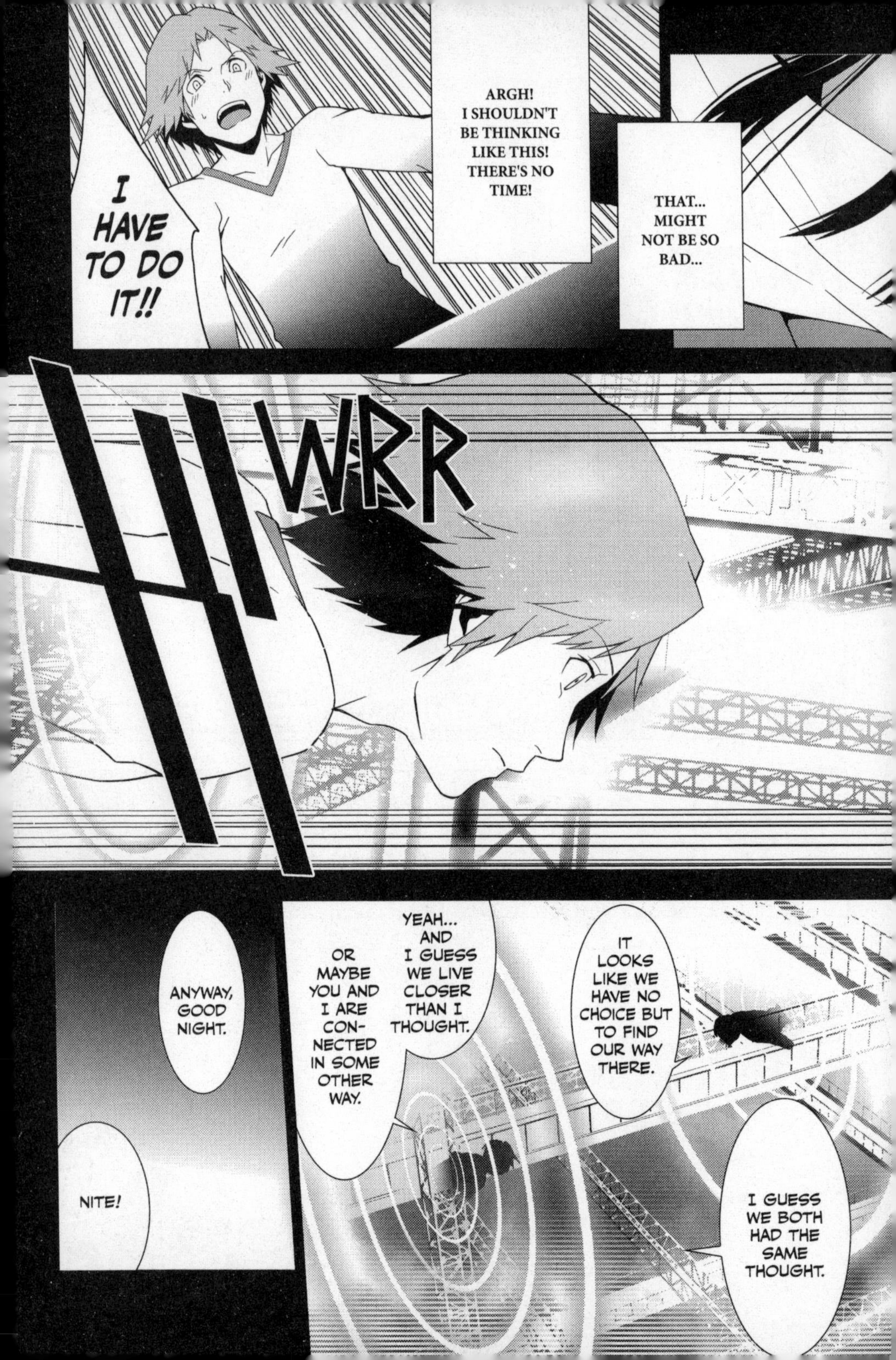
THAT... MIGHT NOT BE SO BAD...
ARGH! I SHOULDN'T BE THINKING LIKE THIS! THERE'S NO TIME!
I HAVE TO DO IT!!
WRR
IT LOOKS LIKE WE HAVE NO CHOICE BUT TO FIND OUR WAY THERE.
I GUESS WE BOTH HAD THE SAME THOUGHT.
YEAH... AND I GUESS WE LIVE CLOSER THAN I THOUGHT.
OR MAYBE YOU AND I ARE CON-NECTED IN SOME OTHER WAY.
ANYWAY, GOOD NIGHT.
NITE!

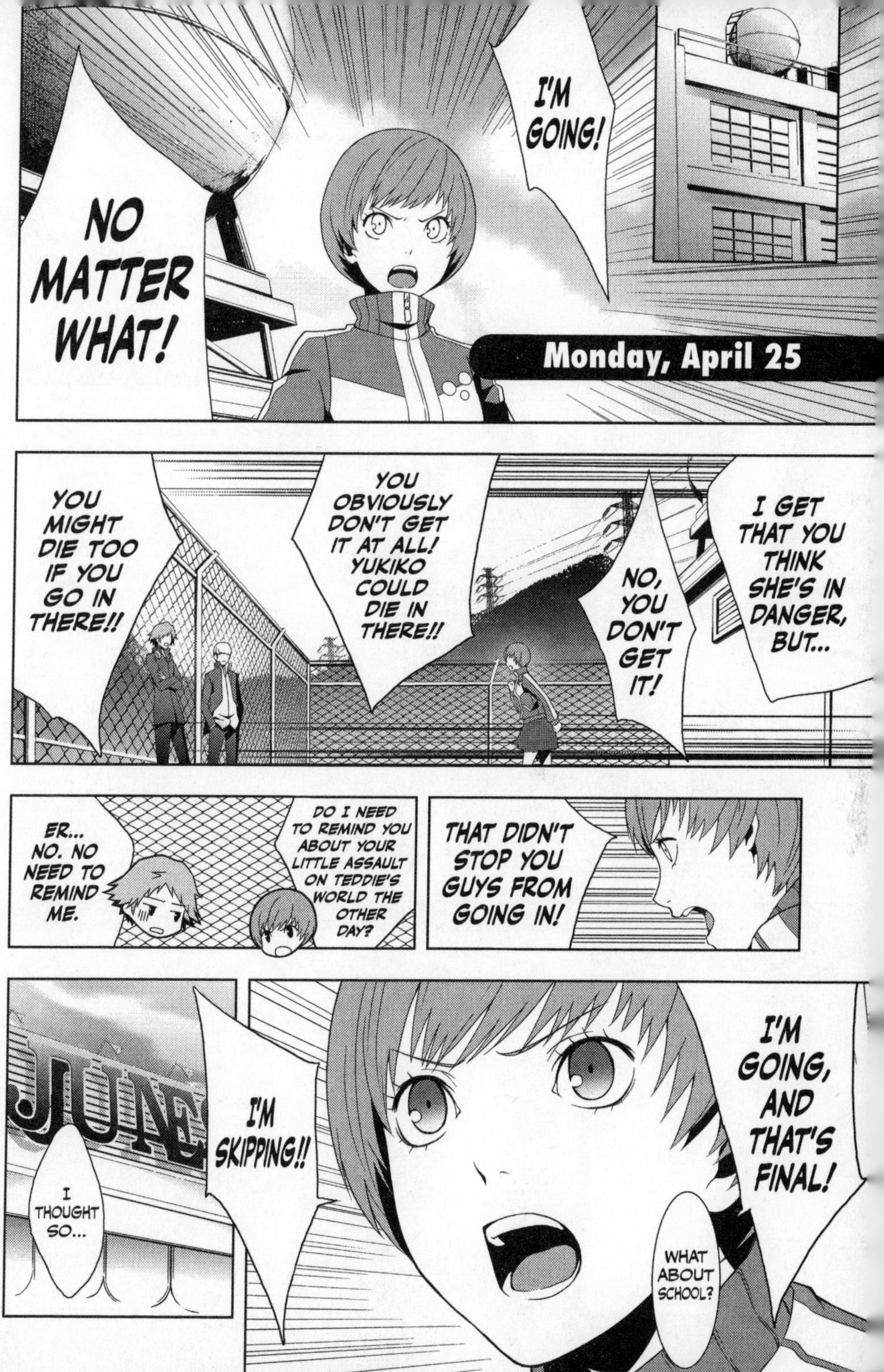
I'M GOING!
NO MATTER WHAT!
Monday, April 25
I GET THAT YOU THINK SHE'S IN DANGER, BUT...
NO, YOU DON'T GET IT!
YOU OBVIOUSLY DON'T GET IT AT ALL! YUKIKO COULD DIE IN THERE!!
YOU MIGHT DIE TOO IF YOU GO IN THERE!!
THAT DIDN'T STOP YOU GUYS FROM GOING IN!
DO I NEED TO REMIND YOU ABOUT YOUR LITTLE ASSAULT ON TEDDIE'S WORLD THE OTHER DAY?
ER... NO. NO NEED TO REMIND ME.
I'M GOING, AND THAT'S FINAL!
WHAT ABOUT SCHOOL?
I'M SKIPPING!!
I THOUGHT SO...

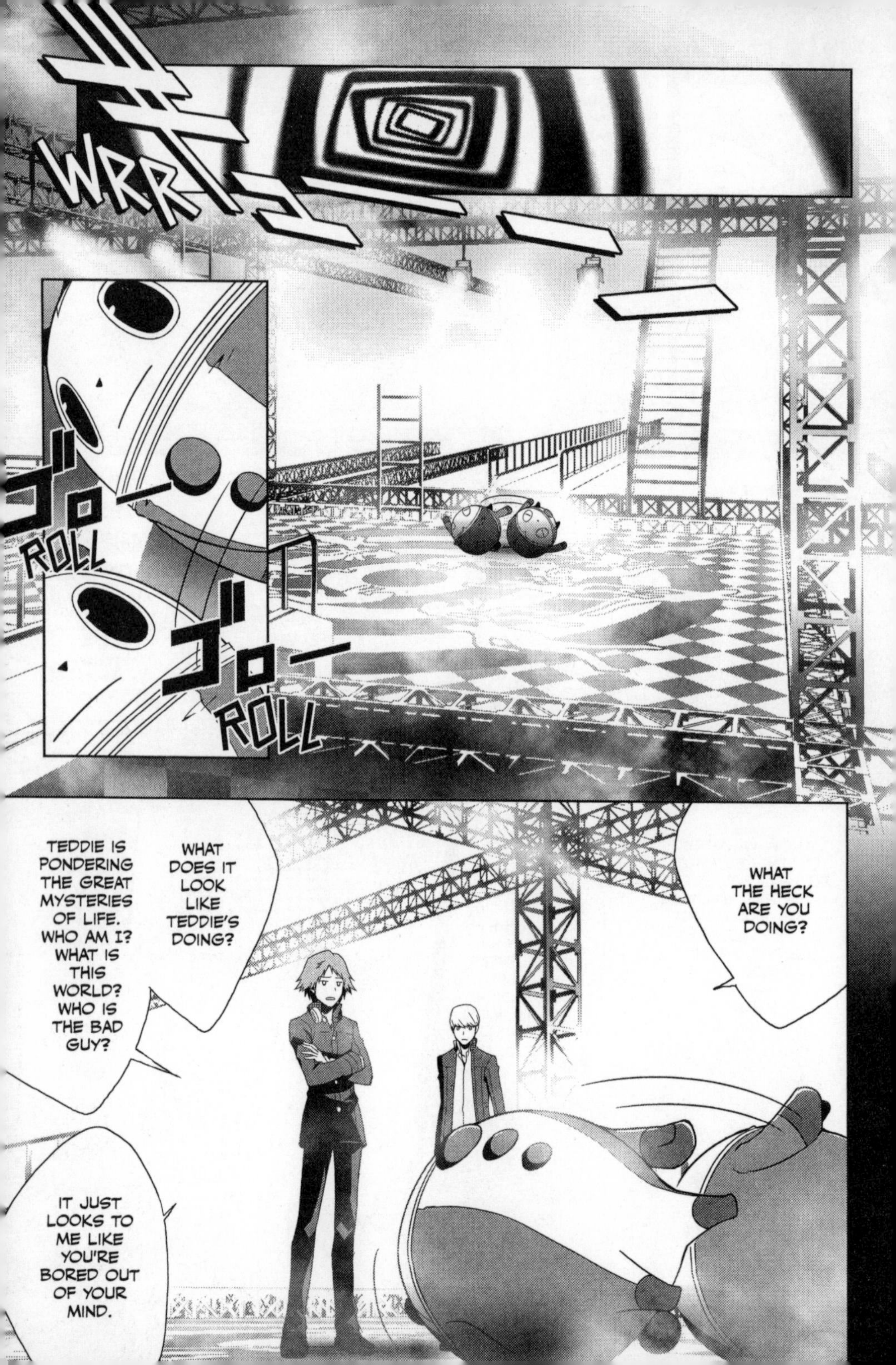
WRR
ゴロー
ROLL
ゴロー
ROLL
WHAT THE HECK ARE YOU DOING?
WHAT DOES IT LOOK LIKE TEDDIE'S DOING?
TEDDIE IS PONDERING THE GREAT MYSTERIES OF LIFE. WHO AM I? WHAT IS THIS WORLD? WHO IS THE BAD GUY?
IT JUST LOOKS TO ME LIKE YOU'RE BORED OUT OF YOUR MIND.

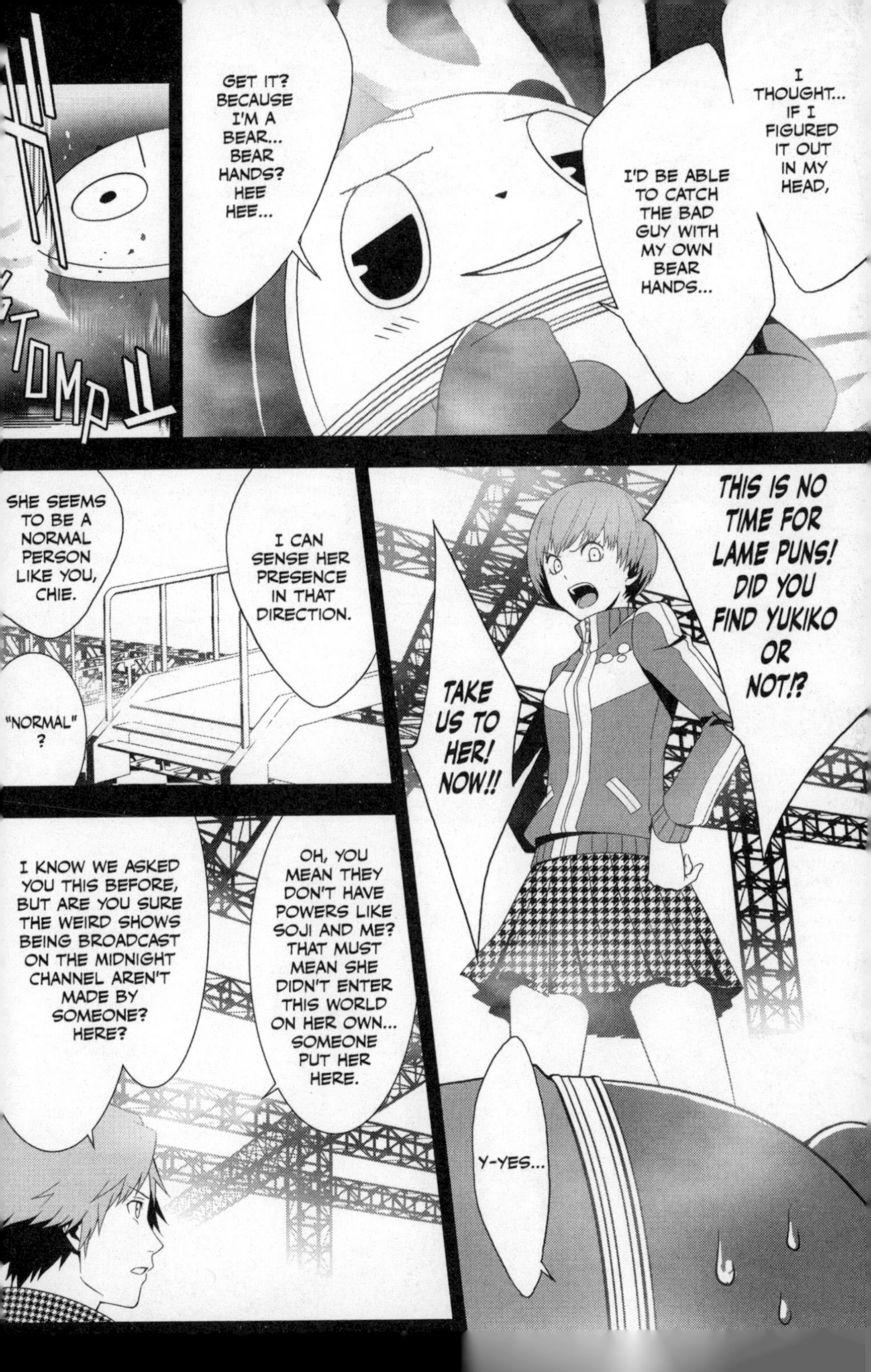
I THOUGHT... IF I FIGURED IT OUT IN MY HEAD,
I'D BE ABLE TO CATCH THE BAD GUY WITH MY OWN BEAR HANDS...
GET IT? BECAUSE I'M A BEAR... BEAR HANDS? HEE HEE...
STOMP!!
THIS IS NO TIME FOR LAME PUNS! DID YOU FIND YUKIKO OR NOT!?
TAKE US TO HER! NOW!!
Y-YES...
I CAN SENSE HER PRESENCE IN THAT DIRECTION.
SHE SEEMS TO BE A NORMAL PERSON LIKE YOU, CHIE.
"NORMAL"?
OH, YOU MEAN THEY DON'T HAVE POWERS LIKE SOJI AND ME? THAT MUST MEAN SHE DIDN'T ENTER THIS WORLD ON HER OWN... SOMEONE PUT HER HERE.
I KNOW WE ASKED YOU THIS BEFORE, BUT ARE YOU SURE THE WEIRD SHOWS BEING BROADCAST ON THE MIDNIGHT CHANNEL AREN'T MADE BY SOMEONE? HERE?

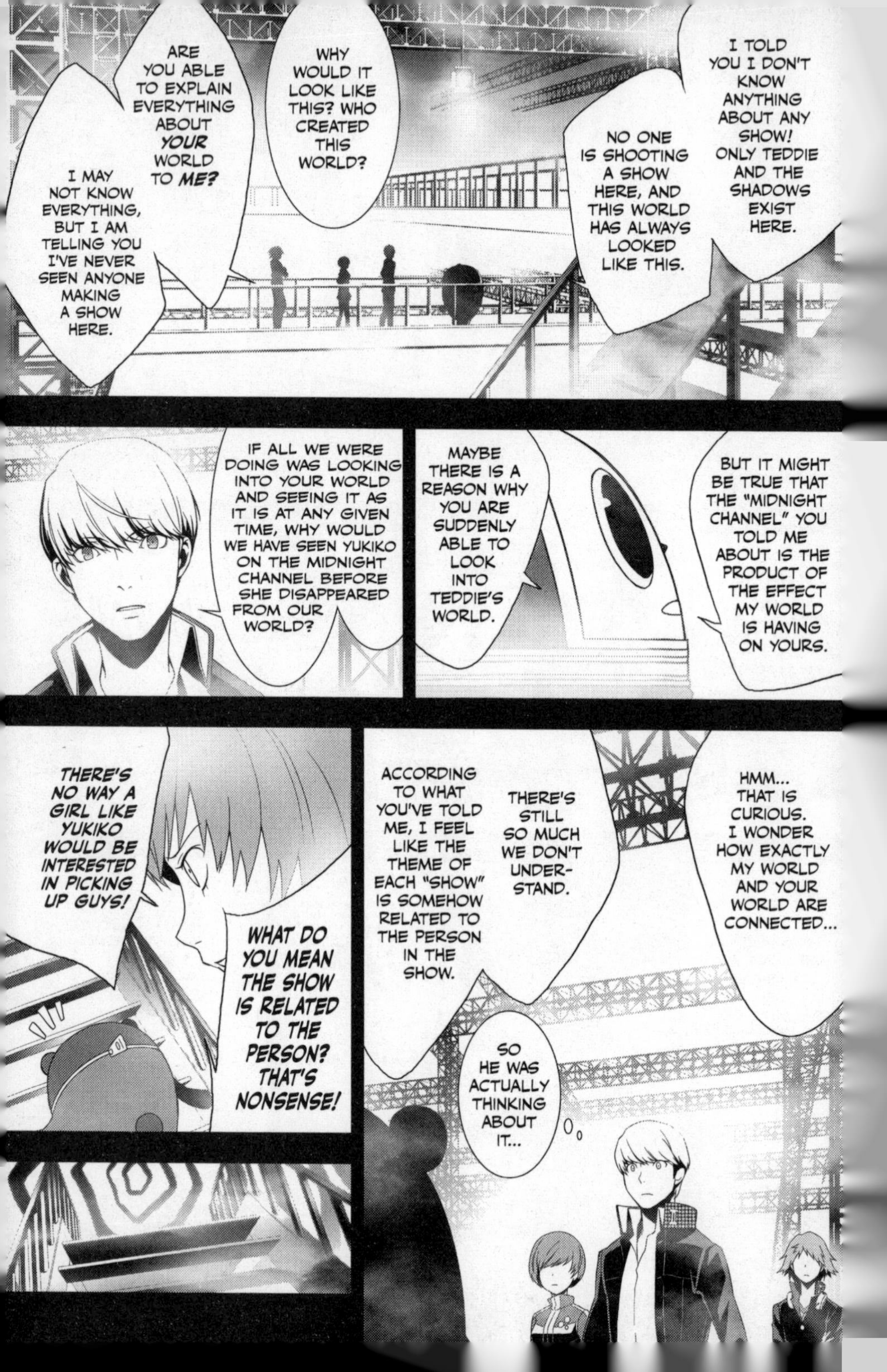
I TOLD YOU I DON'T KNOW ANYTHING ABOUT ANY SHOW! ONLY TEDDIE AND THE SHADOWS EXIST HERE.
NO ONE IS SHOOTING A SHOW HERE, AND THIS WORLD HAS ALWAYS LOOKED LIKE THIS.
WHY WOULD IT LOOK LIKE THIS? WHO CREATED THIS WORLD?
ARE YOU ABLE TO EXPLAIN EVERYTHING ABOUT *YOUR* WORLD TO *ME?*
I MAY NOT KNOW EVERYTHING, BUT I AM TELLING YOU I'VE NEVER SEEN ANYONE MAKING A SHOW HERE.
BUT IT MIGHT BE TRUE THAT THE "MIDNIGHT CHANNEL" YOU TOLD ME ABOUT IS THE PRODUCT OF THE EFFECT MY WORLD IS HAVING ON YOURS.
MAYBE THERE IS A REASON WHY YOU ARE SUDDENLY ABLE TO LOOK INTO TEDDIE'S WORLD.
IF ALL WE WERE DOING WAS LOOKING INTO YOUR WORLD AND SEEING IT AS IT IS AT ANY GIVEN TIME, WHY WOULD WE HAVE SEEN YUKIKO ON THE MIDNIGHT CHANNEL BEFORE SHE DISAPPEARED FROM OUR WORLD?
HMM... THAT IS CURIOUS. I WONDER HOW EXACTLY MY WORLD AND YOUR WORLD ARE CONNECTED...
THERE'S STILL SO MUCH WE DON'T UNDER-STAND.
ACCORDING TO WHAT YOU'VE TOLD ME, I FEEL LIKE THE THEME OF EACH "SHOW" IS SOMEHOW RELATED TO THE PERSON IN THE SHOW.
SO HE WAS ACTUALLY THINKING ABOUT IT...
WHAT DO YOU MEAN THE SHOW IS RELATED TO THE PERSON? THAT'S NONSENSE!
THERE'S NO WAY A GIRL LIKE YUKIKO WOULD BE INTERESTED IN PICKING UP GUYS!

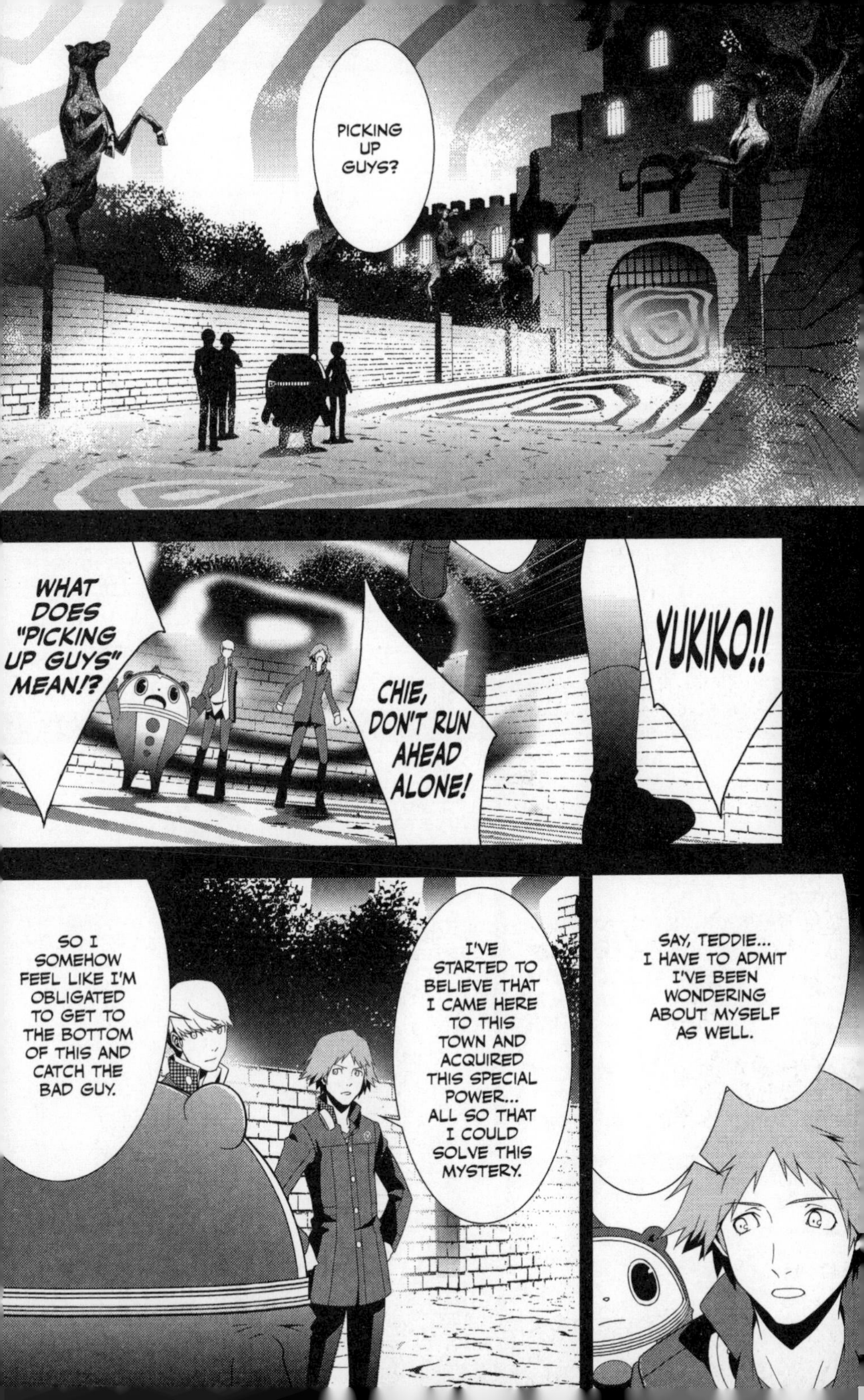
PICKING UP GUYS?
YUKIKO!!
CHIE, DON'T RUN AHEAD ALONE!
WHAT DOES "PICKING UP GUYS" MEAN!?
SAY, TEDDIE... I HAVE TO ADMIT I'VE BEEN WONDERING ABOUT MYSELF AS WELL.
I'VE STARTED TO BELIEVE THAT I CAME HERE TO THIS TOWN AND ACQUIRED THIS SPECIAL POWER... ALL SO THAT I COULD SOLVE THIS MYSTERY.
SO I SOMEHOW FEEL LIKE I'M OBLIGATED TO GET TO THE BOTTOM OF THIS AND CATCH THE BAD GUY.

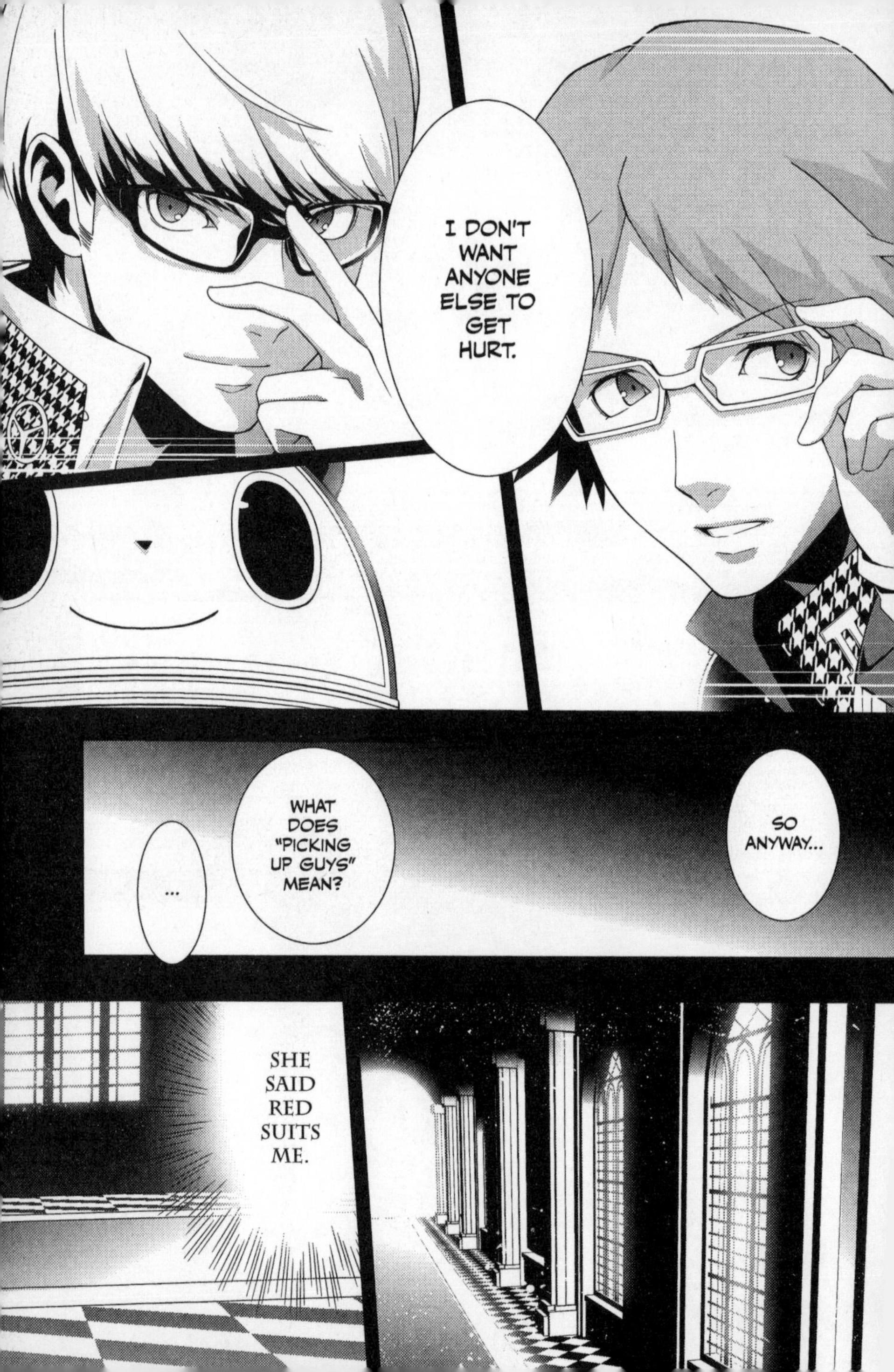
I DON'T WANT ANYONE ELSE TO GET HURT.
SO ANYWAY...
WHAT DOES "PICKING UP GUYS" MEAN?
...
SHE SAID RED SUITS ME.

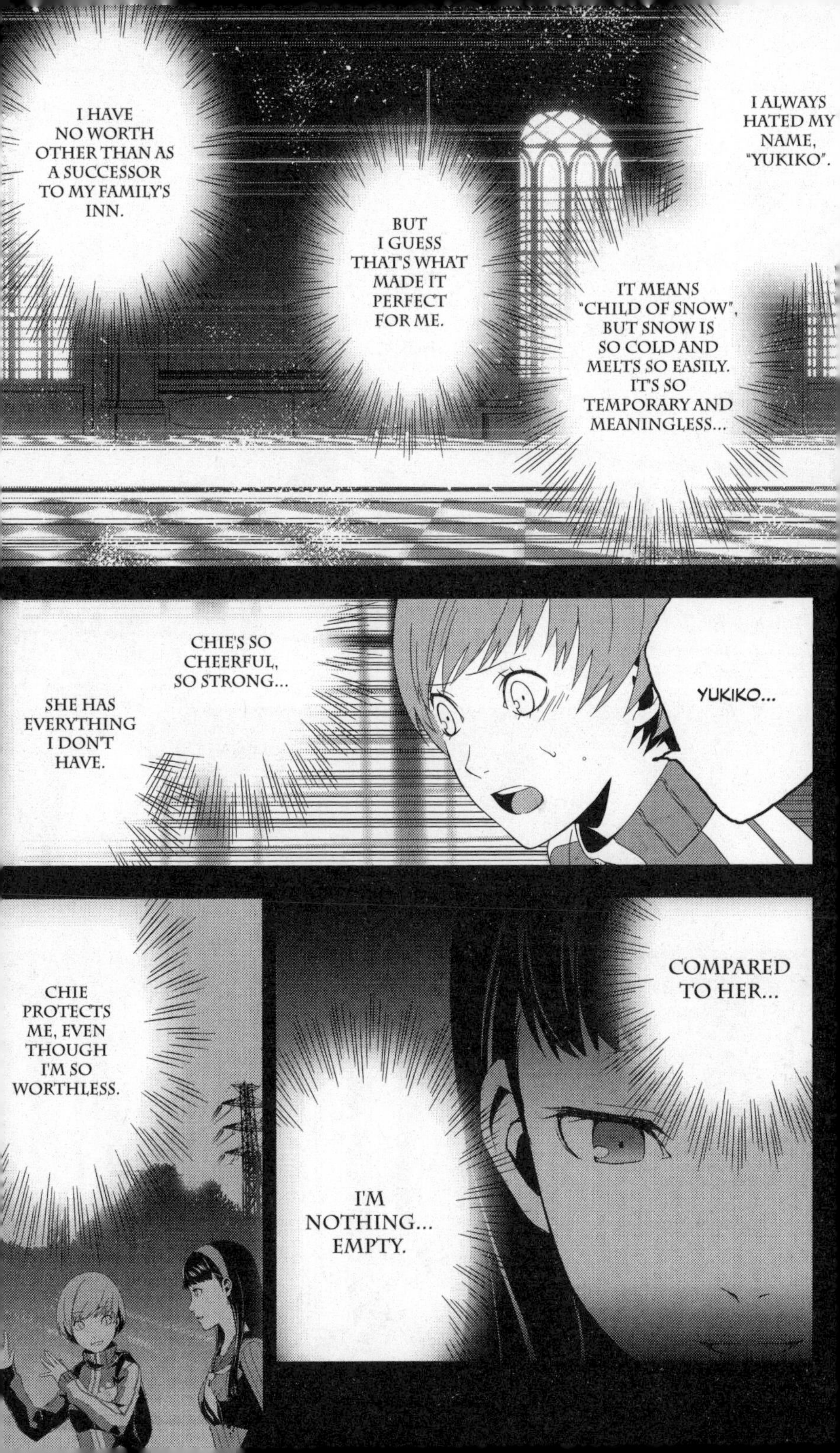
I ALWAYS HATED MY NAME, "YUKIKO".
IT MEANS "CHILD OF SNOW", BUT SNOW IS SO COLD AND MELTS SO EASILY. IT'S SO TEMPORARY AND MEANINGLESS...
I HAVE NO WORTH OTHER THAN AS A SUCCESSOR TO MY FAMILY'S INN.
BUT I GUESS THAT'S WHAT MADE IT PERFECT FOR ME.
YUKIKO...
CHIE'S SO CHEERFUL, SO STRONG...
SHE HAS EVERYTHING I DON'T HAVE.
COMPARED TO HER...
I'M NOTHING... EMPTY.
CHIE PROTECTS ME, EVEN THOUGH I'M SO WORTHLESS.

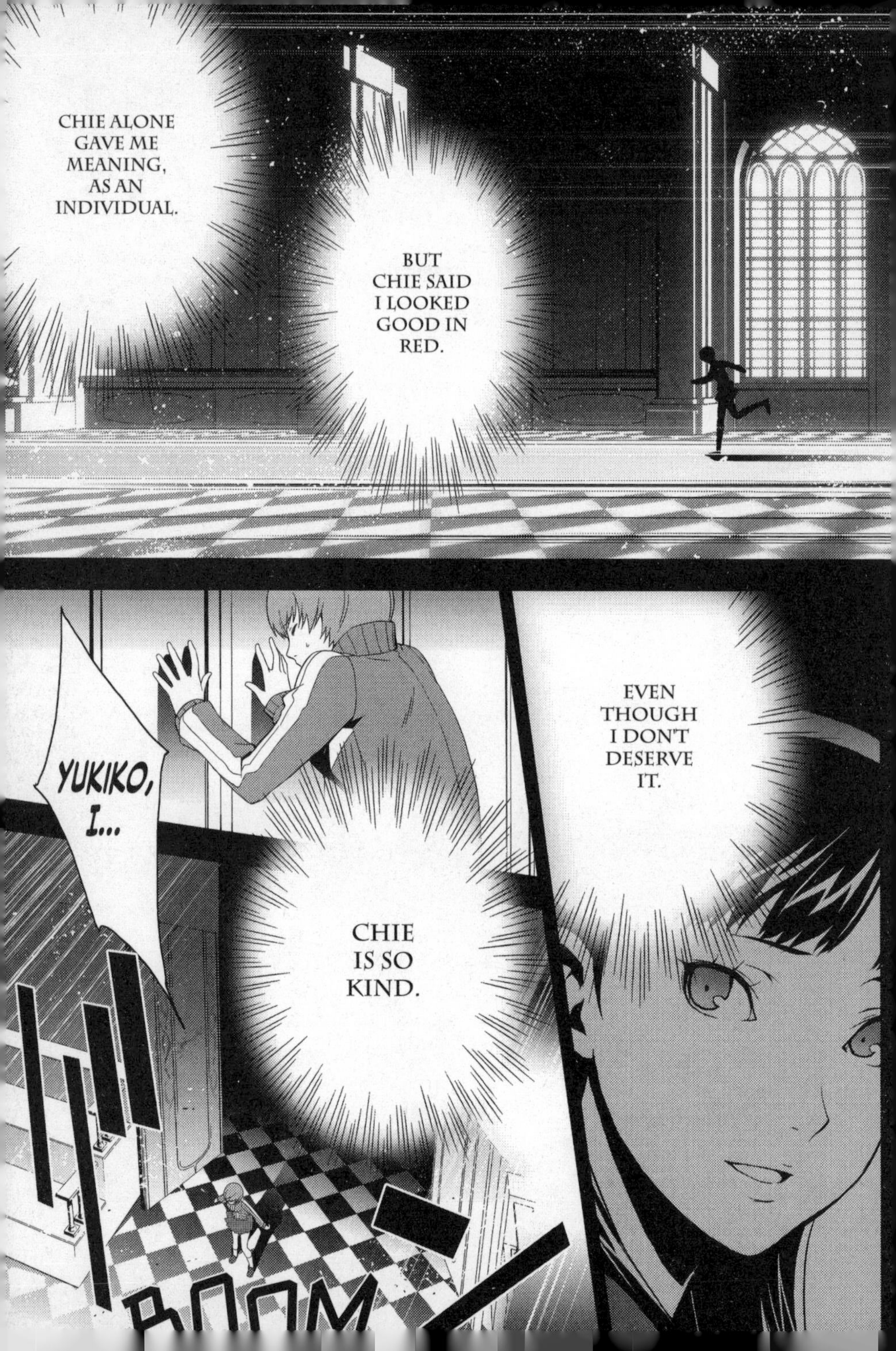

CHIE ALONE GAVE ME MEANING, AS AN INDIVIDUAL.
BUT CHIE SAID I LOOKED GOOD IN RED.
EVEN THOUGH I DON'T DESERVE IT.
CHIE IS SO KIND.
YUKIKO, I...
BOOM

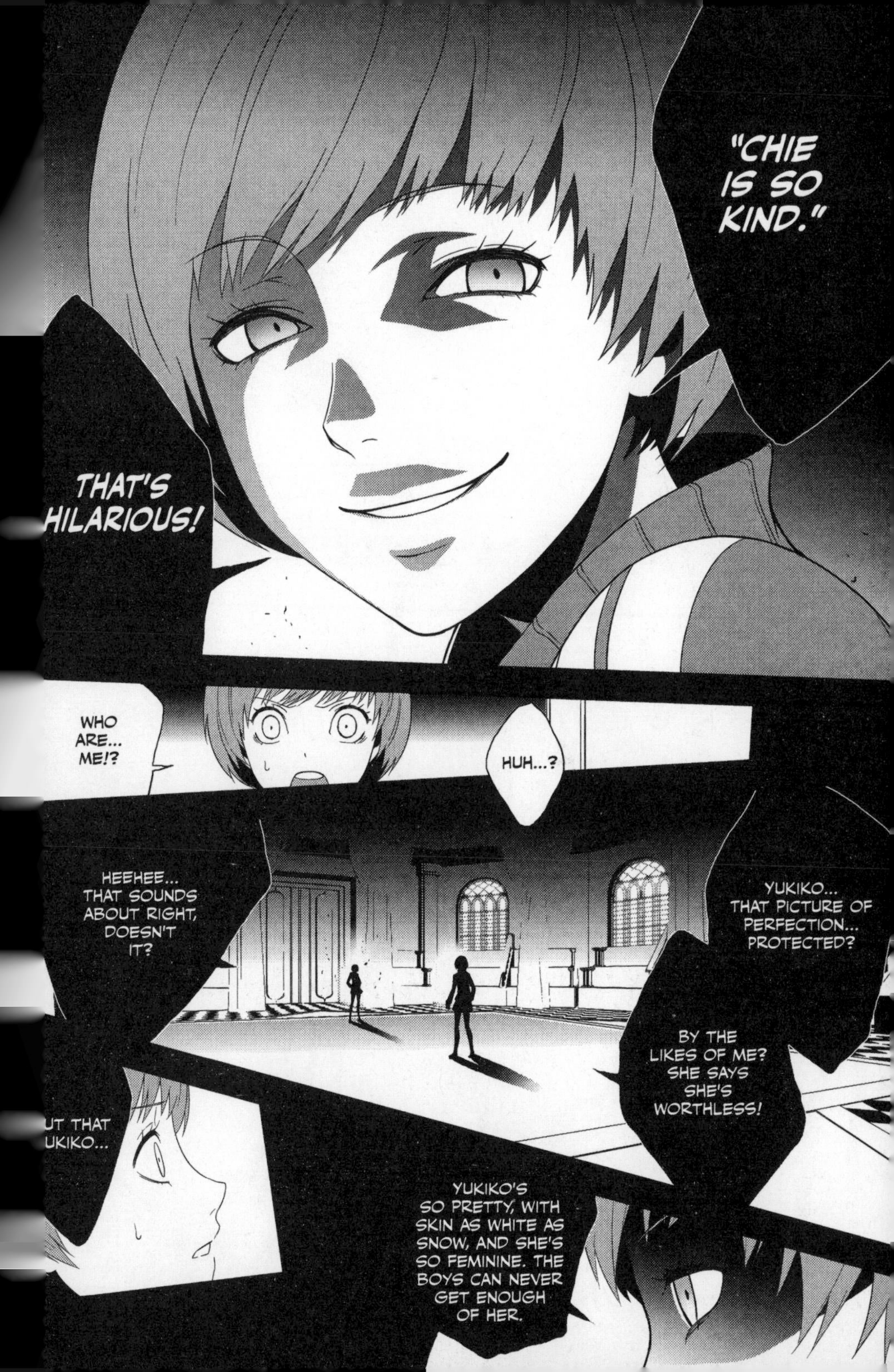
"CHIE IS SO KIND."
THAT'S HILARIOUS!
HUH...?
WHO ARE... ME!?
YUKIKO... THAT PICTURE OF PERFECTION... PROTECTED?
BY THE LIKES OF ME? SHE SAYS SHE'S WORTHLESS!
HEEHEE... THAT SOUNDS ABOUT RIGHT, DOESN'T IT?
YUKIKO'S SO PRETTY, WITH SKIN AS WHITE AS SNOW, AND SHE'S SO FEMININE. THE BOYS CAN NEVER GET ENOUGH OF HER.
UT THAT UKIKO...

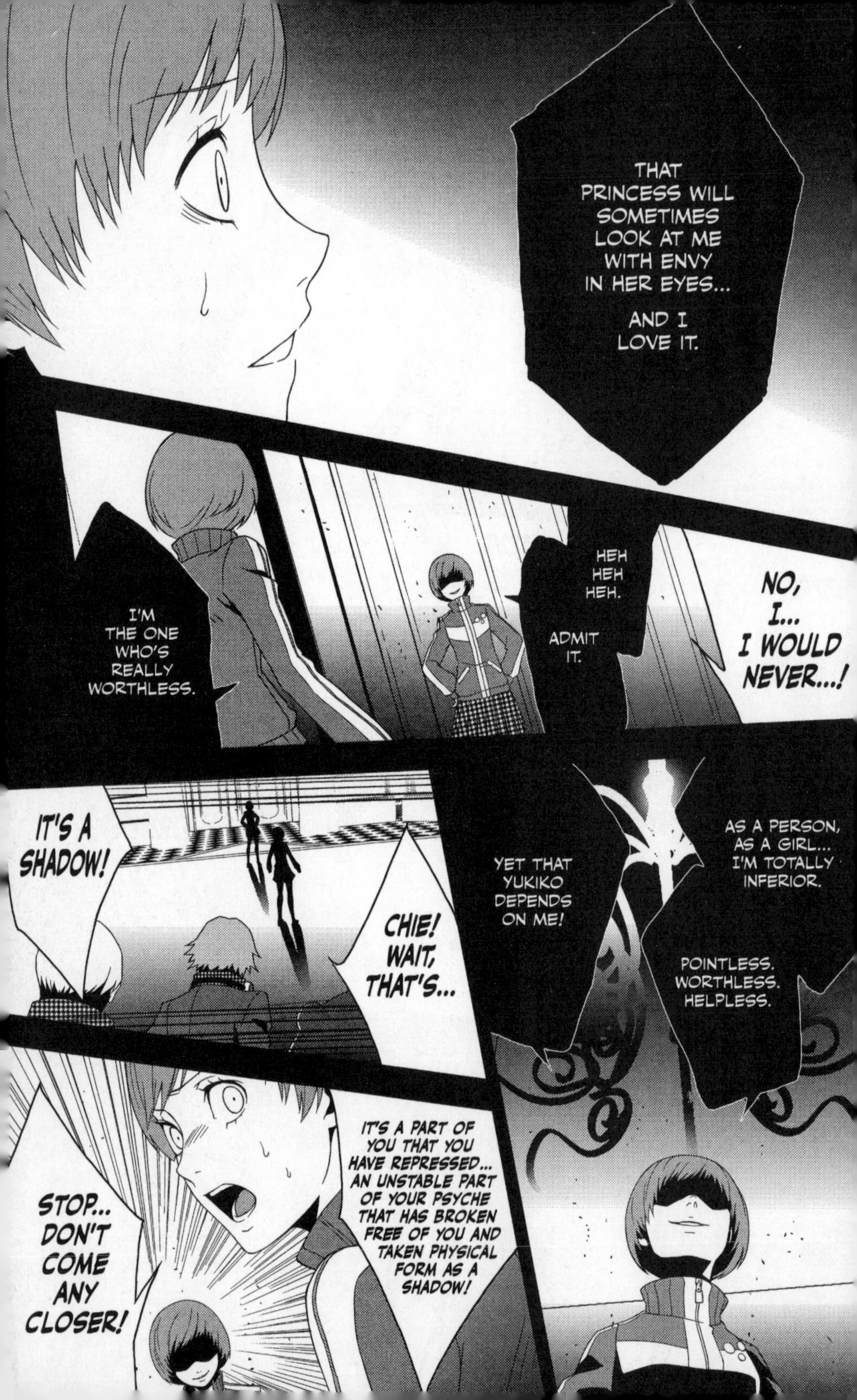

THAT PRINCESS WILL SOMETIMES LOOK AT ME WITH ENVY IN HER EYES...
AND I LOVE IT.
NO, I... I WOULD NEVER...!
HEH HEH HEH.
ADMIT IT.
I'M THE ONE WHO'S REALLY WORTHLESS.
AS A PERSON, AS A GIRL... I'M TOTALLY INFERIOR.
YET THAT YUKIKO DEPENDS ON ME!
POINTLESS. WORTHLESS. HELPLESS.
CHIE! WAIT, THAT'S...
IT'S A SHADOW!
IT'S A PART OF YOU THAT YOU HAVE REPRESSED... AN UNSTABLE PART OF YOUR PSYCHE THAT HAS BROKEN FREE OF YOU AND TAKEN PHYSICAL FORM AS A SHADOW!
STOP... DON'T COME ANY CLOSER!

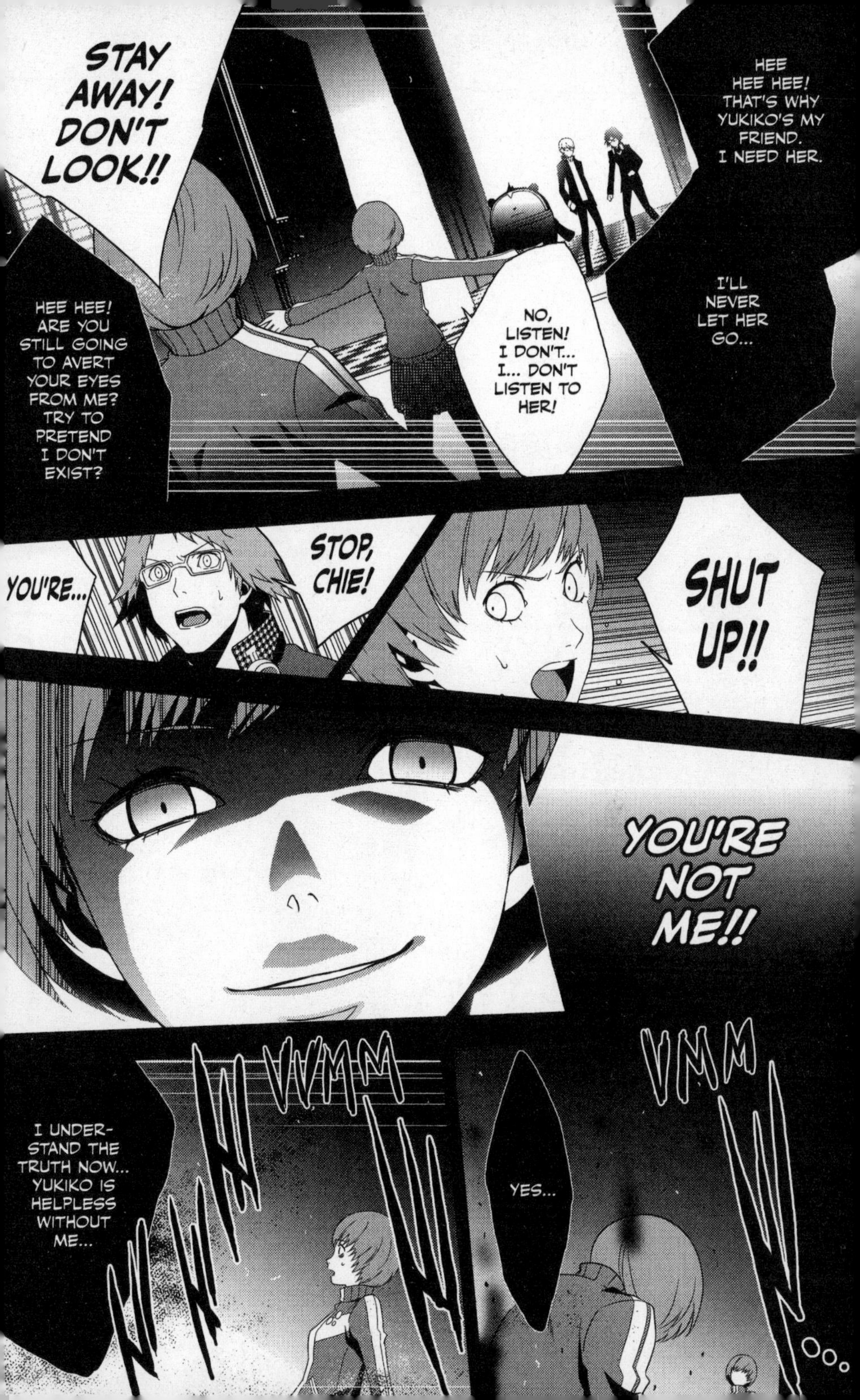
HEE HEE HEE! THAT'S WHY YUKIKO'S MY FRIEND. I NEED HER.
STAY AWAY! DON'T LOOK!!
I'LL NEVER LET HER GO...
NO, LISTEN! I DON'T... I... DON'T LISTEN TO HER!
HEE HEE! ARE YOU STILL GOING TO AVERT YOUR EYES FROM ME? TRY TO PRETEND I DON'T EXIST?
SHUT UP!!
STOP, CHIE!
YOU'RE...
YOU'RE NOT ME!!
VMM
YES...
VVMM
I UNDER-STAND THE TRUTH NOW... YUKIKO IS HELPLESS WITHOUT ME...
Ooo

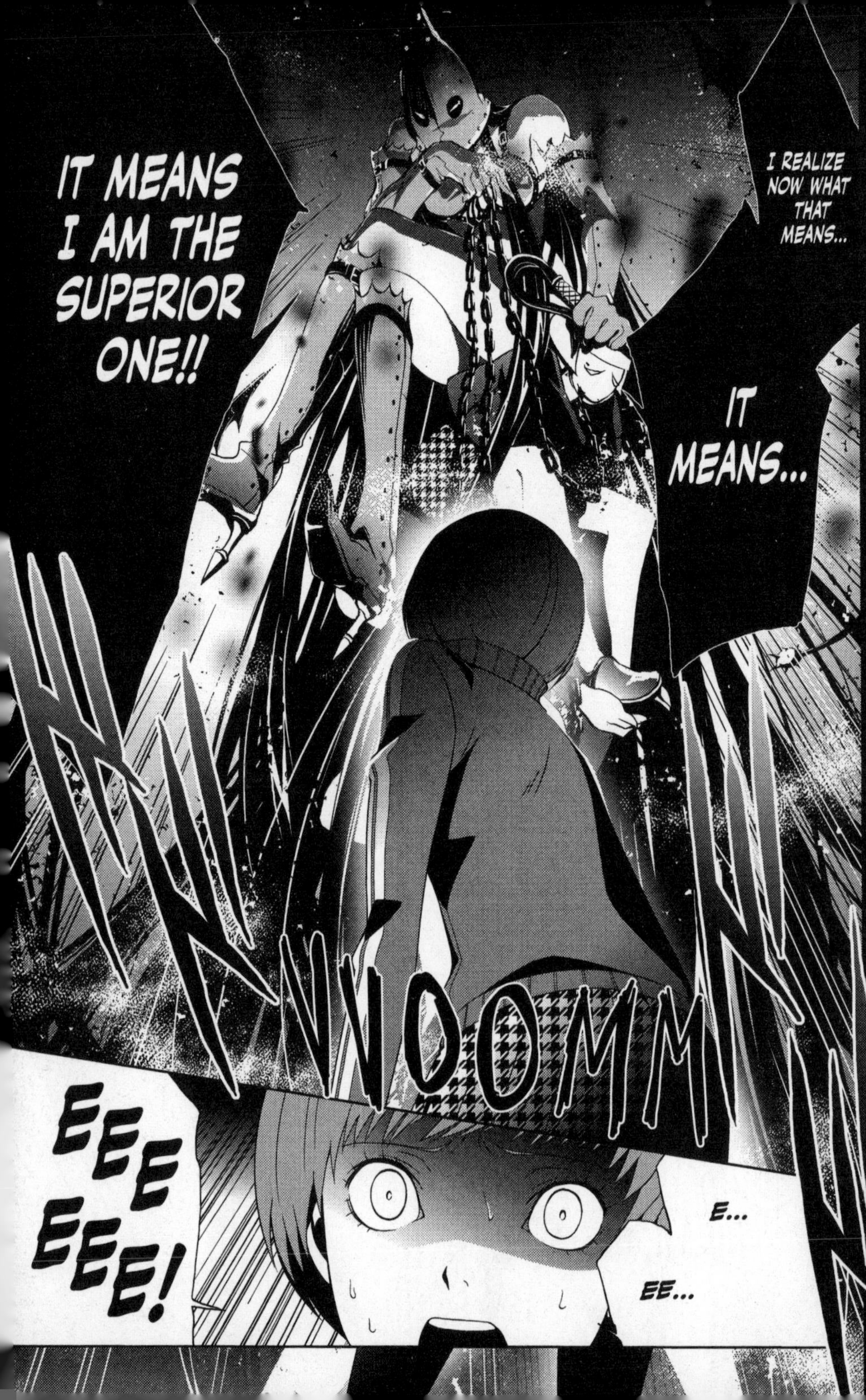
I REALIZE NOW WHAT THAT MEANS...
IT MEANS...
IT MEANS I AM THE SUPERIOR ONE!!
VOOMM
E...
EE...
EEEEEEE!

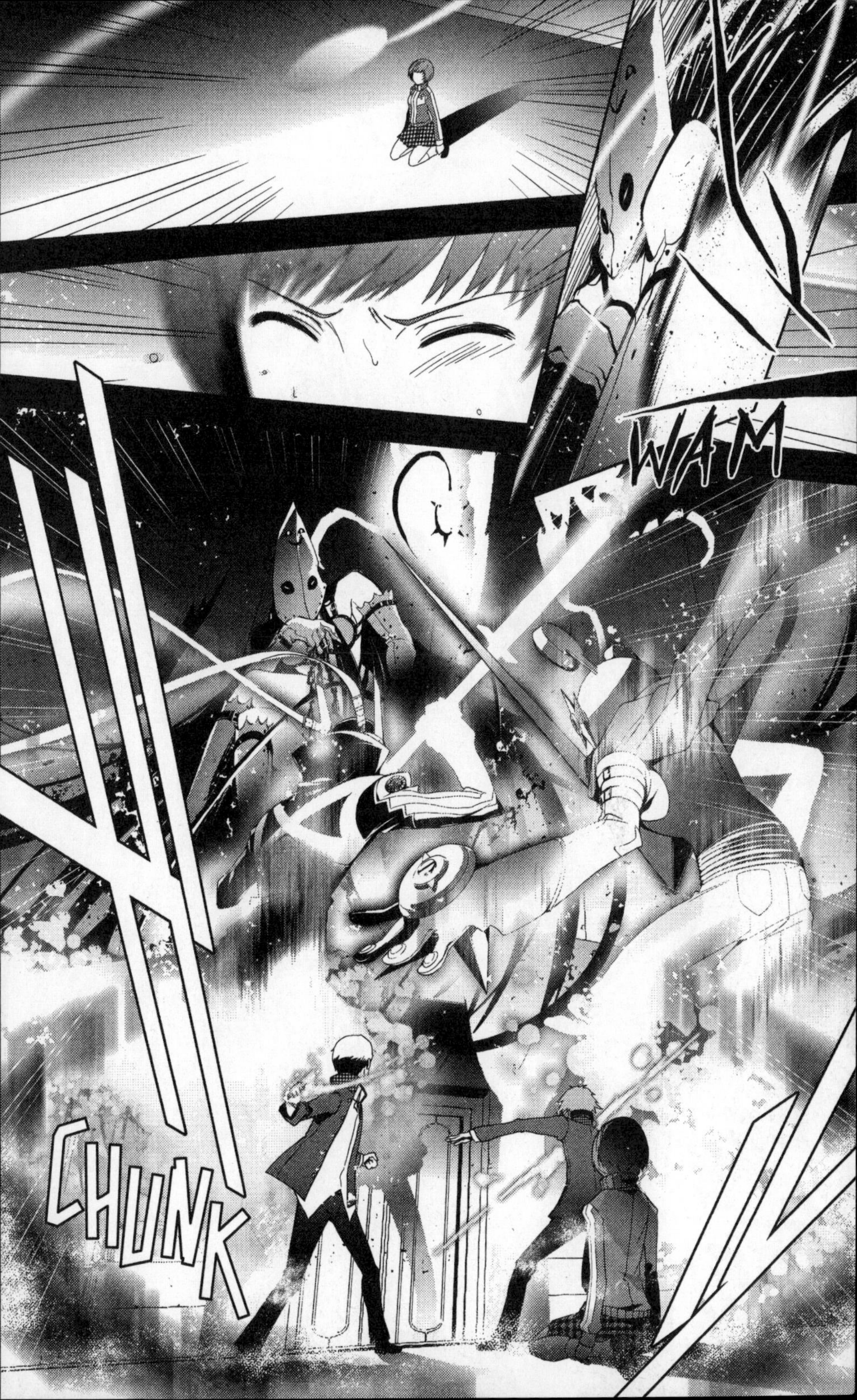
WAM
CHUNK

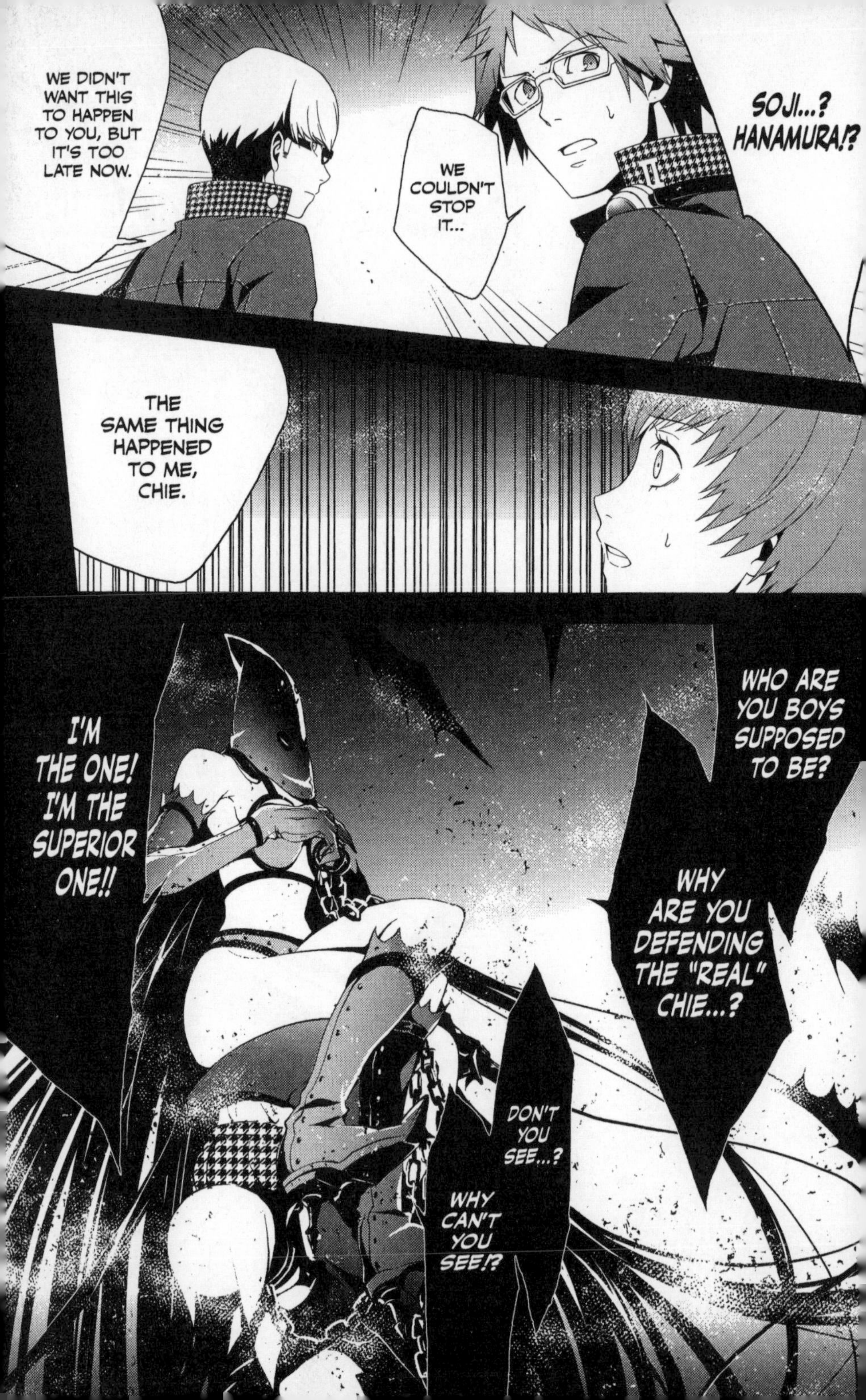
SOJI...? HANAMURA!?
WE COULDN'T STOP IT...
WE DIDN'T WANT THIS TO HAPPEN TO YOU, BUT IT'S TOO LATE NOW.
THE SAME THING HAPPENED TO ME, CHIE.
WHO ARE YOU BOYS SUPPOSED TO BE?
WHY ARE YOU DEFENDING THE "REAL" CHIE...?
DON'T YOU SEE...?
WHY CAN'T YOU SEE!?
I'M THE ONE! I'M THE SUPERIOR ONE!!

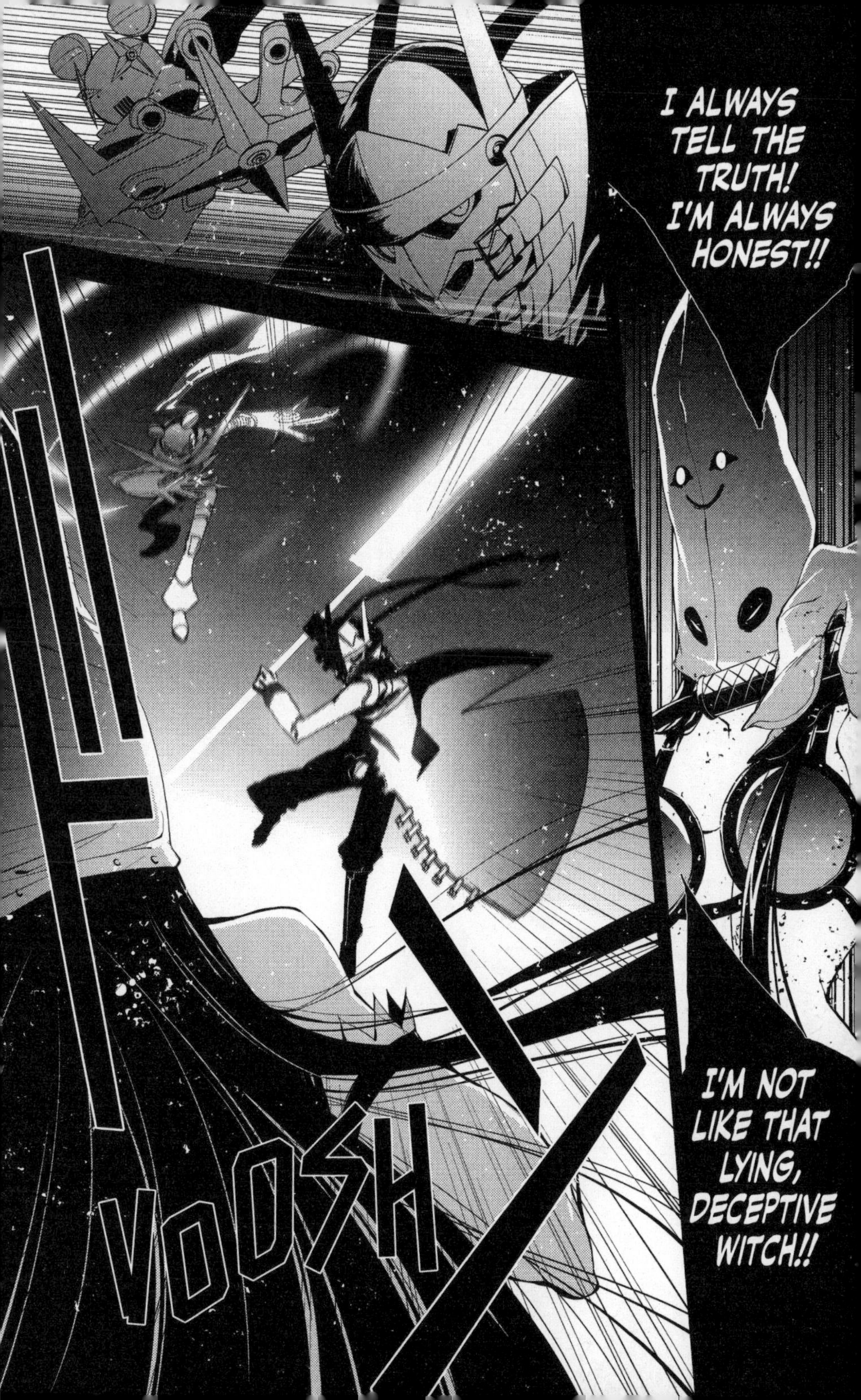
I ALWAYS TELL THE TRUTH! I'M ALWAYS HONEST!!
I'M NOT LIKE THAT LYING, DECEPTIVE WITCH!!
VOOSH

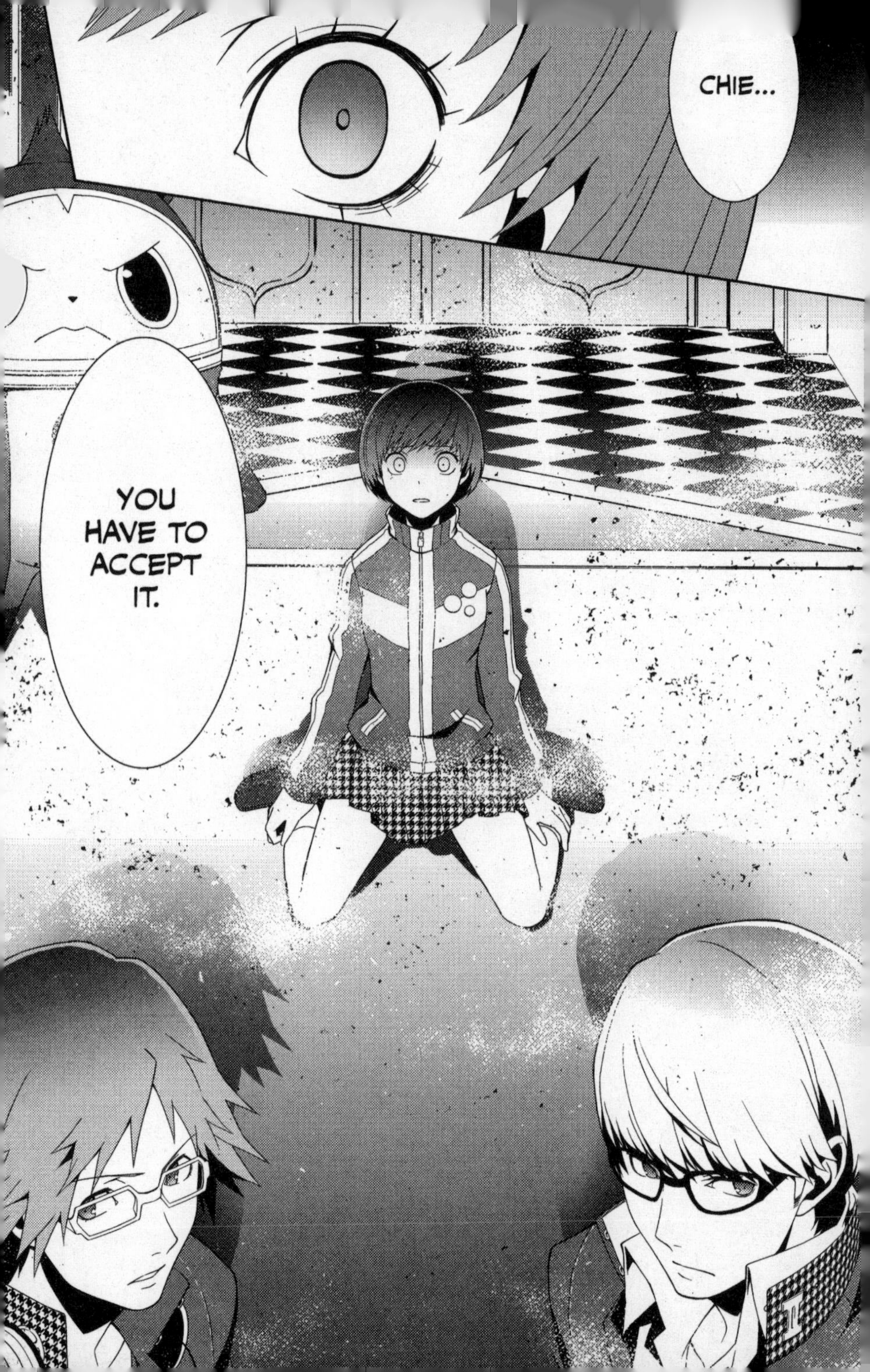
CHIE...
YOU HAVE TO ACCEPT IT.

里中千枝
Chie Satonaka

Chie is a lively girl with a healthy passion for kung fu. In the game, she was all over the place. She was sometimes the voice of common sense, while at other times she seemed totally clueless. She often acted like a total tomboy, but she also proved to be quite emotionally vulnerable. She's probably the strongest person in the whole group physically, and her intuition has proven to be quite keen at times! I was drawn to so many aspects of Chie's character that I didn't hesitate to pick her during my first playthrough. (Don't ask me for what…)

Alongside Yosuke, Chie is a member of the "make funny faces whenever possible" club, and I've had her making some pretty great faces in this manga. The portraits in the game had to be restricted to a limited selection of poses and facial expressions, but the dialogue and voice actors did such a great job of tickling my imagination! I could imagine for myself how Chie would come to life, what kinds of faces she might make, or how she would move.

It's a little off-topic, but I swear there's this certain idol who looks quite similar to Shadow Chie. I'm not saying she has an evil grin or anything, but… there's just something about her that reminds me of Shadow Chie. I won't name any names, of course, but I am a huge fan. (I know no one asked…)

PERSONA 4 CHARACTER NOTE

#09: CHIE SATONAKA PART 2

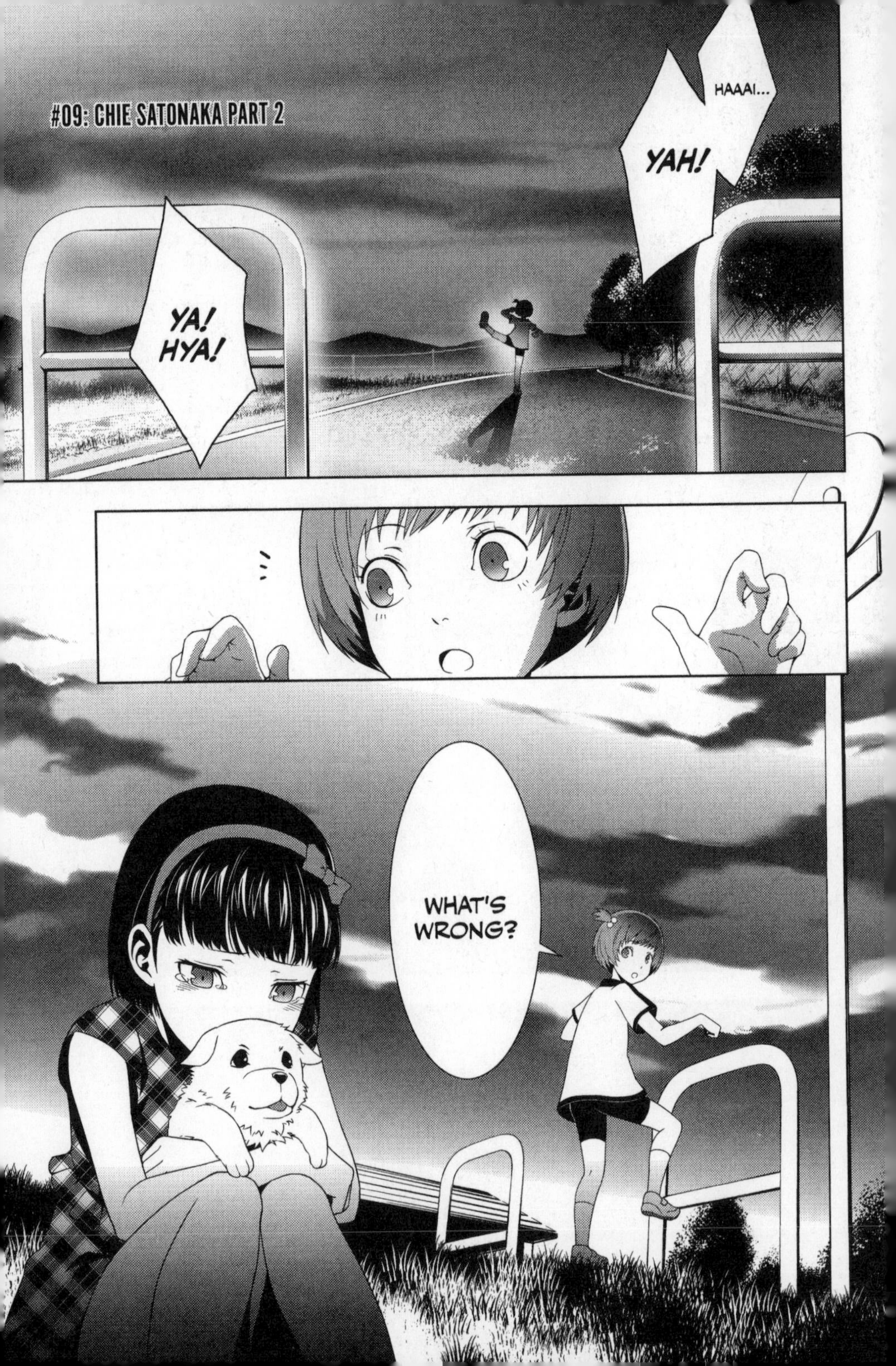

HAAAI...
YAH!
YA! HYA!
WHAT'S WRONG?

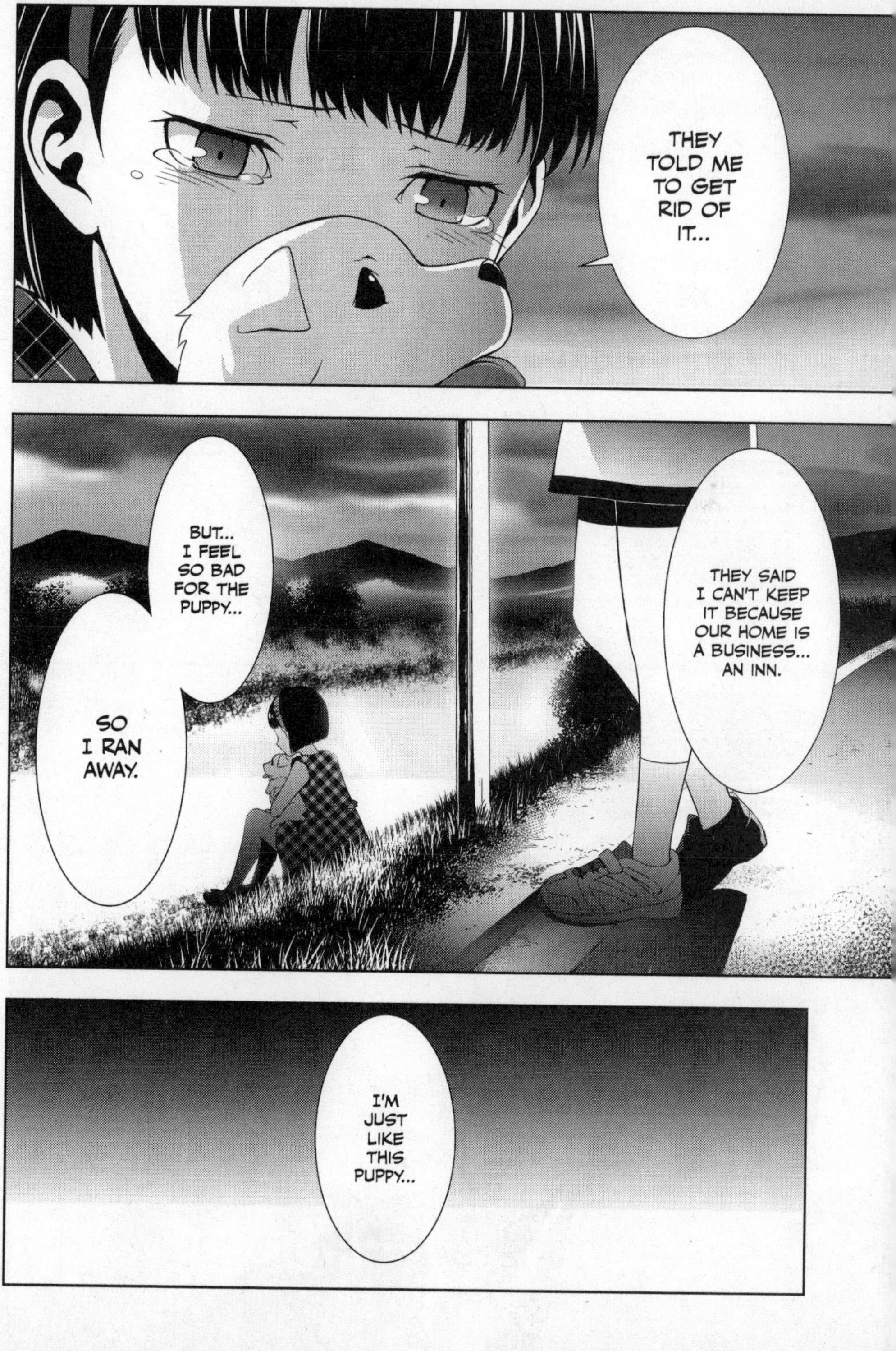
THEY TOLD ME TO GET RID OF IT...
THEY SAID I CAN'T KEEP IT BECAUSE OUR HOME IS A BUSINESS... AN INN.
BUT... I FEEL SO BAD FOR THE PUPPY...
SO I RAN AWAY.
I'M JUST LIKE THIS PUPPY...

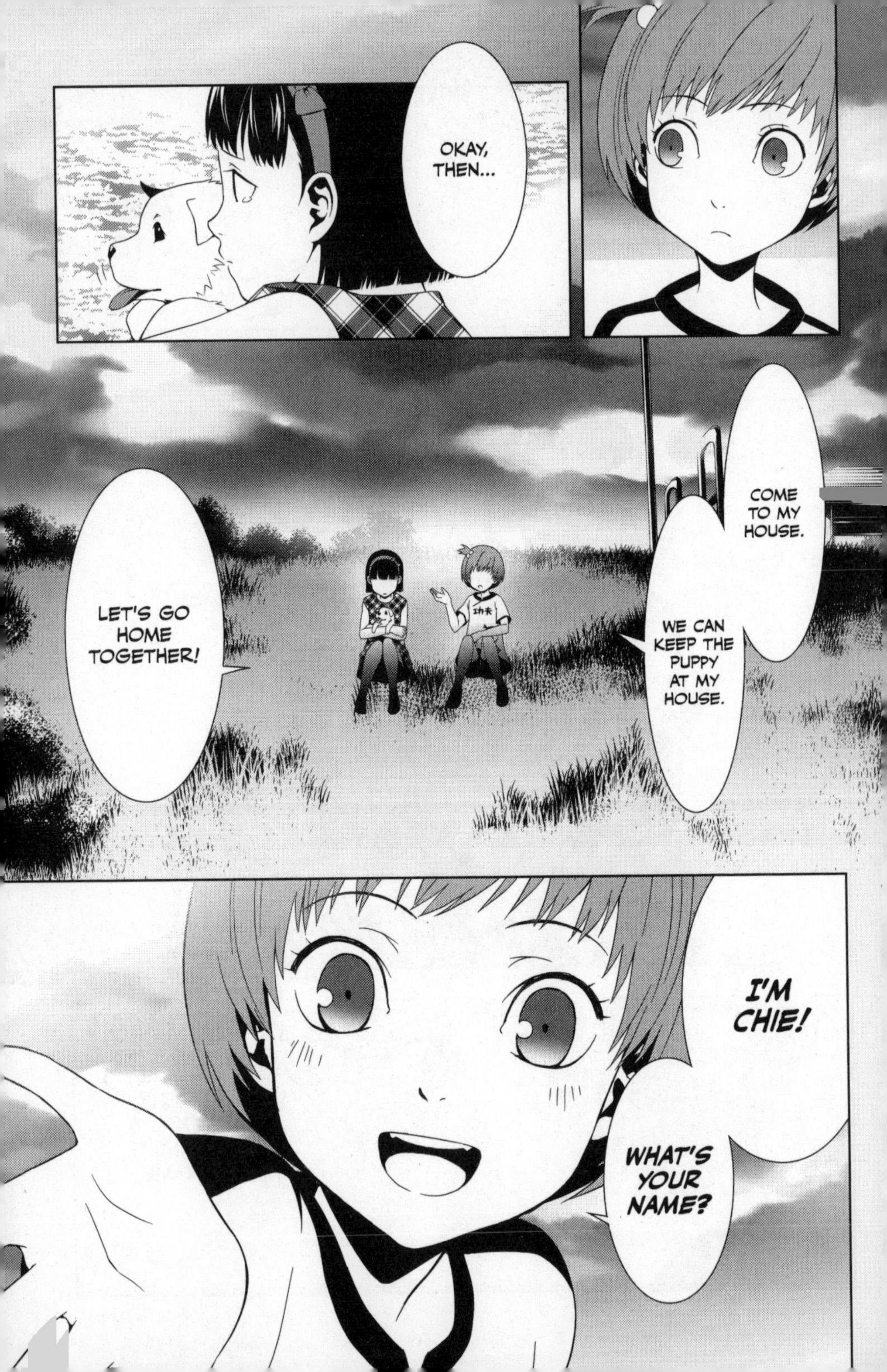
OKAY, THEN...
COME TO MY HOUSE.
WE CAN KEEP THE PUPPY AT MY HOUSE.
LET'S GO HOME TOGETHER!
I'M CHIE!
WHAT'S YOUR NAME?

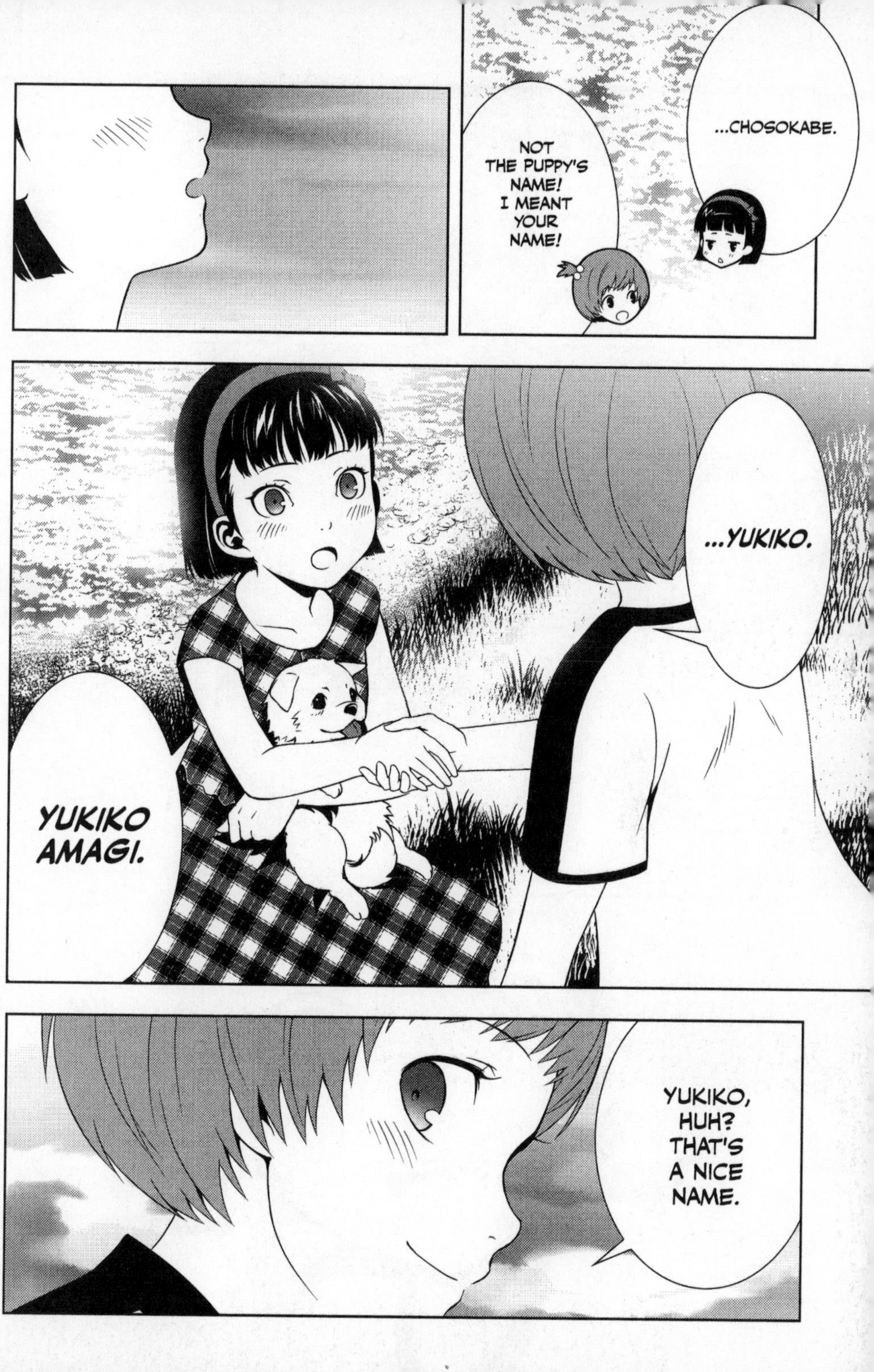
...CHOSOKABE.
NOT THE PUPPY'S NAME! I MEANT YOUR NAME!
...YUKIKO.
YUKIKO AMAGI.
YUKIKO, HUH? THAT'S A NICE NAME.

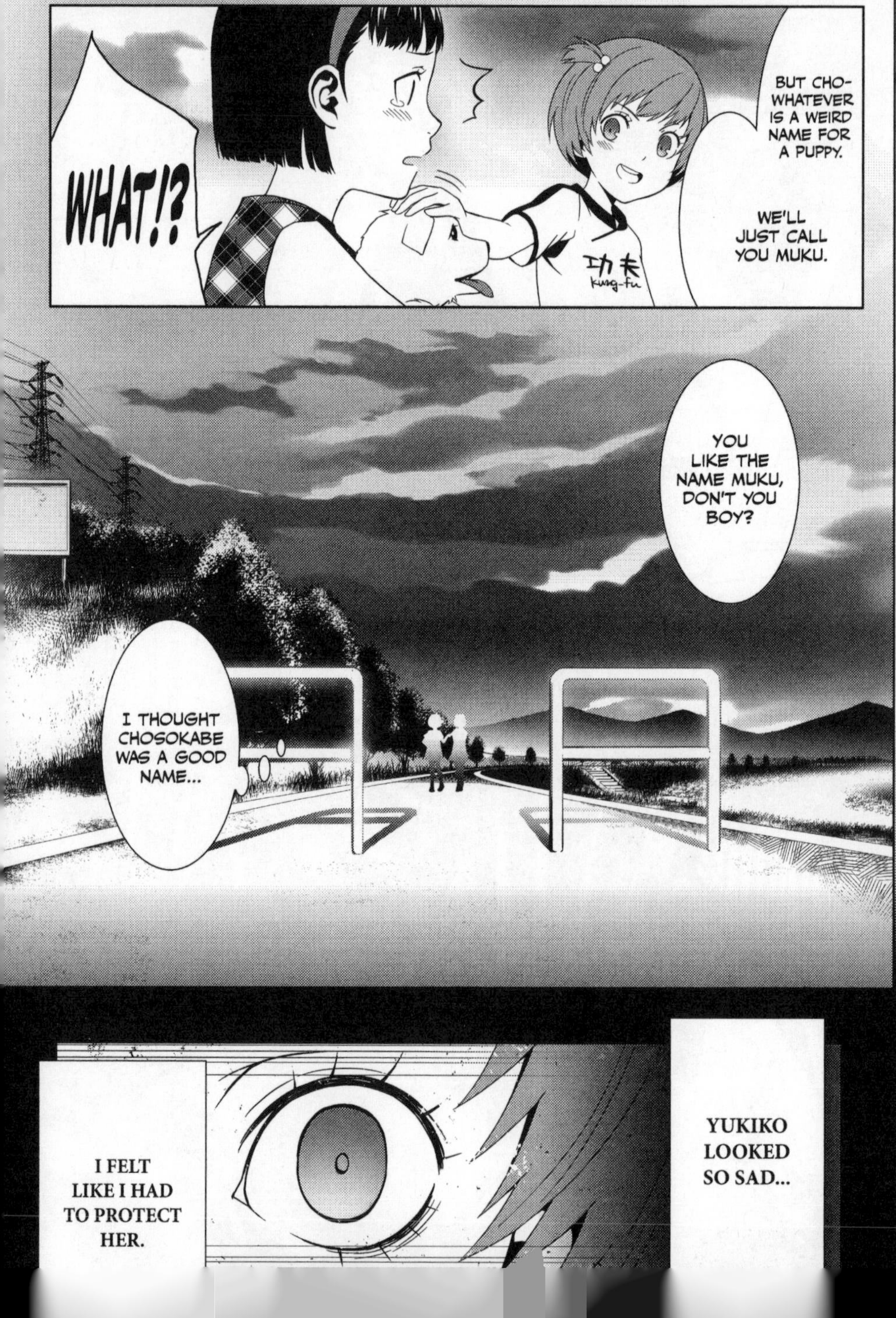
BUT CHO-WHATEVER IS A WEIRD NAME FOR A PUPPY.
WE'LL JUST CALL YOU MUKU.
WHAT!?
工夫 kung-fu
YOU LIKE THE NAME MUKU, DON'T YOU BOY?
I THOUGHT CHOSOKABE WAS A GOOD NAME...
YUKIKO LOOKED SO SAD...
I FELT LIKE I HAD TO PROTECT HER.

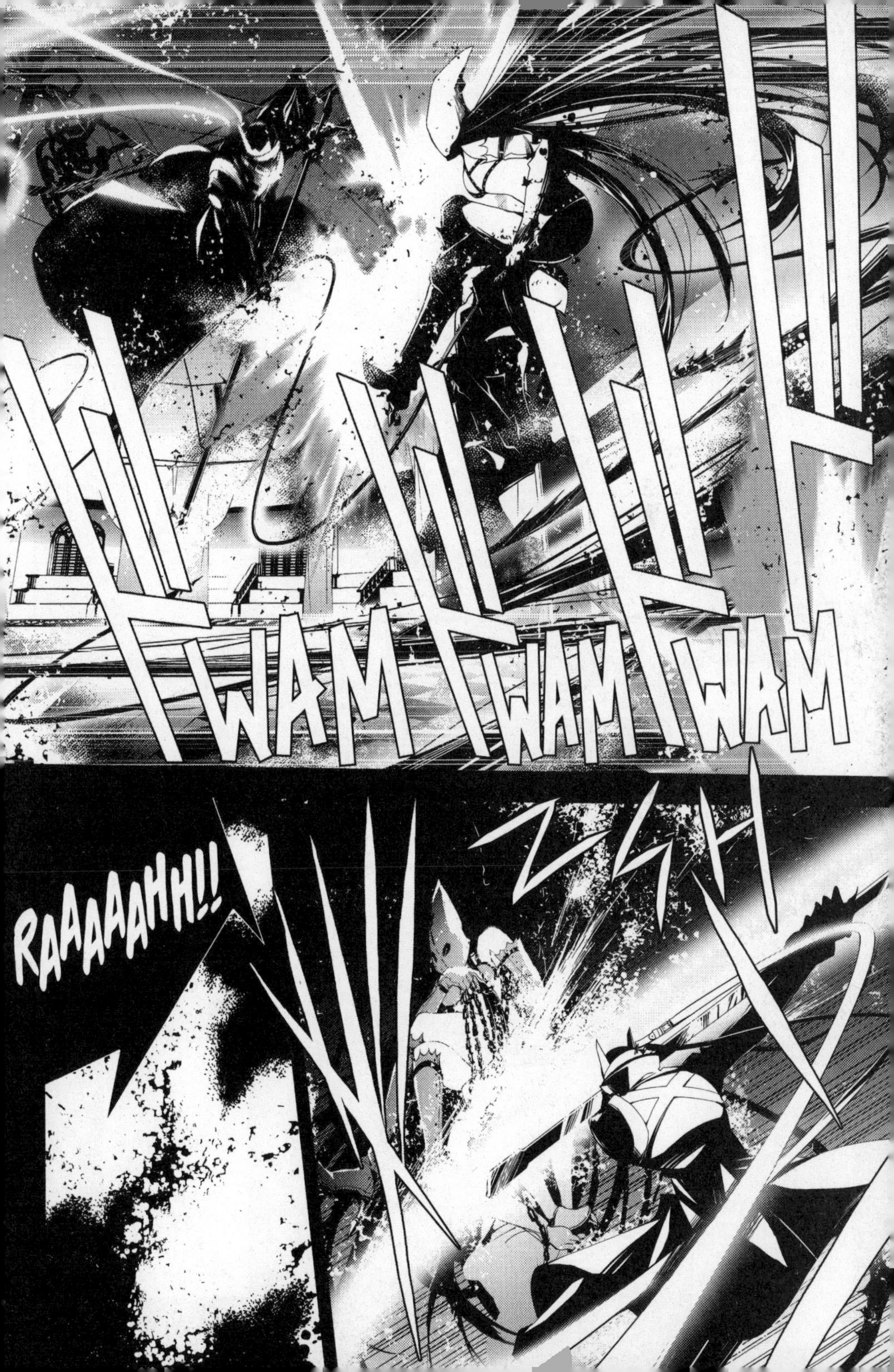
WAM WAM WAM
ZSSH
RAAAAAHH!!

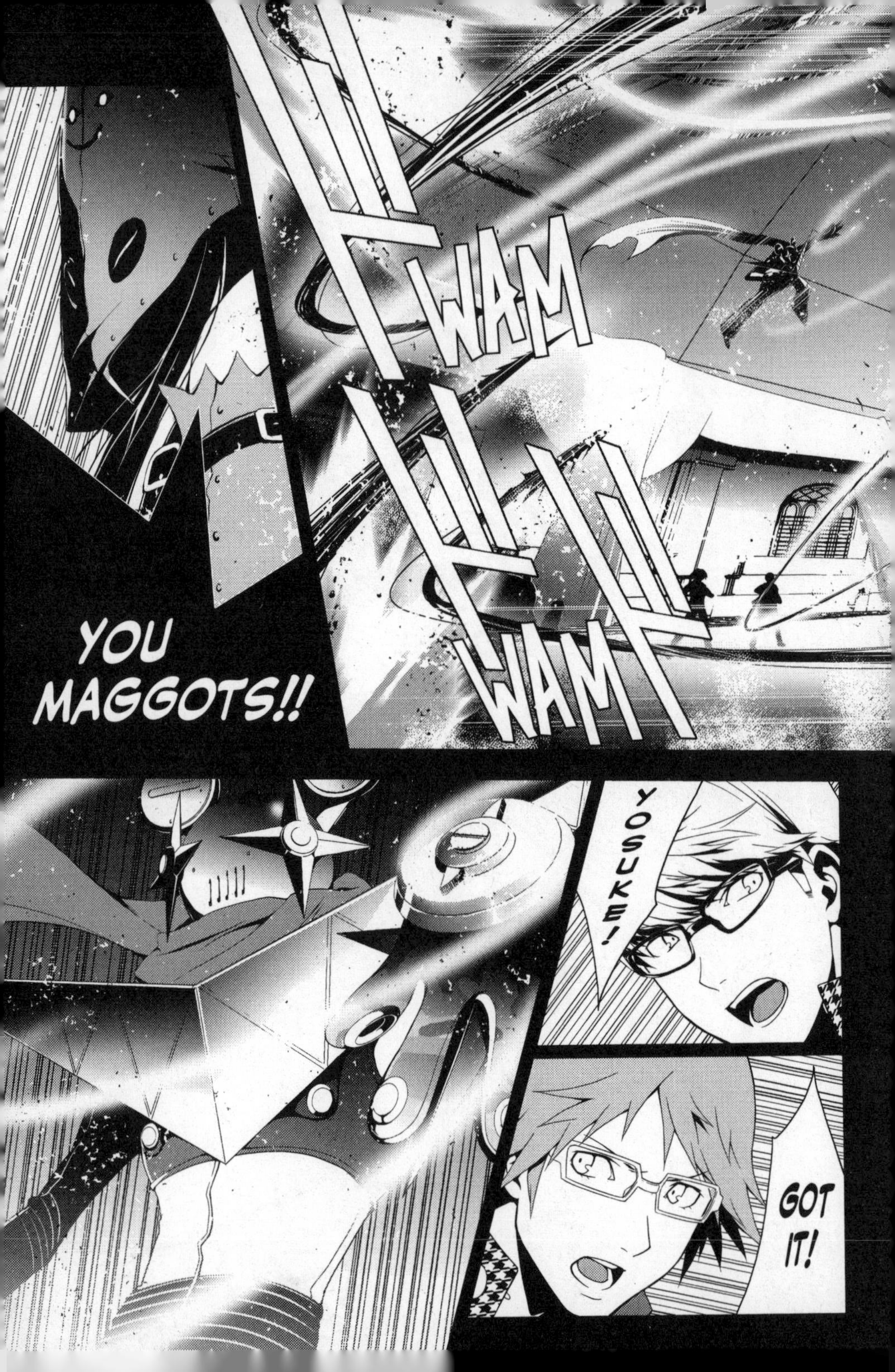
WAM
WAM
WAM
YOU MAGGOTS!!
YOSUKE!
GOT IT!

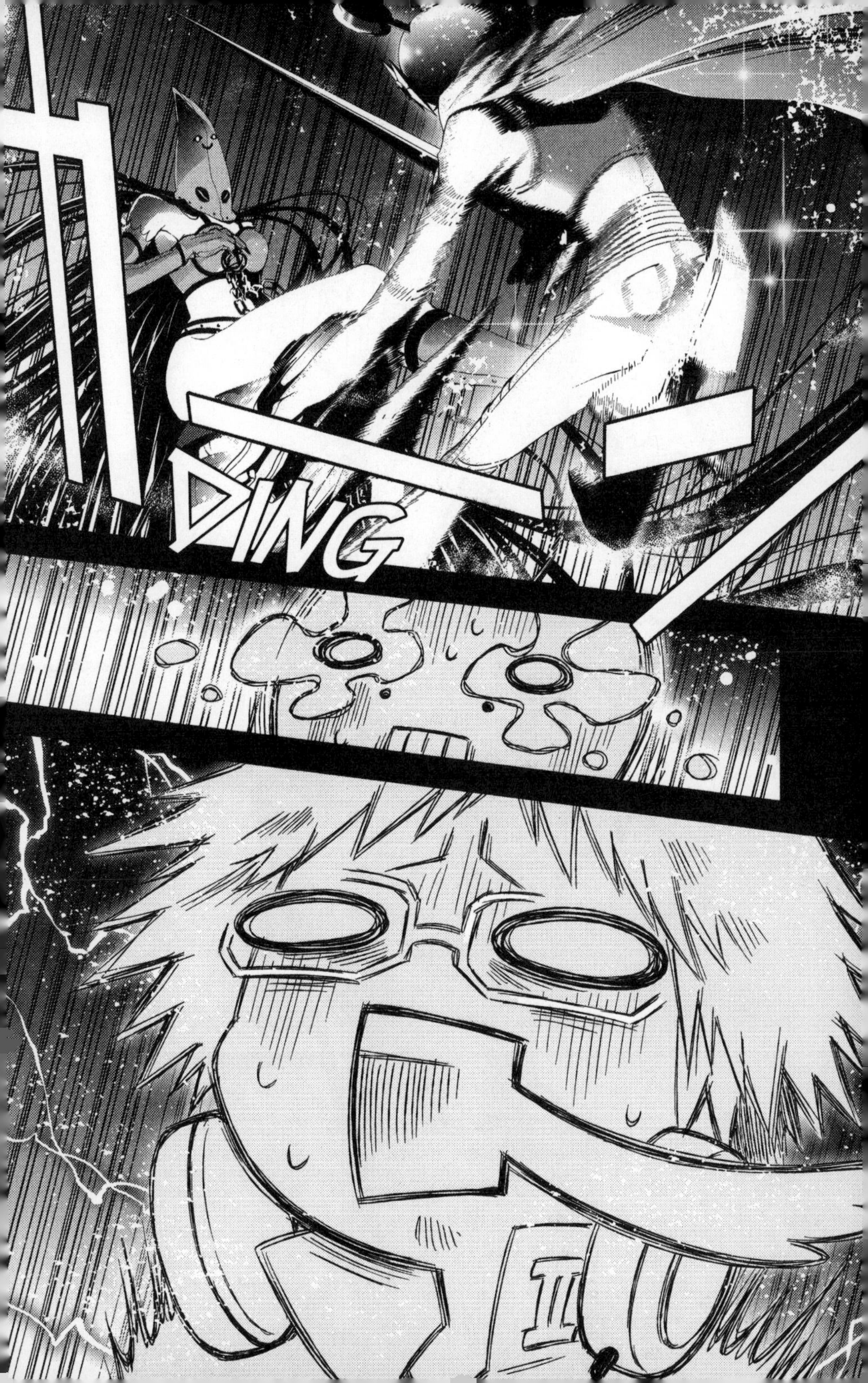
DING

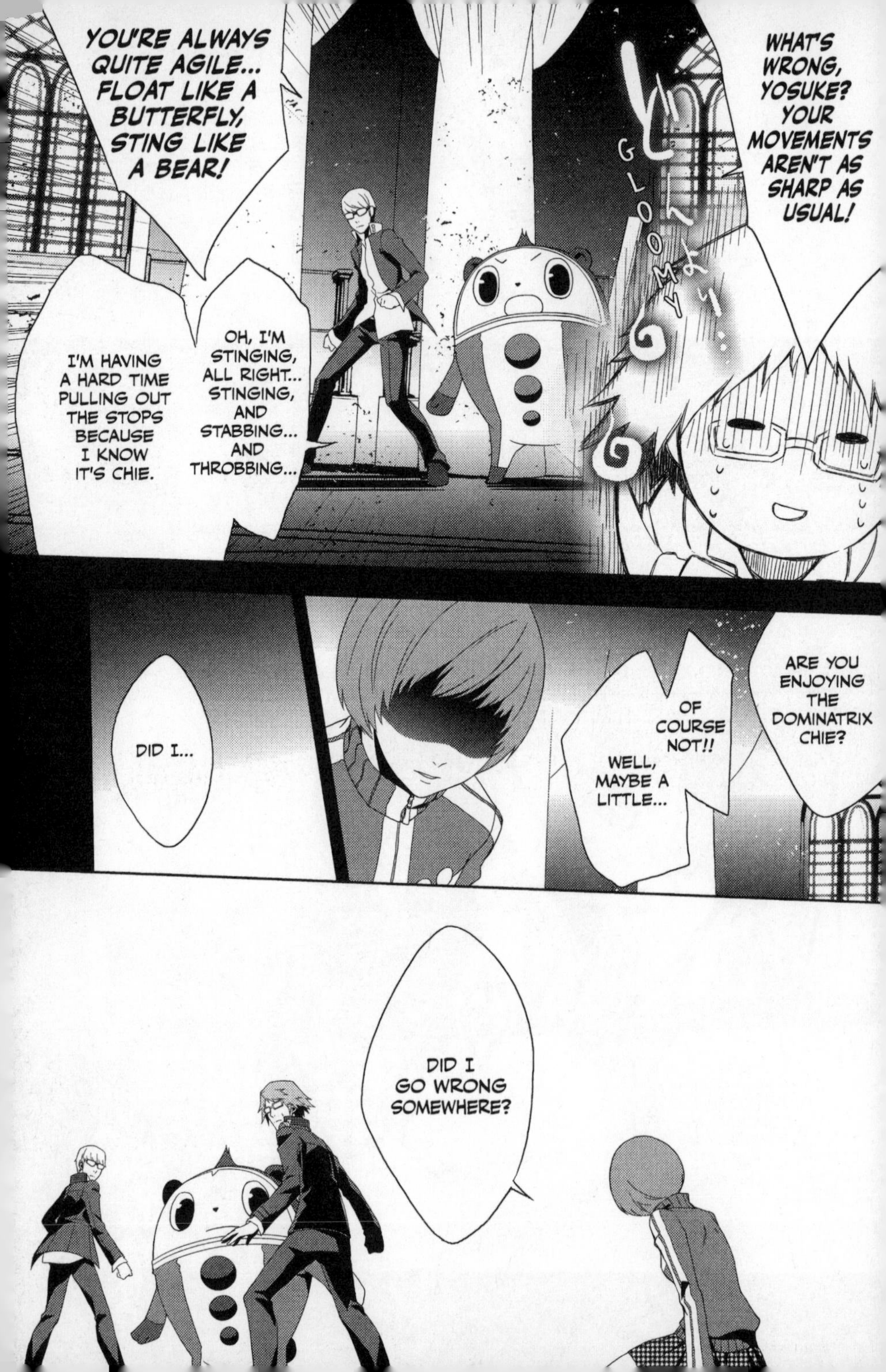
WHAT'S WRONG, YOSUKE? YOUR MOVEMENTS AREN'T AS SHARP AS USUAL!
GLOOMY
YOU'RE ALWAYS QUITE AGILE... FLOAT LIKE A BUTTERFLY, STING LIKE A BEAR!
OH, I'M STINGING, ALL RIGHT... STINGING, AND STABBING... AND THROBBING...
I'M HAVING A HARD TIME PULLING OUT THE STOPS BECAUSE I KNOW IT'S CHIE.
ARE YOU ENJOYING THE DOMINATRIX CHIE?
OF COURSE NOT!!
WELL, MAYBE A LITTLE...
DID I...
DID I GO WRONG SOMEWHERE?

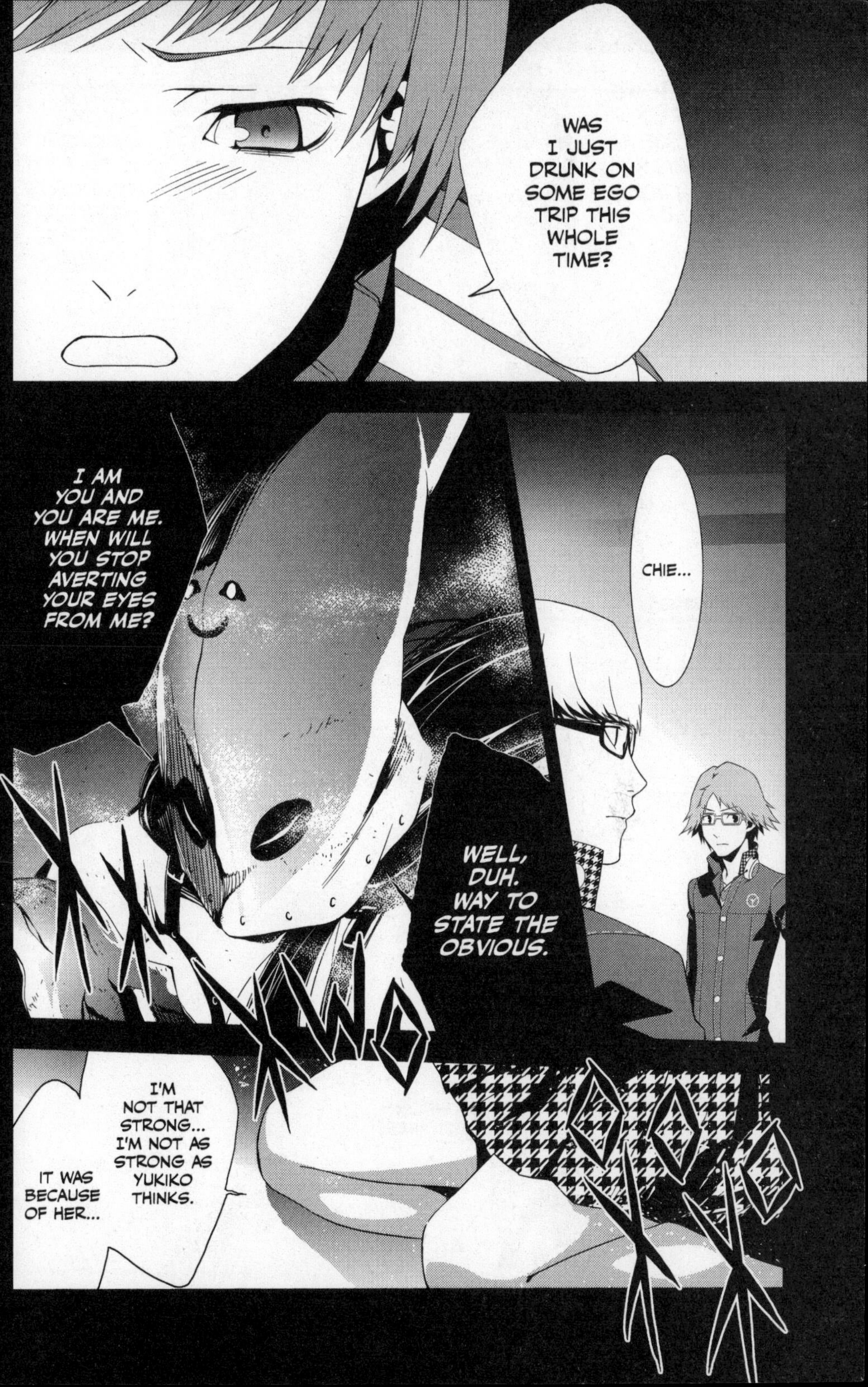

WAS I JUST DRUNK ON SOME EGO TRIP THIS WHOLE TIME?
CHIE...
WELL, DUH. WAY TO STATE THE OBVIOUS.
I AM YOU AND YOU ARE ME. WHEN WILL YOU STOP AVERTING YOUR EYES FROM ME?
I'M NOT THAT STRONG... I'M NOT AS STRONG AS YUKIKO THINKS.
IT WAS BECAUSE OF HER...

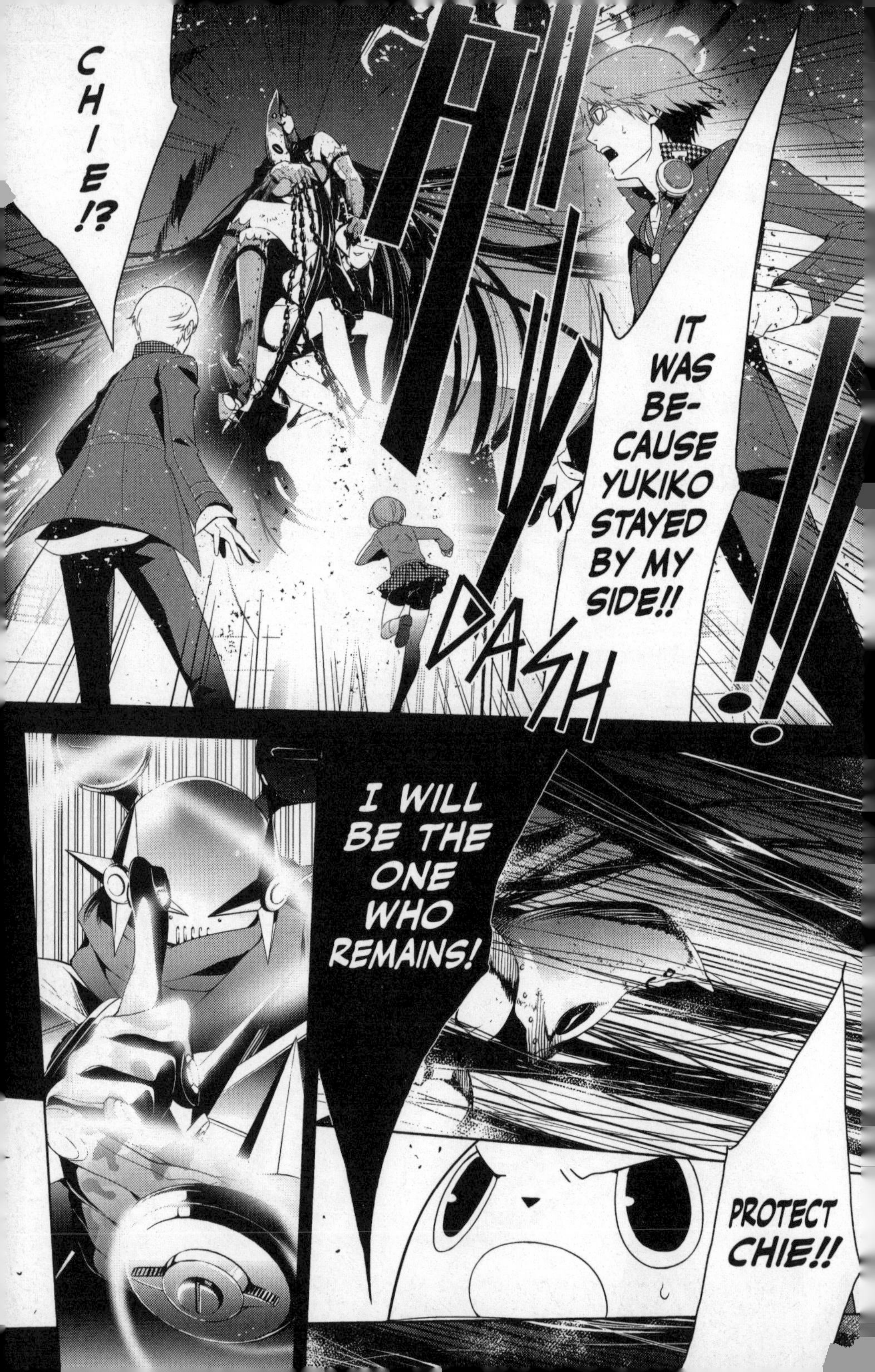
IT WAS BE-CAUSE YUKIKO STAYED BY MY SIDE!!
DASH
CHIE!?
I WILL BE THE ONE WHO REMAINS!
PROTECT CHIE!!

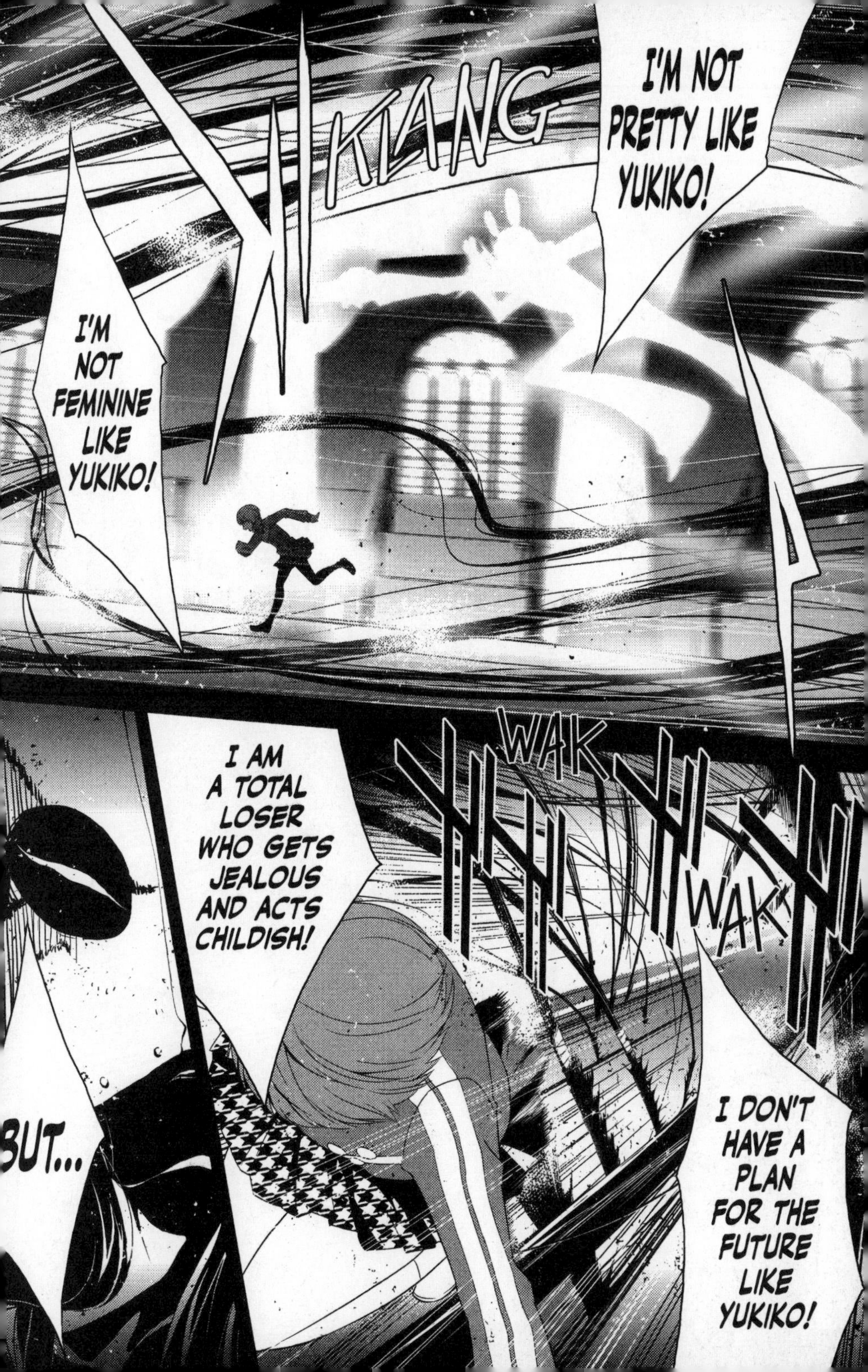
I'M NOT PRETTY LIKE YUKIKO!
KLANG
I'M NOT FEMININE LIKE YUKIKO!
WAK
WAK
I AM A TOTAL LOSER WHO GETS JEALOUS AND ACTS CHILDISH!
I DON'T HAVE A PLAN FOR THE FUTURE LIKE YUKIKO!
BUT...

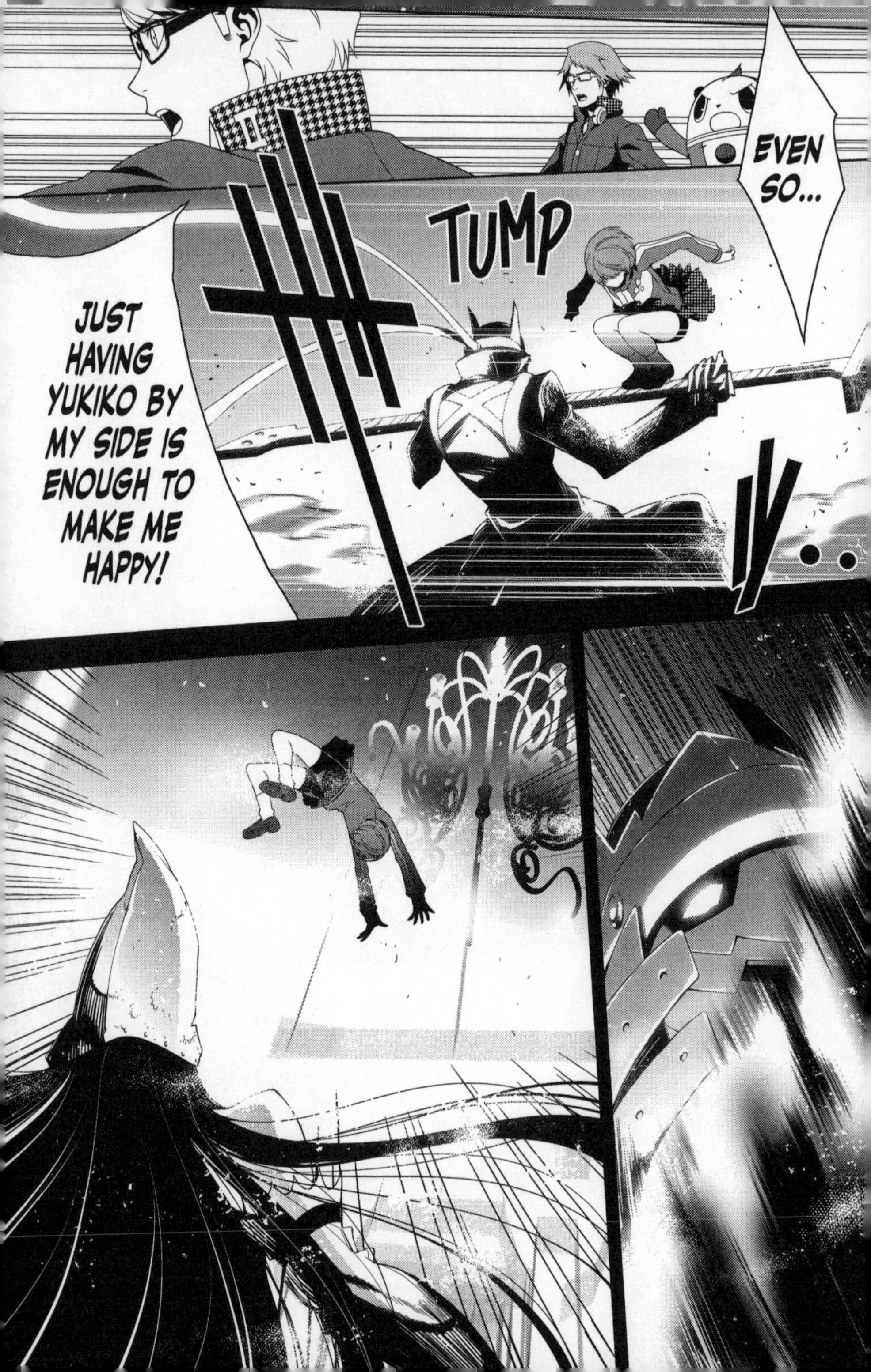
EVEN SO...
TUMP
JUST HAVING YUKIKO BY MY SIDE IS ENOUGH TO MAKE ME HAPPY!

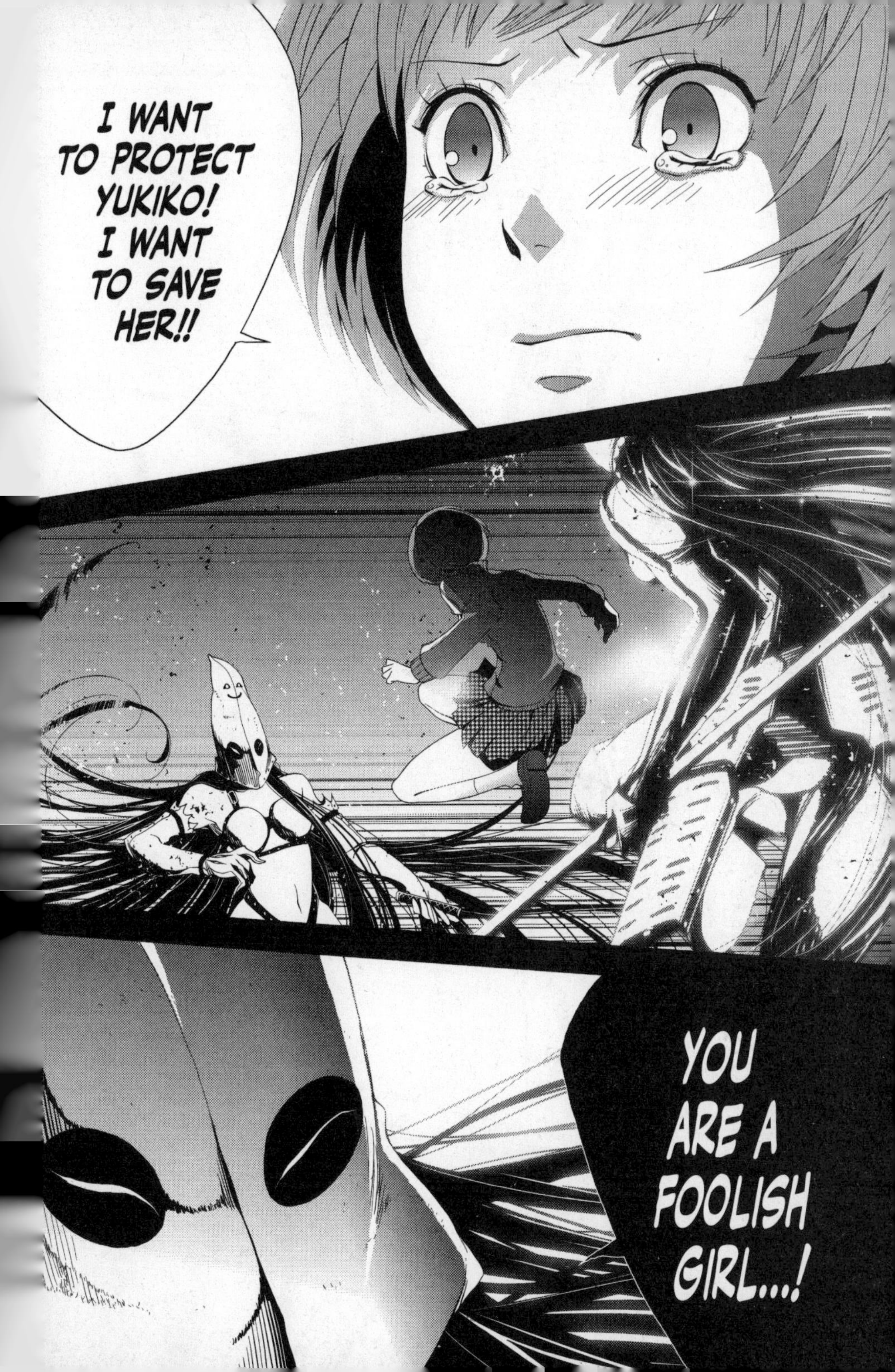
I WANT TO PROTECT YUKIKO! I WANT TO SAVE HER!!
YOU ARE A FOOLISH GIRL...!

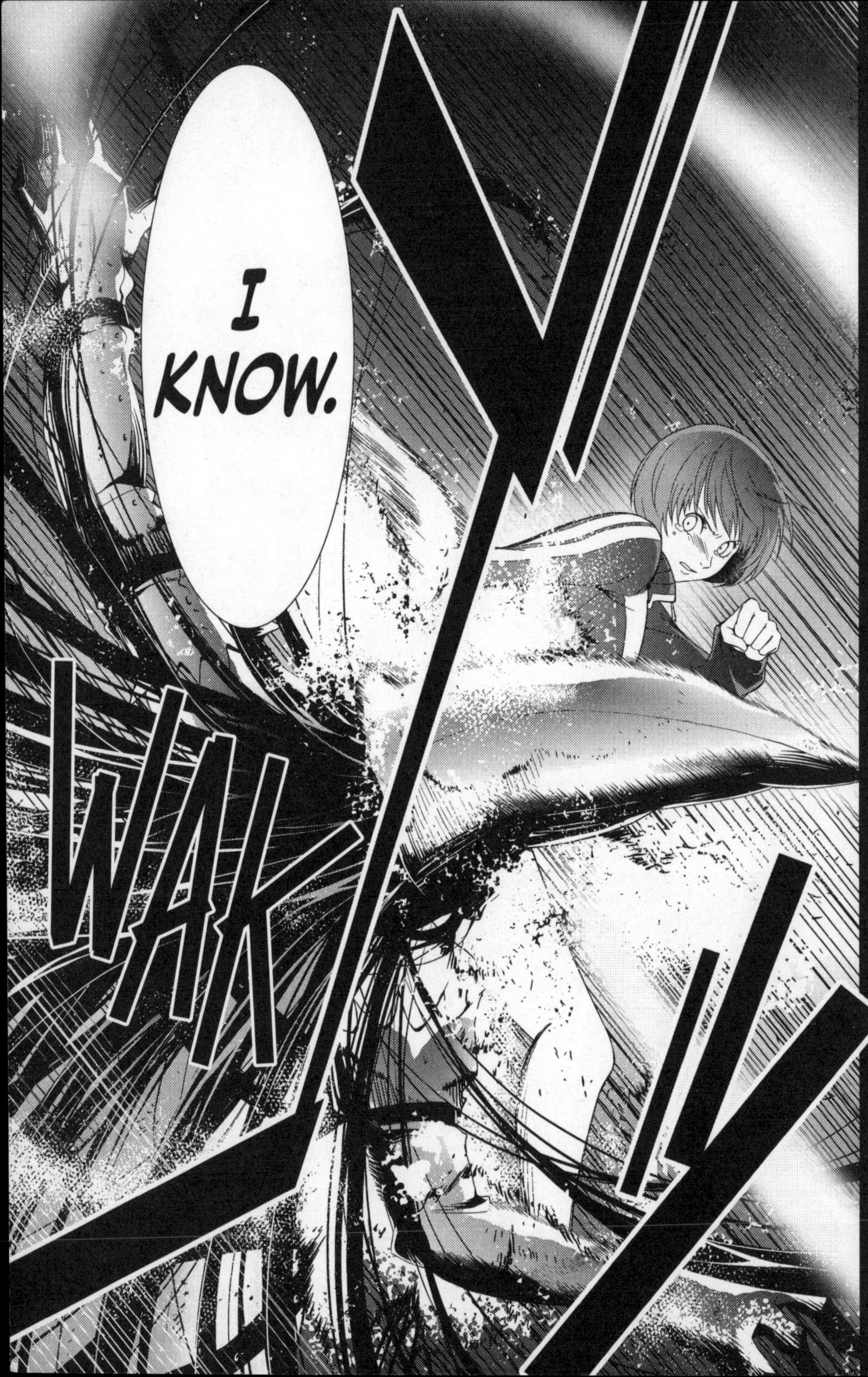
I KNOW.
WAK

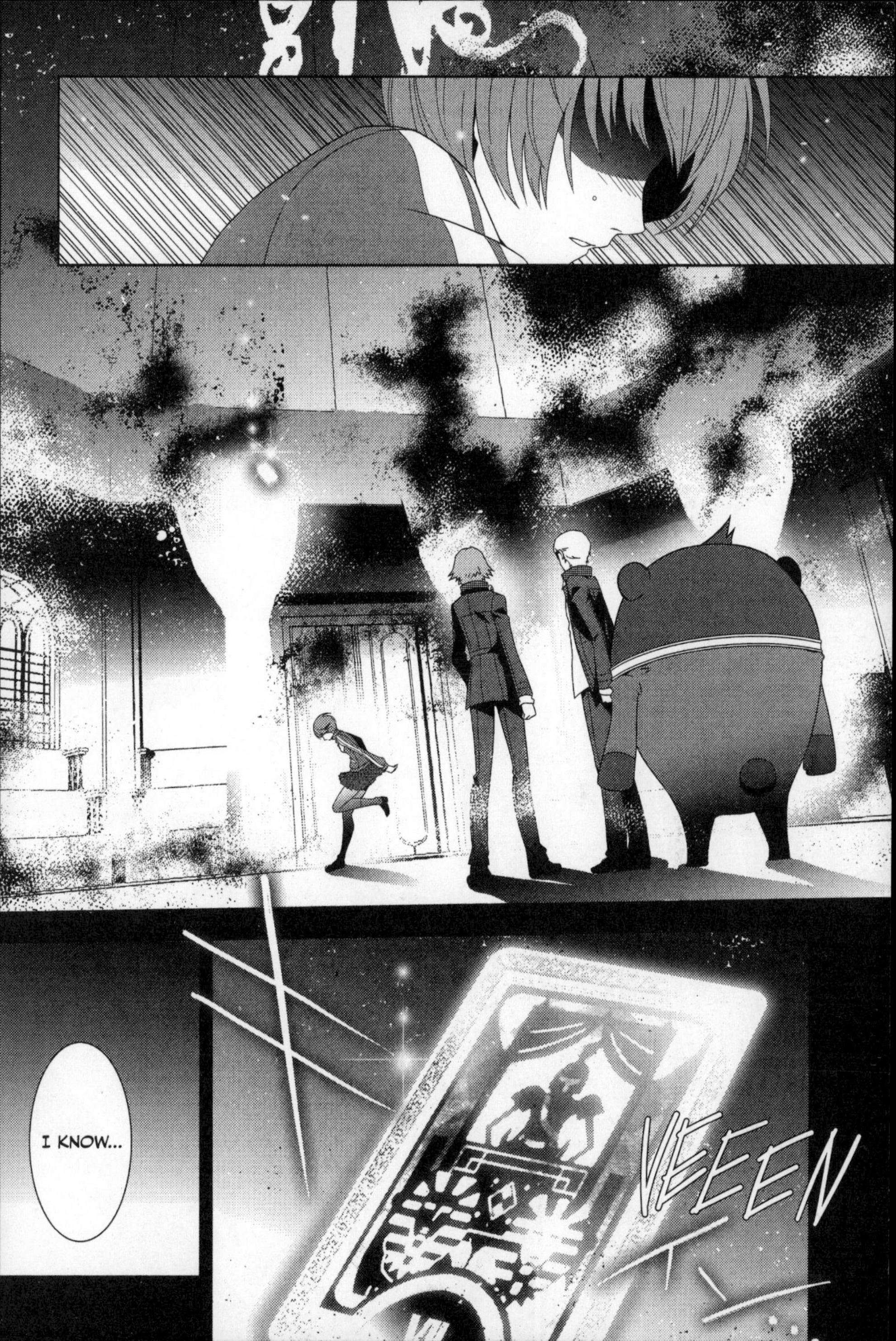
VEEEN
I KNOW...

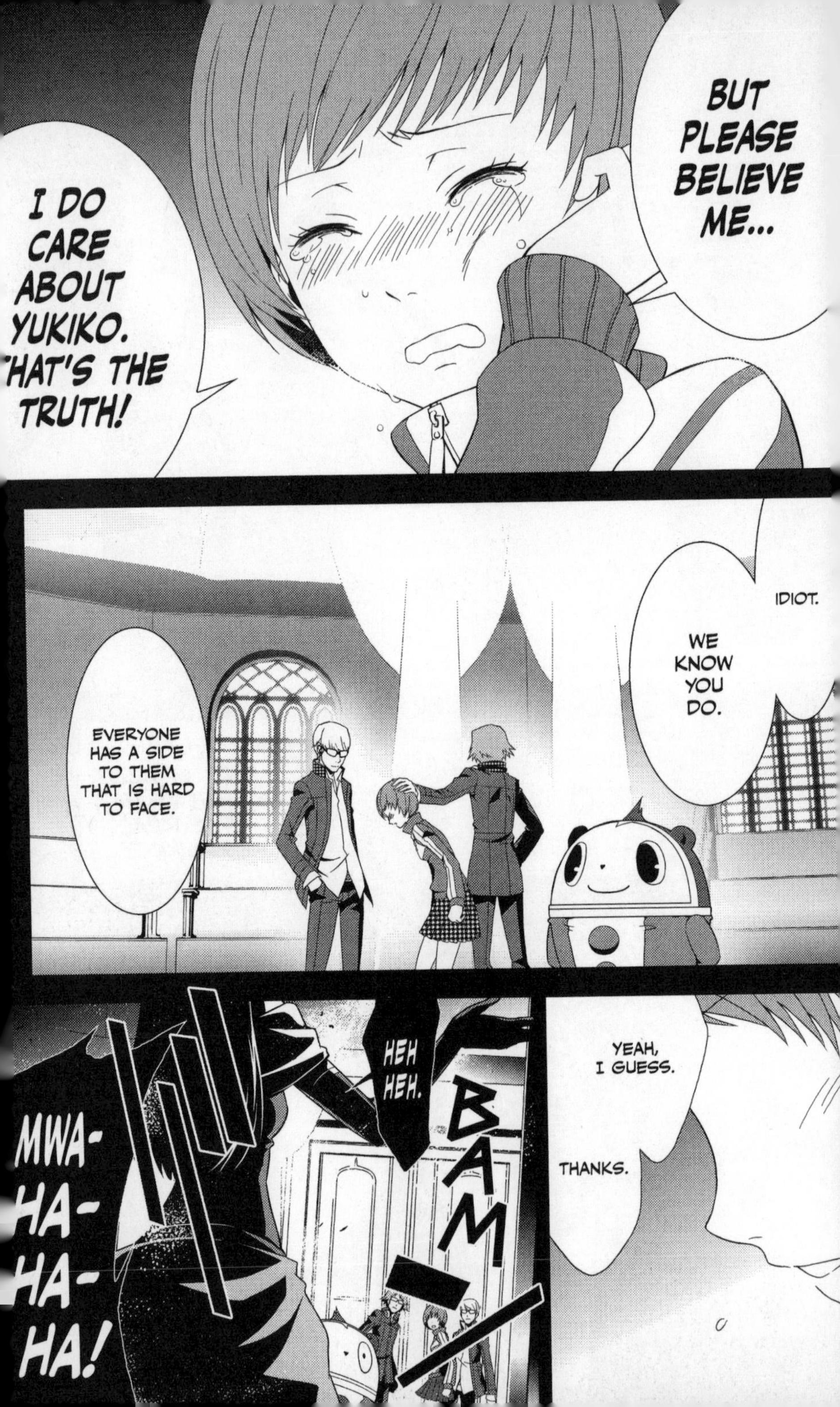
BUT PLEASE BELIEVE ME...
I DO CARE ABOUT YUKIKO. 'HAT'S THE TRUTH!
IDIOT.
WE KNOW YOU DO.
EVERYONE HAS A SIDE TO THEM THAT IS HARD TO FACE.
YEAH, I GUESS.
THANKS.
HEH HEH.
BAM
MWA-HA-HA-HA-HA!

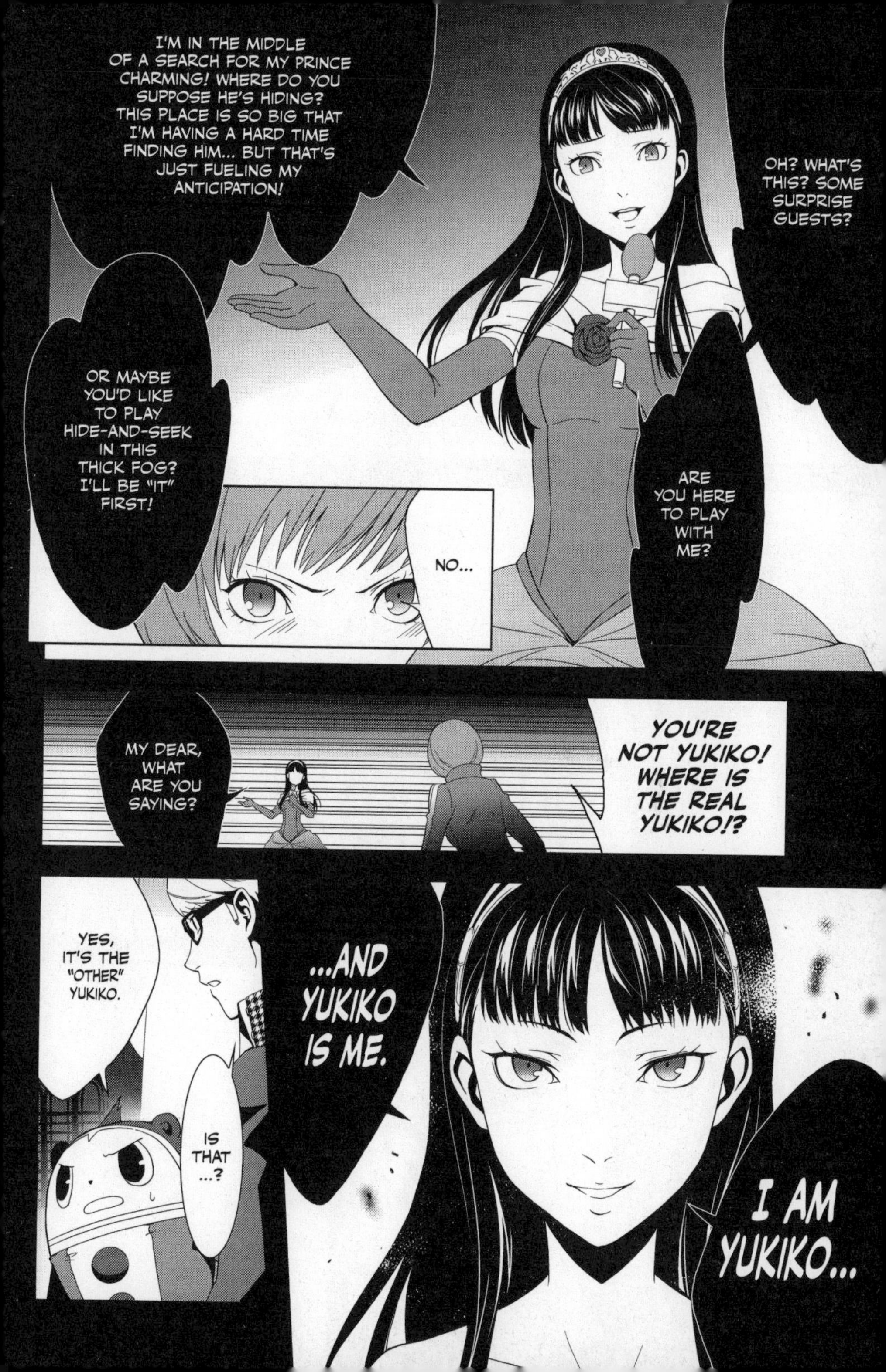
OH? WHAT'S THIS? SOME SURPRISE GUESTS?
I'M IN THE MIDDLE OF A SEARCH FOR MY PRINCE CHARMING! WHERE DO YOU SUPPOSE HE'S HIDING? THIS PLACE IS SO BIG THAT I'M HAVING A HARD TIME FINDING HIM... BUT THAT'S JUST FUELING MY ANTICIPATION!
ARE YOU HERE TO PLAY WITH ME?
OR MAYBE YOU'D LIKE TO PLAY HIDE-AND-SEEK IN THIS THICK FOG? I'LL BE "IT" FIRST!
NO...
YOU'RE NOT YUKIKO! WHERE IS THE REAL YUKIKO!?
MY DEAR, WHAT ARE YOU SAYING?
I AM YUKIKO...
...AND YUKIKO IS ME.
YES, IT'S THE "OTHER" YUKIKO.
IS THAT ...?

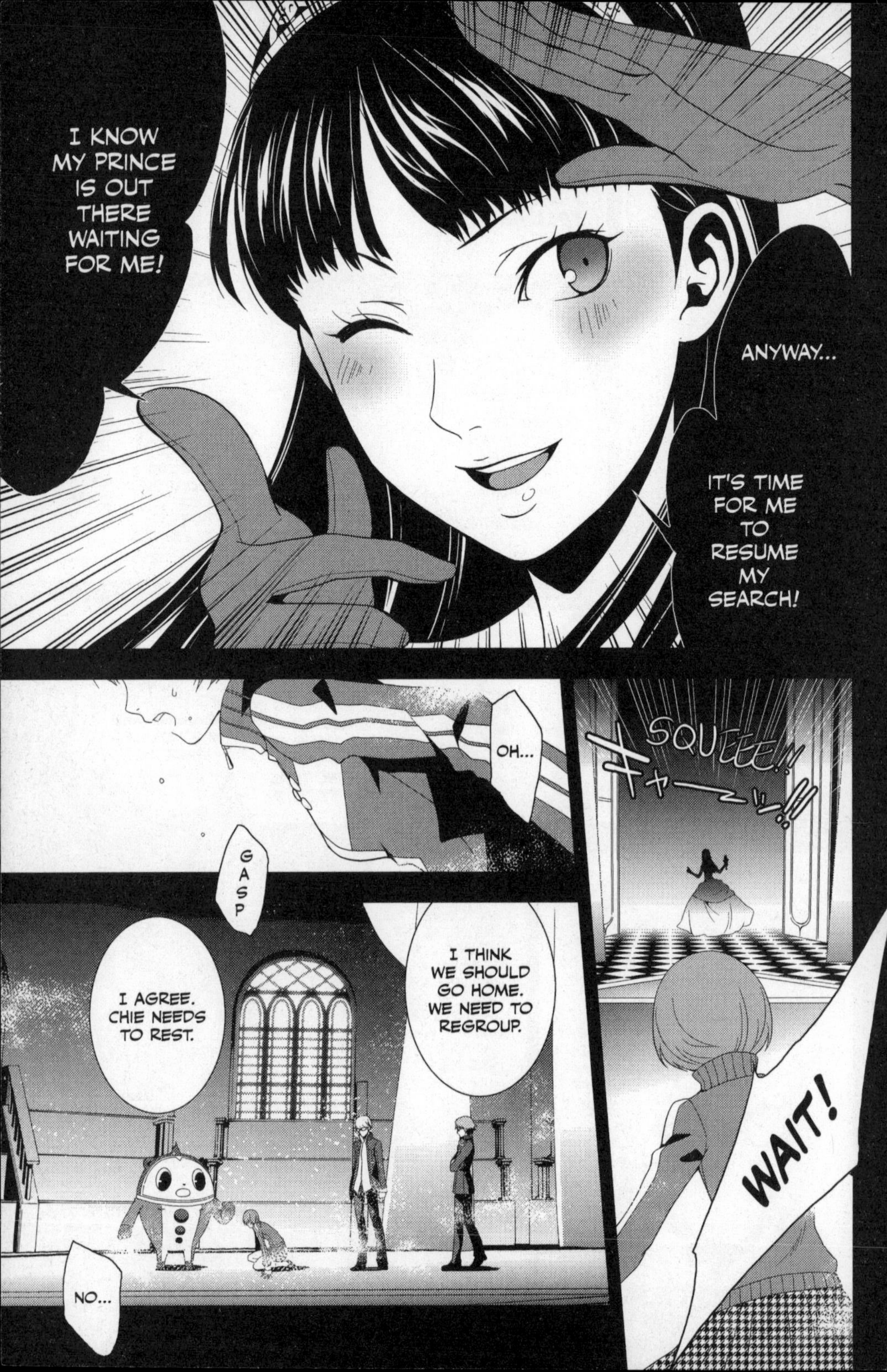
I KNOW MY PRINCE IS OUT THERE WAITING FOR ME!
ANYWAY...
IT'S TIME FOR ME TO RESUME MY SEARCH!
SQUEEEE!!
キャーーッ!!
WAIT!
OH...
GASP
I THINK WE SHOULD GO HOME. WE NEED TO REGROUP.
I AGREE. CHIE NEEDS TO REST.
NO...

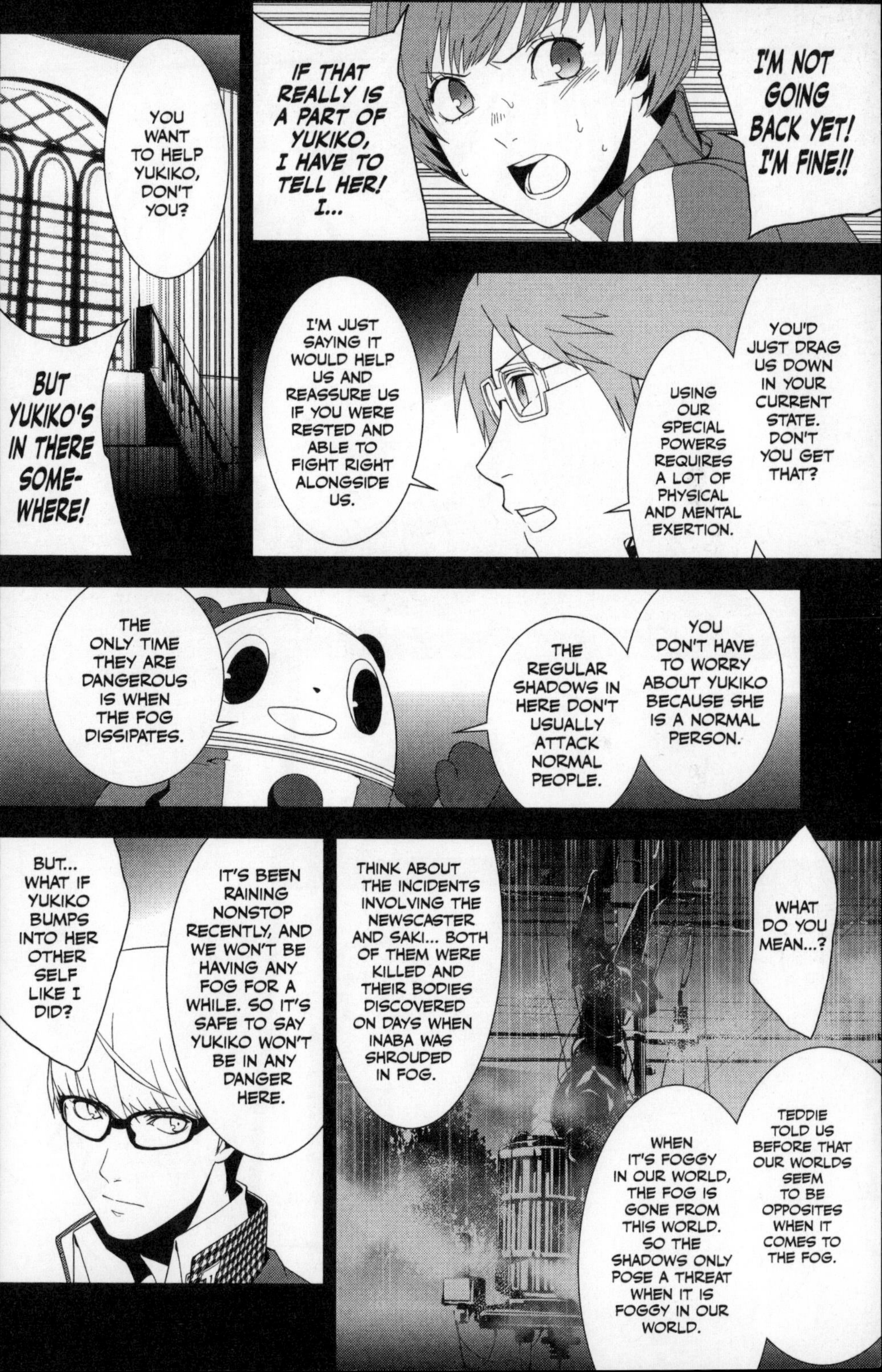
I'M NOT GOING BACK YET! I'M FINE!!
IF THAT REALLY IS A PART OF YUKIKO, I HAVE TO TELL HER! I...
YOU'D JUST DRAG US DOWN IN YOUR CURRENT STATE. DON'T YOU GET THAT?
USING OUR SPECIAL POWERS REQUIRES A LOT OF PHYSICAL AND MENTAL EXERTION.
I'M JUST SAYING IT WOULD HELP US AND REASSURE US IF YOU WERE RESTED AND ABLE TO FIGHT RIGHT ALONGSIDE US.
YOU WANT TO HELP YUKIKO, DON'T YOU?
BUT YUKIKO'S IN THERE SOME-WHERE!
YOU DON'T HAVE TO WORRY ABOUT YUKIKO BECAUSE SHE IS A NORMAL PERSON.
THE REGULAR SHADOWS IN HERE DON'T USUALLY ATTACK NORMAL PEOPLE.
THE ONLY TIME THEY ARE DANGEROUS IS WHEN THE FOG DISSIPATES.
WHAT DO YOU MEAN...?
TEDDIE TOLD US BEFORE THAT OUR WORLDS SEEM TO BE OPPOSITES WHEN IT COMES TO THE FOG.
WHEN IT'S FOGGY IN OUR WORLD, THE FOG IS GONE FROM THIS WORLD. SO THE SHADOWS ONLY POSE A THREAT WHEN IT IS FOGGY IN OUR WORLD.
THINK ABOUT THE INCIDENTS INVOLVING THE NEWSCASTER AND SAKI... BOTH OF THEM WERE KILLED AND THEIR BODIES DISCOVERED ON DAYS WHEN INABA WAS SHROUDED IN FOG.
IT'S BEEN RAINING NONSTOP RECENTLY, AND WE WON'T BE HAVING ANY FOG FOR A WHILE. SO IT'S SAFE TO SAY YUKIKO WON'T BE IN ANY DANGER HERE.
BUT... WHAT IF YUKIKO BUMPS INTO HER OTHER SELF LIKE I DID?

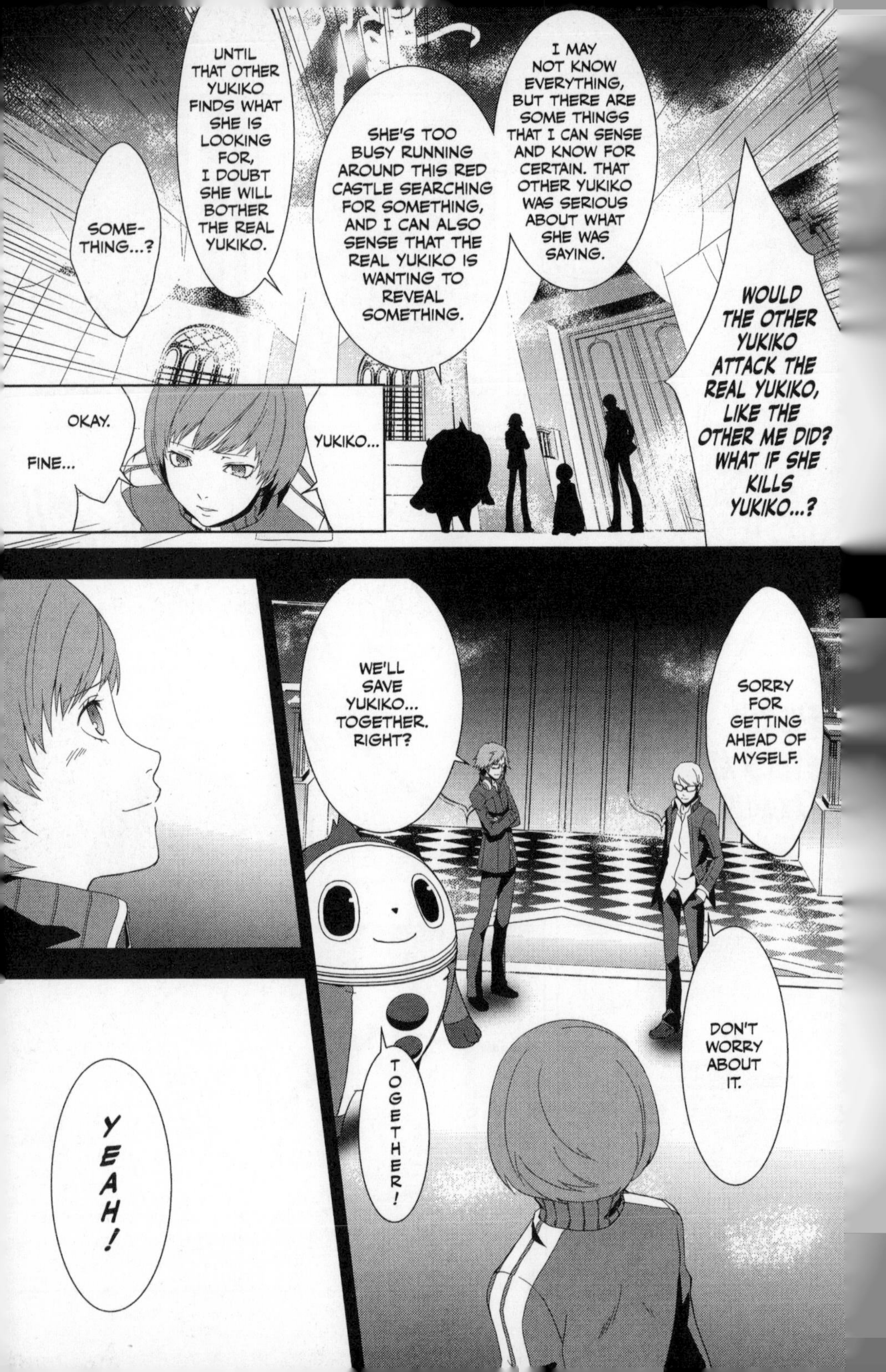
WOULD THE OTHER YUKIKO ATTACK THE REAL YUKIKO, LIKE THE OTHER ME DID? WHAT IF SHE KILLS YUKIKO...?
I MAY NOT KNOW EVERYTHING, BUT THERE ARE SOME THINGS THAT I CAN SENSE AND KNOW FOR CERTAIN. THAT OTHER YUKIKO WAS SERIOUS ABOUT WHAT SHE WAS SAYING.
SHE'S TOO BUSY RUNNING AROUND THIS RED CASTLE SEARCHING FOR SOMETHING, AND I CAN ALSO SENSE THAT THE REAL YUKIKO IS WANTING TO REVEAL SOMETHING.
UNTIL THAT OTHER YUKIKO FINDS WHAT SHE IS LOOKING FOR, I DOUBT SHE WILL BOTHER THE REAL YUKIKO.
SOME-THING...?
YUKIKO...
OKAY.
FINE...
SORRY FOR GETTING AHEAD OF MYSELF.
WE'LL SAVE YUKIKO... TOGETHER. RIGHT?
DON'T WORRY ABOUT IT.
TOGETHER!
YEAH!

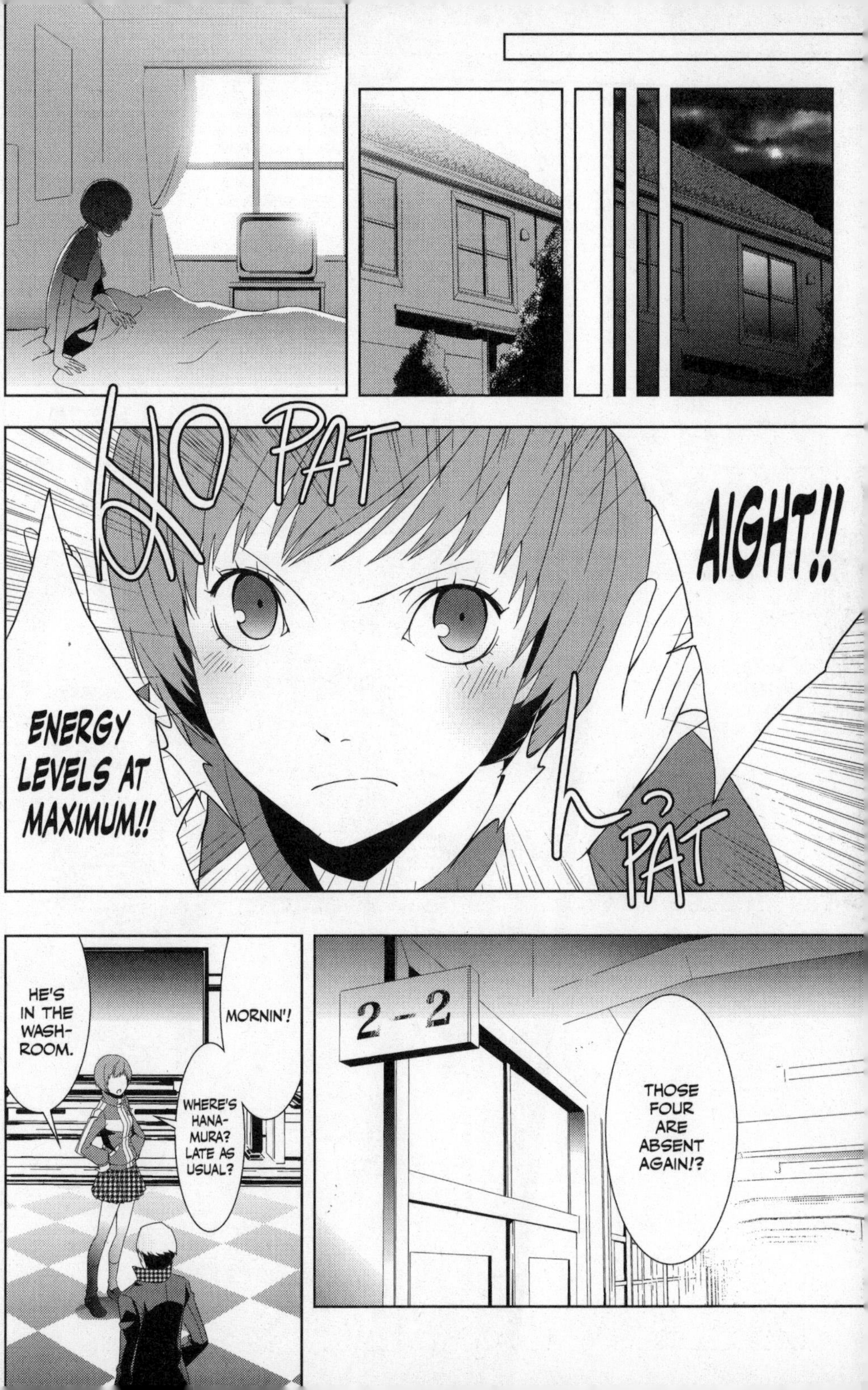
AIGHT!!
HO PAT
PAT
ENERGY LEVELS AT MAXIMUM!!
2-2
THOSE FOUR ARE ABSENT AGAIN!?
MORNIN'!
WHERE'S HANA-MURA? LATE AS USUAL?
HE'S IN THE WASH-ROOM.

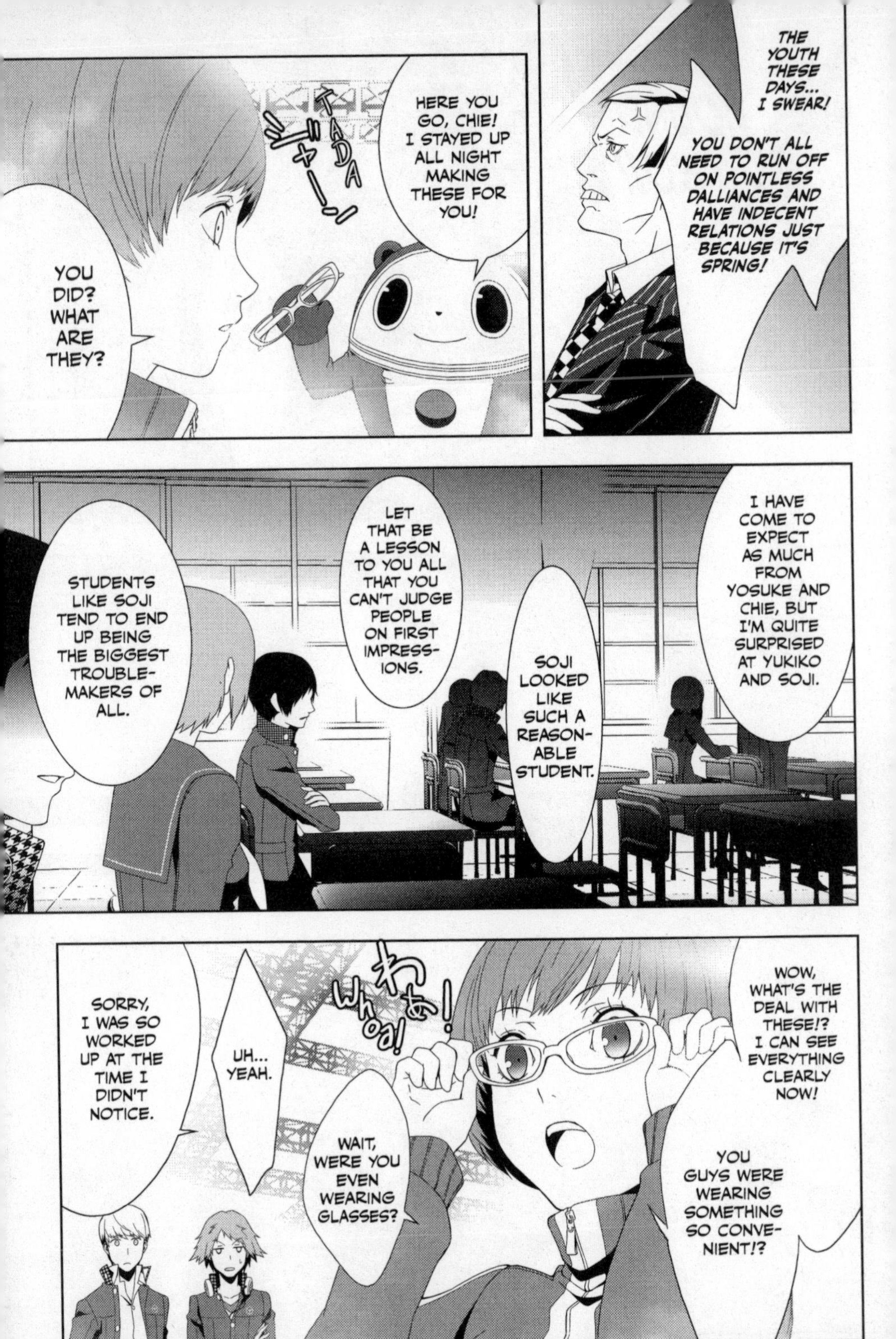

THE YOUTH THESE DAYS... I SWEAR!
YOU DON'T ALL NEED TO RUN OFF ON POINTLESS DALLIANCES AND HAVE INDECENT RELATIONS JUST BECAUSE IT'S SPRING!
HERE YOU GO, CHIE! I STAYED UP ALL NIGHT MAKING THESE FOR YOU!
TADA
YOU DID? WHAT ARE THEY?
I HAVE COME TO EXPECT AS MUCH FROM YOSUKE AND CHIE, BUT I'M QUITE SURPRISED AT YUKIKO AND SOJI.
SOJI LOOKED LIKE SUCH A REASONABLE STUDENT.
LET THAT BE A LESSON TO YOU ALL THAT YOU CAN'T JUDGE PEOPLE ON FIRST IMPRESSIONS.
STUDENTS LIKE SOJI TEND TO END UP BEING THE BIGGEST TROUBLE-MAKERS OF ALL.
WOW, WHAT'S THE DEAL WITH THESE!? I CAN SEE EVERYTHING CLEARLY NOW!
YOU GUYS WERE WEARING SOMETHING SO CONVENIENT!?
WHOA!
WAIT, WERE YOU EVEN WEARING GLASSES?
UH... YEAH.
SORRY, I WAS SO WORKED UP AT THE TIME I DIDN'T NOTICE.

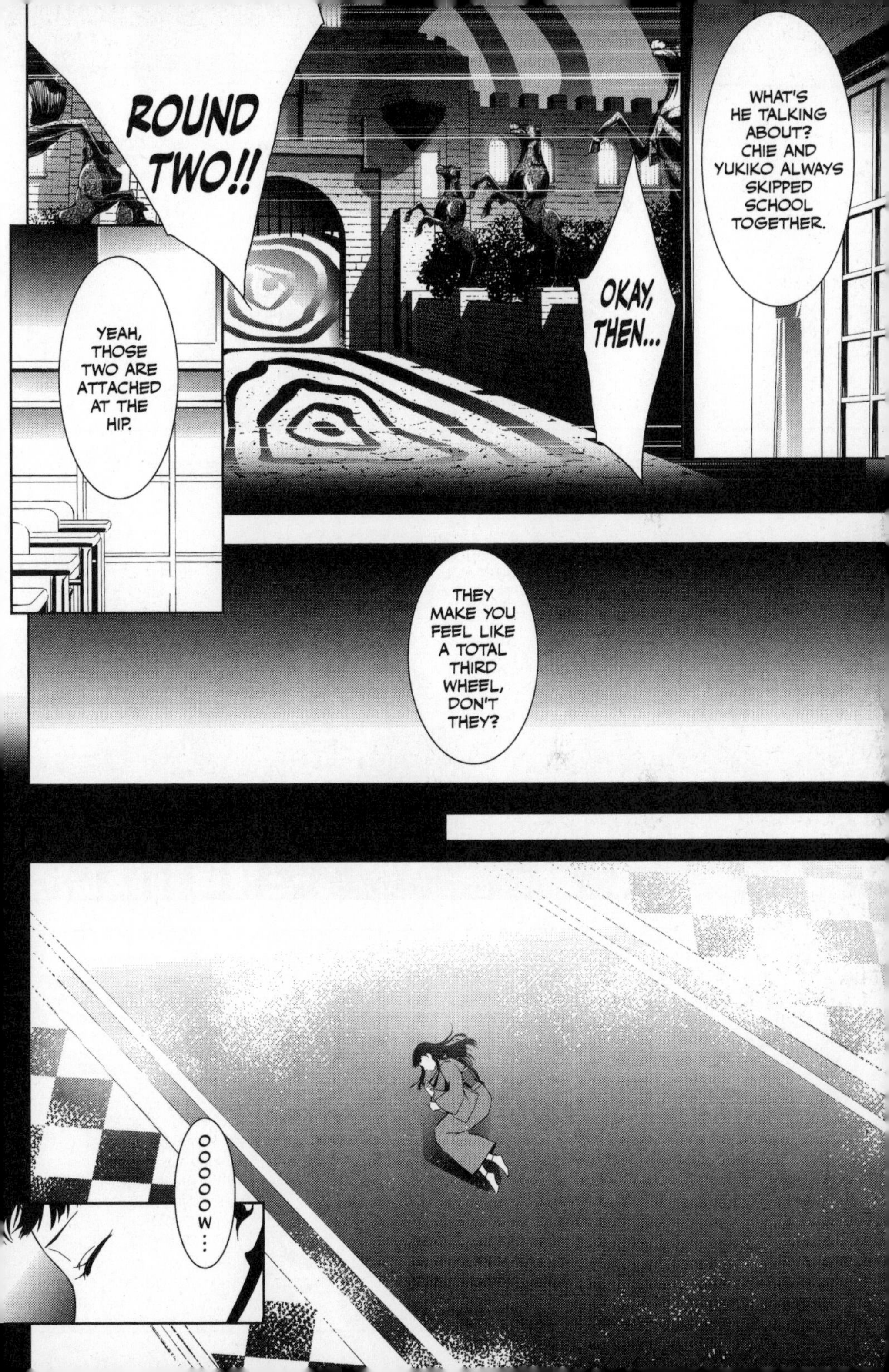
WHAT'S HE TALKING ABOUT? CHIE AND YUKIKO ALWAYS SKIPPED SCHOOL TOGETHER.
OKAY, THEN...
ROUND TWO!!
YEAH, THOSE TWO ARE ATTACHED AT THE HIP.
THEY MAKE YOU FEEL LIKE A TOTAL THIRD WHEEL, DON'T THEY?
OOOOOW...

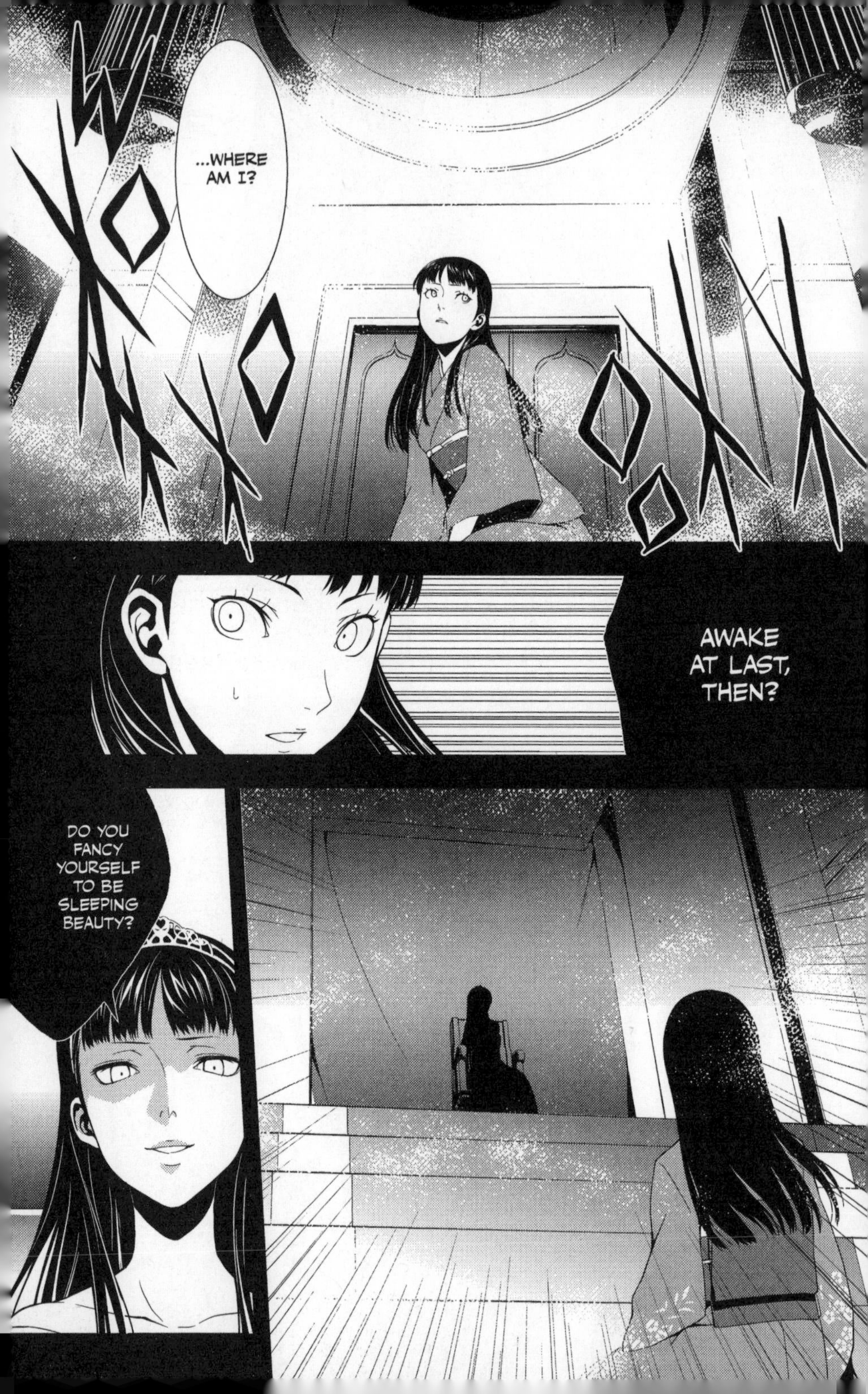
...WHERE AM I?
AWAKE AT LAST, THEN?
DO YOU FANCY YOURSELF TO BE SLEEPING BEAUTY?

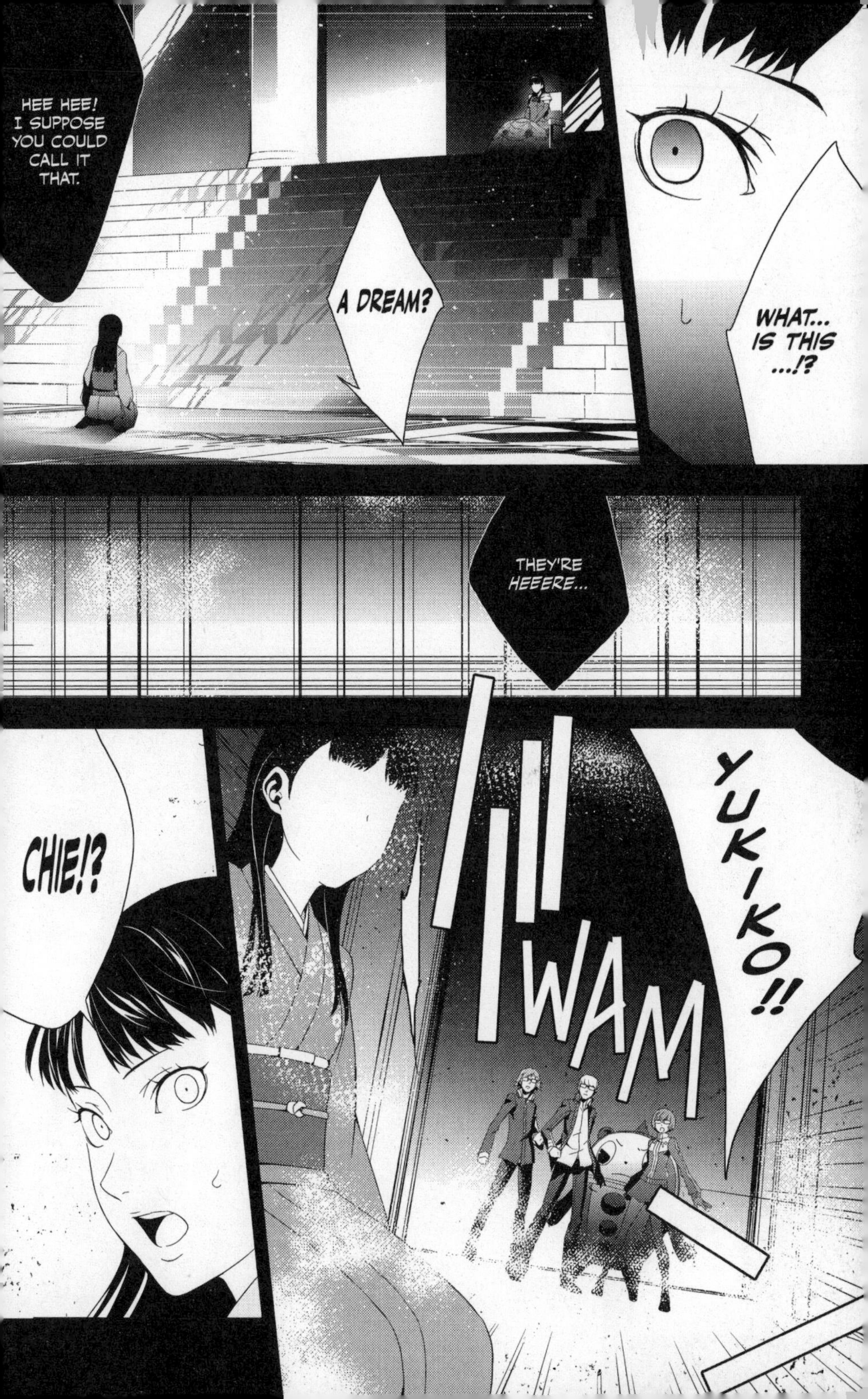
WHAT... IS THIS ...!?
A DREAM?
HEE HEE! I SUPPOSE YOU COULD CALL IT THAT.
THEY'RE HEEERE...
YUKIKO!!
WAM
CHIE!?

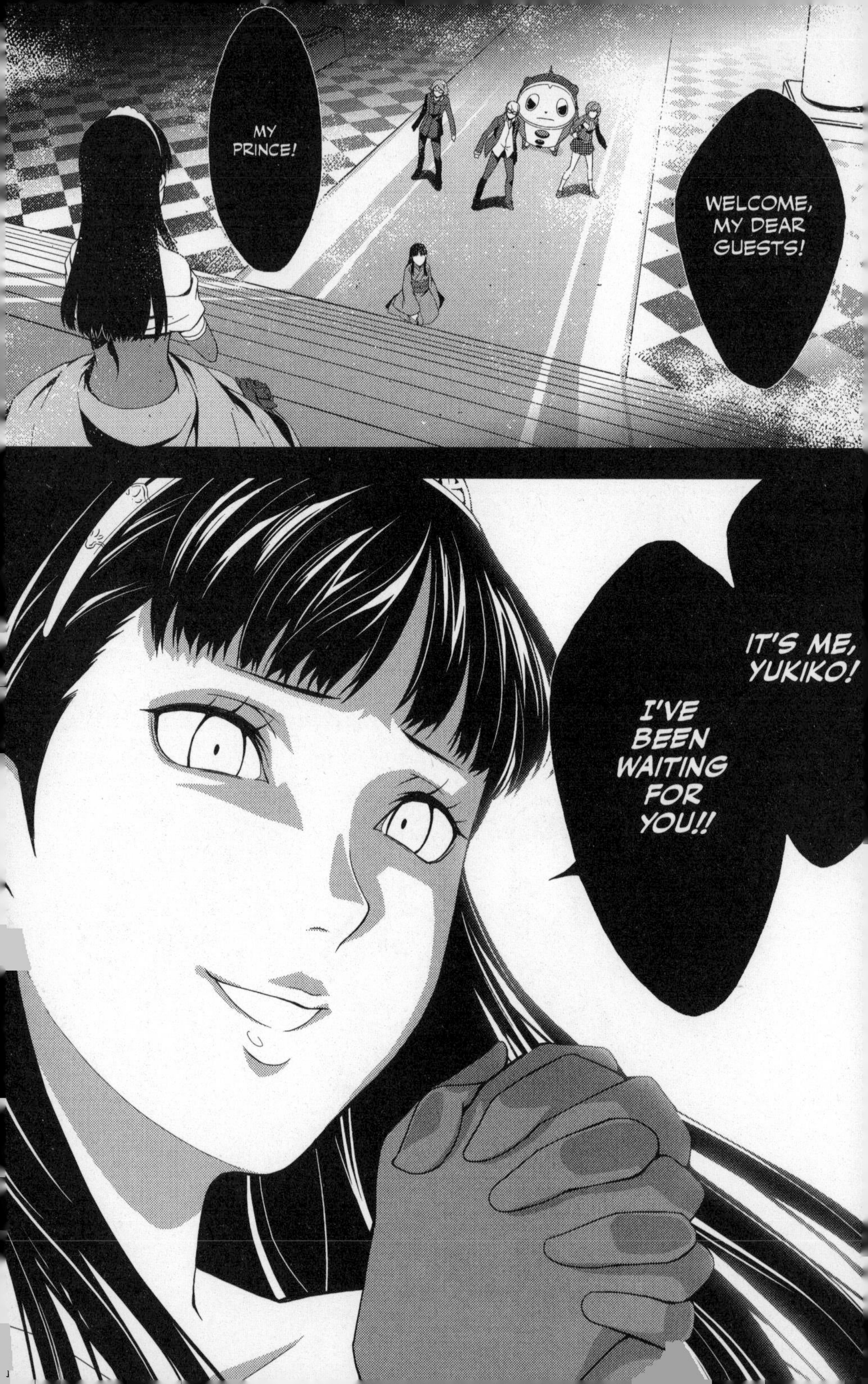
WELCOME, MY DEAR GUESTS!
MY PRINCE!
IT'S ME, YUKIKO!
I'VE BEEN WAITING FOR YOU!!

Design sketch

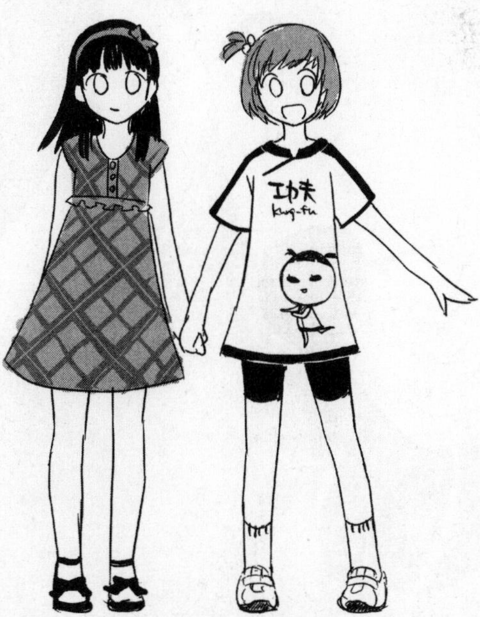

工夫
kung-fu

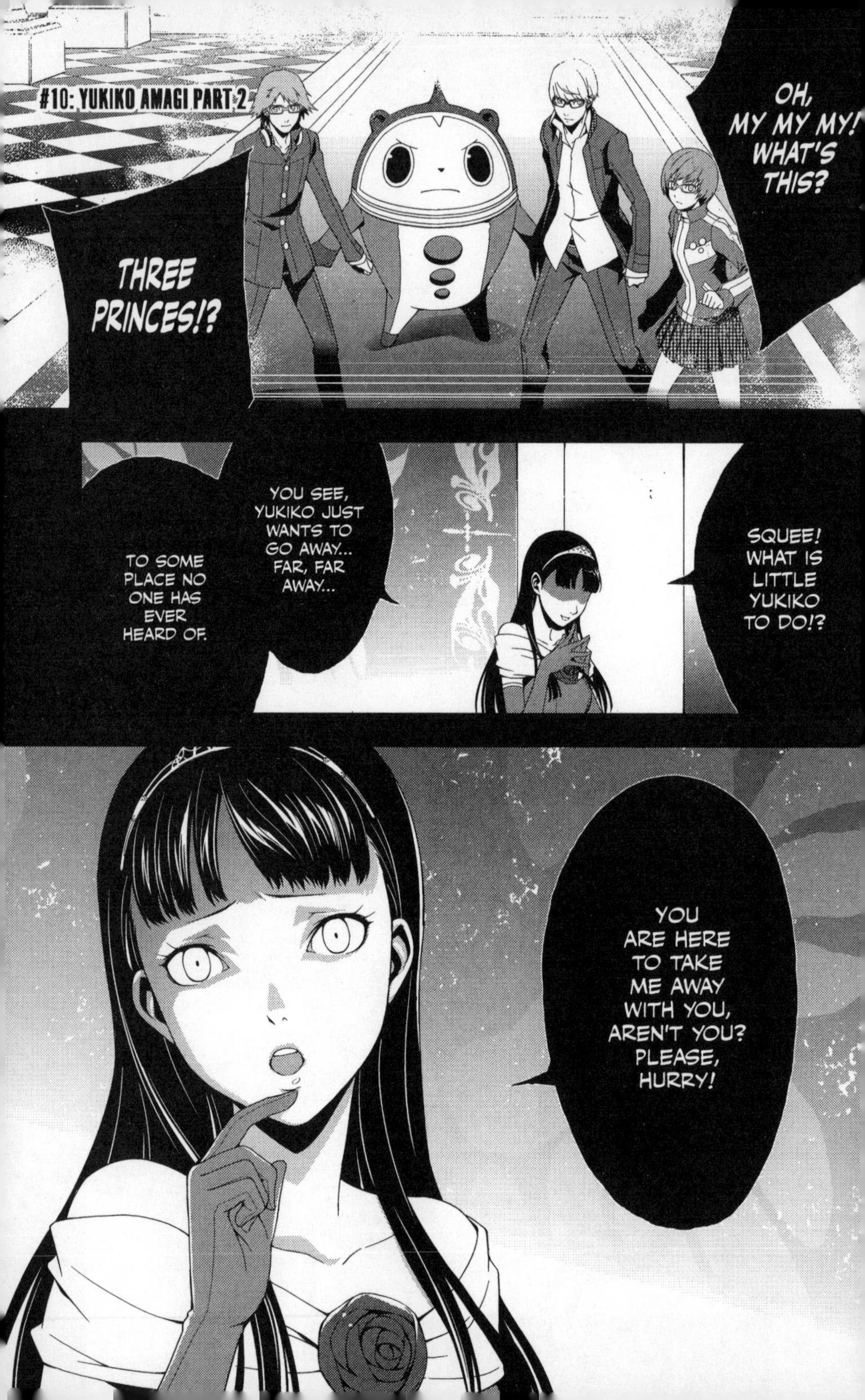
#10: YUKIKO AMAGI PART 2
OH, MY MY MY! WHAT'S THIS?
THREE PRINCES!?
SQUEE! WHAT IS LITTLE YUKIKO TO DO!?
YOU SEE, YUKIKO JUST WANTS TO GO AWAY... FAR, FAR AWAY...
TO SOME PLACE NO ONE HAS EVER HEARD OF.
YOU ARE HERE TO TAKE ME AWAY WITH YOU, AREN'T YOU? PLEASE, HURRY!

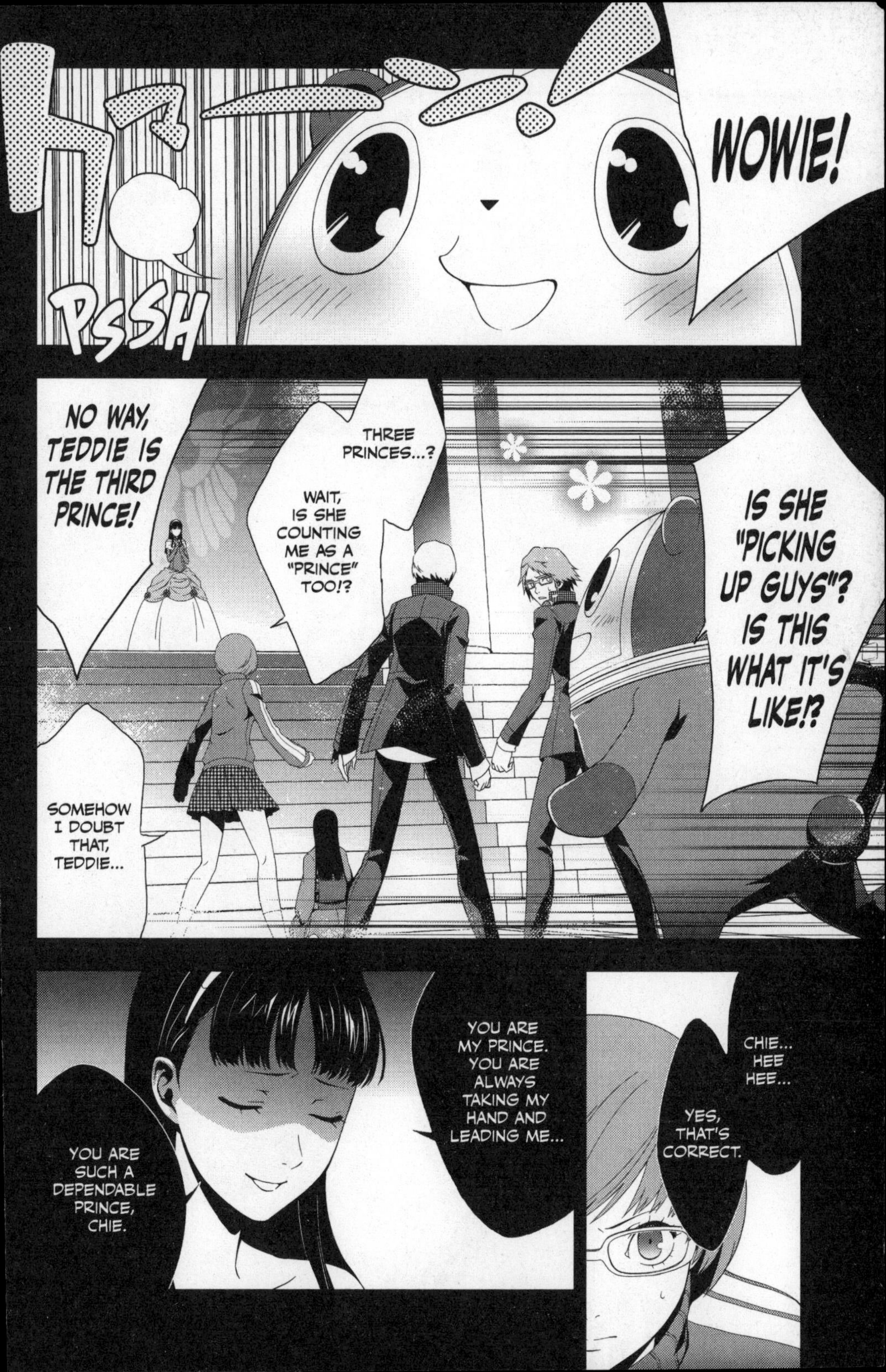
WOWIE!
PSSH
IS SHE "PICKING UP GUYS"? IS THIS WHAT IT'S LIKE!?
THREE PRINCES...?
WAIT, IS SHE COUNTING ME AS A "PRINCE" TOO!?
NO WAY, TEDDIE IS THE THIRD PRINCE!
SOMEHOW I DOUBT THAT, TEDDIE...
CHIE... HEE HEE...
YES, THAT'S CORRECT.
YOU ARE MY PRINCE. YOU ARE ALWAYS TAKING MY HAND AND LEADING ME...
YOU ARE SUCH A DEPENDABLE PRINCE, CHIE.

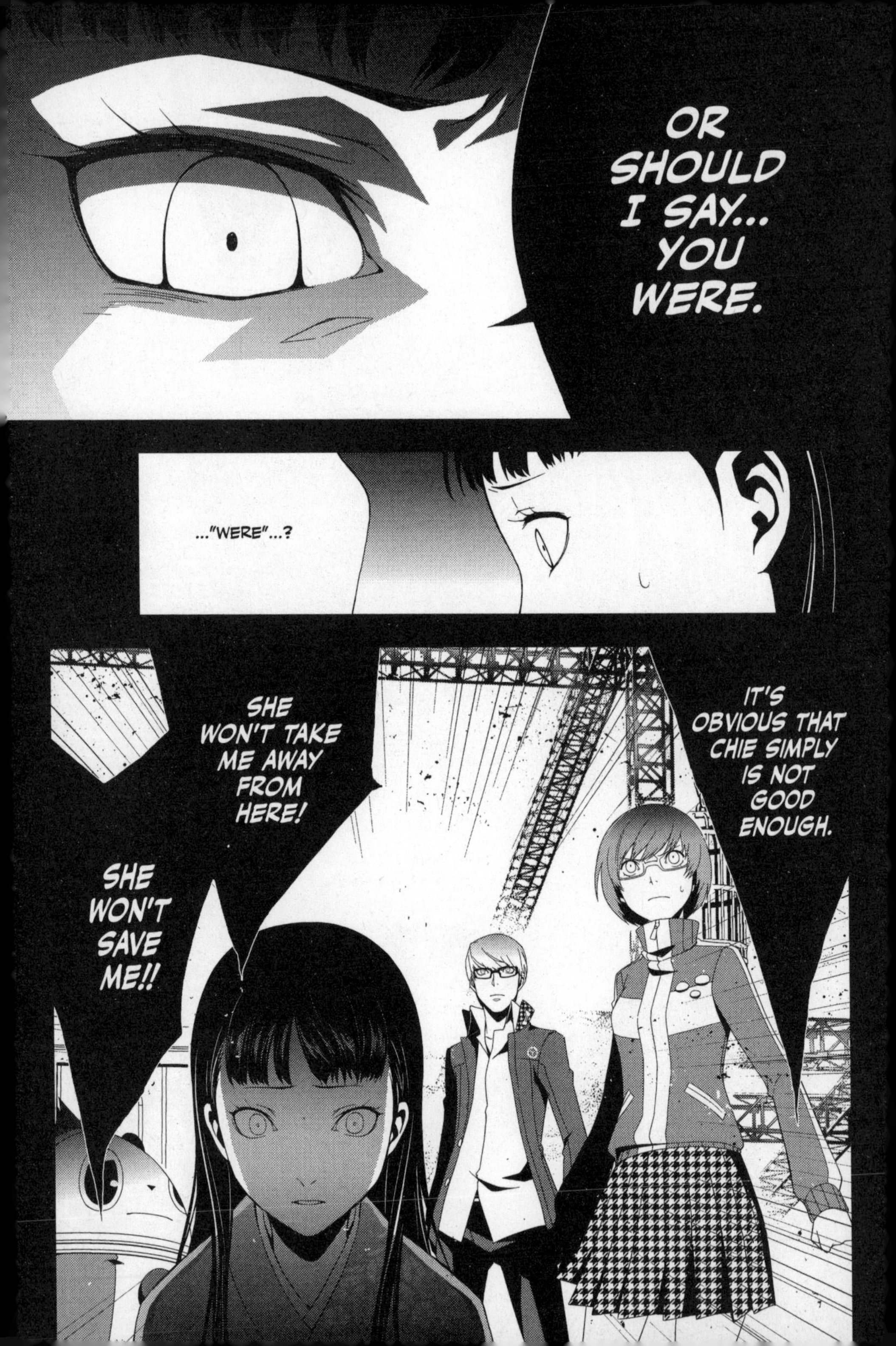
OR SHOULD I SAY... YOU WERE.
..."WERE"...?
IT'S OBVIOUS THAT CHIE SIMPLY IS NOT GOOD ENOUGH.
SHE WON'T TAKE ME AWAY FROM HERE!
SHE WON'T SAVE ME!!

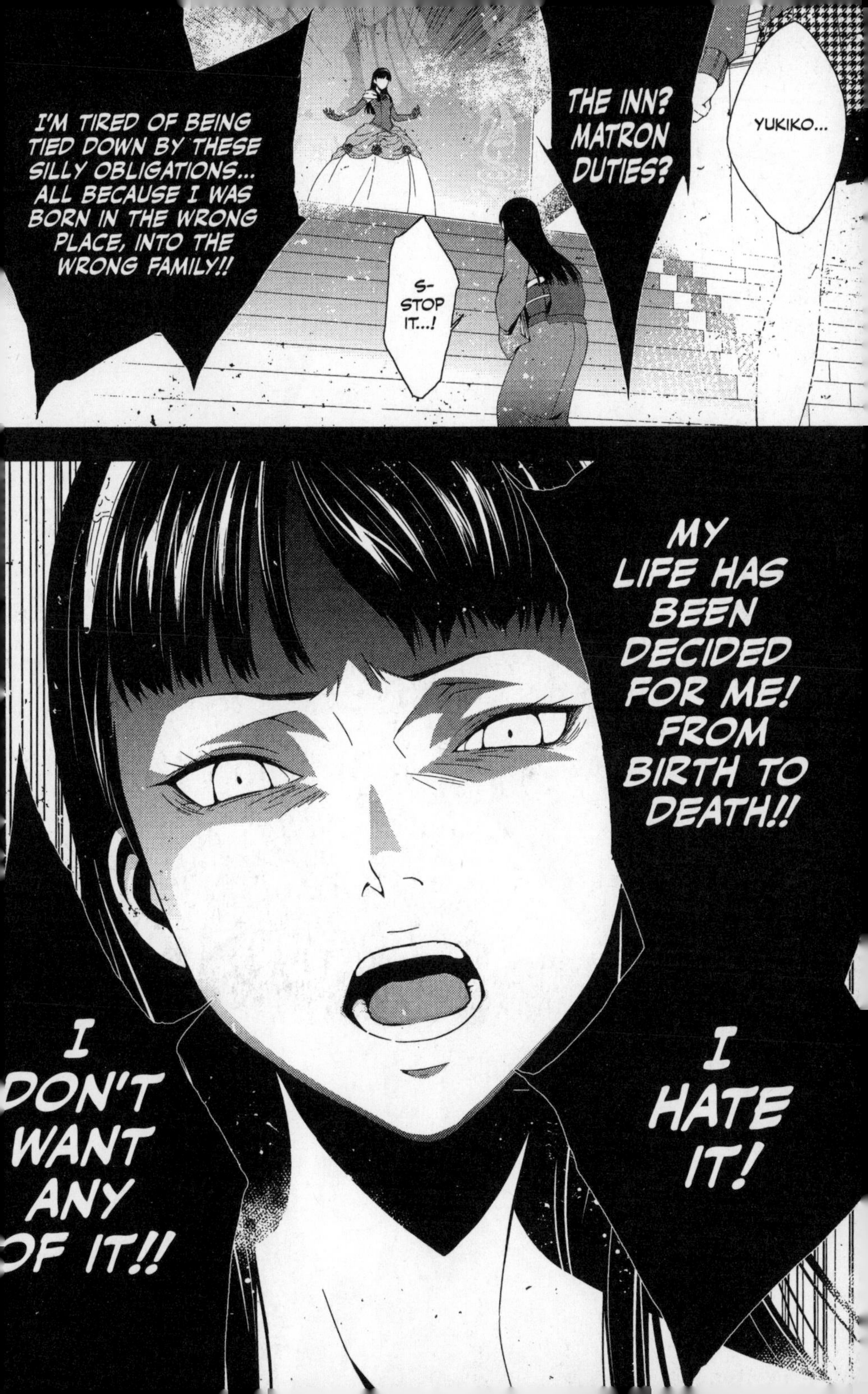
YUKIKO...
THE INN? MATRON DUTIES?
I'M TIRED OF BEING TIED DOWN BY THESE SILLY OBLIGATIONS... ALL BECAUSE I WAS BORN IN THE WRONG PLACE, INTO THE WRONG FAMILY!!
S-STOP IT...!
MY LIFE HAS BEEN DECIDED FOR ME! FROM BIRTH TO DEATH!!
I HATE IT!
I DON'T WANT ANY OF IT!!

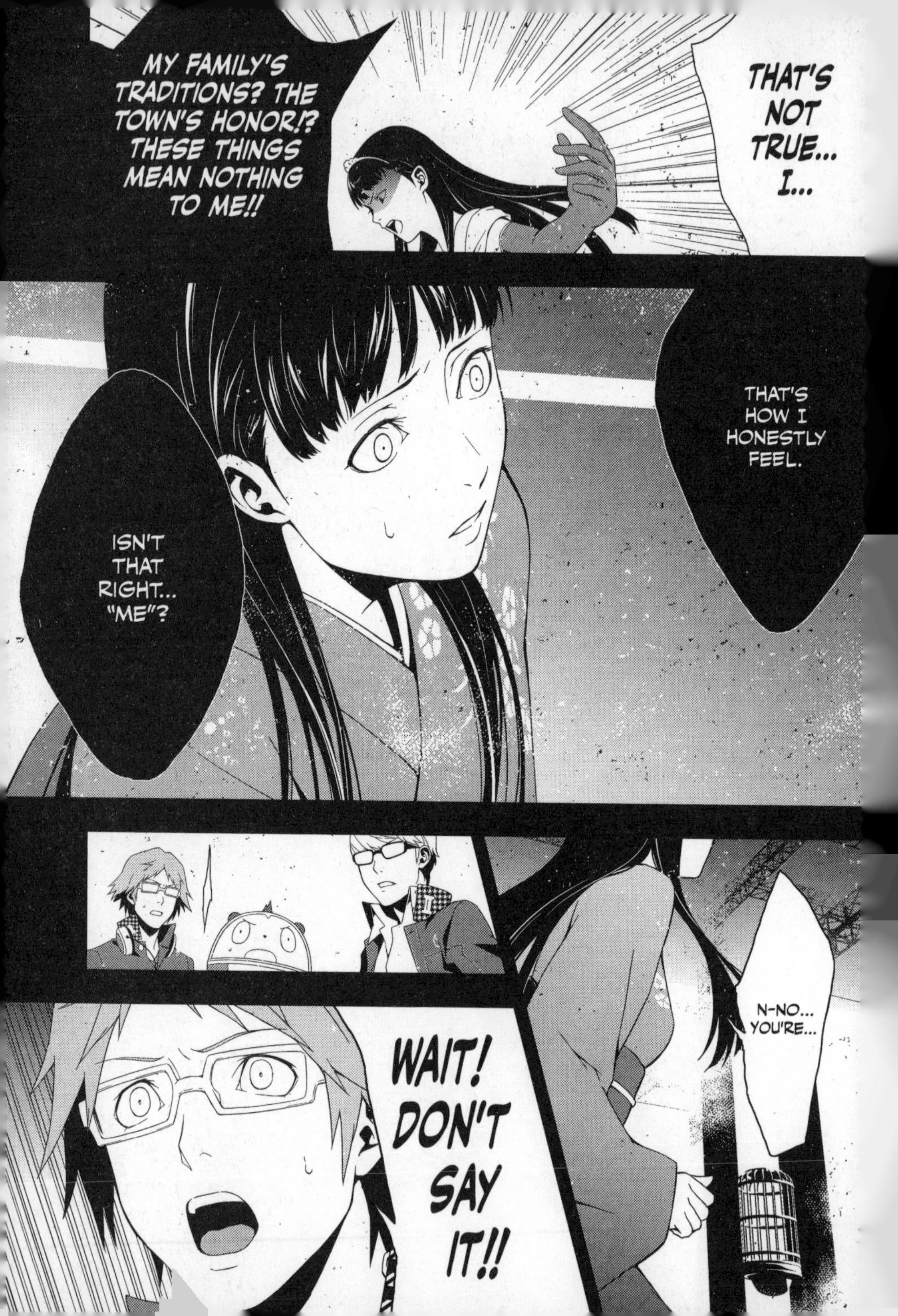
MY FAMILY'S TRADITIONS? THE TOWN'S HONOR!? THESE THINGS MEAN NOTHING TO ME!!
THAT'S NOT TRUE... I...
THAT'S HOW I HONESTLY FEEL.
ISN'T THAT RIGHT... "ME"?
N-NO... YOU'RE...
WAIT! DON'T SAY IT!!

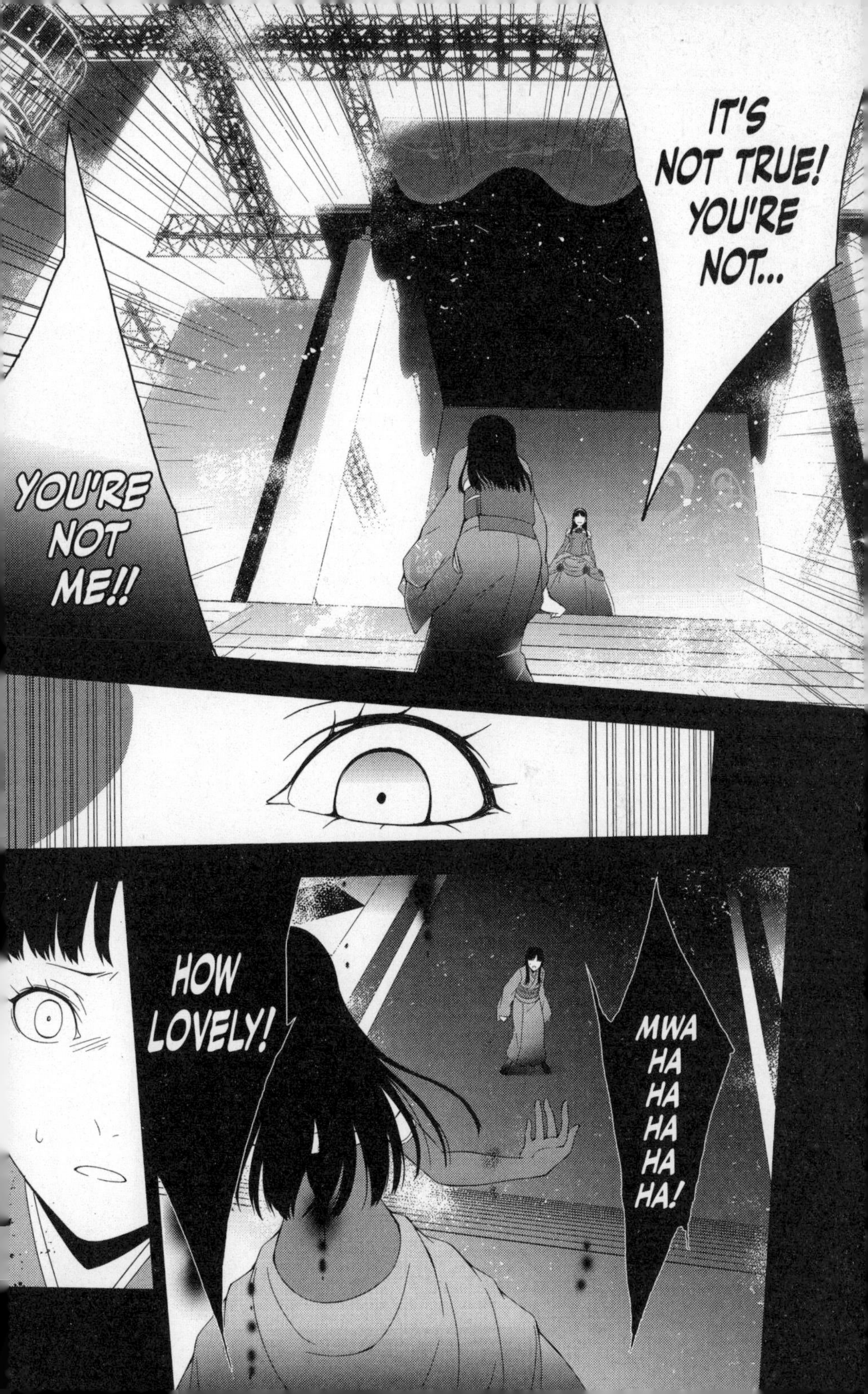
IT'S NOT TRUE! YOU'RE NOT...
YOU'RE NOT ME!!
MWA HA HA HA HA HA!
HOW LOVELY!

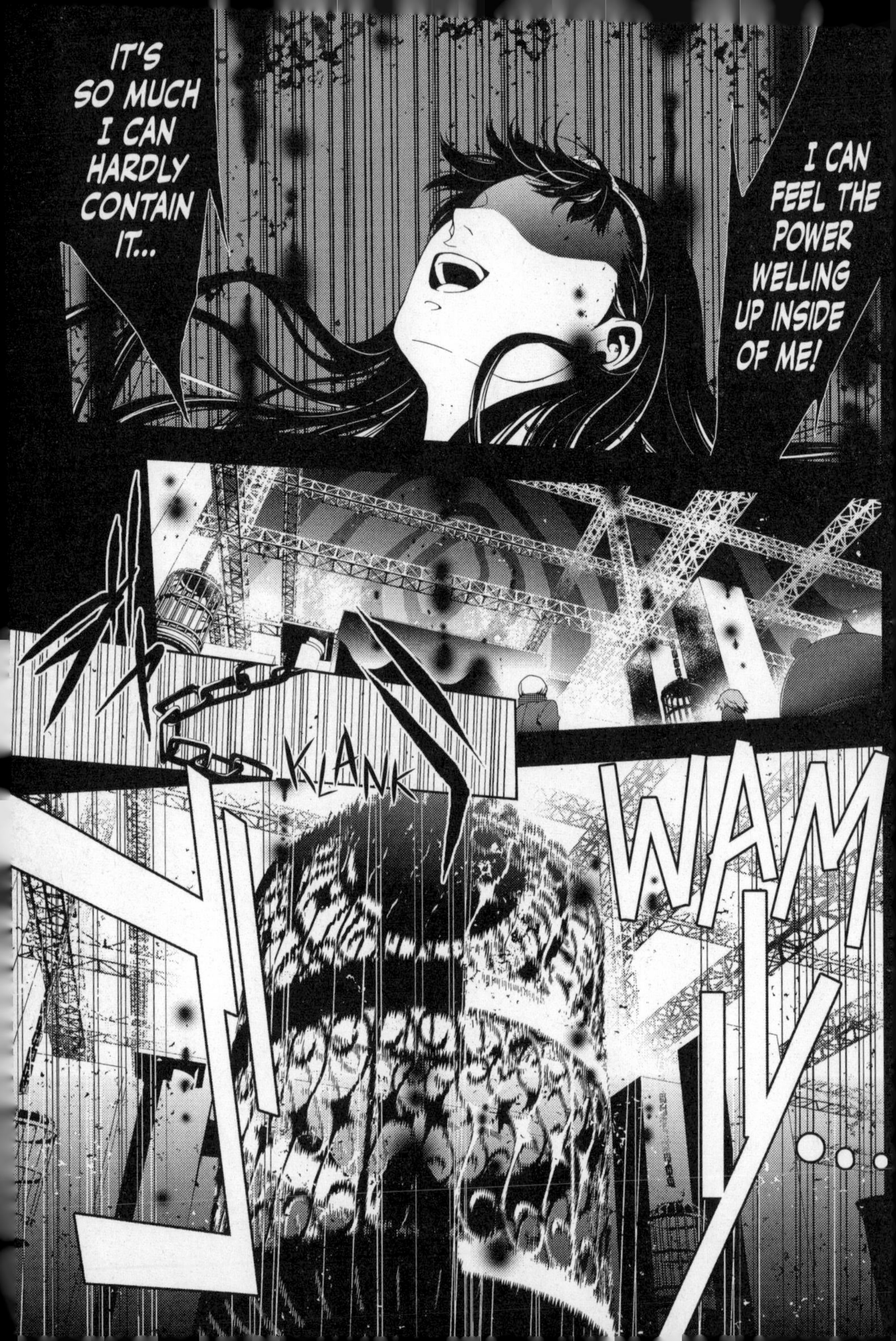
I CAN FEEL THE POWER WELLING UP INSIDE OF ME!
IT'S SO MUCH I CAN HARDLY CONTAIN IT...
KLANK
WAM

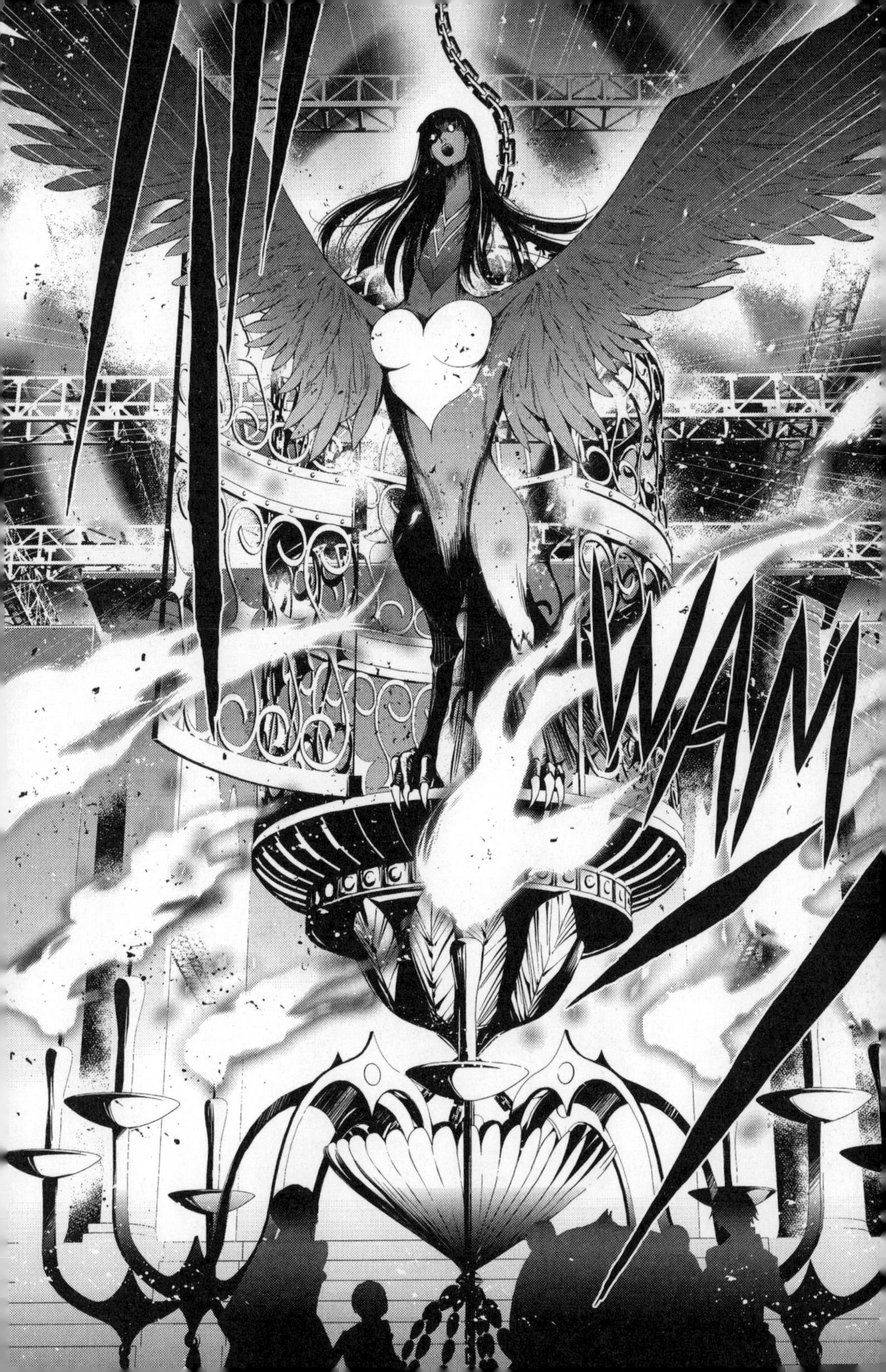
WAM

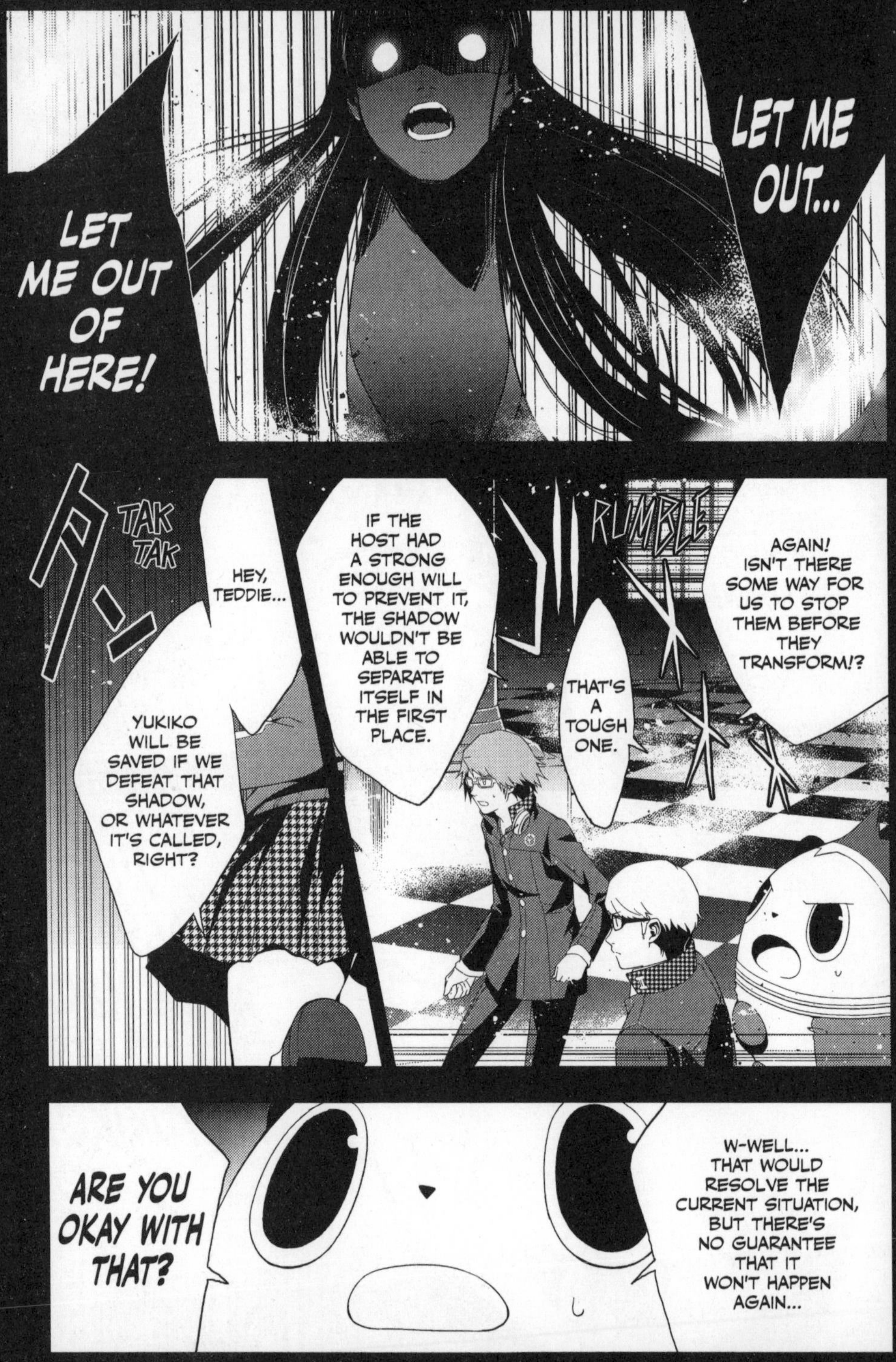

LET ME OUT...
LET ME OUT OF HERE!
AGAIN! ISN'T THERE SOME WAY FOR US TO STOP THEM BEFORE THEY TRANSFORM!?
RUMBLE
THAT'S A TOUGH ONE.
IF THE HOST HAD A STRONG ENOUGH WILL TO PREVENT IT, THE SHADOW WOULDN'T BE ABLE TO SEPARATE ITSELF IN THE FIRST PLACE.
HEY, TEDDIE...
TAK TAK
YUKIKO WILL BE SAVED IF WE DEFEAT THAT SHADOW, OR WHATEVER IT'S CALLED, RIGHT?
W-WELL... THAT WOULD RESOLVE THE CURRENT SITUATION, BUT THERE'S NO GUARANTEE THAT IT WON'T HAPPEN AGAIN...
ARE YOU OKAY WITH THAT?

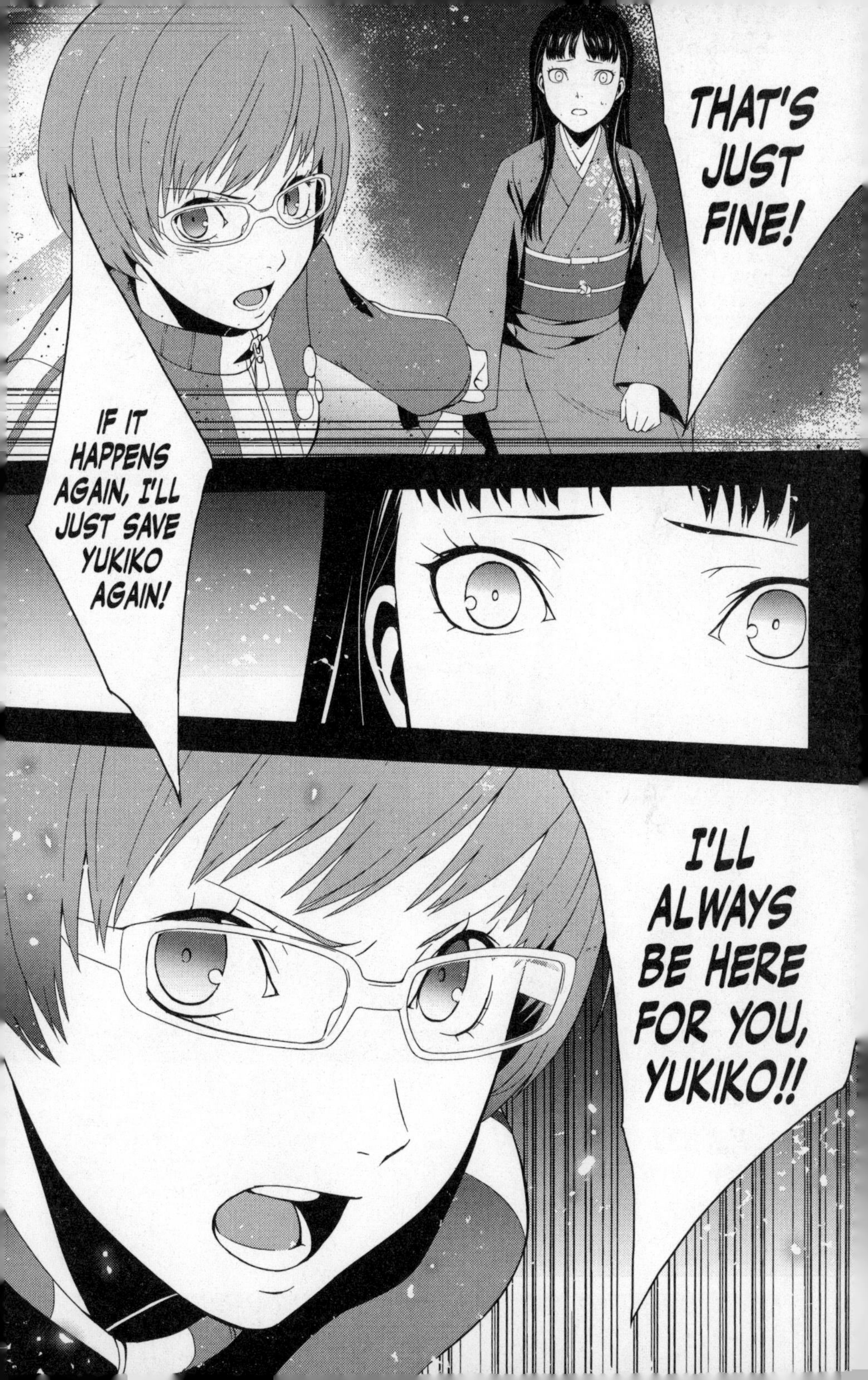
THAT'S JUST FINE!
IF IT HAPPENS AGAIN, I'LL JUST SAVE YUKIKO AGAIN!
I'LL ALWAYS BE HERE FOR YOU, YUKIKO!!

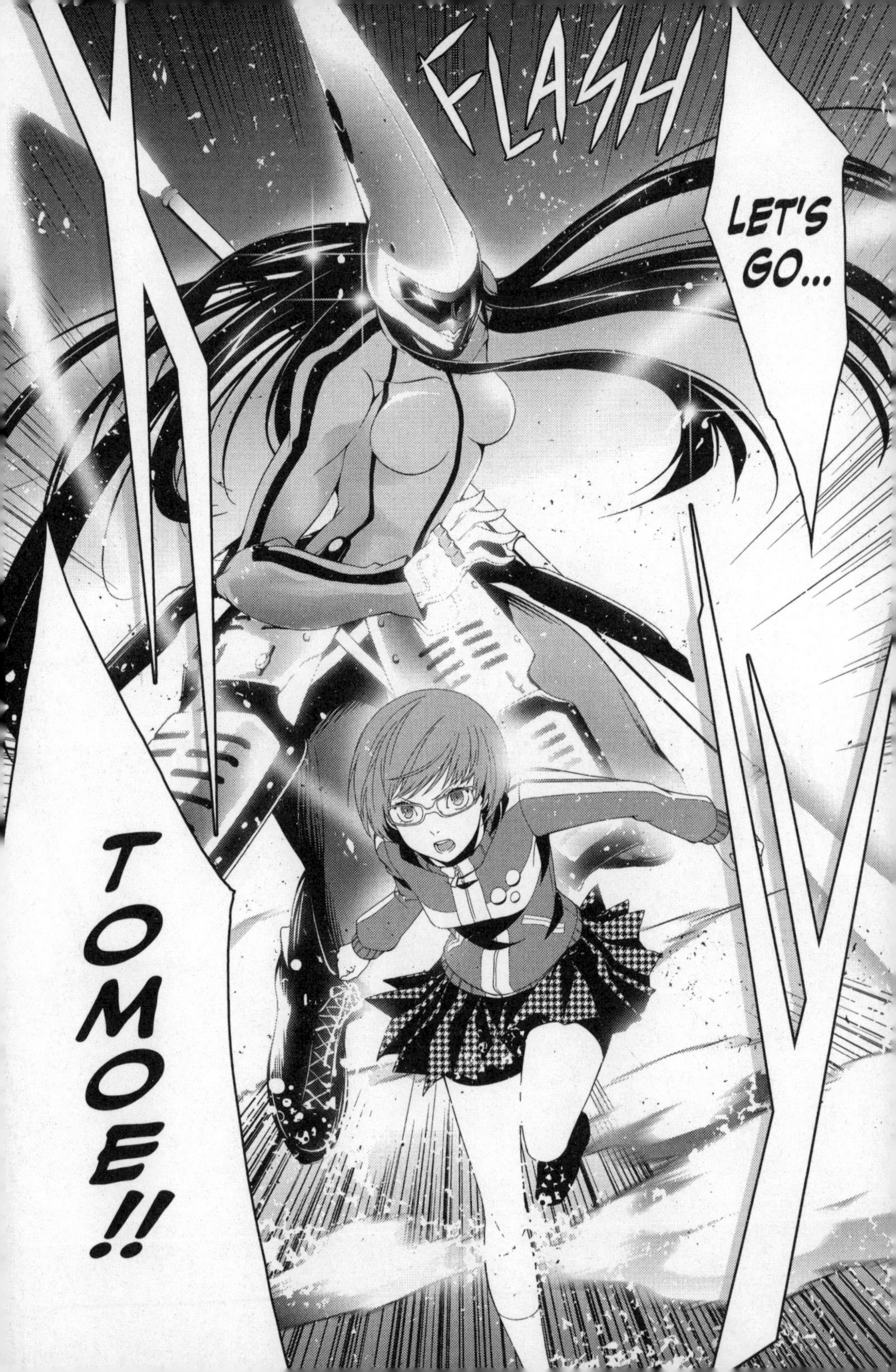
FLASH
LET'S GO...
TOMOE!!

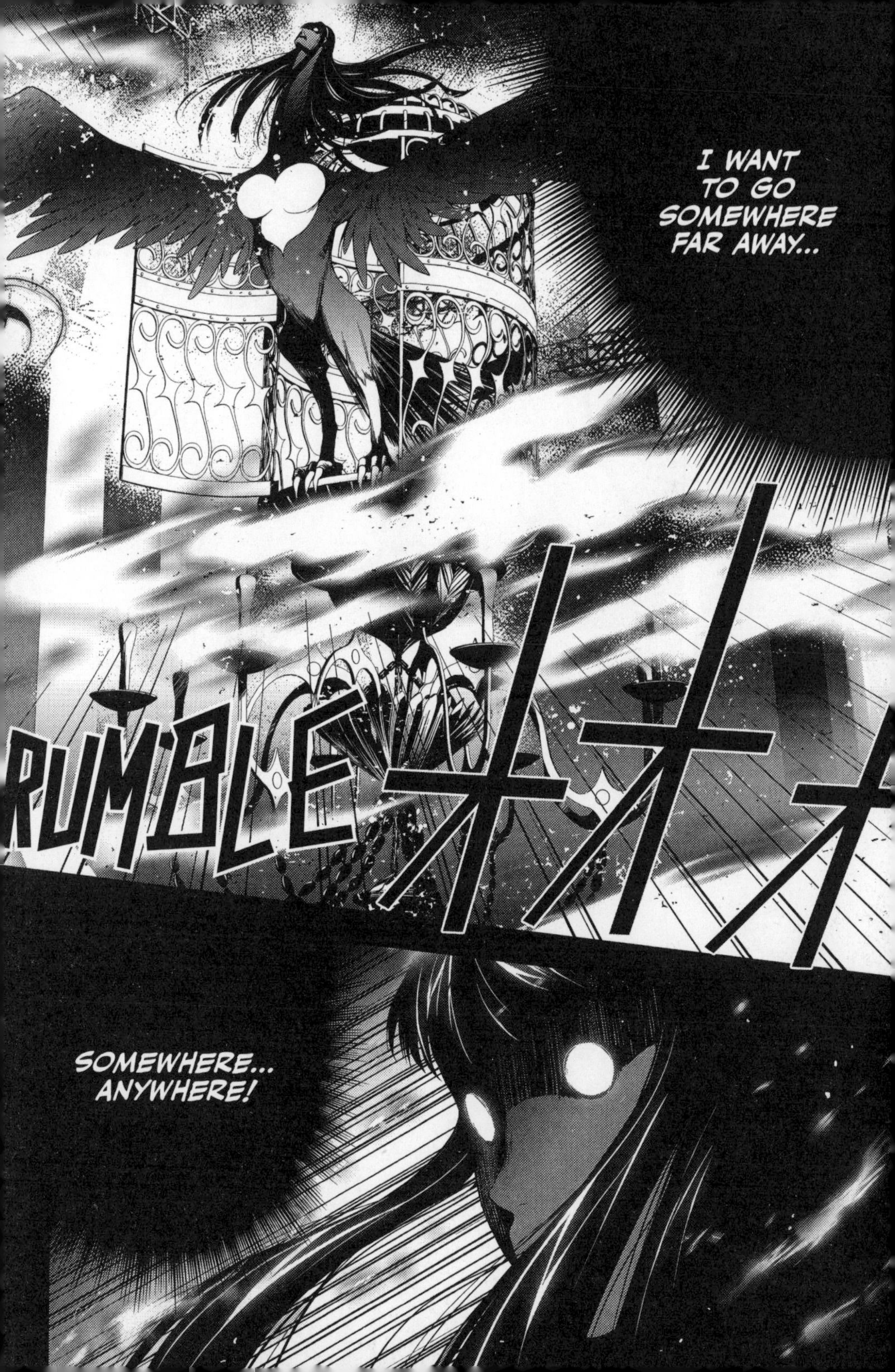
I WANT TO GO SOMEWHERE FAR AWAY...
RUMBLE
SOMEWHERE... ANYWHERE!

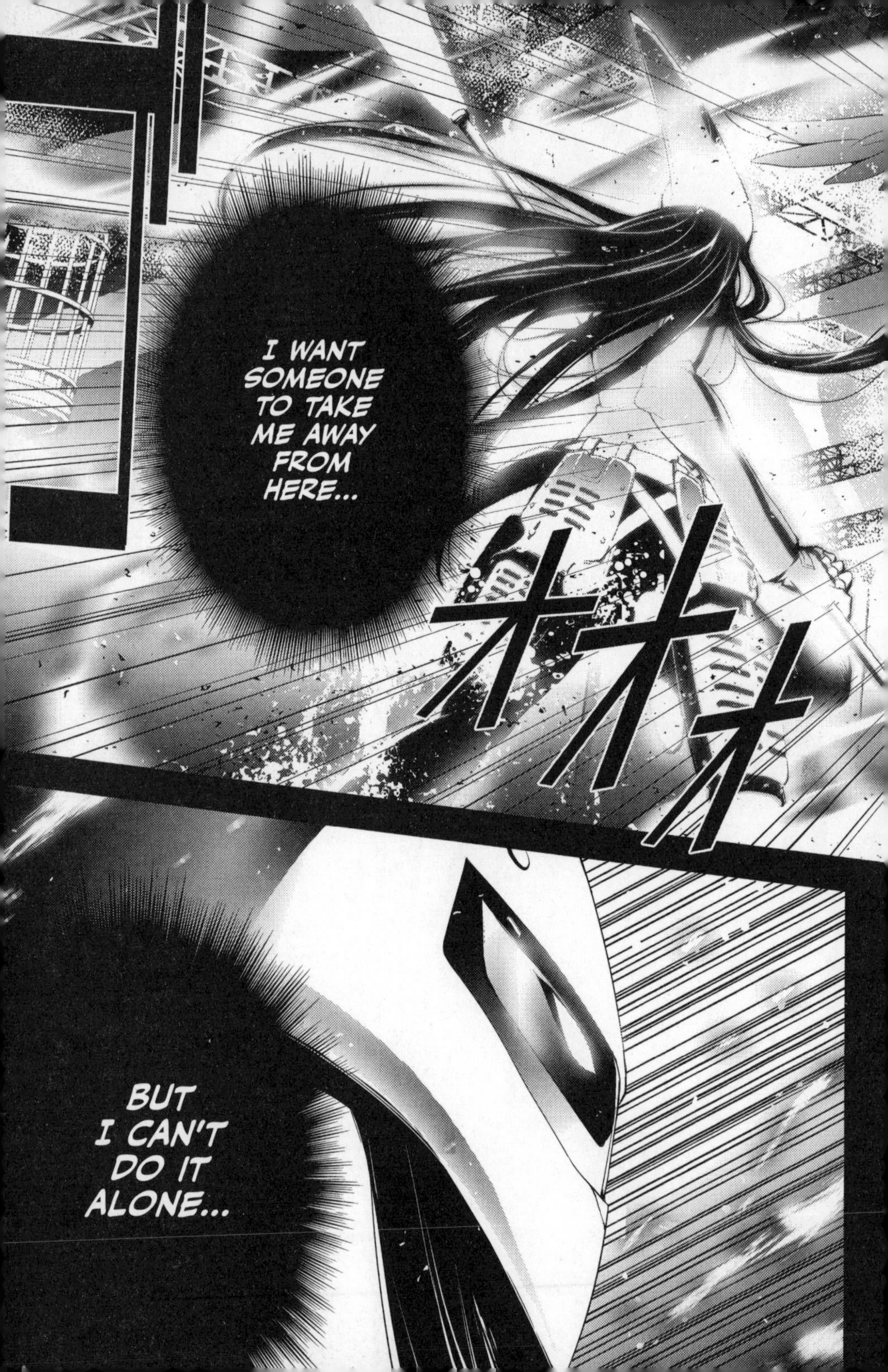
I WANT SOMEONE TO TAKE ME AWAY FROM HERE...
オオオ
BUT I CAN'T DO IT ALONE...

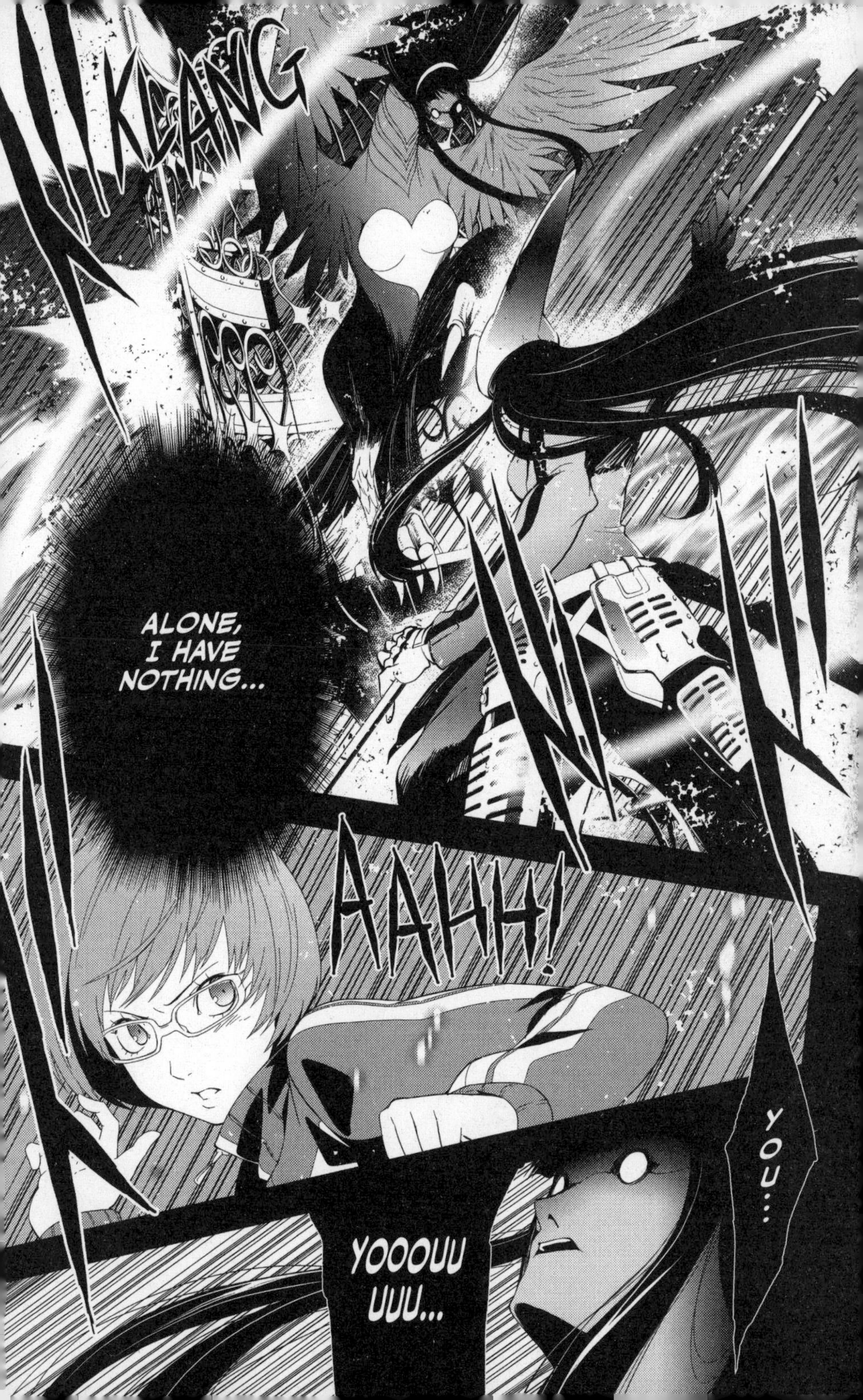
KLANG
ALONE, I HAVE NOTHING...
AAHH!
YOU...
YOOOUU UUU...

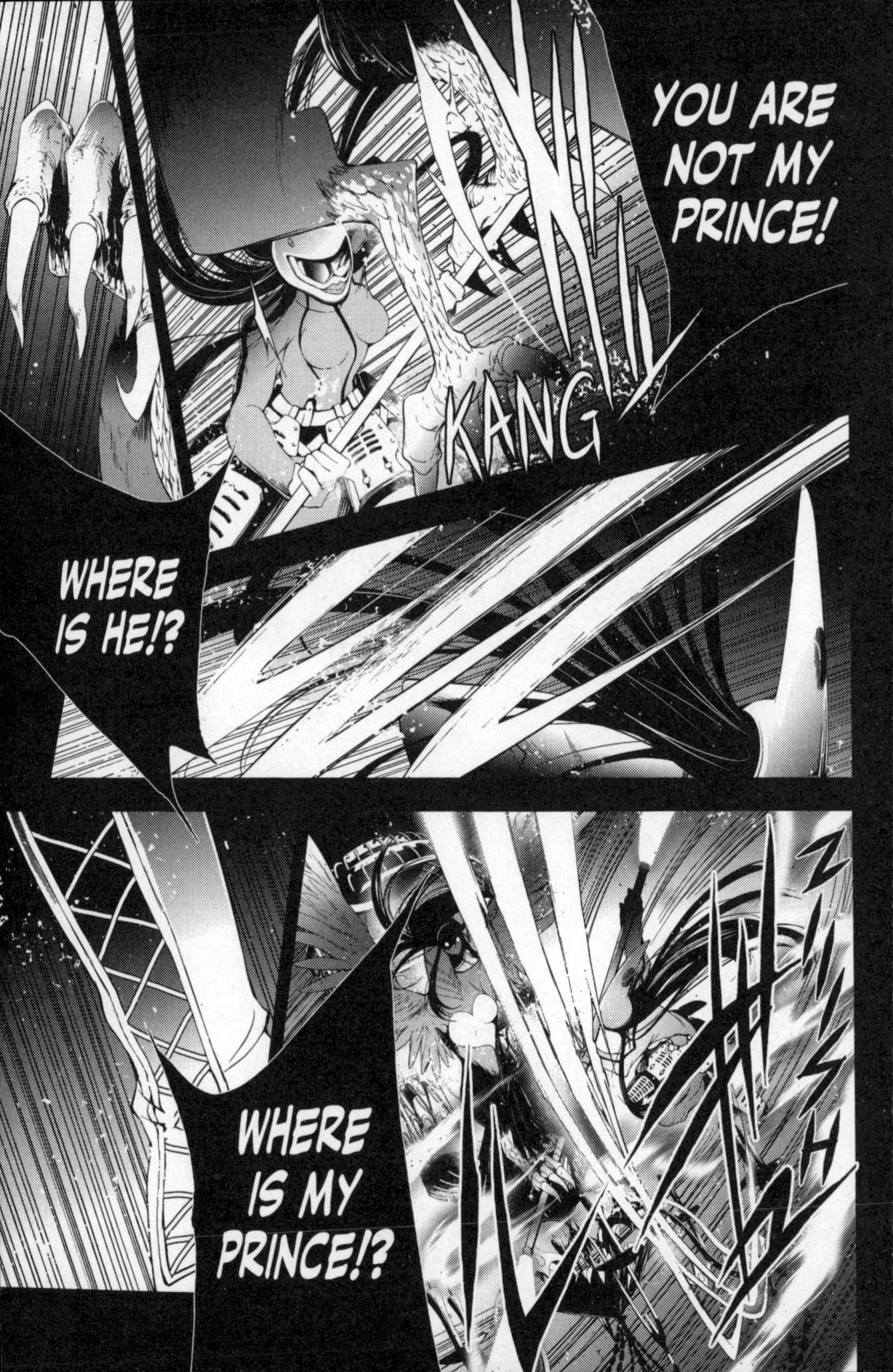
YOU ARE NOT MY PRINCE!
KANG
WHERE IS HE!?
WHERE IS MY PRINCE!?

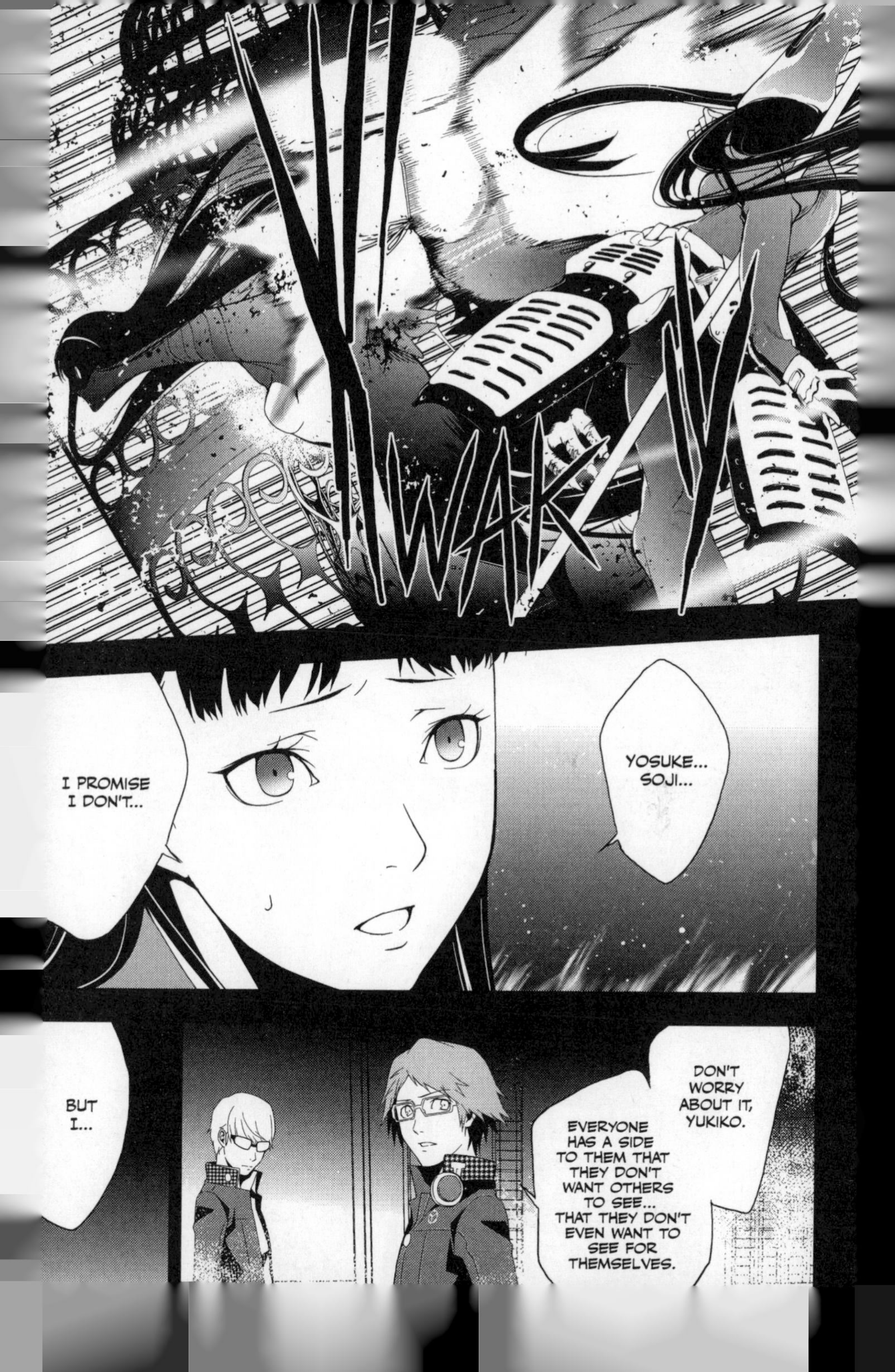
WAK
YOSUKE... SOJI...
I PROMISE I DON'T...
DON'T WORRY ABOUT IT, YUKIKO.
EVERYONE HAS A SIDE TO THEM THAT THEY DON'T WANT OTHERS TO SEE... THAT THEY DON'T EVEN WANT TO SEE FOR THEMSELVES.
BUT I...

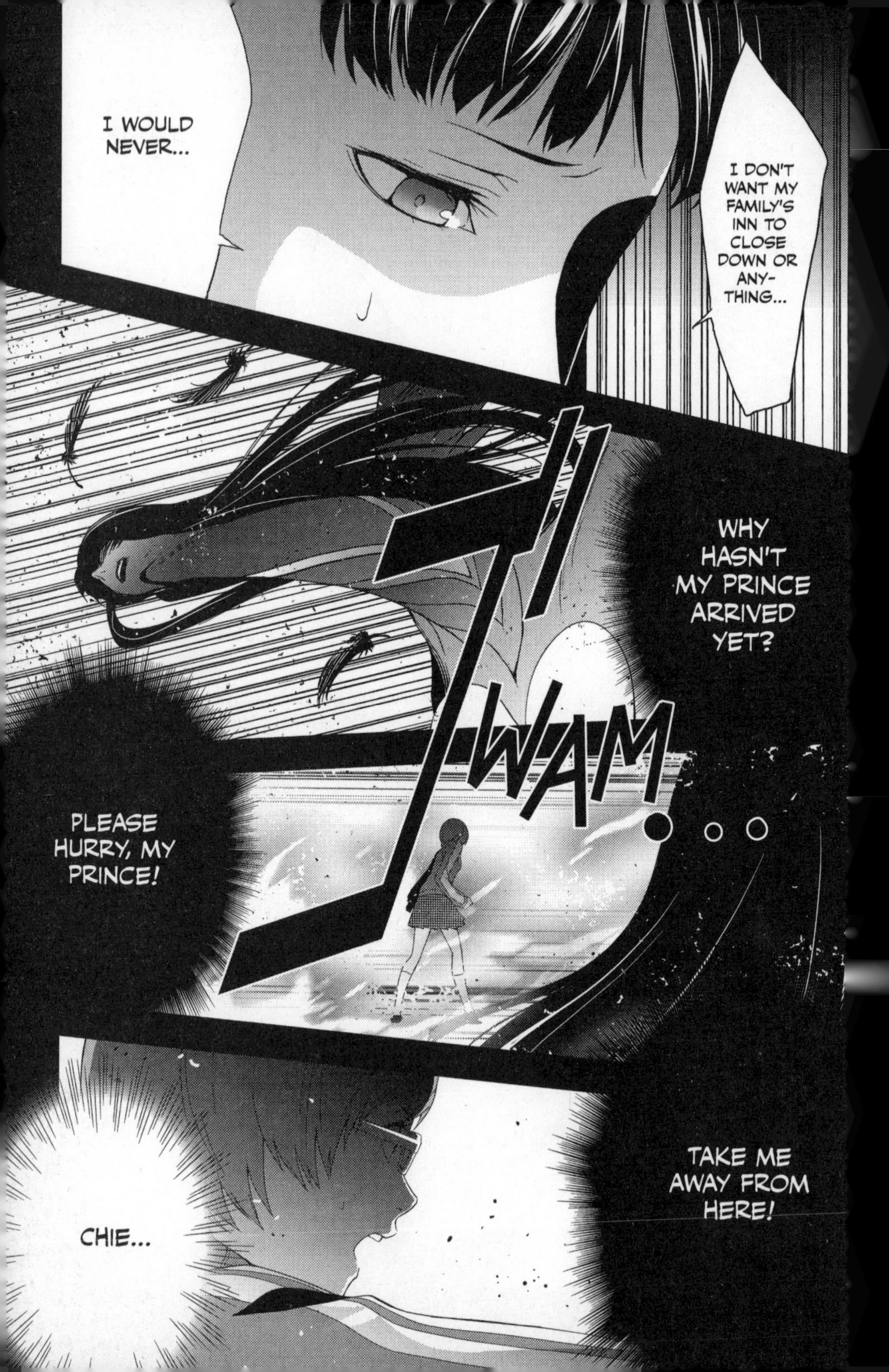
I DON'T WANT MY FAMILY'S INN TO CLOSE DOWN OR ANY-THING...
I WOULD NEVER...
WHY HASN'T MY PRINCE ARRIVED YET?
WAM...
PLEASE HURRY, MY PRINCE!
TAKE ME AWAY FROM HERE!
CHIE...

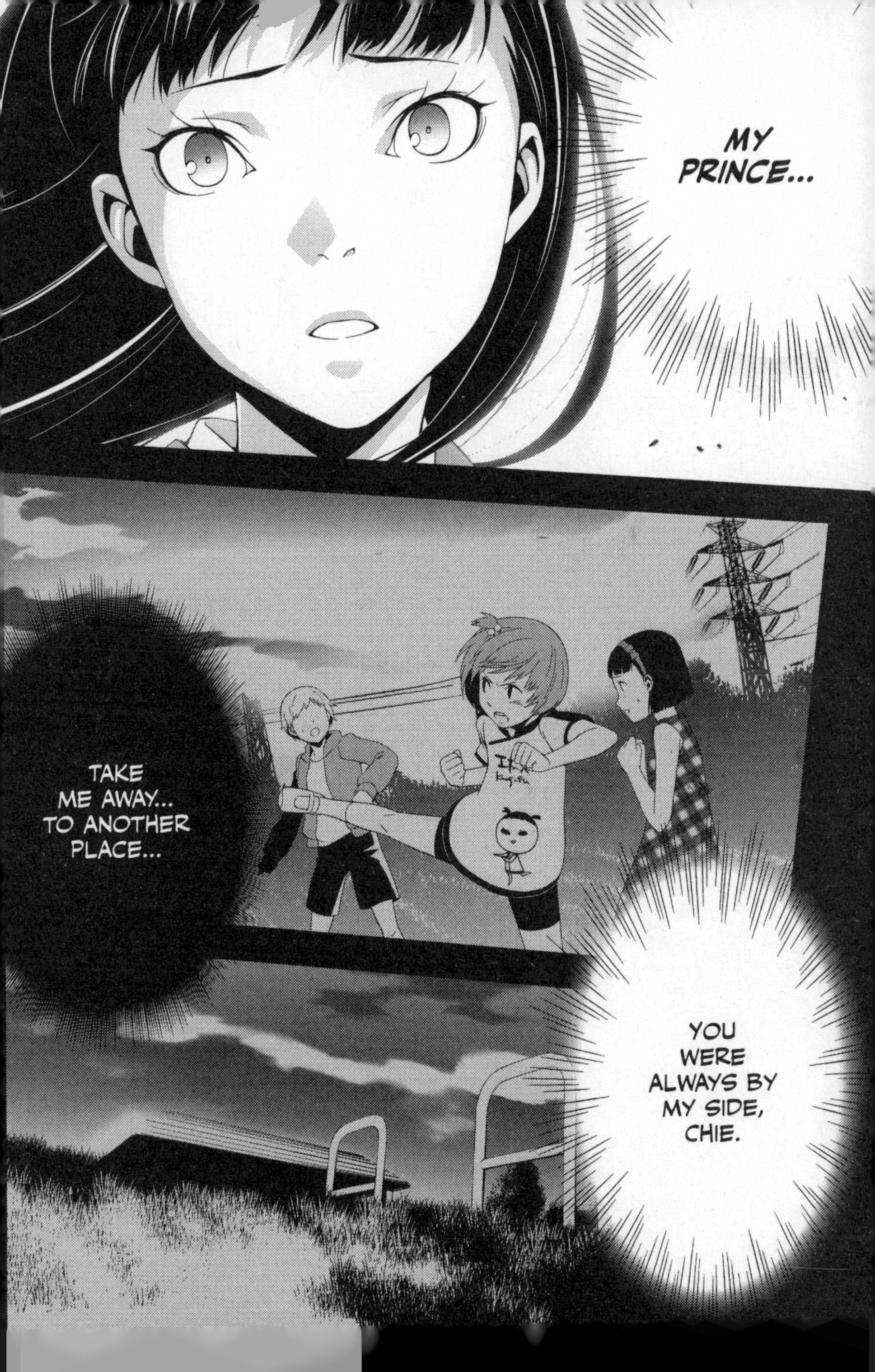
MY PRINCE...
TAKE ME AWAY... TO ANOTHER PLACE...
YOU WERE ALWAYS BY MY SIDE, CHIE.

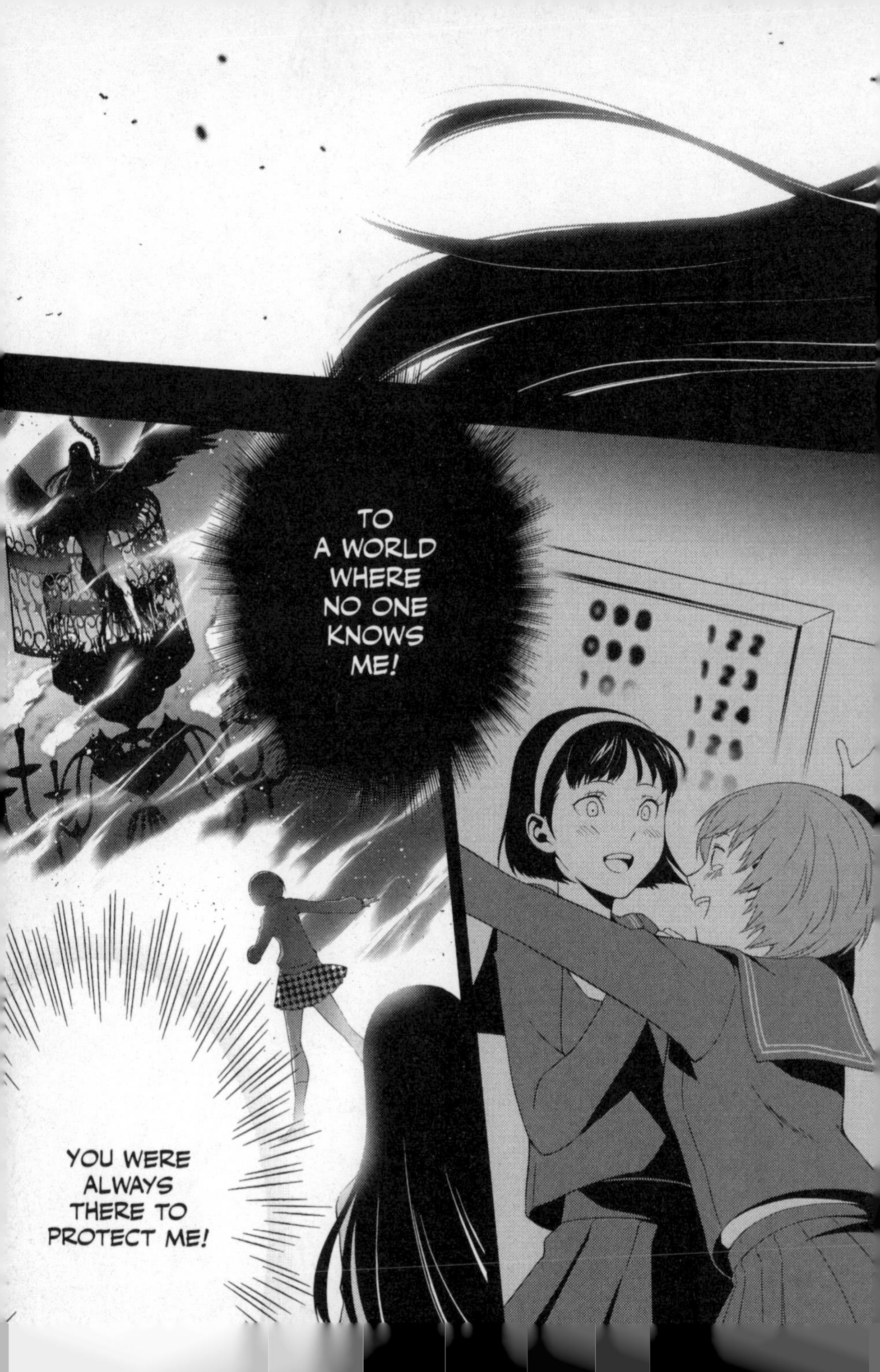
TO A WORLD WHERE NO ONE KNOWS ME!
YOU WERE ALWAYS THERE TO PROTECT ME!

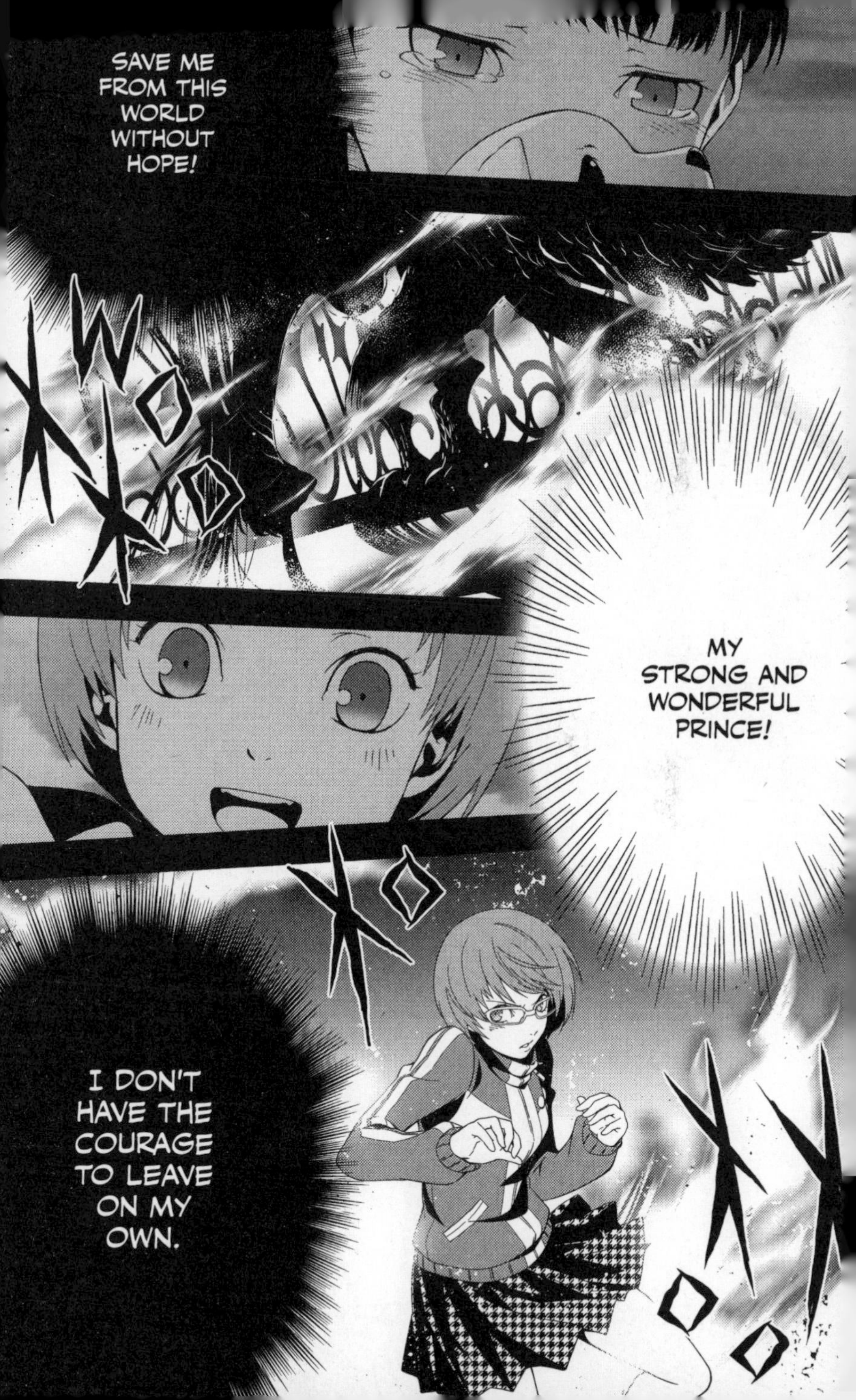
SAVE ME FROM THIS WORLD WITHOUT HOPE!
MY STRONG AND WONDERFUL PRINCE!
I DON'T HAVE THE COURAGE TO LEAVE ON MY OWN.

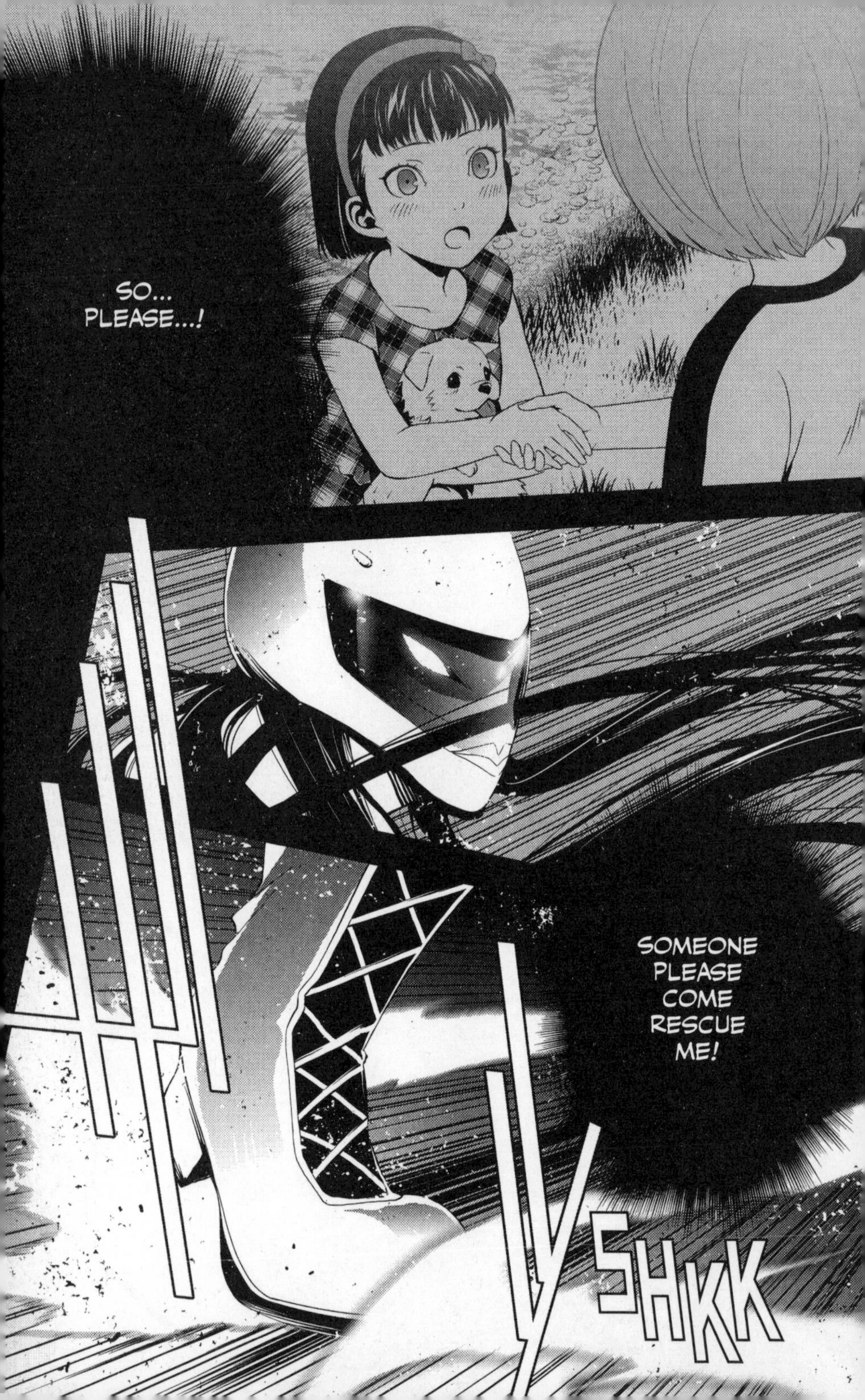
SO... PLEASE...!
SOMEONE PLEASE COME RESCUE ME!
SHKK

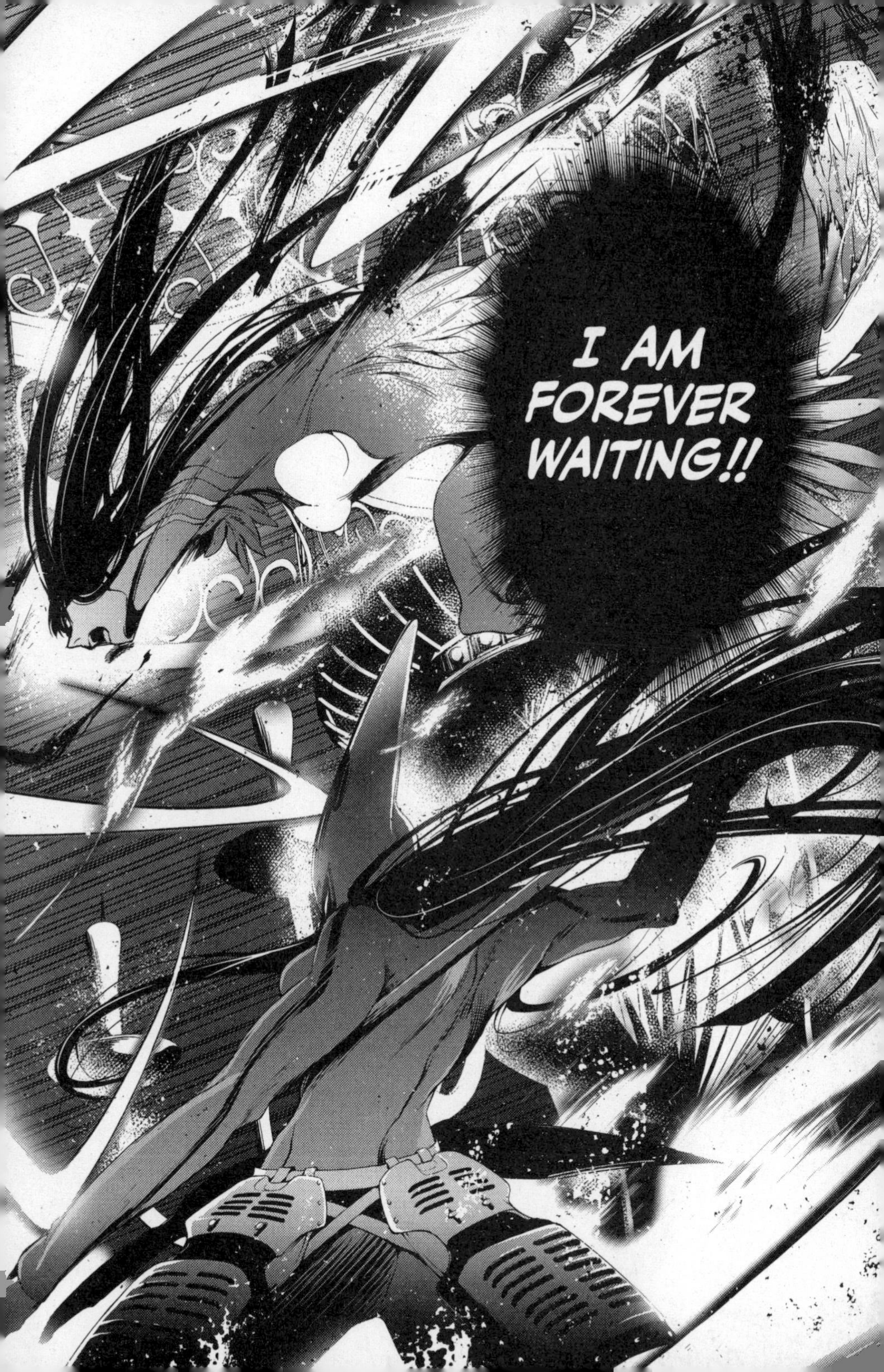
I AM FOREVER WAITING!!

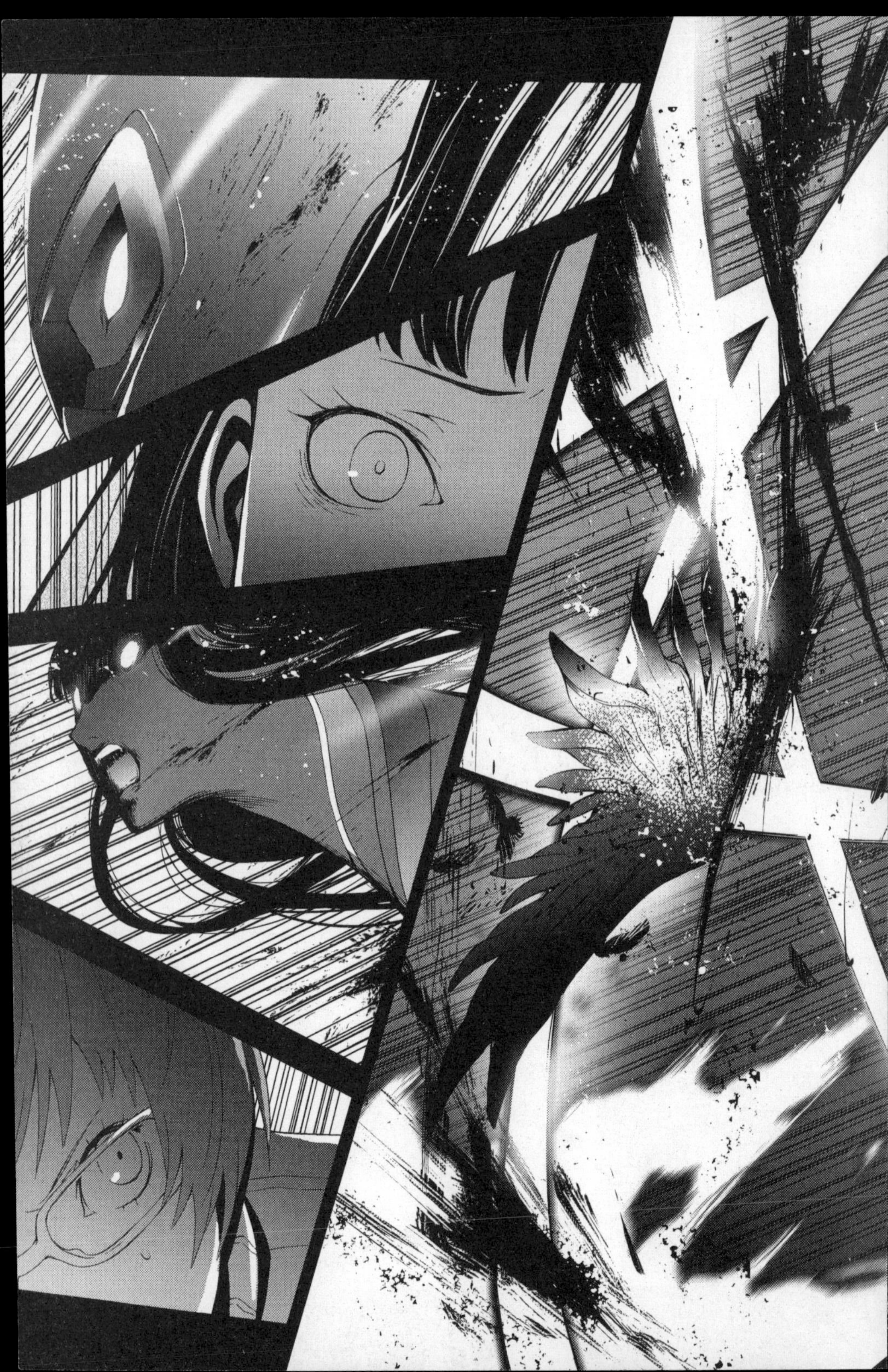

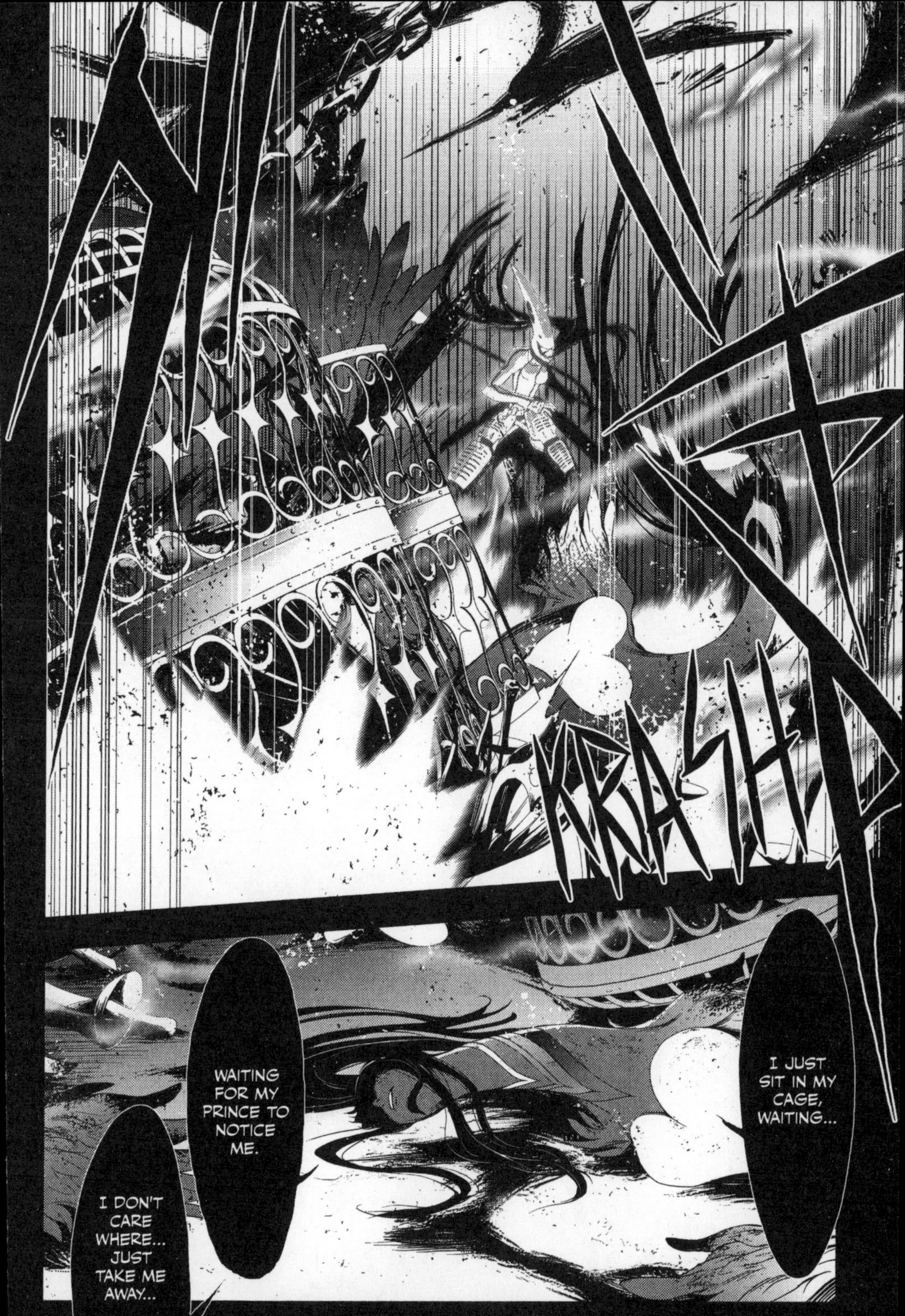
KRASH
I JUST SIT IN MY CAGE, WAITING...
WAITING FOR MY PRINCE TO NOTICE ME.
I DON'T CARE WHERE... JUST TAKE ME AWAY...

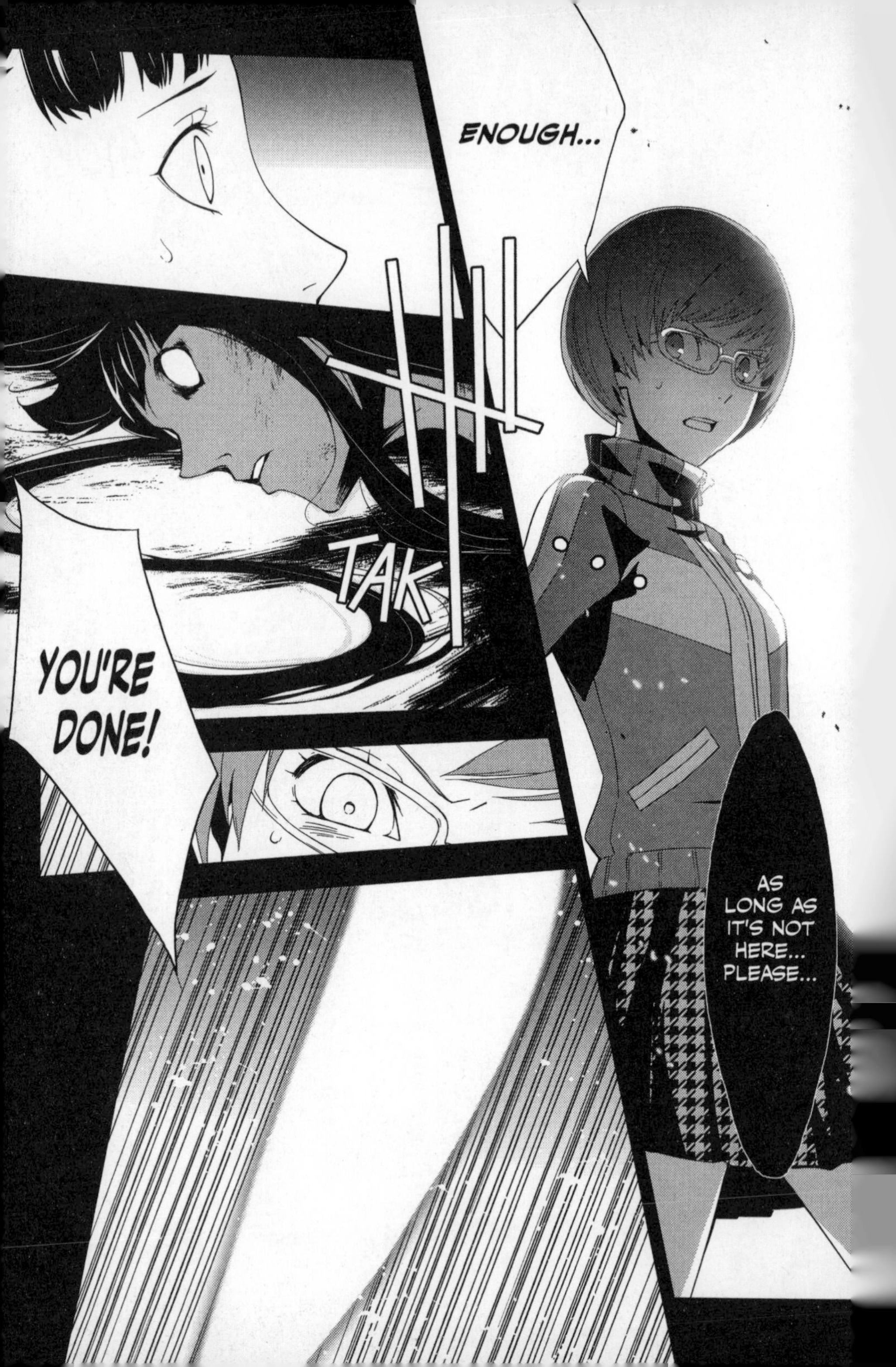
ENOUGH...
AS LONG AS IT'S NOT HERE... PLEASE...
TAK
YOU'RE DONE!

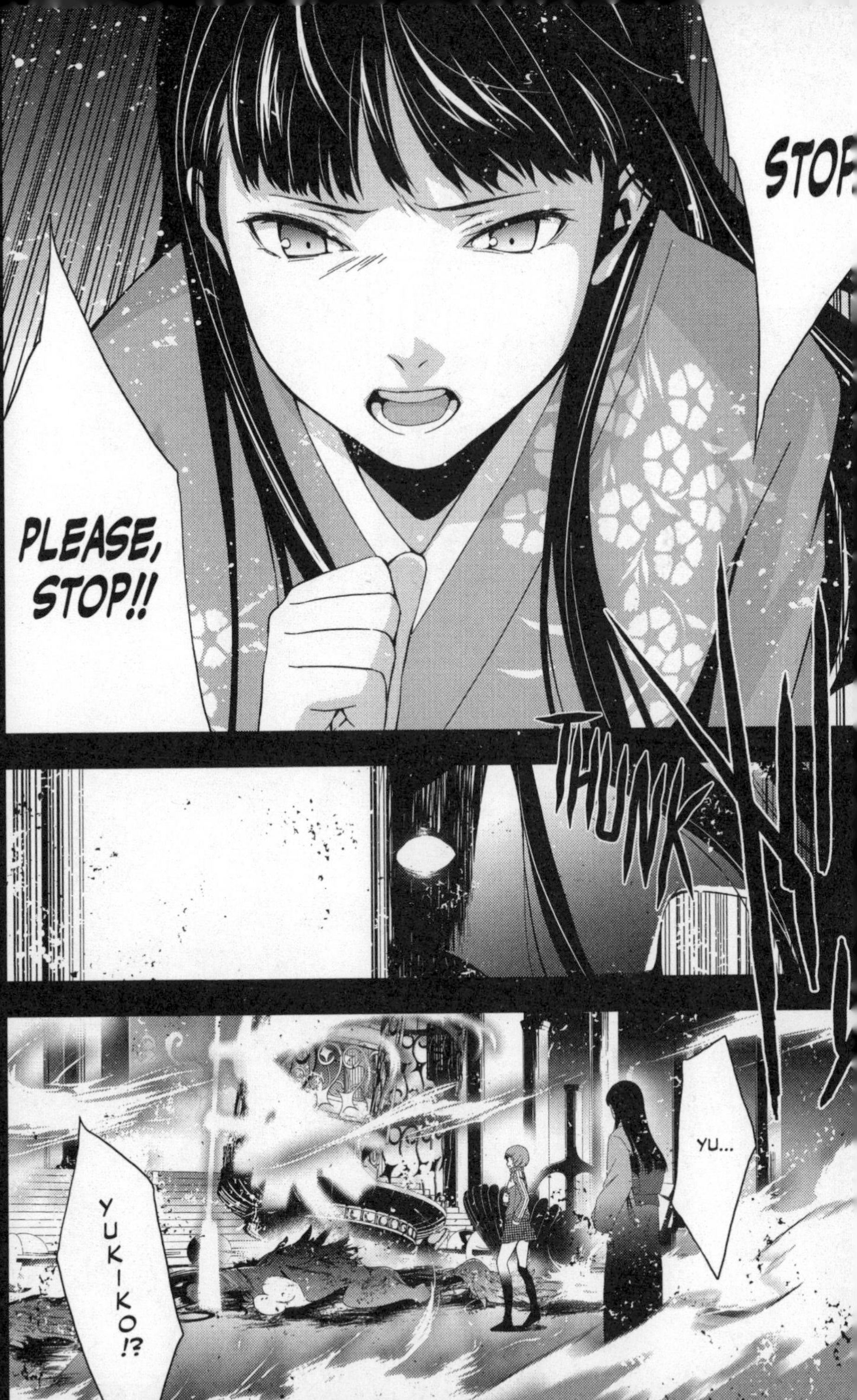
STOP
PLEASE, STOP!!
THUNK
YU...
YUKIKO!?

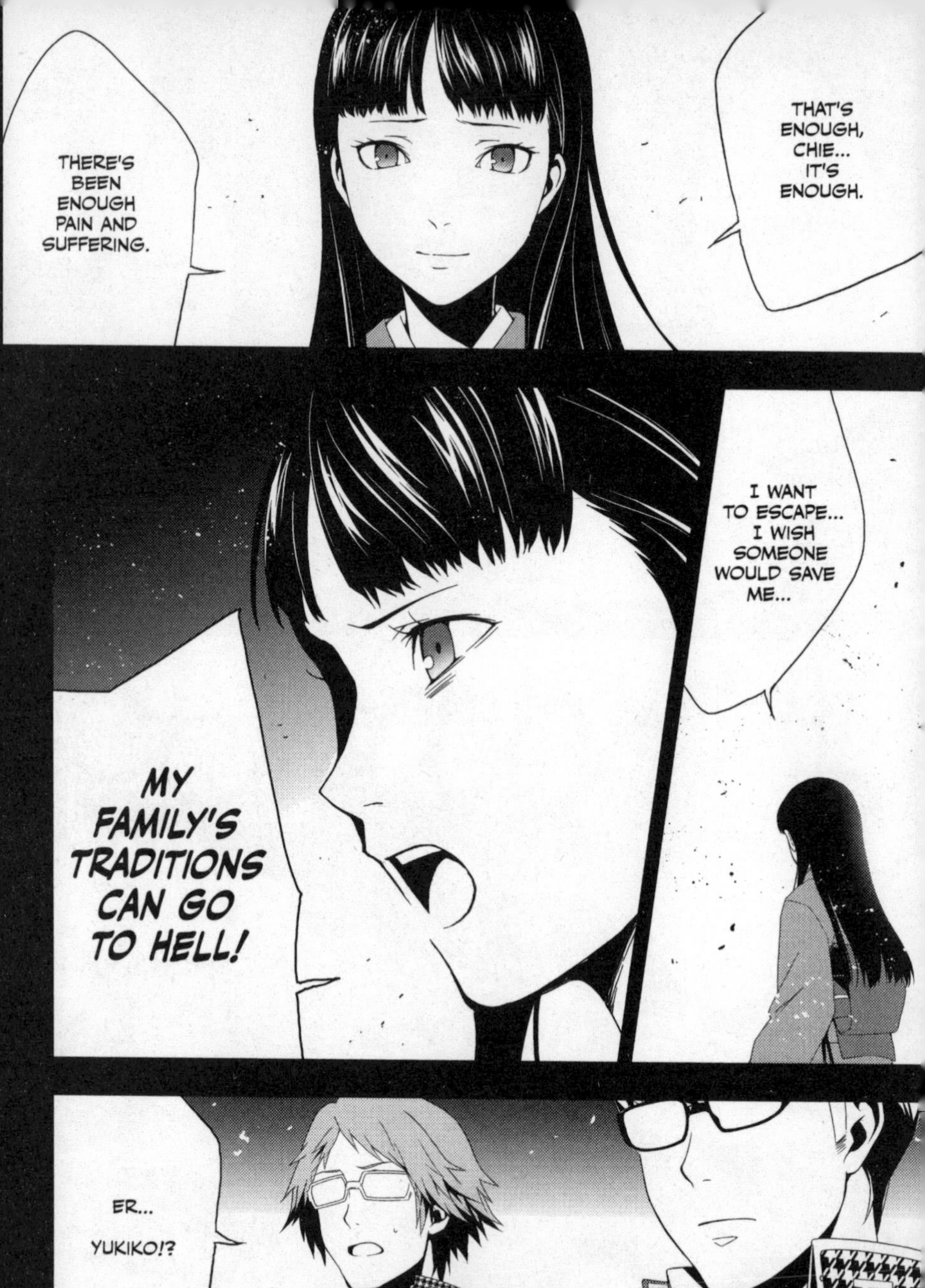
THAT'S ENOUGH, CHIE... IT'S ENOUGH.
THERE'S BEEN ENOUGH PAIN AND SUFFERING.
I WANT TO ESCAPE... I WISH SOMEONE WOULD SAVE ME...
MY FAMILY'S TRADITIONS CAN GO TO HELL!
ER...
YUKIKO!?

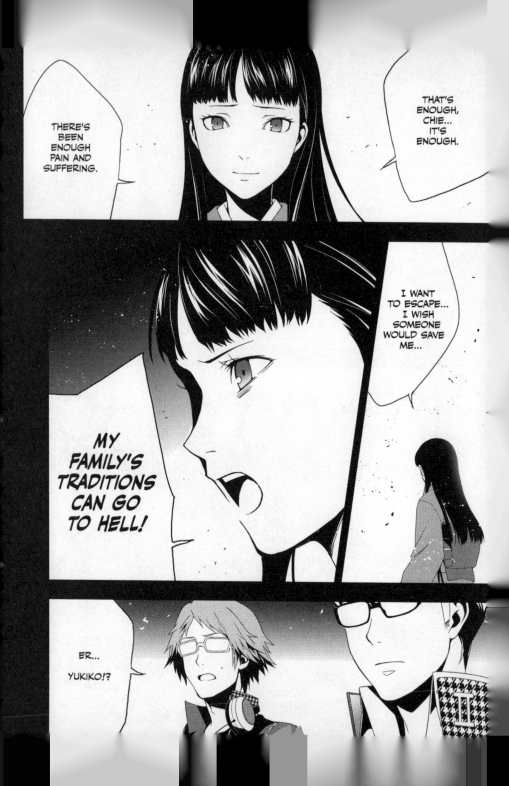

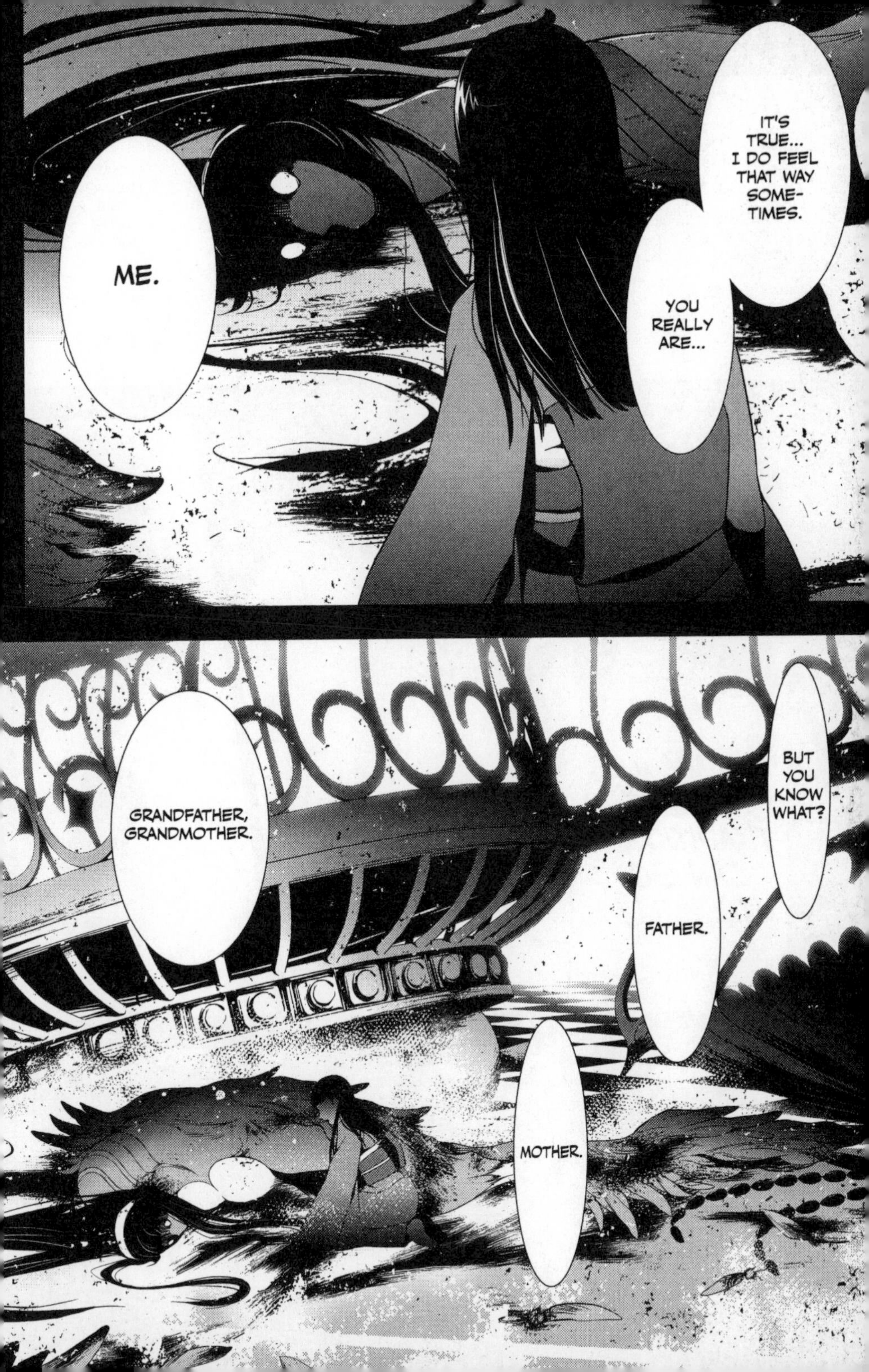
IT'S TRUE... I DO FEEL THAT WAY SOME-TIMES.
YOU REALLY ARE...
ME.
BUT YOU KNOW WHAT?
FATHER.
MOTHER.
GRANDFATHER, GRANDMOTHER.

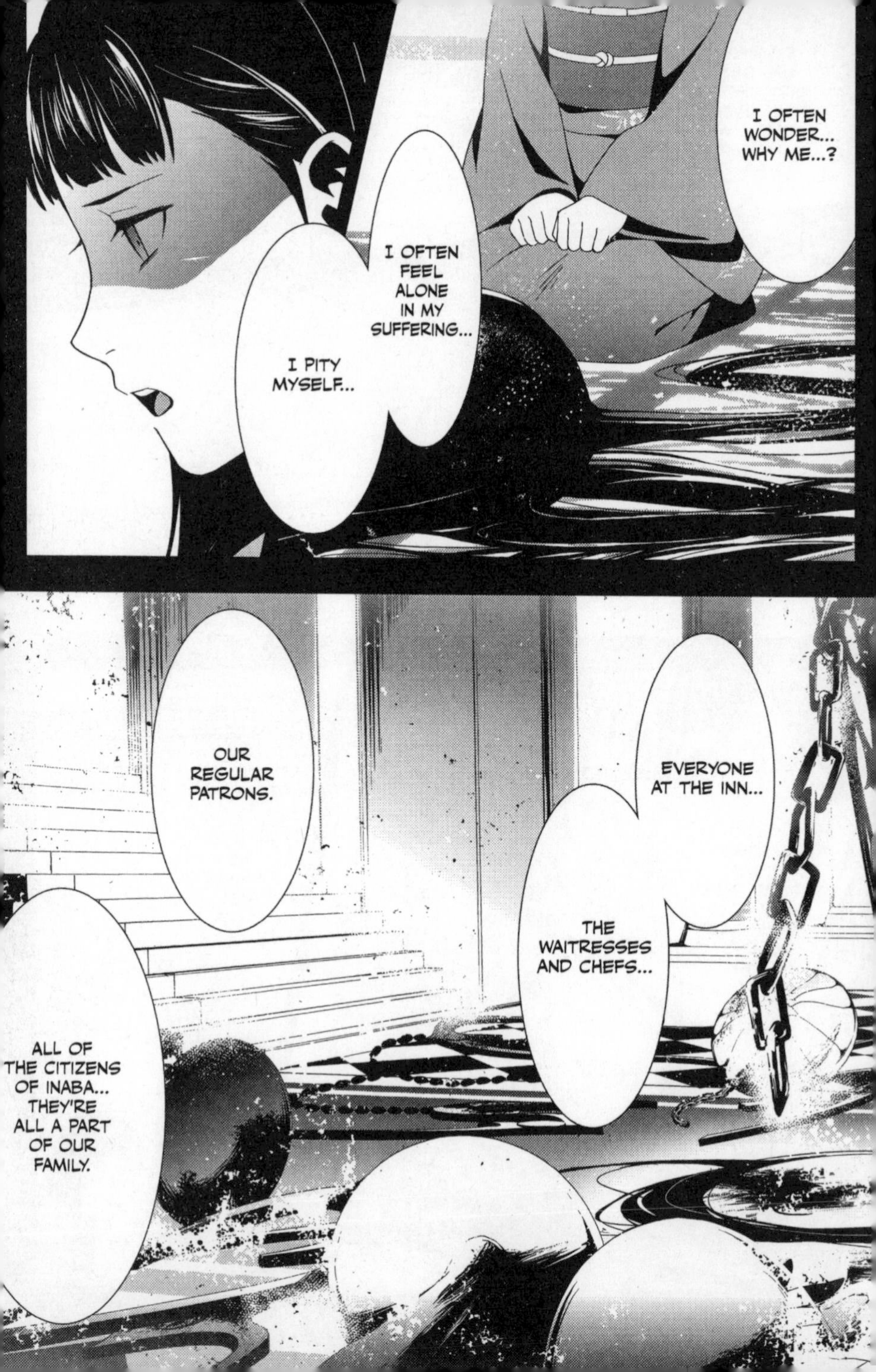
I OFTEN WONDER... WHY ME...?
I OFTEN FEEL ALONE IN MY SUFFERING...
I PITY MYSELF...
EVERYONE AT THE INN...
THE WAITRESSES AND CHEFS...
OUR REGULAR PATRONS.
ALL OF THE CITIZENS OF INABA... THEY'RE ALL A PART OF OUR FAMILY.

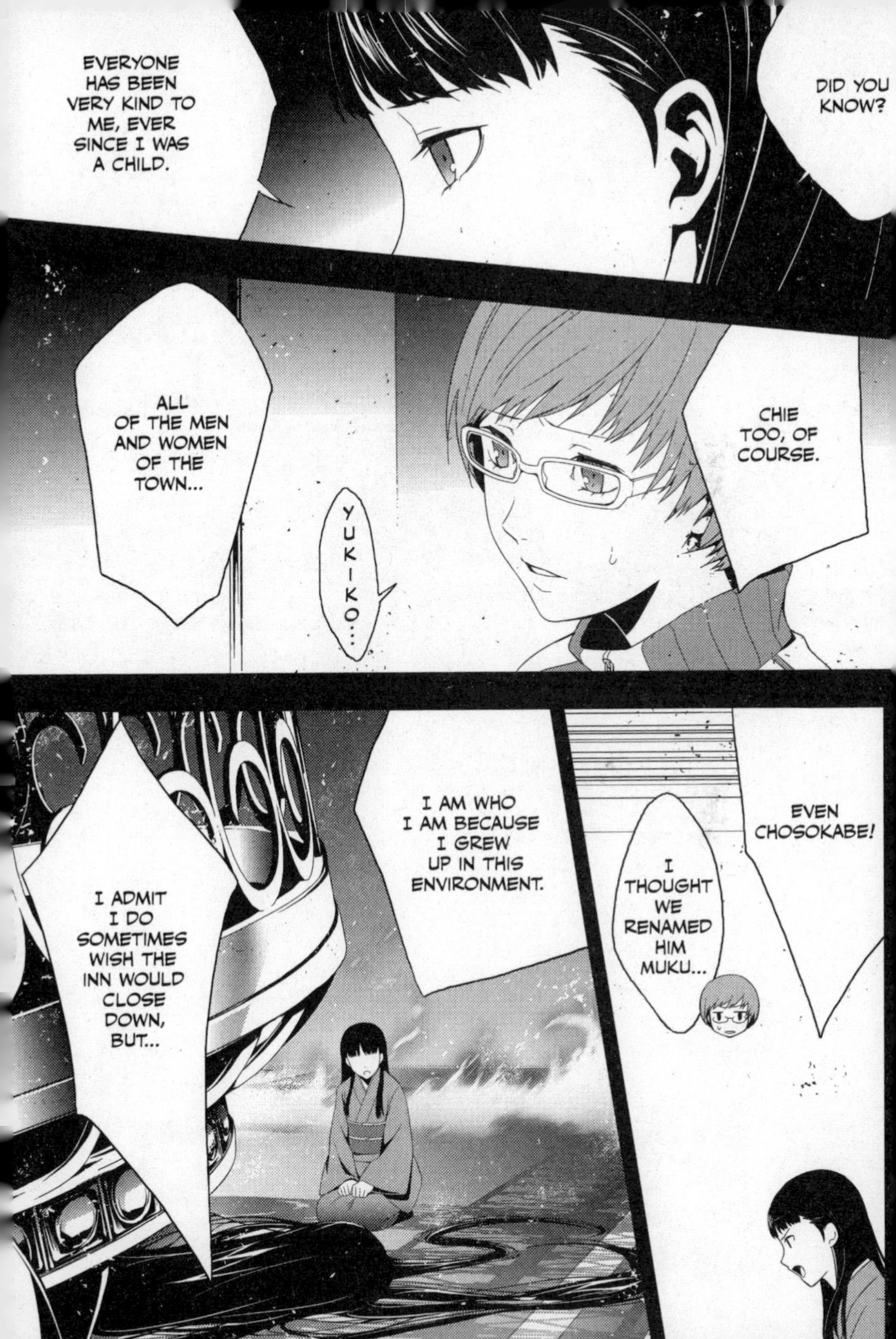
DID YOU KNOW?
EVERYONE HAS BEEN VERY KIND TO ME, EVER SINCE I WAS A CHILD.
CHIE TOO, OF COURSE.
YUKIKO...
ALL OF THE MEN AND WOMEN OF THE TOWN...
EVEN CHOSOKABE!
I THOUGHT WE RENAMED HIM MUKU...
I AM WHO I AM BECAUSE I GREW UP IN THIS ENVIRONMENT.
I ADMIT I DO SOMETIMES WISH THE INN WOULD CLOSE DOWN, BUT...

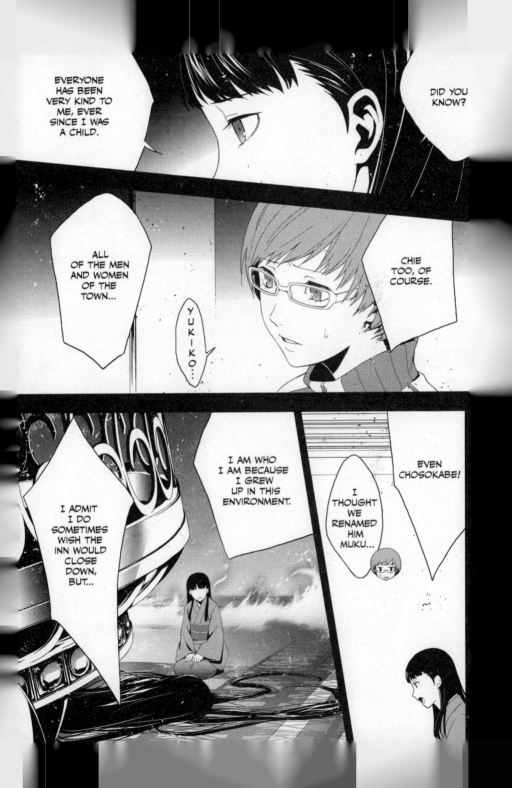

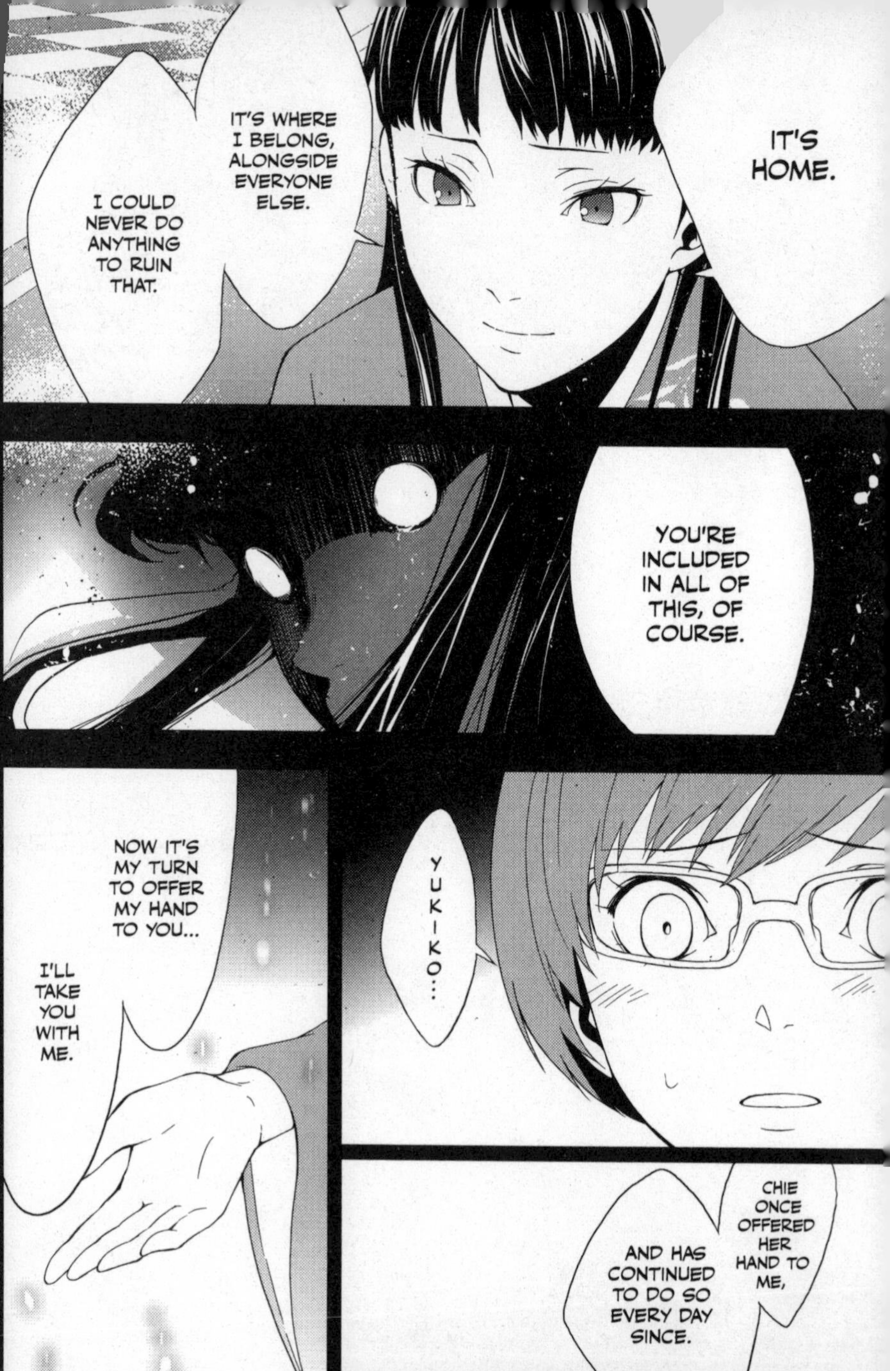
IT'S HOME.
IT'S WHERE I BELONG, ALONGSIDE EVERYONE ELSE.
I COULD NEVER DO ANYTHING TO RUIN THAT.
YOU'RE INCLUDED IN ALL OF THIS, OF COURSE.
YUKIKO...
CHIE ONCE OFFERED HER HAND TO ME,
AND HAS CONTINUED TO DO SO EVERY DAY SINCE.
NOW IT'S MY TURN TO OFFER MY HAND TO YOU...
I'LL TAKE YOU WITH ME.

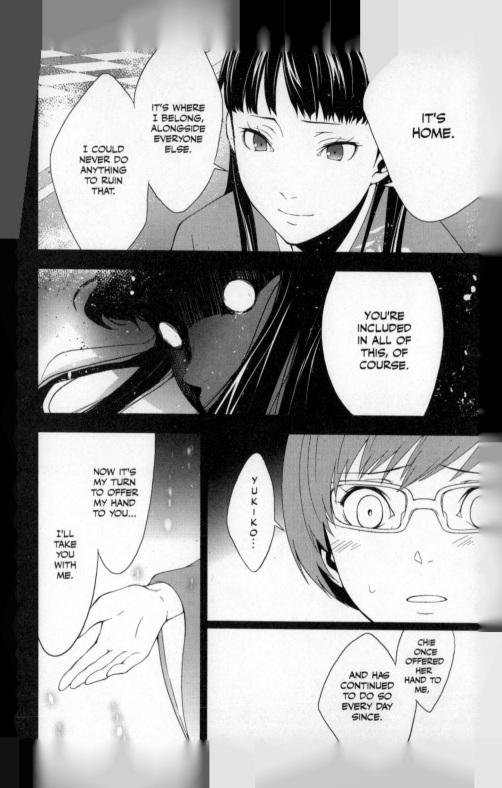

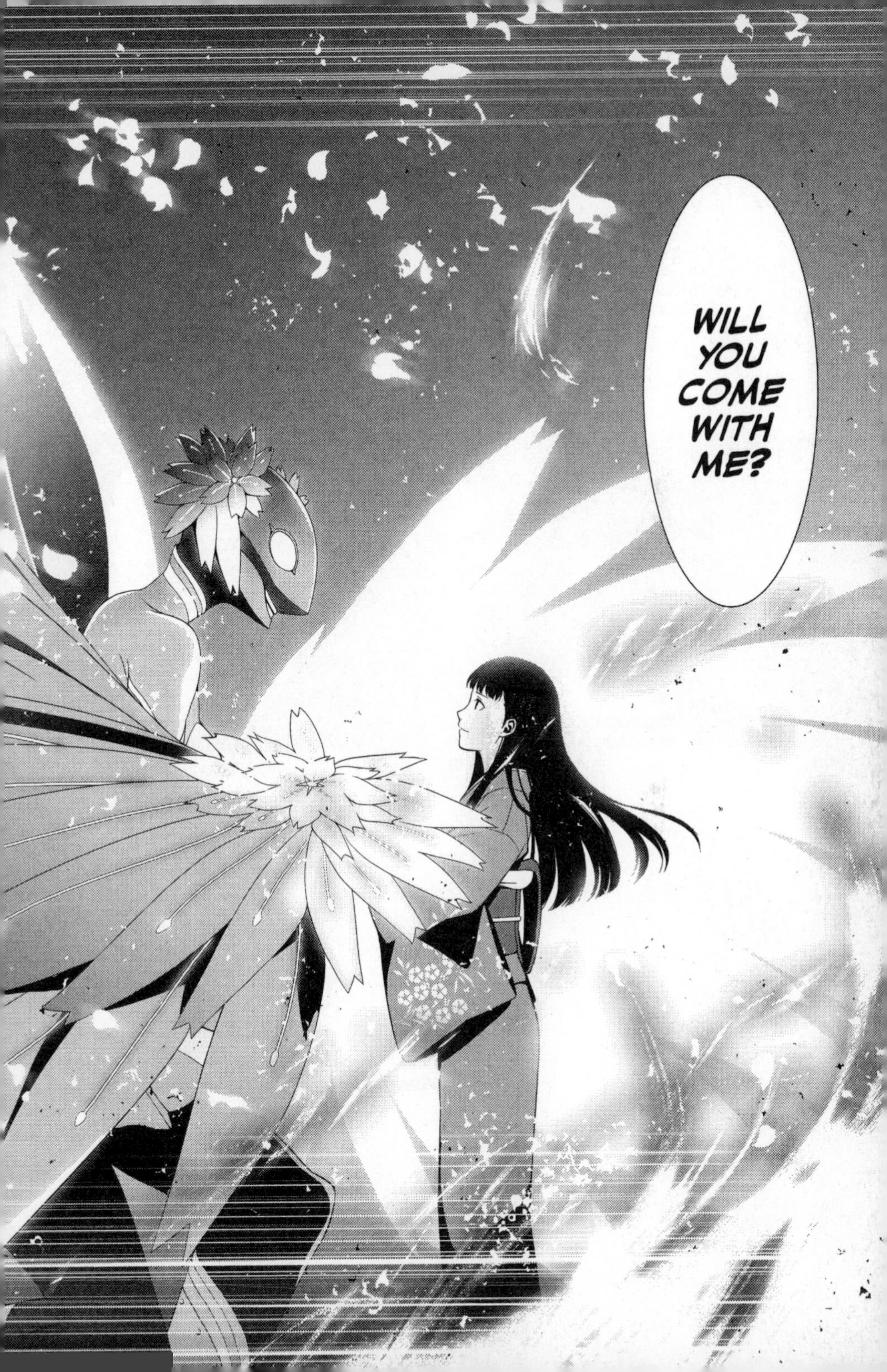
WILL YOU COME WITH ME?

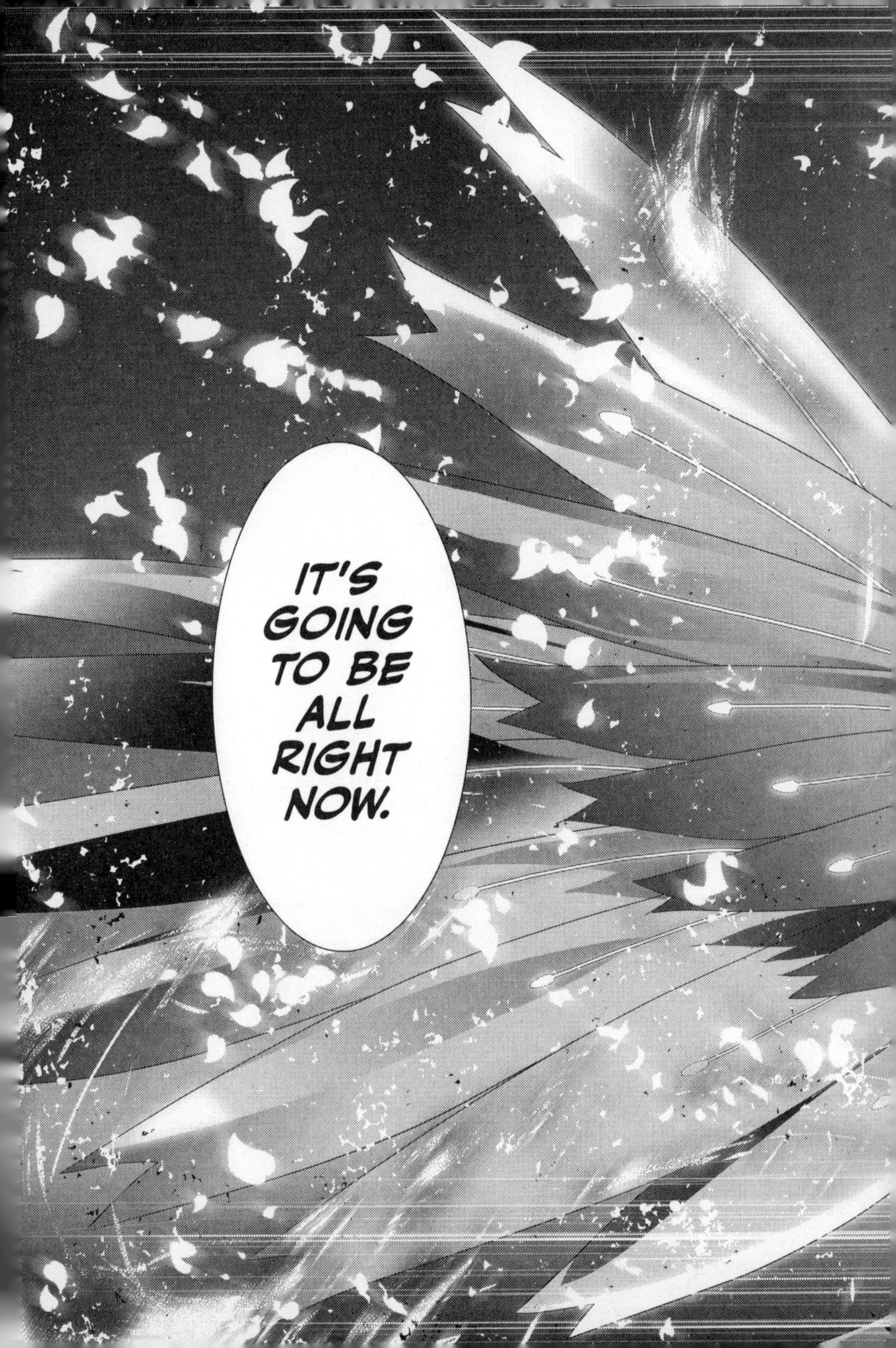
IT'S GOING TO BE ALL RIGHT NOW.

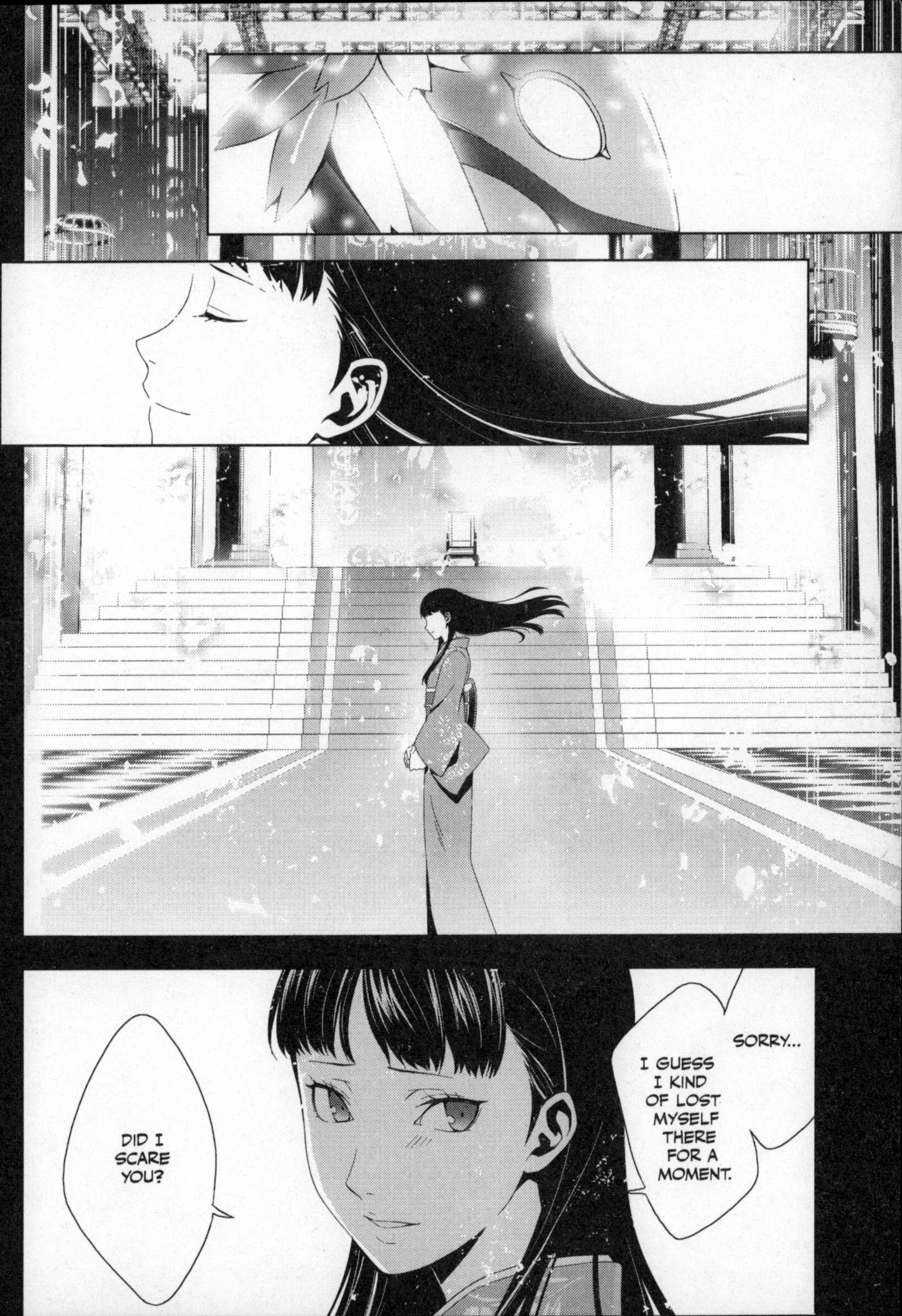
SORRY...
I GUESS I KIND OF LOST MYSELF THERE FOR A MOMENT.
DID I SCARE YOU?

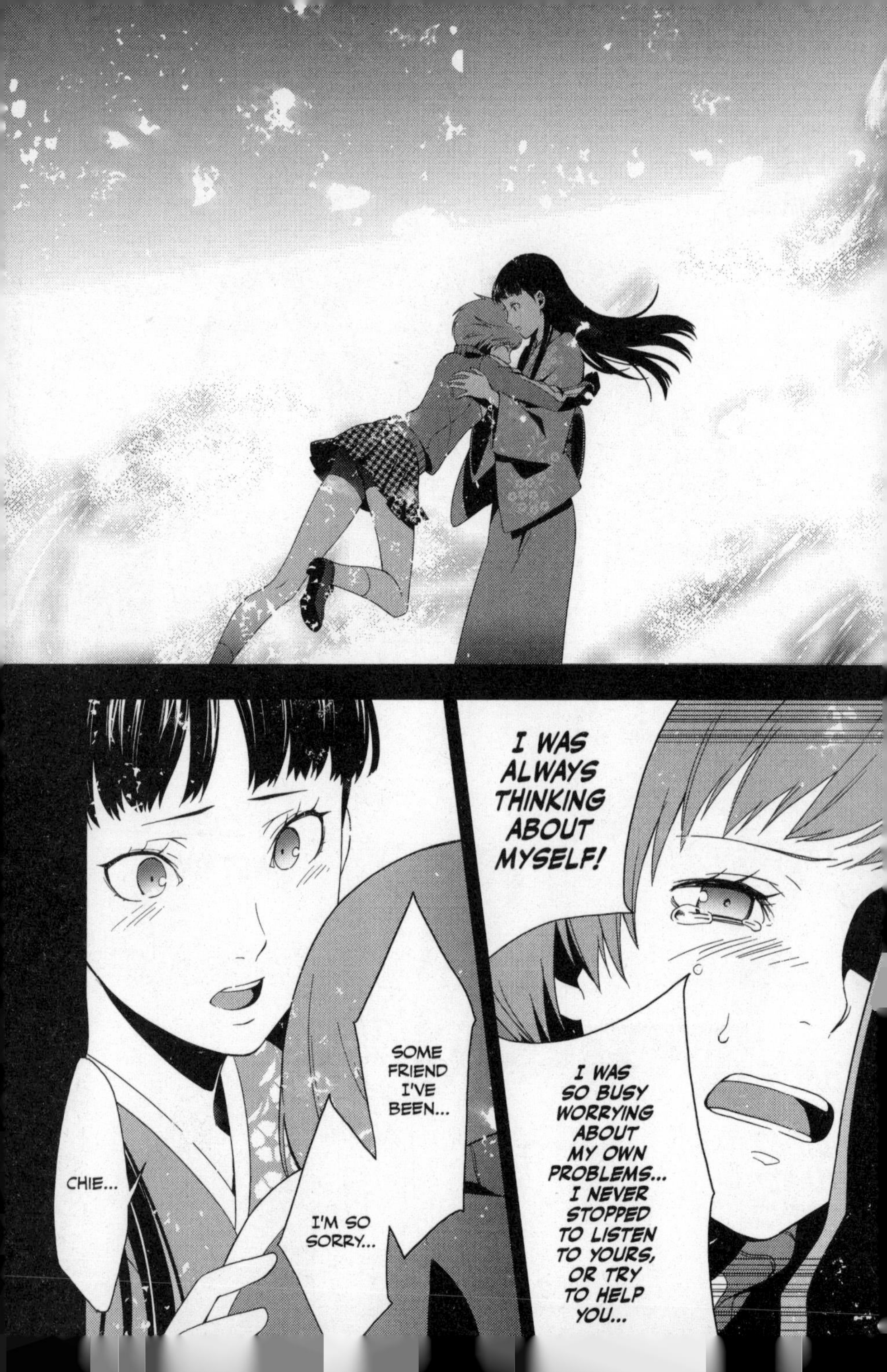
I WAS ALWAYS THINKING ABOUT MYSELF!
I WAS SO BUSY WORRYING ABOUT MY OWN PROBLEMS... I NEVER STOPPED TO LISTEN TO YOURS, OR TRY TO HELP YOU...
SOME FRIEND I'VE BEEN...
I'M SO SORRY...
CHIE...

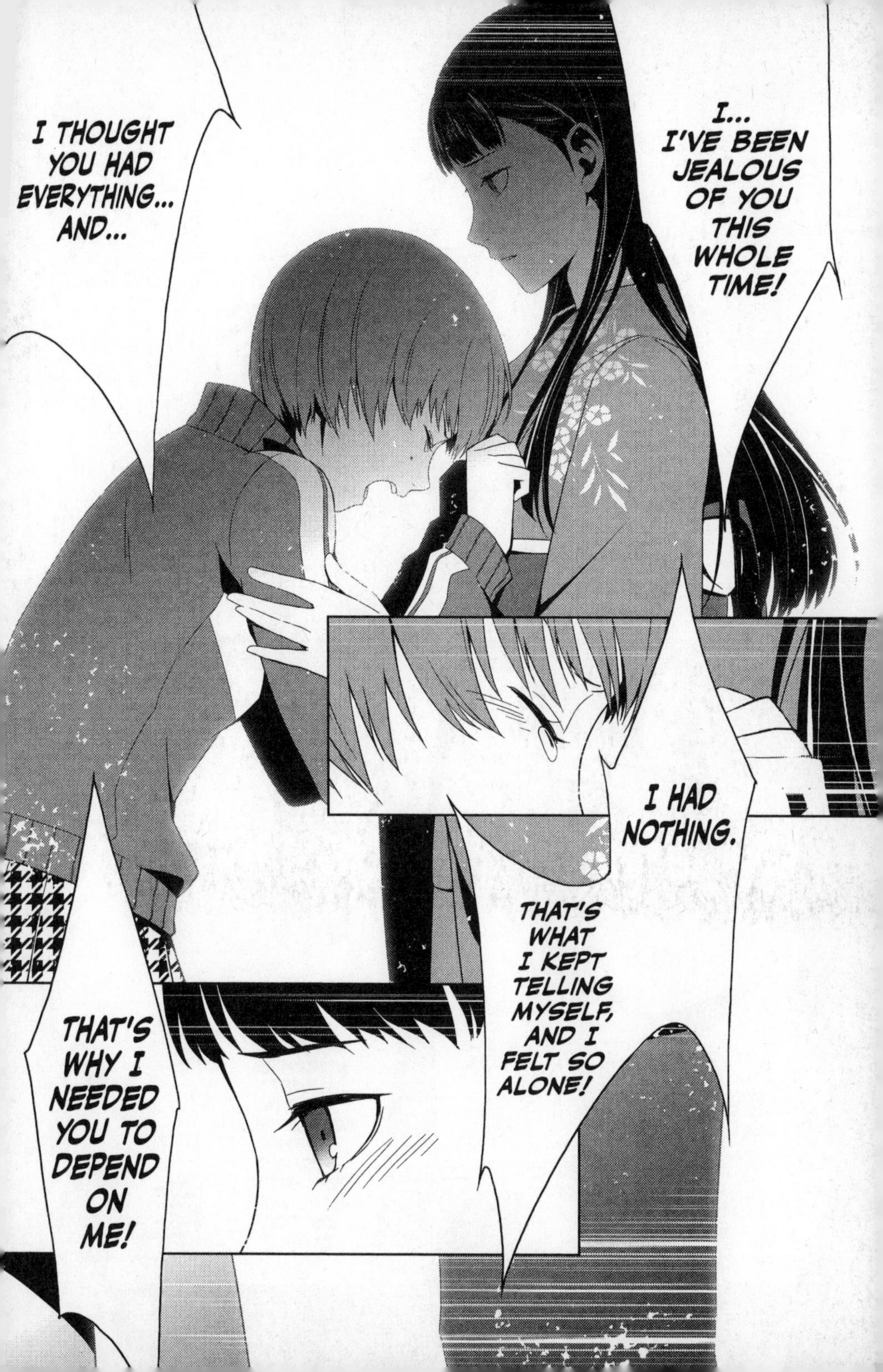
I... I'VE BEEN JEALOUS OF YOU THIS WHOLE TIME!
I THOUGHT YOU HAD EVERYTHING... AND...
I HAD NOTHING.
THAT'S WHAT I KEPT TELLING MYSELF, AND I FELT SO ALONE!
THAT'S WHY I NEEDED YOU TO DEPEND ON ME!

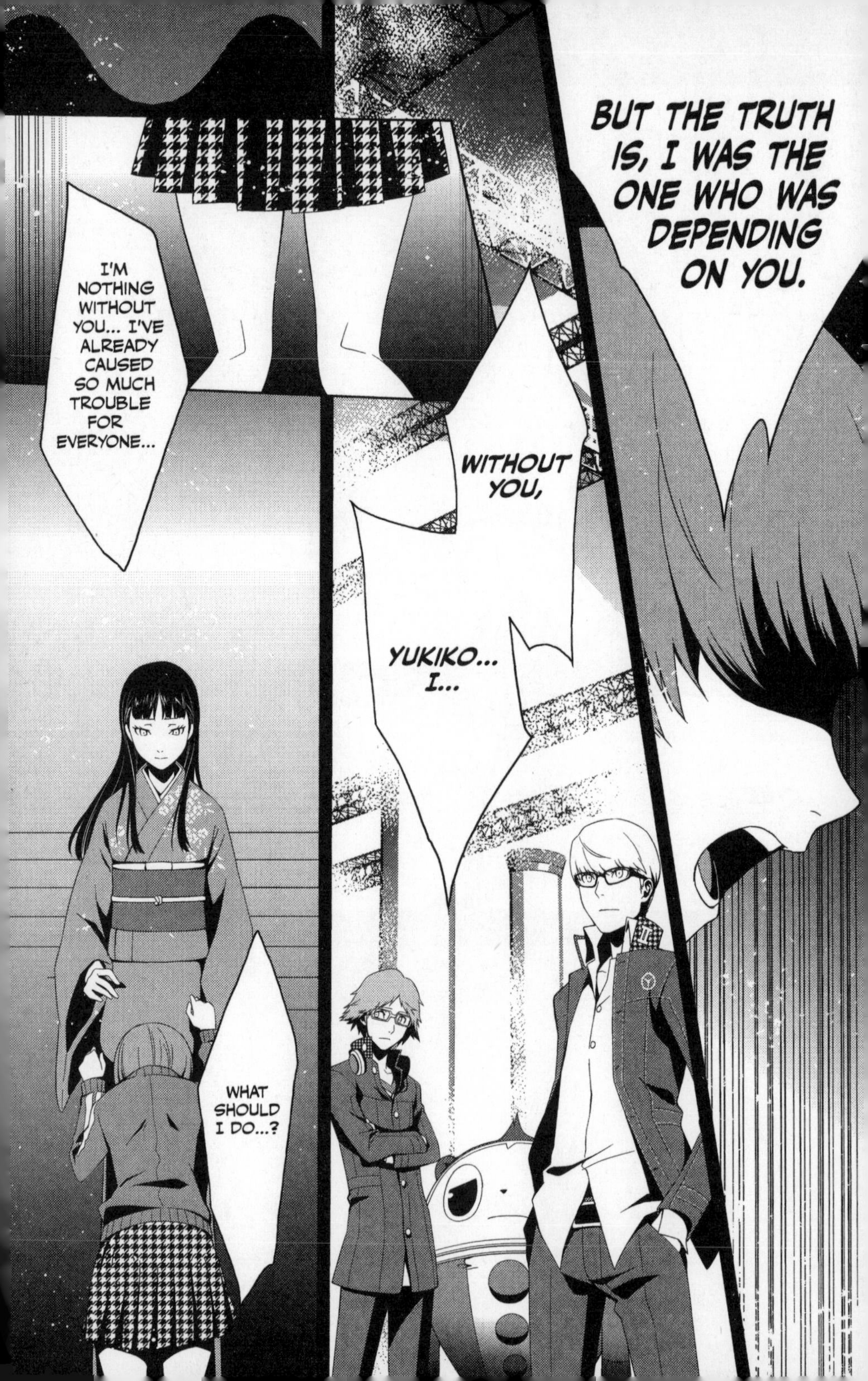
BUT THE TRUTH IS, I WAS THE ONE WHO WAS DEPENDING ON YOU.
WITHOUT YOU,
YUKIKO... I...
I'M NOTHING WITHOUT YOU... I'VE ALREADY CAUSED SO MUCH TROUBLE FOR EVERYONE...
WHAT SHOULD I DO...?

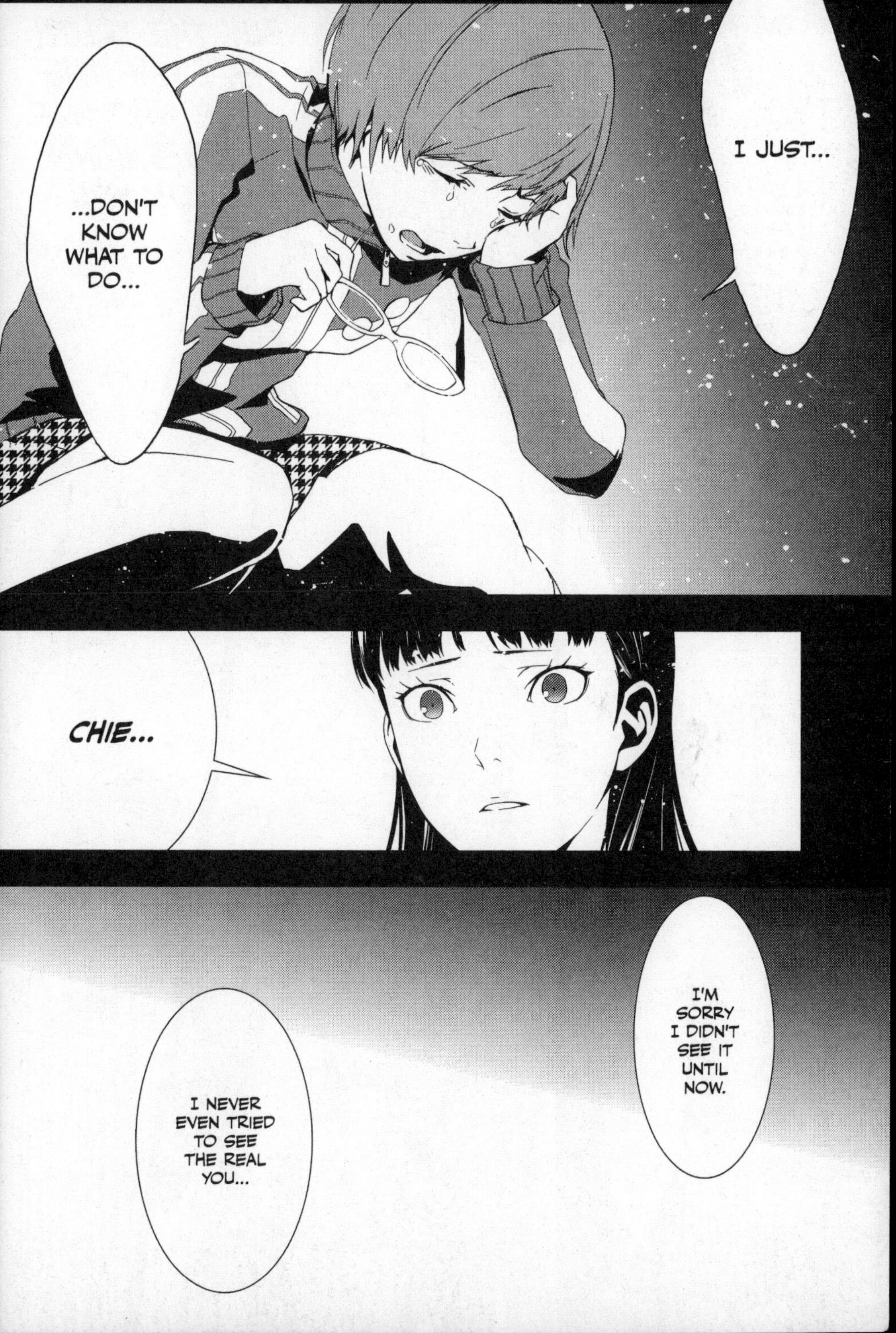
I JUST...
...DON'T KNOW WHAT TO DO...
CHIE...
I'M SORRY I DIDN'T SEE IT UNTIL NOW.
I NEVER EVEN TRIED TO SEE THE REAL YOU...

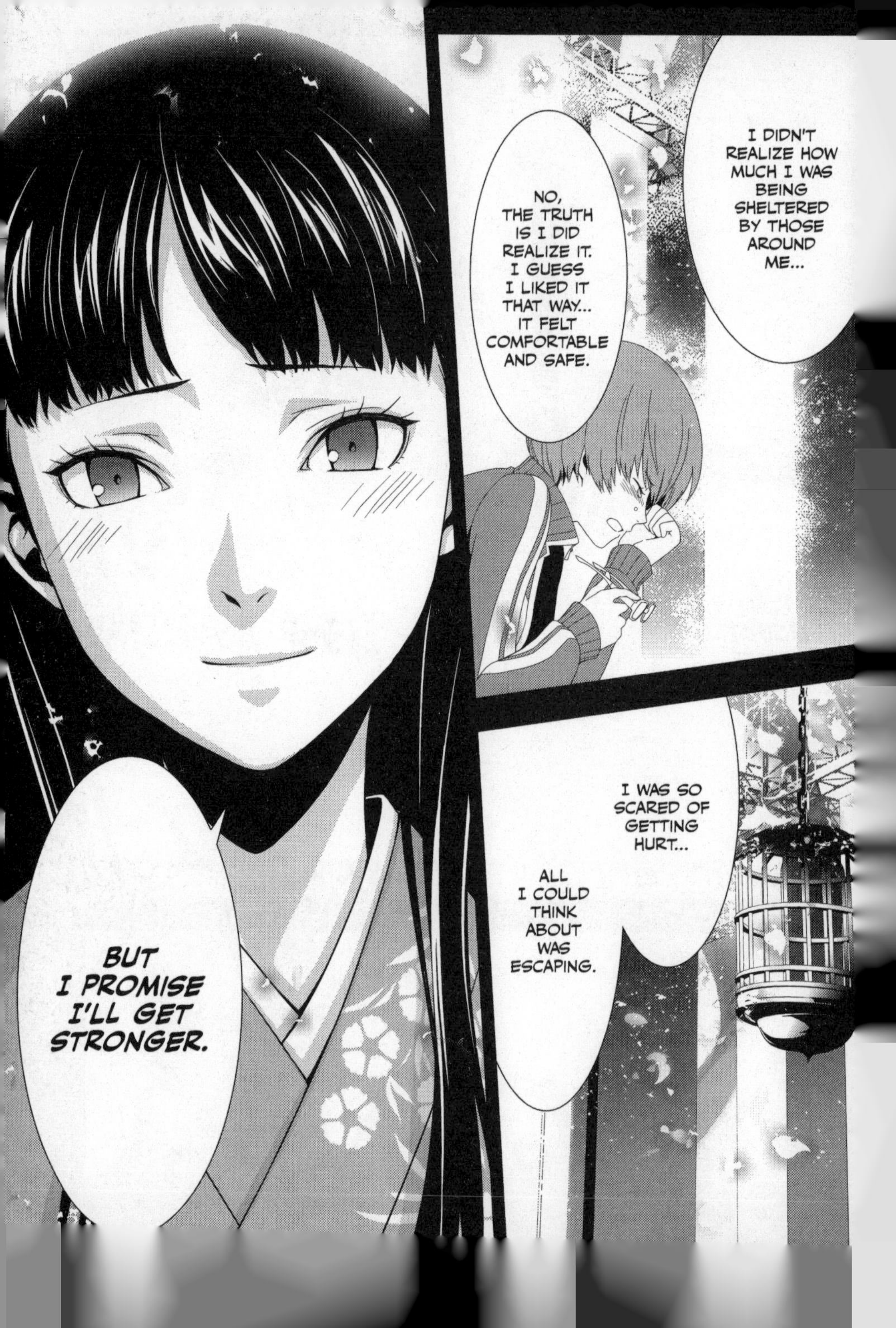
I DIDN'T REALIZE HOW MUCH I WAS BEING SHELTERED BY THOSE AROUND ME...
NO, THE TRUTH IS I DID REALIZE IT. I GUESS I LIKED IT THAT WAY... IT FELT COMFORTABLE AND SAFE.
I WAS SO SCARED OF GETTING HURT...
ALL I COULD THINK ABOUT WAS ESCAPING.
BUT I PROMISE I'LL GET STRONGER.

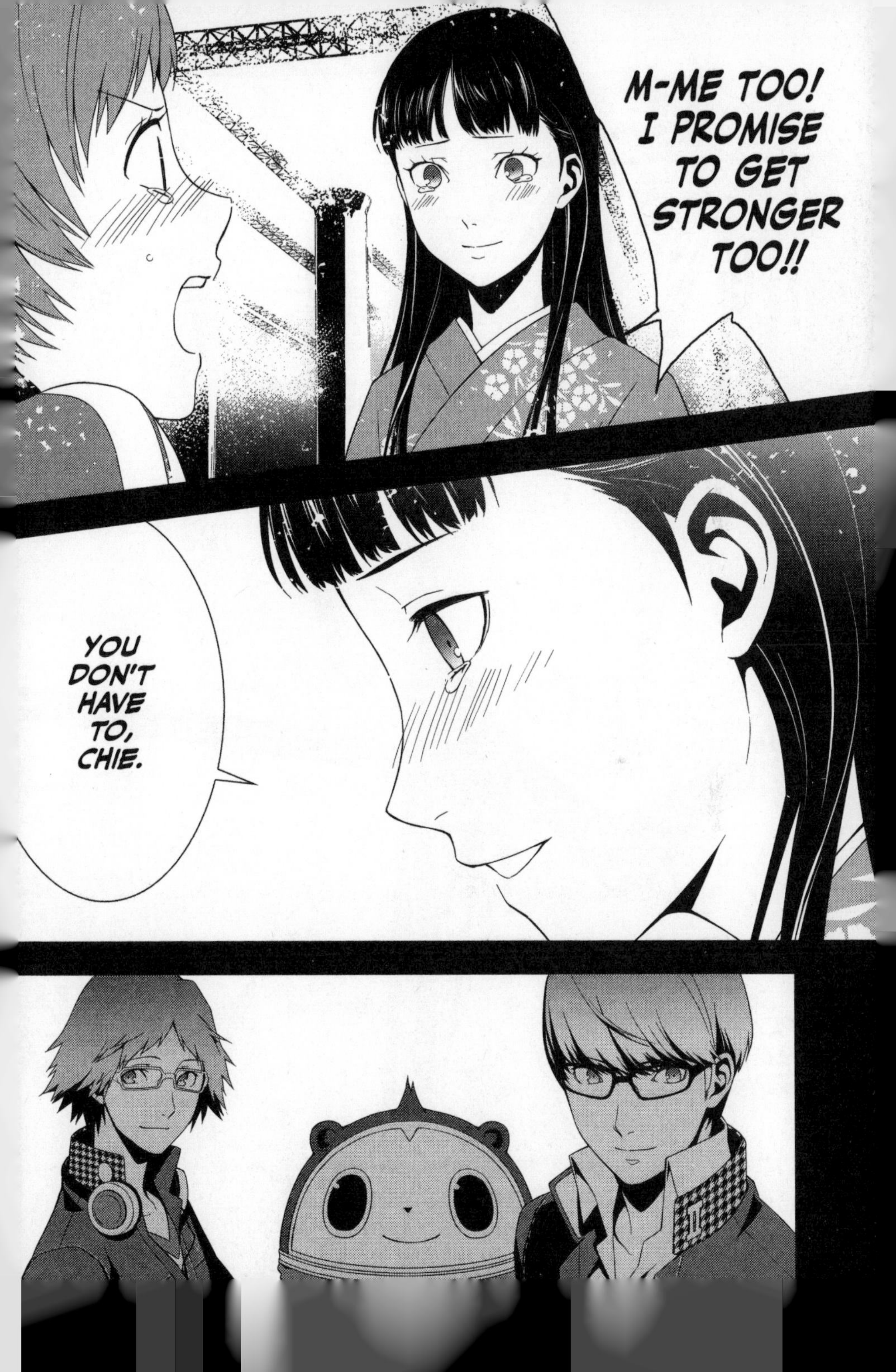
M-ME TOO! I PROMISE TO GET STRONGER TOO!!
YOU DON'T HAVE TO, CHIE.

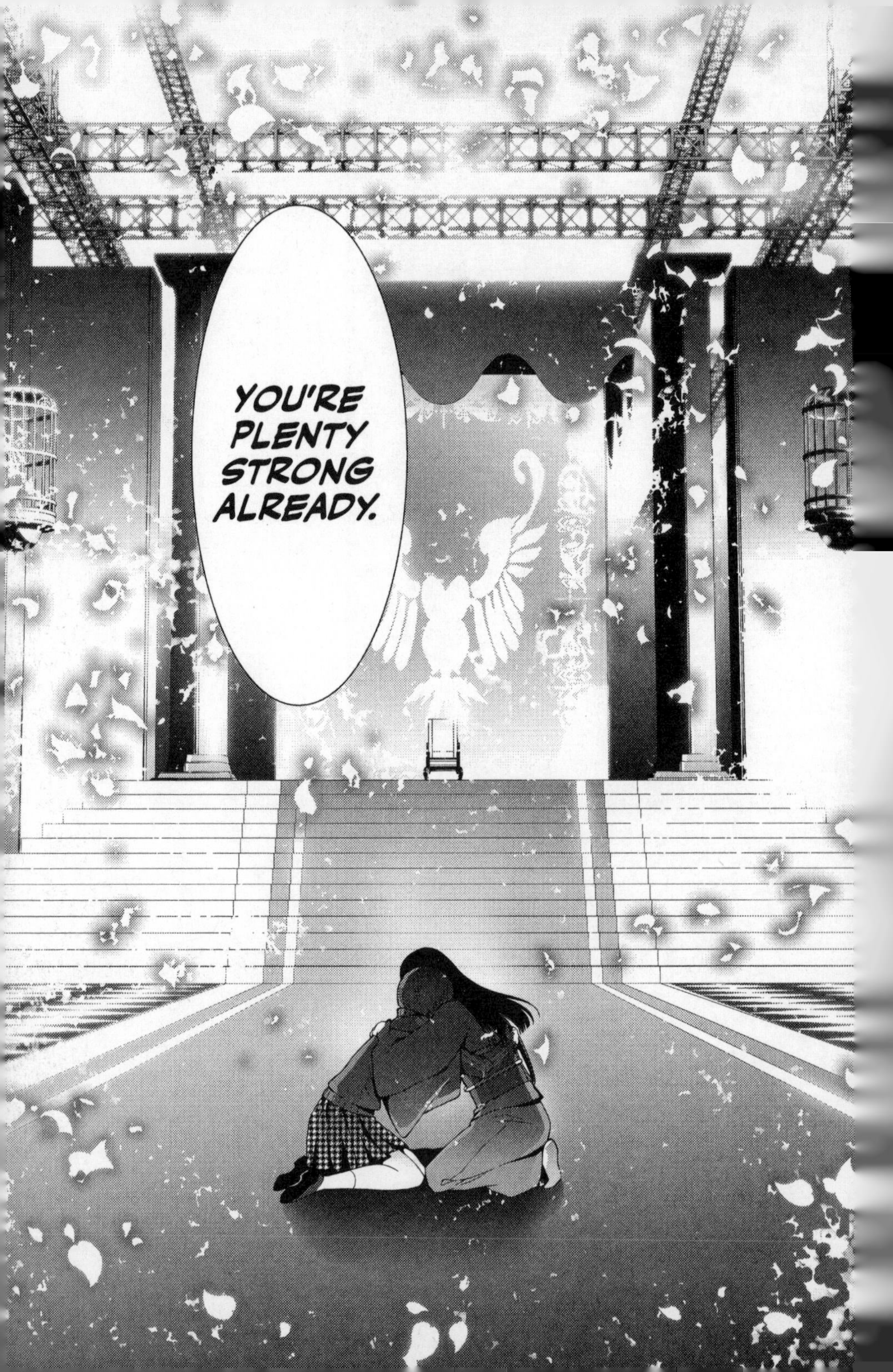
YOU'RE PLENTY STRONG ALREADY.

天城雪子
Yukiko Amagi

Yukiko is the epitome of Japanese beauty, complete with long black hair. To top it off, she is the heiress to the Amagi Inn. I like to call that combo a one-hit K.O. (I don't care if that doesn't make sense.) First of all, her name is fantastic. Yukiko Amagi... it just rolls off the tongue and it sounds like it belongs to a famous enka singer or something. She carries a fan in the opening sequence and in battle, which just adds to her awesome vibe. Her name has this ring to it, a kind of aura or passion that I usually associate with northeastern Japan.

It was over a decade ago now, but there was a certain show with three sisters, and the eldest was named Yukiko. The actress playing the role of that Yukiko had a distinctive nose, and I sometimes wonder if she was the model for this character. I feel like her image really matches this character, so I do find my illustrations of Yukiko Amagi being influenced by that from time to time. I am careful not to let it influence my drawing too much, though.

Yukiko will sometimes say the weirdest things with a straight face, and in such cases I feel like the whole scene takes on a surreal aspect, visually speaking.

PERSONA 4 CHARACTER NOTE

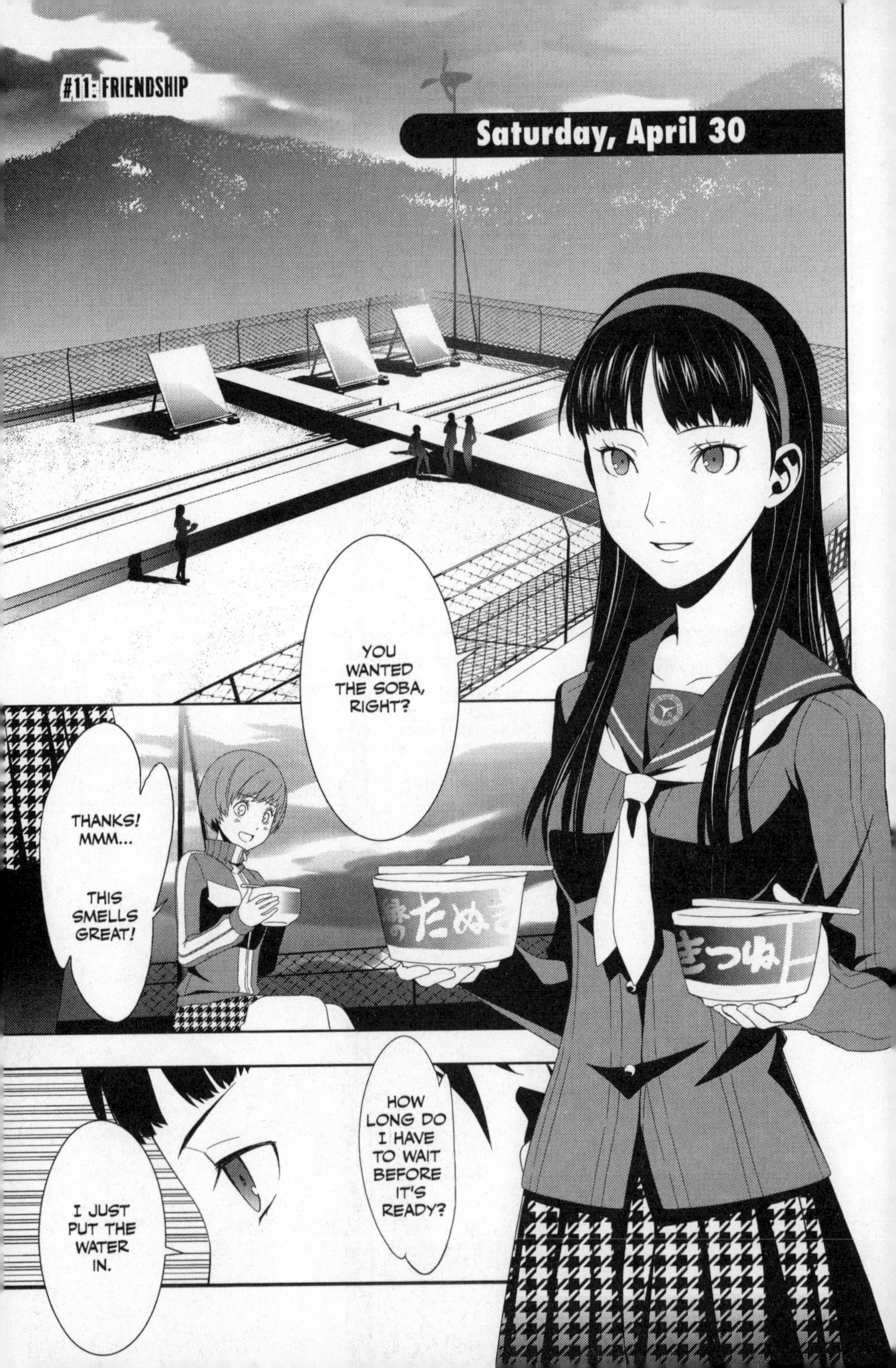
#11: FRIENDSHIP
Saturday, April 30
YOU WANTED THE SOBA, RIGHT?
THANKS! MMM...
THIS SMELLS GREAT!
HOW LONG DO I HAVE TO WAIT BEFORE IT'S READY?
I JUST PUT THE WATER IN.

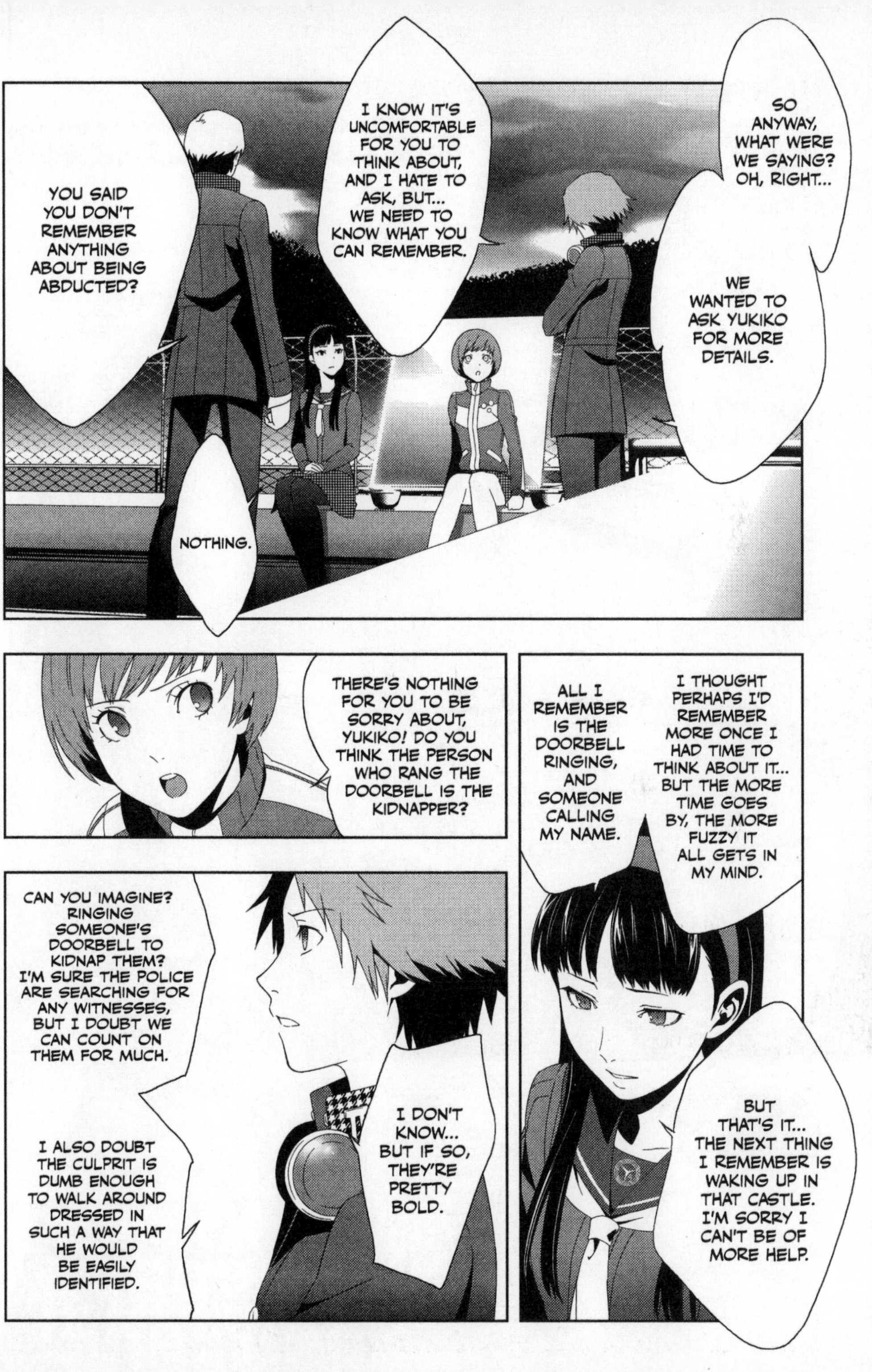
SO ANYWAY, WHAT WERE WE SAYING? OH, RIGHT...
WE WANTED TO ASK YUKIKO FOR MORE DETAILS.
I KNOW IT'S UNCOMFORTABLE FOR YOU TO THINK ABOUT, AND I HATE TO ASK, BUT... WE NEED TO KNOW WHAT YOU CAN REMEMBER.
YOU SAID YOU DON'T REMEMBER ANYTHING ABOUT BEING ABDUCTED?
NOTHING.
I THOUGHT PERHAPS I'D REMEMBER MORE ONCE I HAD TIME TO THINK ABOUT IT... BUT THE MORE TIME GOES BY, THE MORE FUZZY IT ALL GETS IN MY MIND.
ALL I REMEMBER IS THE DOORBELL RINGING, AND SOMEONE CALLING MY NAME.
BUT THAT'S IT... THE NEXT THING I REMEMBER IS WAKING UP IN THAT CASTLE. I'M SORRY I CAN'T BE OF MORE HELP.
THERE'S NOTHING FOR YOU TO BE SORRY ABOUT, YUKIKO! DO YOU THINK THE PERSON WHO RANG THE DOORBELL IS THE KIDNAPPER?
I DON'T KNOW... BUT IF SO, THEY'RE PRETTY BOLD.
CAN YOU IMAGINE? RINGING SOMEONE'S DOORBELL TO KIDNAP THEM? I'M SURE THE POLICE ARE SEARCHING FOR ANY WITNESSES, BUT I DOUBT WE CAN COUNT ON THEM FOR MUCH.
I ALSO DOUBT THE CULPRIT IS DUMB ENOUGH TO WALK AROUND DRESSED IN SUCH A WAY THAT HE WOULD BE EASILY IDENTIFIED.

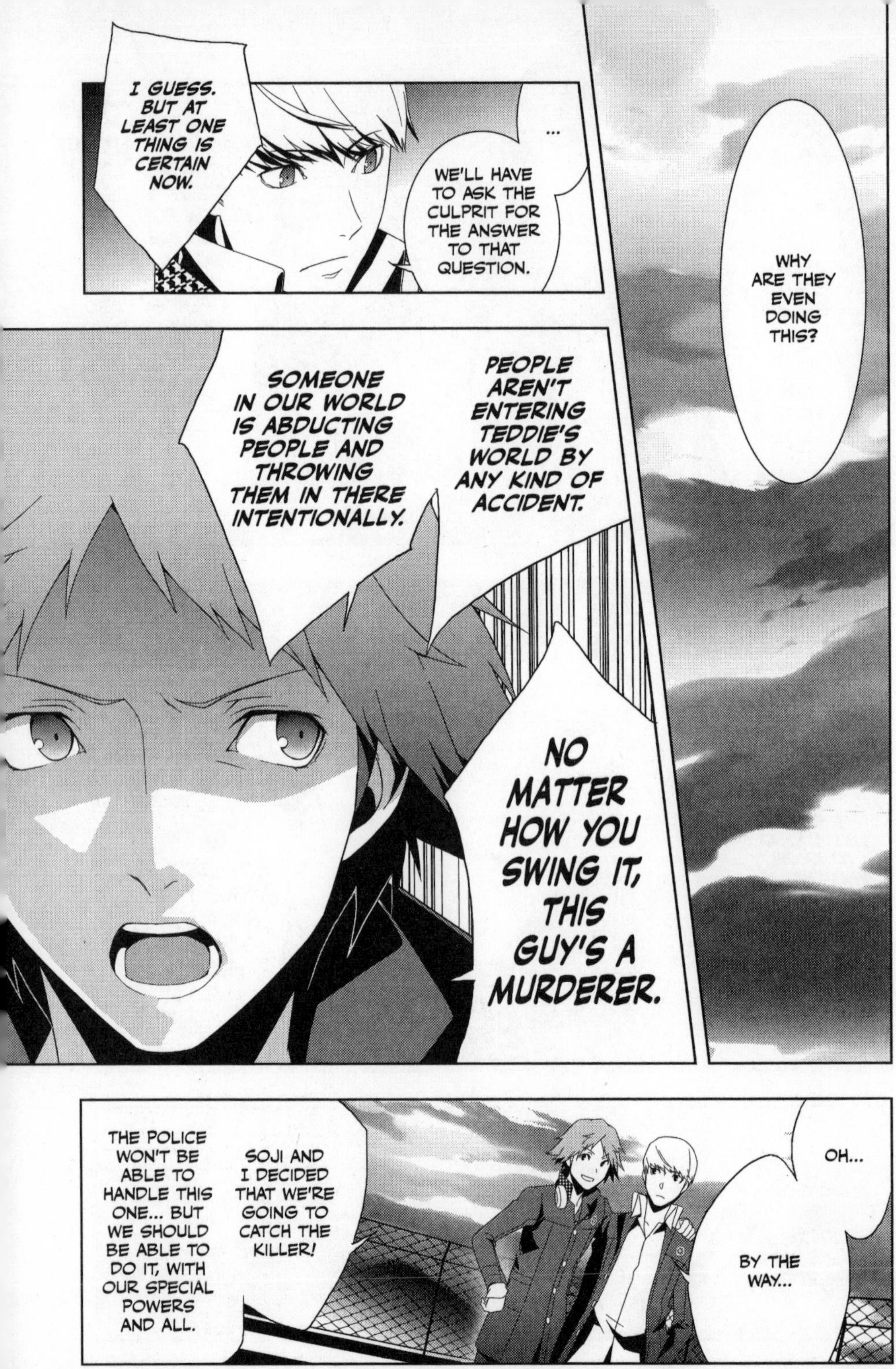
WHY ARE THEY EVEN DOING THIS?
...
WE'LL HAVE TO ASK THE CULPRIT FOR THE ANSWER TO THAT QUESTION.
I GUESS. BUT AT LEAST ONE THING IS CERTAIN NOW.
PEOPLE AREN'T ENTERING TEDDIE'S WORLD BY ANY KIND OF ACCIDENT.
SOMEONE IN OUR WORLD IS ABDUCTING PEOPLE AND THROWING THEM IN THERE INTENTIONALLY.
NO MATTER HOW YOU SWING IT, THIS GUY'S A MURDERER.
OH...
BY THE WAY...
SOJI AND I DECIDED THAT WE'RE GOING TO CATCH THE KILLER!
THE POLICE WON'T BE ABLE TO HANDLE THIS ONE... BUT WE SHOULD BE ABLE TO DO IT, WITH OUR SPECIAL POWERS AND ALL.

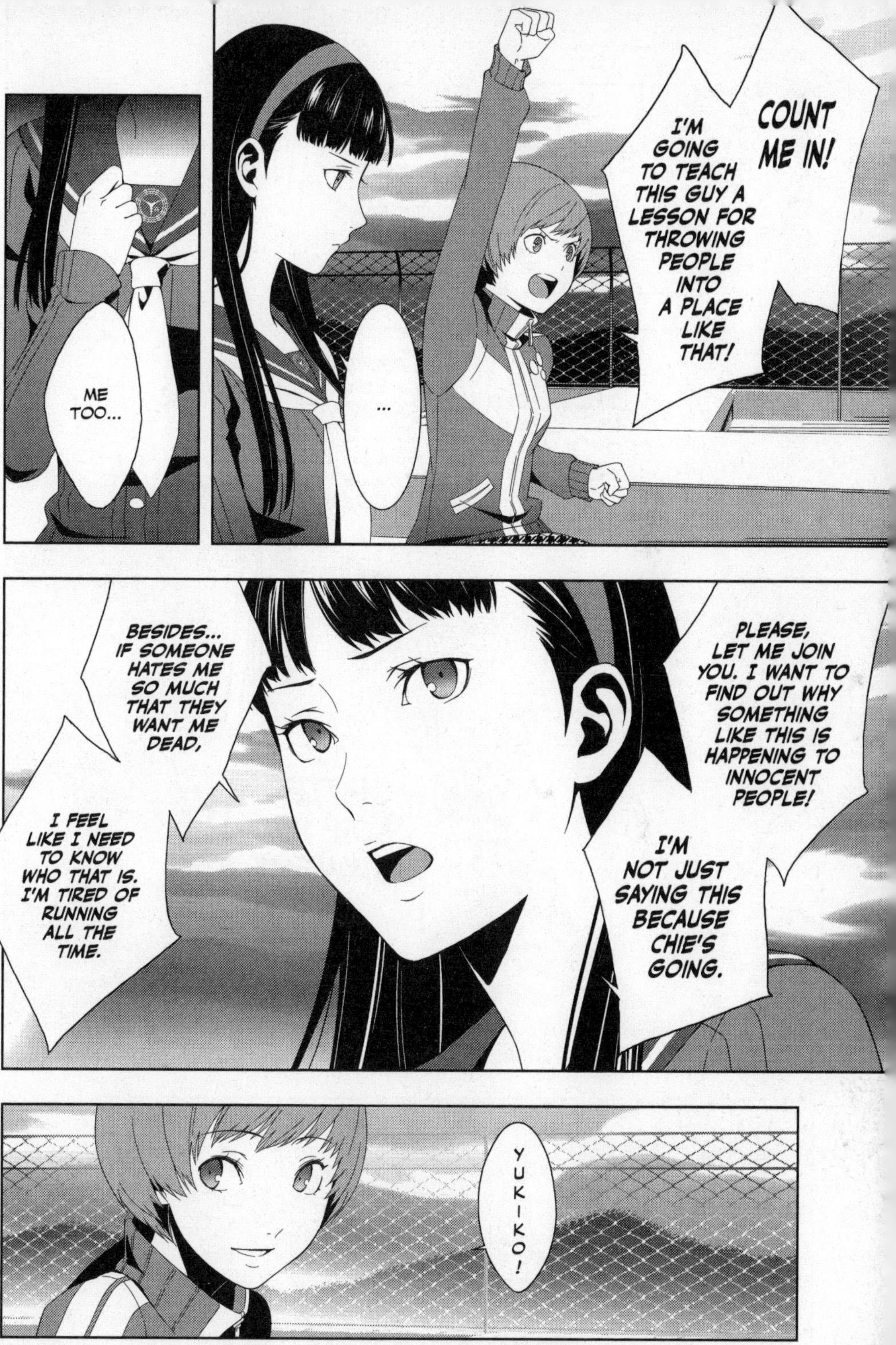
COUNT ME IN! I'M GOING TO TEACH THIS GUY A LESSON FOR THROWING PEOPLE INTO A PLACE LIKE THAT!
...
ME TOO...
PLEASE, LET ME JOIN YOU. I WANT TO FIND OUT WHY SOMETHING LIKE THIS IS HAPPENING TO INNOCENT PEOPLE!
I'M NOT JUST SAYING THIS BECAUSE CHIE'S GOING.
BESIDES... IF SOMEONE HATES ME SO MUCH THAT THEY WANT ME DEAD,
I FEEL LIKE I NEED TO KNOW WHO THAT IS. I'M TIRED OF RUNNING ALL THE TIME.
YUKIKO!

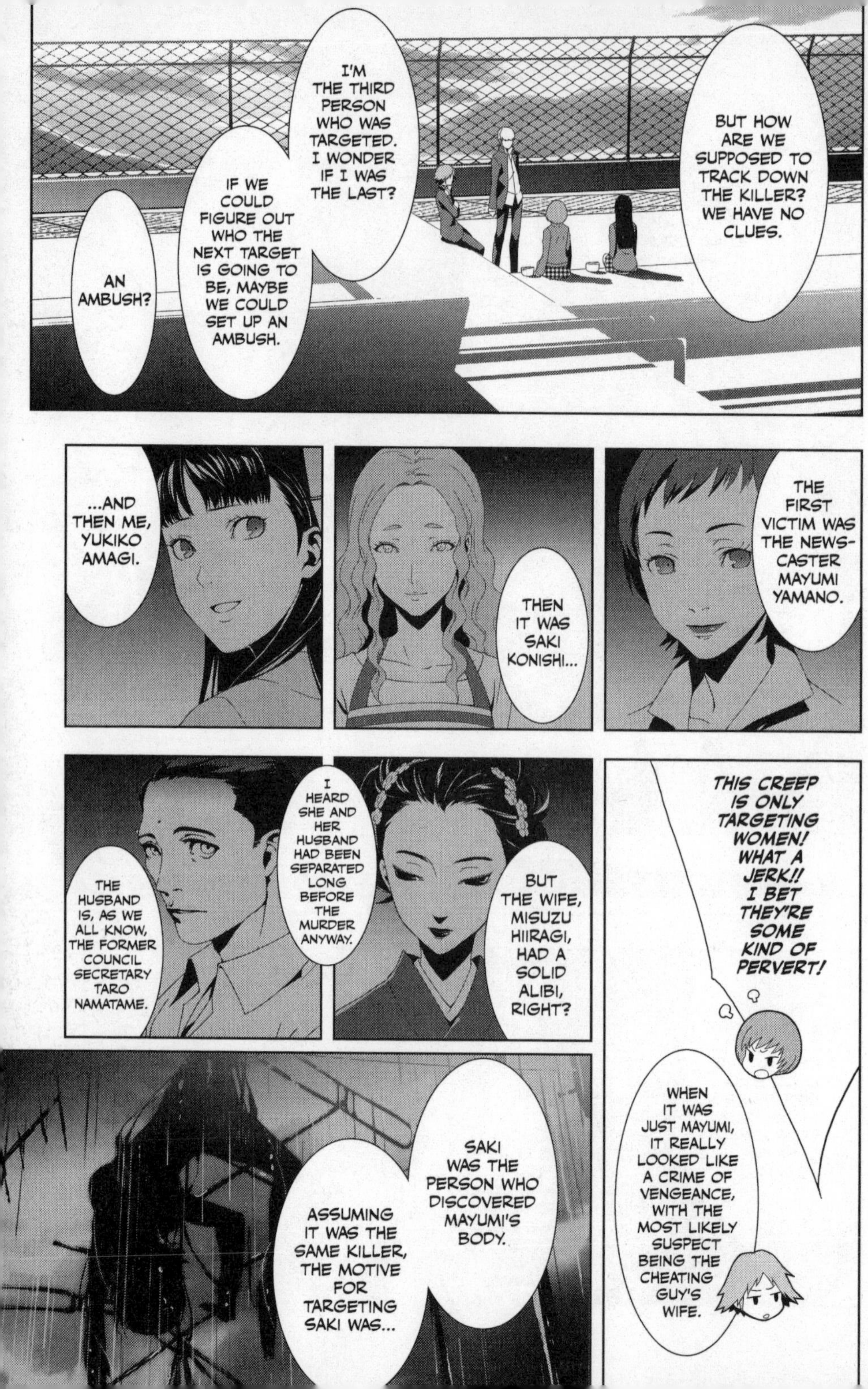

BUT HOW ARE WE SUPPOSED TO TRACK DOWN THE KILLER? WE HAVE NO CLUES.
I'M THE THIRD PERSON WHO WAS TARGETED. I WONDER IF I WAS THE LAST?
IF WE COULD FIGURE OUT WHO THE NEXT TARGET IS GOING TO BE, MAYBE WE COULD SET UP AN AMBUSH.
AN AMBUSH?
THE FIRST VICTIM WAS THE NEWS-CASTER MAYUMI YAMANO.
THEN IT WAS SAKI KONISHI...
...AND THEN ME, YUKIKO AMAGI.
THIS CREEP IS ONLY TARGETING WOMEN! WHAT A JERK!! I BET THEY'RE SOME KIND OF PERVERT!
WHEN IT WAS JUST MAYUMI, IT REALLY LOOKED LIKE A CRIME OF VENGEANCE, WITH THE MOST LIKELY SUSPECT BEING THE CHEATING GUY'S WIFE.
BUT THE WIFE, MISUZU HIIRAGI, HAD A SOLID ALIBI, RIGHT?
I HEARD SHE AND HER HUSBAND HAD BEEN SEPARATED LONG BEFORE THE MURDER ANYWAY.
THE HUSBAND IS, AS WE ALL KNOW, THE FORMER COUNCIL SECRETARY TARO NAMATAME.
SAKI WAS THE PERSON WHO DISCOVERED MAYUMI'S BODY.
ASSUMING IT WAS THE SAME KILLER, THE MOTIVE FOR TARGETING SAKI WAS...

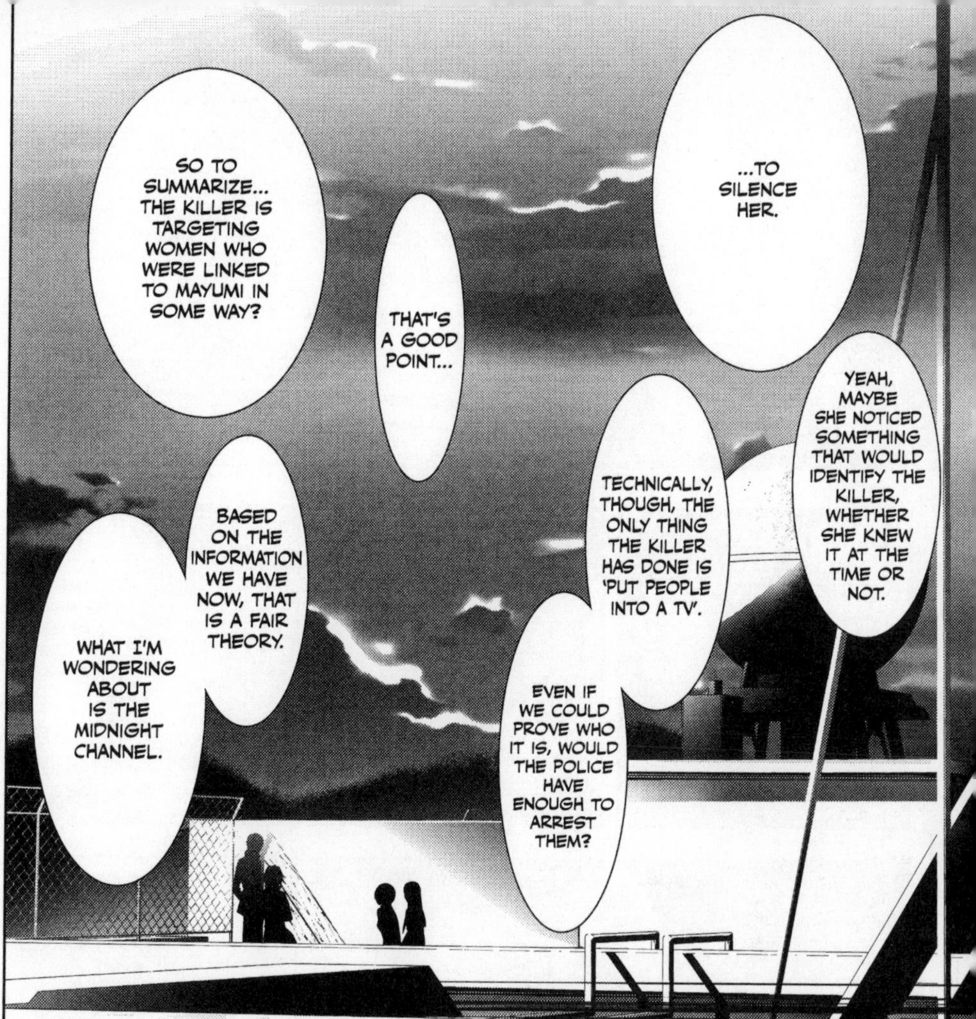
...TO SILENCE HER.
YEAH, MAYBE SHE NOTICED SOMETHING THAT WOULD IDENTIFY THE KILLER, WHETHER SHE KNEW IT AT THE TIME OR NOT.
TECHNICALLY, THOUGH, THE ONLY THING THE KILLER HAS DONE IS 'PUT PEOPLE INTO A TV'.
EVEN IF WE COULD PROVE WHO IT IS, WOULD THE POLICE HAVE ENOUGH TO ARREST THEM?
THAT'S A GOOD POINT...
SO TO SUMMARIZE... THE KILLER IS TARGETING WOMEN WHO WERE LINKED TO MAYUMI IN SOME WAY?
BASED ON THE INFORMATION WE HAVE NOW, THAT IS A FAIR THEORY.
WHAT I'M WONDERING ABOUT IS THE MIDNIGHT CHANNEL.
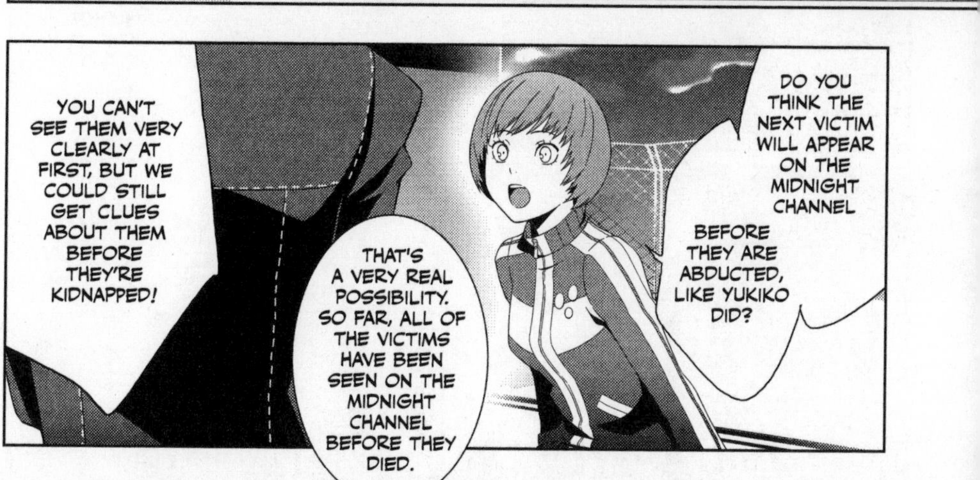
DO YOU THINK THE NEXT VICTIM WILL APPEAR ON THE MIDNIGHT CHANNEL
BEFORE THEY ARE ABDUCTED, LIKE YUKIKO DID?
THAT'S A VERY REAL POSSIBILITY. SO FAR, ALL OF THE VICTIMS HAVE BEEN SEEN ON THE MIDNIGHT CHANNEL BEFORE THEY DIED.
YOU CAN'T SEE THEM VERY CLEARLY AT FIRST, BUT WE COULD STILL GET CLUES ABOUT THEM BEFORE THEY'RE KIDNAPPED!

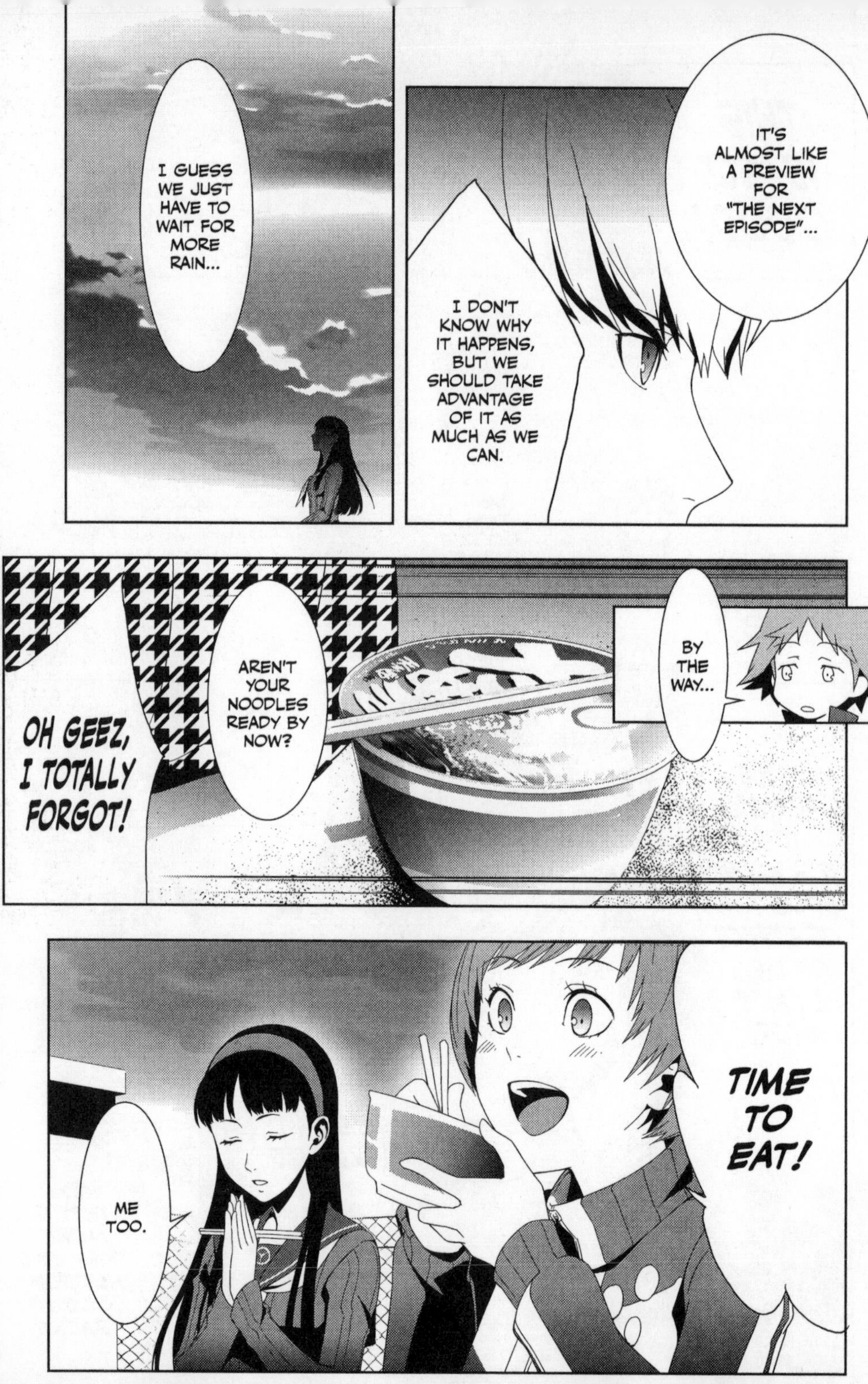
IT'S ALMOST LIKE A PREVIEW FOR "THE NEXT EPISODE"...
I DON'T KNOW WHY IT HAPPENS, BUT WE SHOULD TAKE ADVANTAGE OF IT AS MUCH AS WE CAN.
I GUESS WE JUST HAVE TO WAIT FOR MORE RAIN...
BY THE WAY...
AREN'T YOUR NOODLES READY BY NOW?
OH GEEZ, I TOTALLY FORGOT!
TIME TO EAT!
ME TOO.

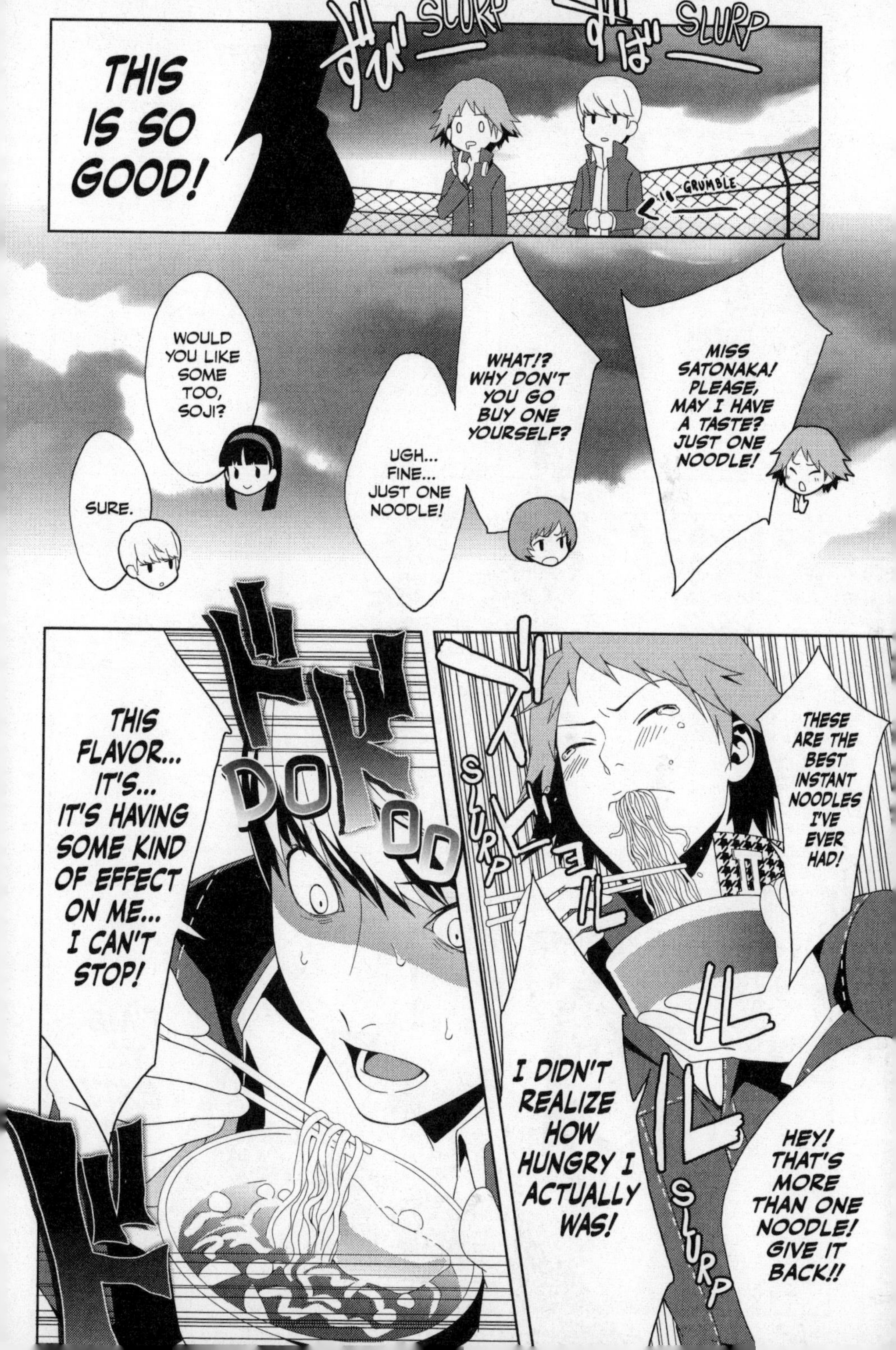
SLURP
SLURP
THIS IS SO GOOD!
GRUMBLE
MISS SATONAKA! PLEASE, MAY I HAVE A TASTE? JUST ONE NOODLE!
WHAT!? WHY DON'T YOU GO BUY ONE YOURSELF?
UGH... FINE... JUST ONE NOODLE!
WOULD YOU LIKE SOME TOO, SOJI?
SURE.
THESE ARE THE BEST INSTANT NOODLES I'VE EVER HAD!
SLURP
I DIDN'T REALIZE HOW HUNGRY I ACTUALLY WAS!
HEY! THAT'S MORE THAN ONE NOODLE! GIVE IT BACK!!
SLURP
DOOOD
THIS FLAVOR... IT'S... IT'S HAVING SOME KIND OF EFFECT ON ME... I CAN'T STOP!

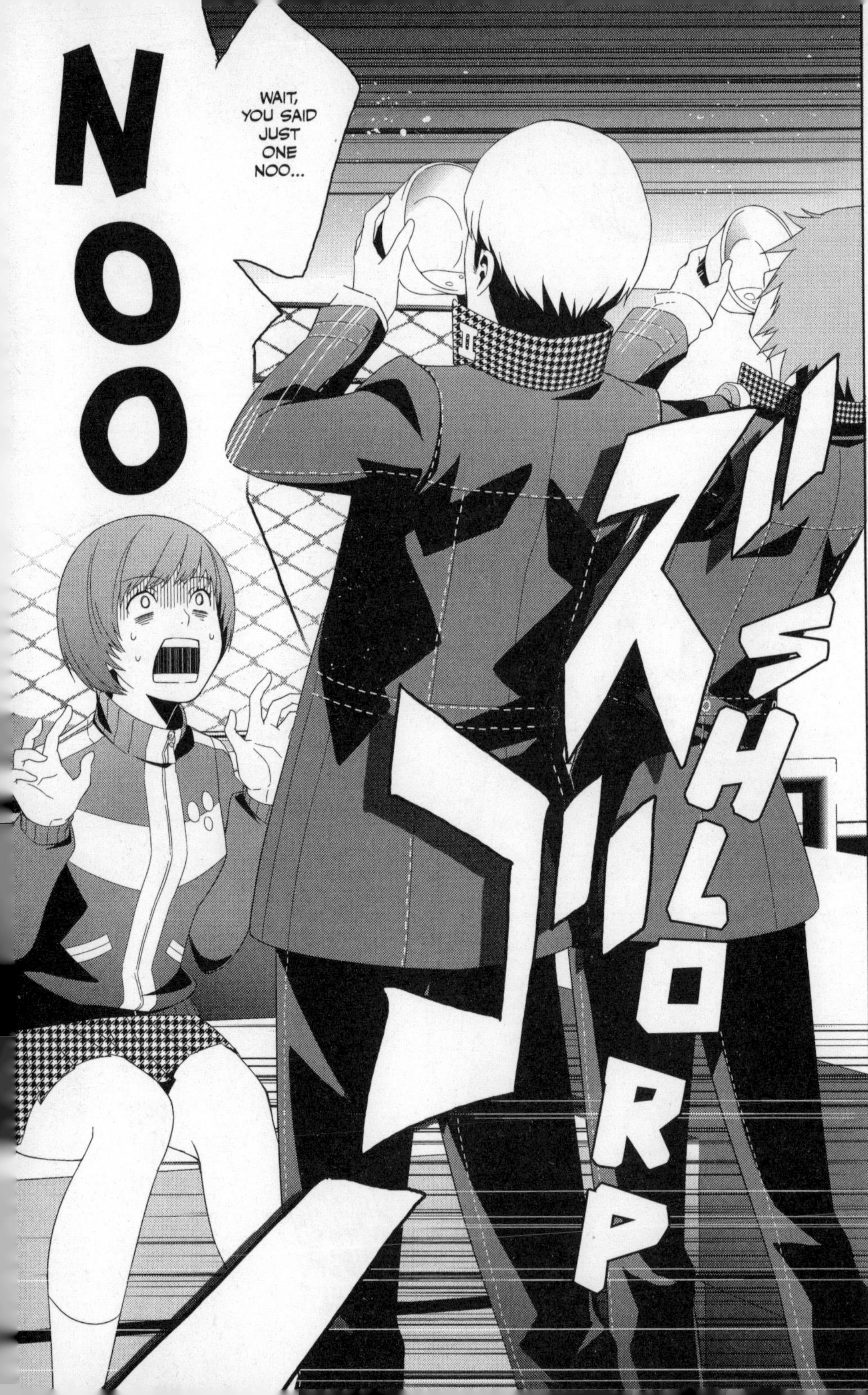
NOO
WAIT, YOU SAID JUST ONE NOO...
SHLORP

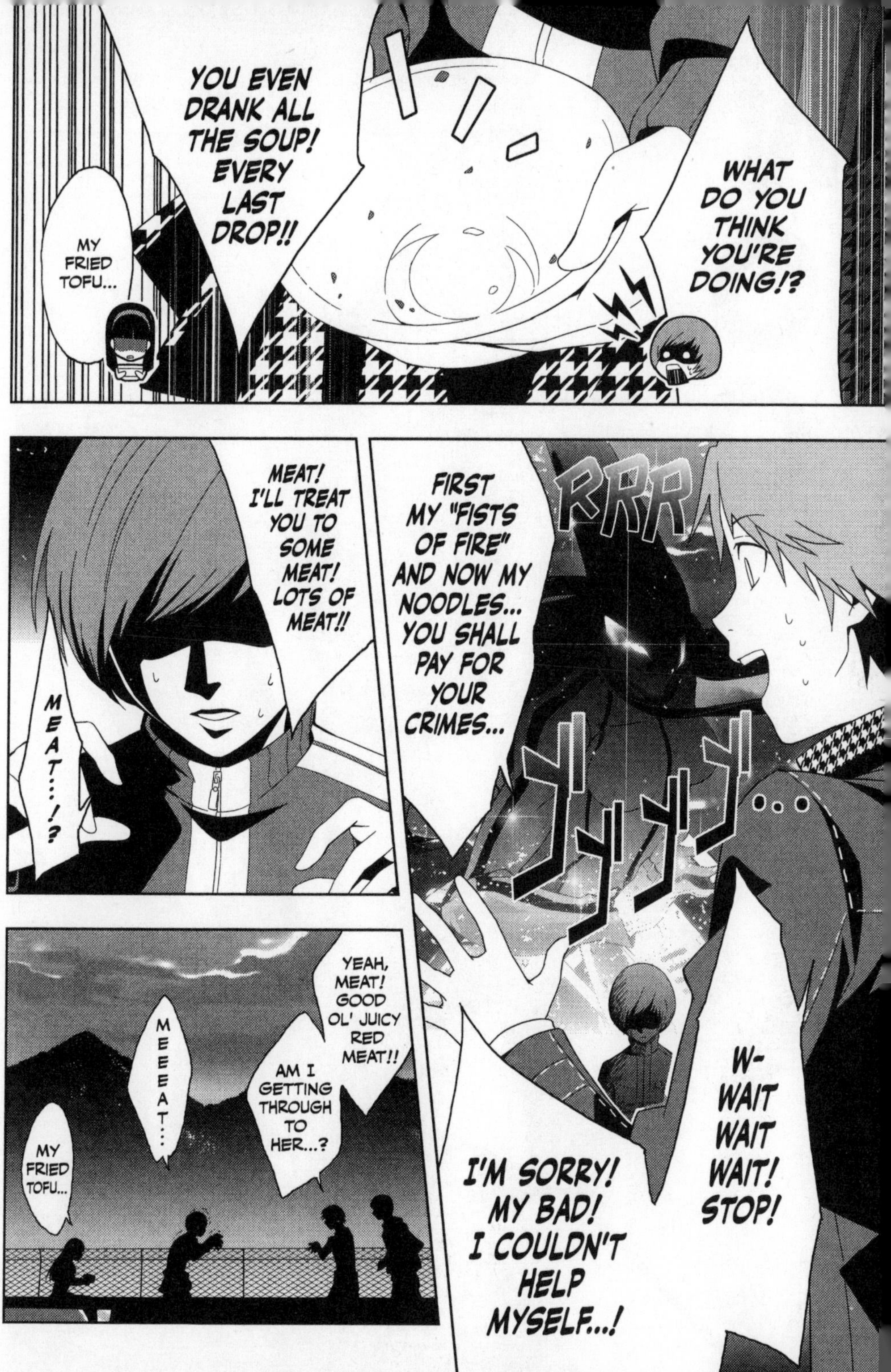
WHAT DO YOU THINK YOU'RE DOING!?
YOU EVEN DRANK ALL THE SOUP! EVERY LAST DROP!!
MY FRIED TOFU...
RRR
FIRST MY "FISTS OF FIRE" AND NOW MY NOODLES... YOU SHALL PAY FOR YOUR CRIMES...
W- WAIT WAIT WAIT! STOP!
I'M SORRY! MY BAD! I COULDN'T HELP MYSELF...!
MEAT! I'LL TREAT YOU TO SOME MEAT! LOTS OF MEAT!!
MEAT...!?
YEAH, MEAT! GOOD OL' JUICY RED MEAT!!
MEEEAT...
AM I GETTING THROUGH TO HER...?
MY FRIED TOFU...

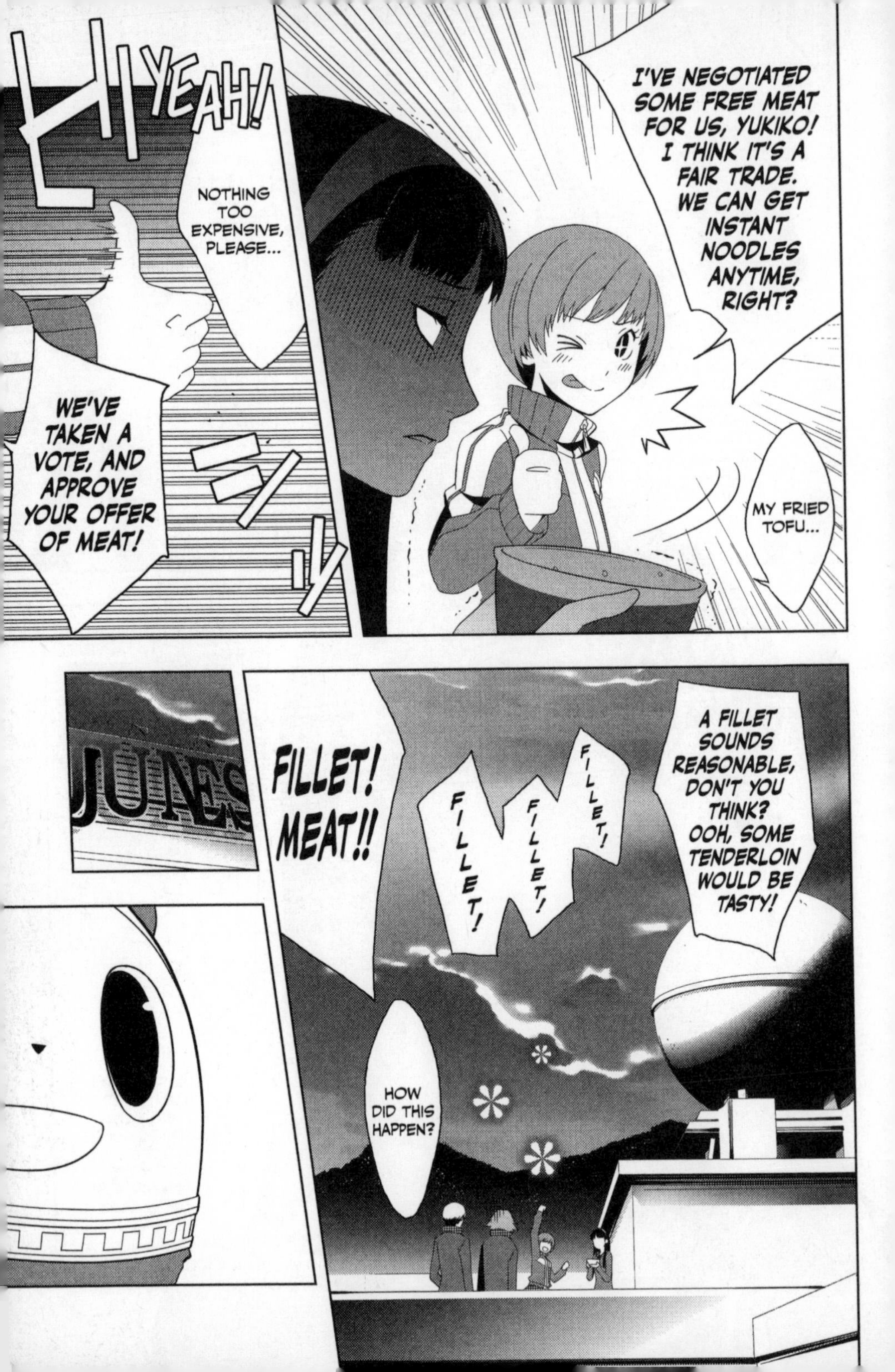

I'VE NEGOTIATED SOME FREE MEAT FOR US, YUKIKO! I THINK IT'S A FAIR TRADE. WE CAN GET INSTANT NOODLES ANYTIME, RIGHT?
MY FRIED TOFU...
HIYEAH!
NOTHING TOO EXPENSIVE, PLEASE...
WE'VE TAKEN A VOTE, AND APPROVE YOUR OFFER OF MEAT!
A FILLET SOUNDS REASONABLE, DON'T YOU THINK? OOH, SOME TENDERLOIN WOULD BE TASTY!
FILLET! FILLET! FILLET!
FILLET! MEAT!!
HOW DID THIS HAPPEN?
JUNES

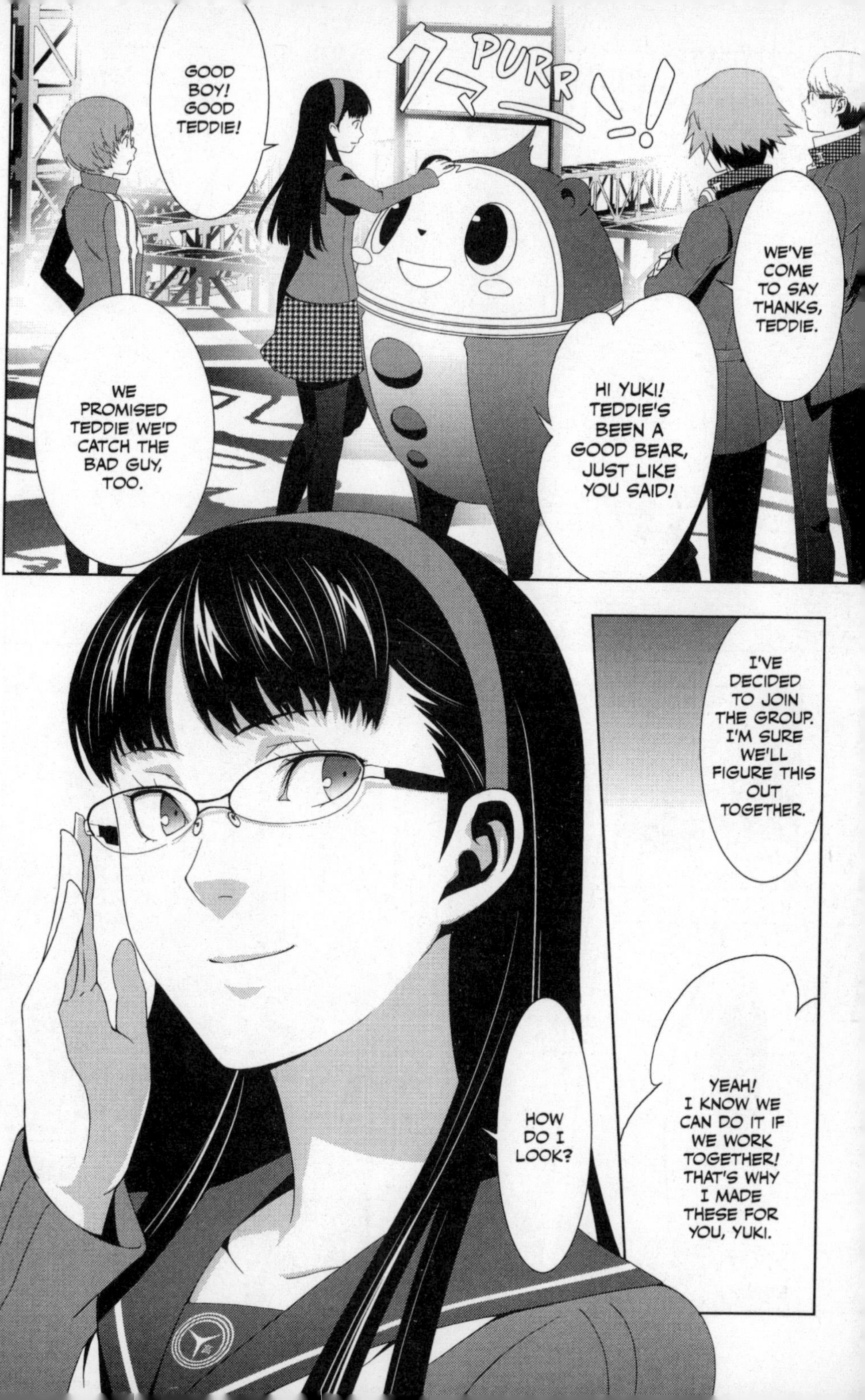
WE'VE COME TO SAY THANKS, TEDDIE.
クマー!
PURR
HI YUKI! TEDDIE'S BEEN A GOOD BEAR, JUST LIKE YOU SAID!
GOOD BOY! GOOD TEDDIE!
WE PROMISED TEDDIE WE'D CATCH THE BAD GUY, TOO.
I'VE DECIDED TO JOIN THE GROUP. I'M SURE WE'LL FIGURE THIS OUT TOGETHER.
YEAH! I KNOW WE CAN DO IT IF WE WORK TOGETHER! THAT'S WHY I MADE THESE FOR YOU, YUKI.
HOW DO I LOOK?

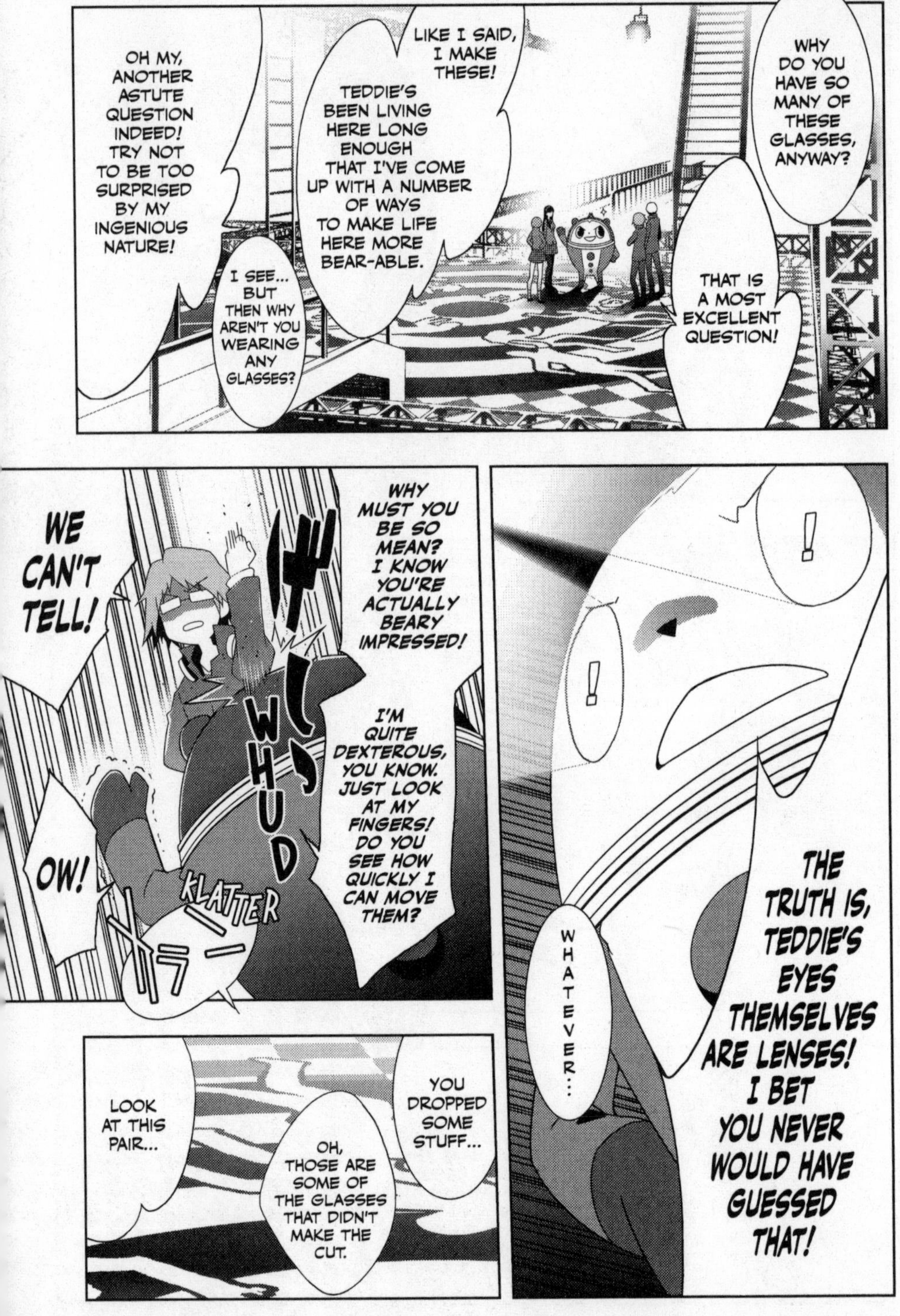
WHY DO YOU HAVE SO MANY OF THESE GLASSES, ANYWAY?
THAT IS A MOST EXCELLENT QUESTION!
LIKE I SAID, I MAKE THESE!
TEDDIE'S BEEN LIVING HERE LONG ENOUGH THAT I'VE COME UP WITH A NUMBER OF WAYS TO MAKE LIFE HERE MORE BEAR-ABLE.
I SEE... BUT THEN WHY AREN'T YOU WEARING ANY GLASSES?
OH MY, ANOTHER ASTUTE QUESTION INDEED! TRY NOT TO BE TOO SURPRISED BY MY INGENIOUS NATURE!
!
!
THE TRUTH IS, TEDDIE'S EYES THEMSELVES ARE LENSES! I BET YOU NEVER WOULD HAVE GUESSED THAT!
WHATEVER...
WHY MUST YOU BE SO MEAN? I KNOW YOU'RE ACTUALLY BEARY IMPRESSED!
I'M QUITE DEXTEROUS, YOU KNOW. JUST LOOK AT MY FINGERS! DO YOU SEE HOW QUICKLY I CAN MOVE THEM?
WHUD
WE CAN'T TELL!
OW!
KLATTER
YOU DROPPED SOME STUFF...
OH, THOSE ARE SOME OF THE GLASSES THAT DIDN'T MAKE THE CUT.
LOOK AT THIS PAIR...

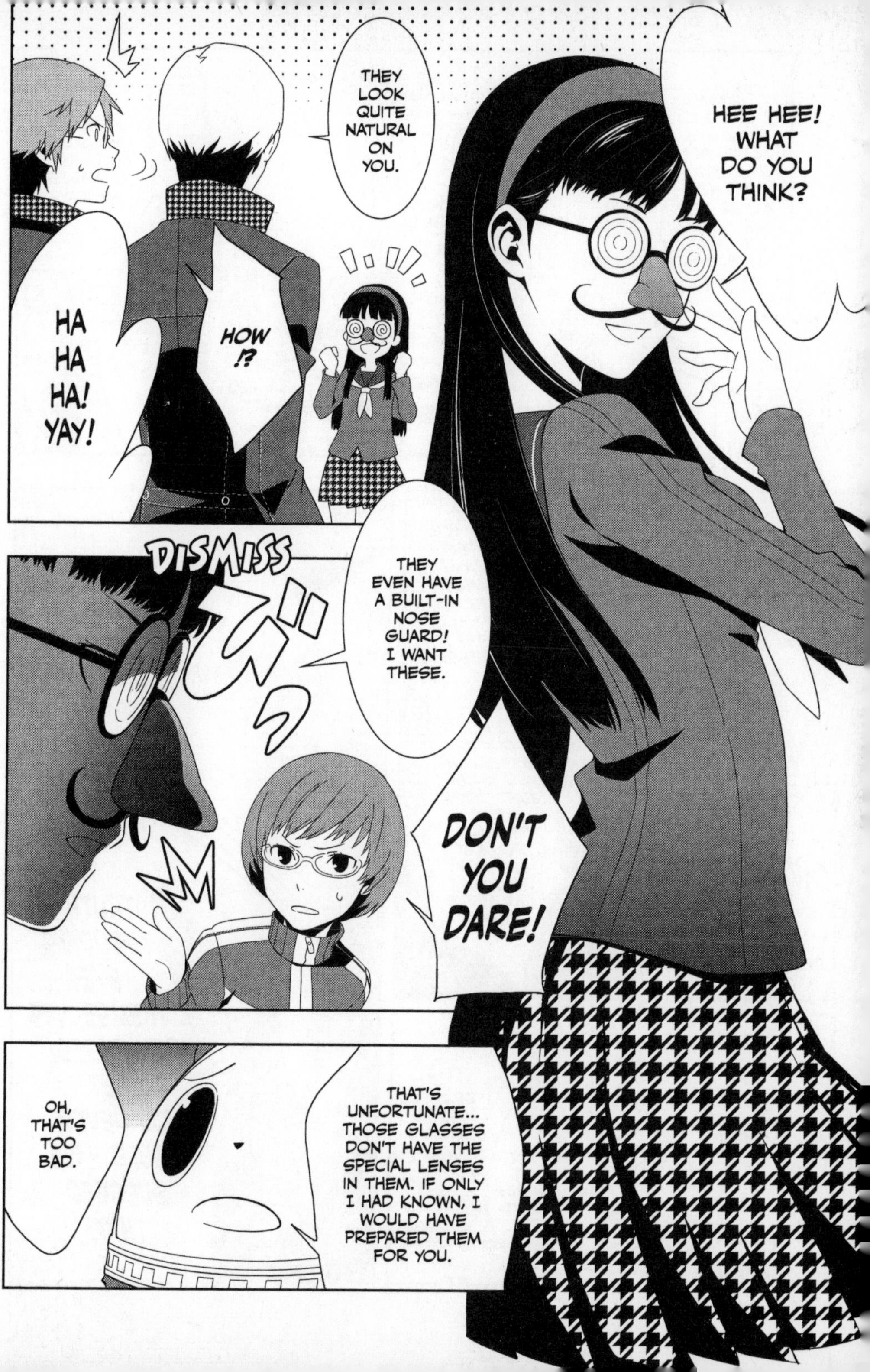
HEE HEE! WHAT DO YOU THINK?
THEY LOOK QUITE NATURAL ON YOU.
HOW !?
HA HA HA! YAY!
DISMISS
THEY EVEN HAVE A BUILT-IN NOSE GUARD! I WANT THESE.
DON'T YOU DARE!
THAT'S UNFORTUNATE... THOSE GLASSES DON'T HAVE THE SPECIAL LENSES IN THEM. IF ONLY I HAD KNOWN, I WOULD HAVE PREPARED THEM FOR YOU.
OH, THAT'S TOO BAD.

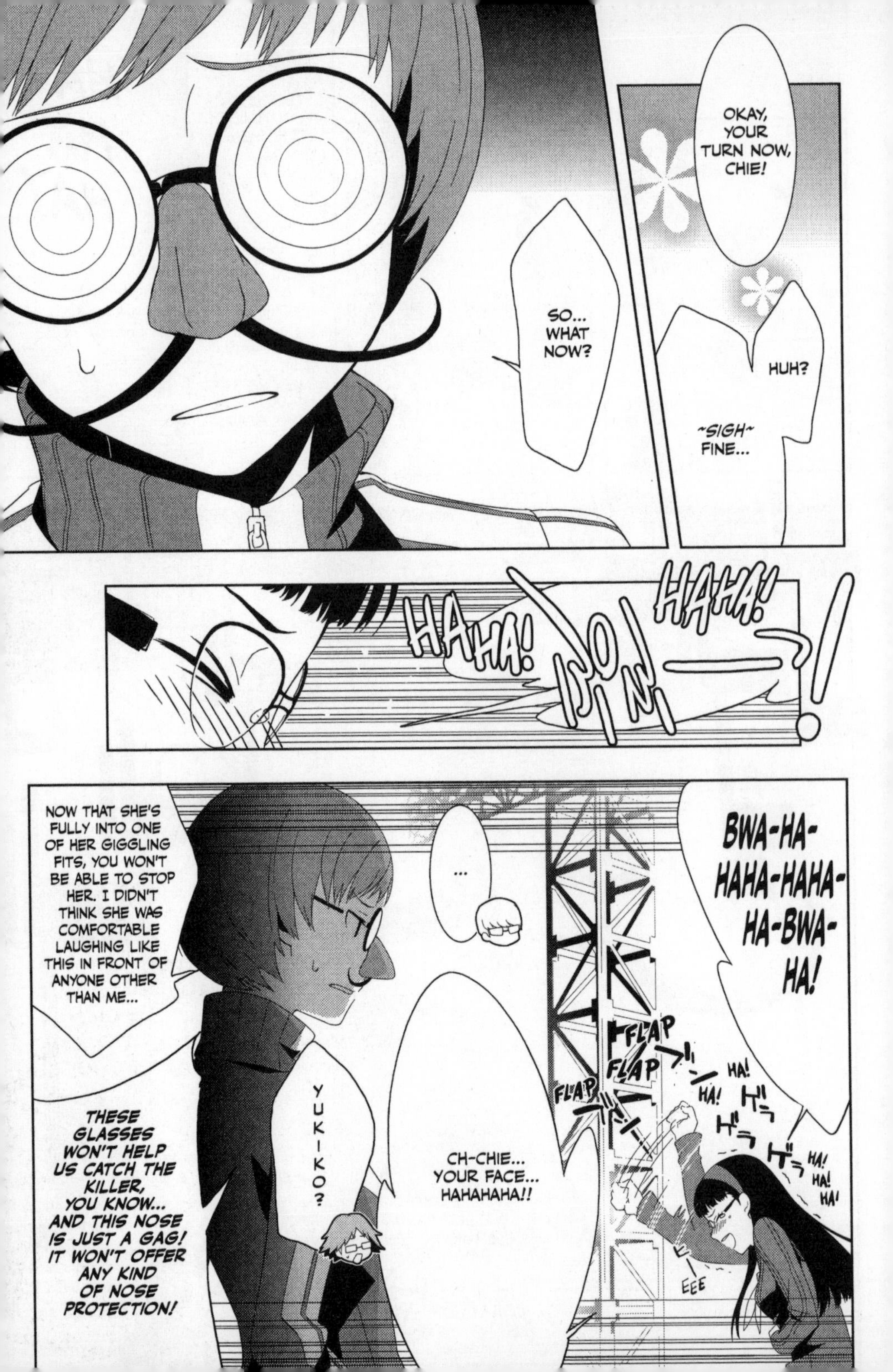
OKAY, YOUR TURN NOW, CHIE!
HUH?
~SIGH~ FINE...
SO... WHAT NOW?
HAHA!
DON—!
HAHA!
BWA-HA-HAHA-HAHAHA-HA-BWA-HA!
...
CH-CHIE... YOUR FACE... HAHAHAHA!!
FLAP
FLAP
FLAP
HA! HA!
HA! HA! HA!
EEE
YUKIKO?
NOW THAT SHE'S FULLY INTO ONE OF HER GIGGLING FITS, YOU WON'T BE ABLE TO STOP HER. I DIDN'T THINK SHE WAS COMFORTABLE LAUGHING LIKE THIS IN FRONT OF ANYONE OTHER THAN ME...
THESE GLASSES WON'T HELP US CATCH THE KILLER, YOU KNOW... AND THIS NOSE IS JUST A GAG! IT WON'T OFFER ANY KIND OF NOSE PROTECTION!

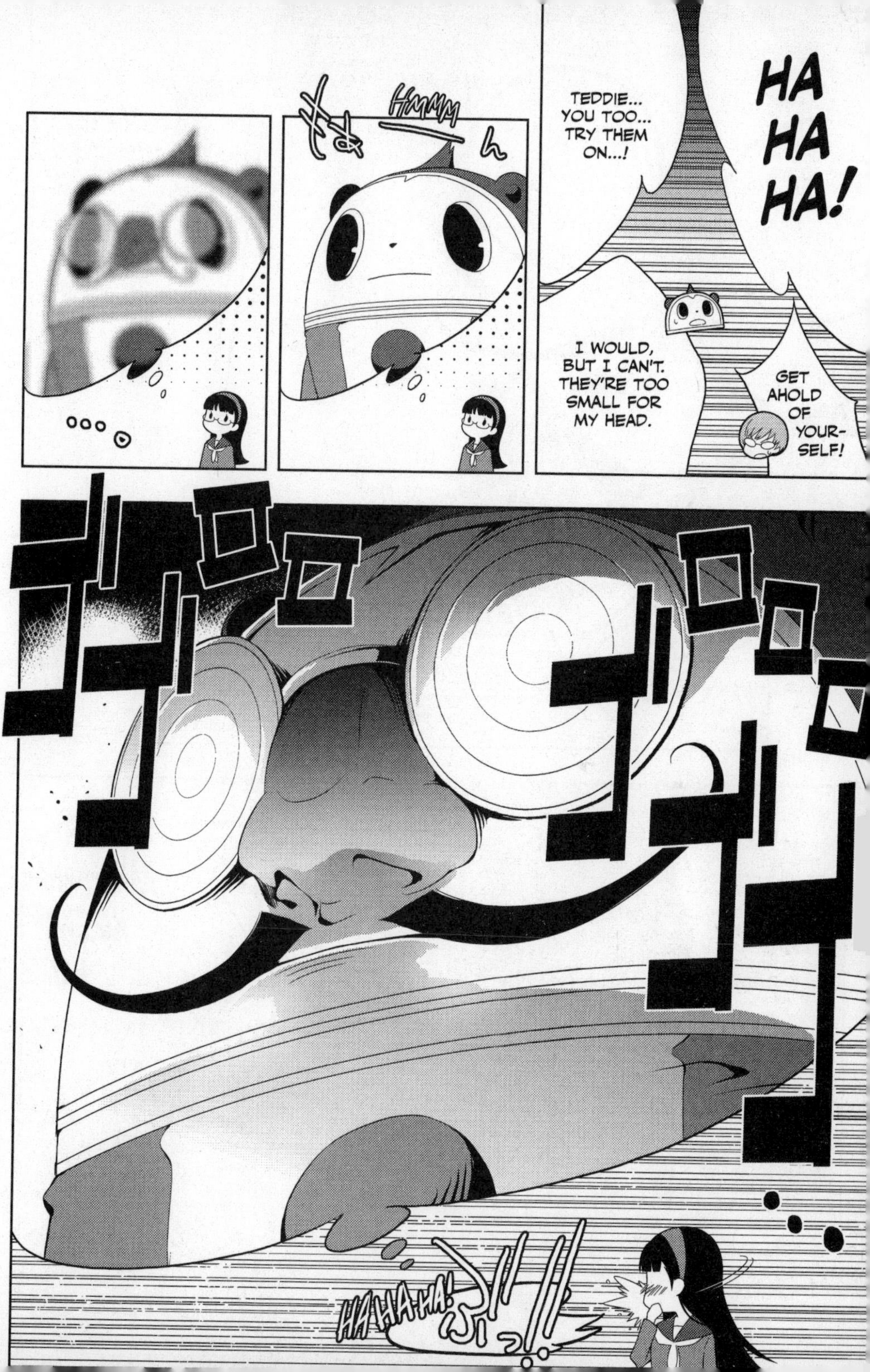
HA HA HA!
GET AHOLD OF YOURSELF!
TEDDIE... YOU TOO... TRY THEM ON...!
I WOULD, BUT I CAN'T. THEY'RE TOO SMALL FOR MY HEAD.
HMMM
HA HA HA!

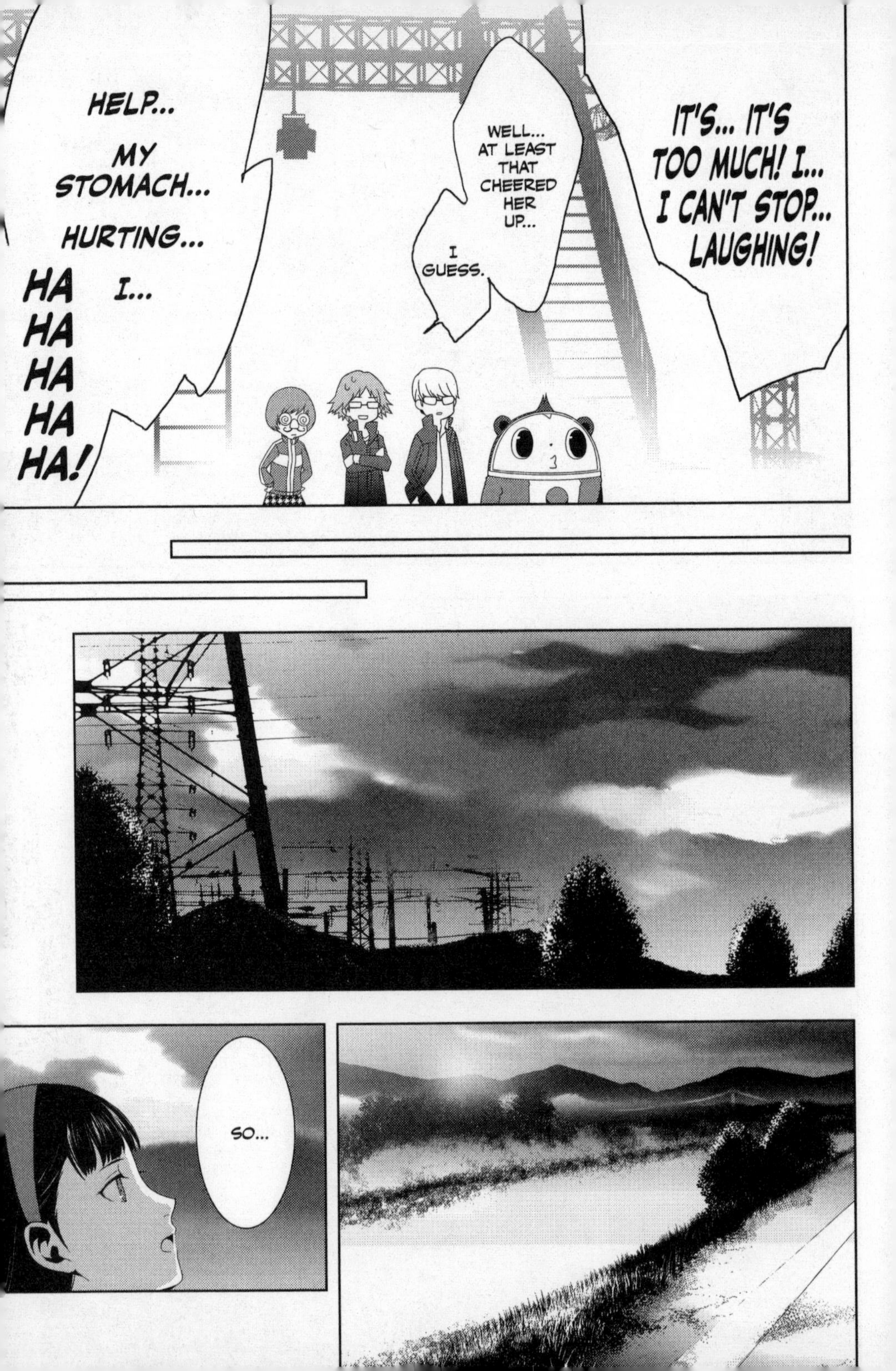
IT'S... IT'S TOO MUCH! I... I CAN'T STOP... LAUGHING!
WELL... AT LEAST THAT CHEERED HER UP...
I GUESS.
HELP... MY STOMACH... HURTING... I...
HA HA HA HA HA HA!
SO...

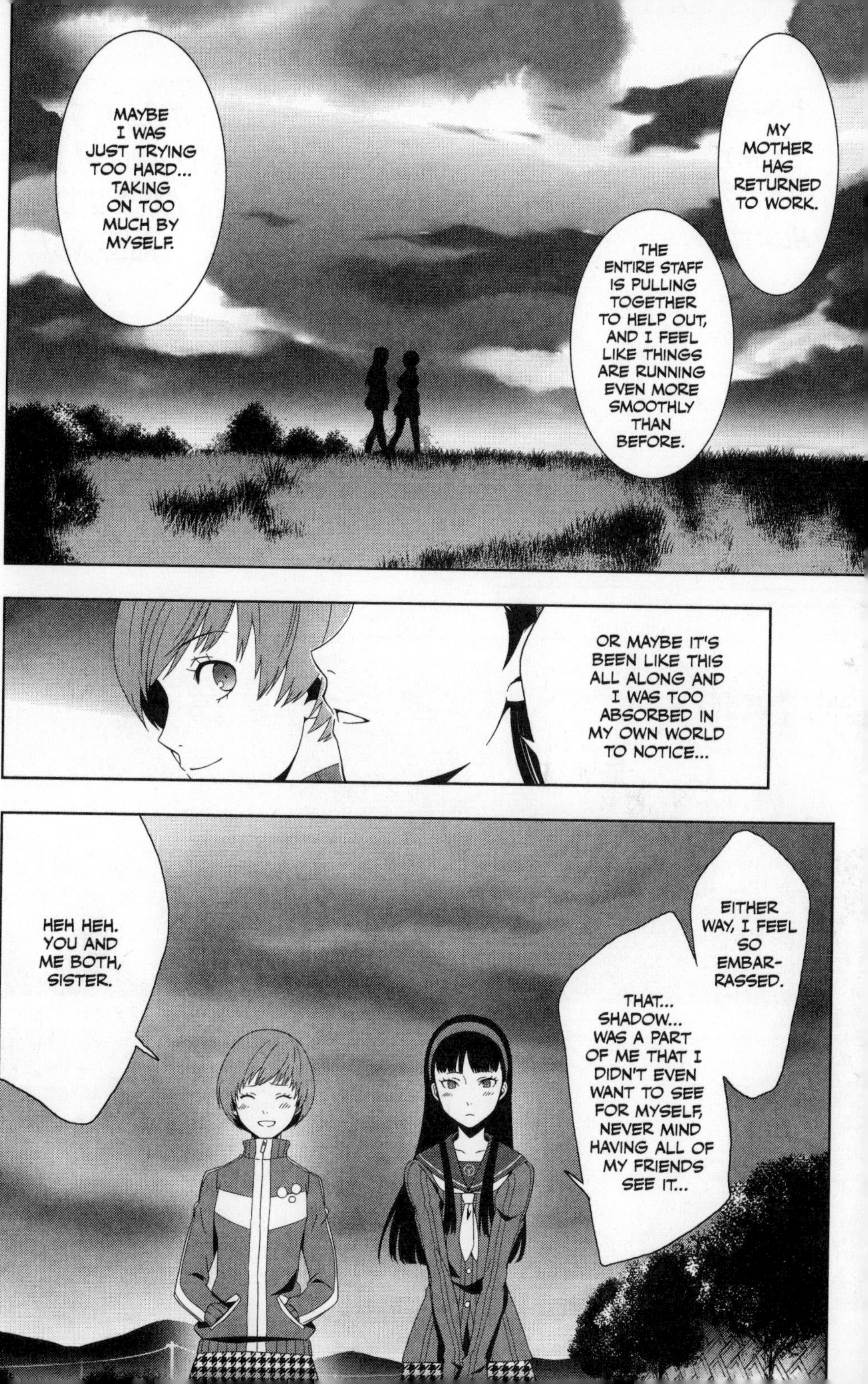
MY MOTHER HAS RETURNED TO WORK.
THE ENTIRE STAFF IS PULLING TOGETHER TO HELP OUT, AND I FEEL LIKE THINGS ARE RUNNING EVEN MORE SMOOTHLY THAN BEFORE.
MAYBE I WAS JUST TRYING TOO HARD... TAKING ON TOO MUCH BY MYSELF.
OR MAYBE IT'S BEEN LIKE THIS ALL ALONG AND I WAS TOO ABSORBED IN MY OWN WORLD TO NOTICE...
EITHER WAY, I FEEL SO EMBAR-RASSED.
THAT... SHADOW... WAS A PART OF ME THAT I DIDN'T EVEN WANT TO SEE FOR MYSELF, NEVER MIND HAVING ALL OF MY FRIENDS SEE IT...
HEH HEH. YOU AND ME BOTH, SISTER.

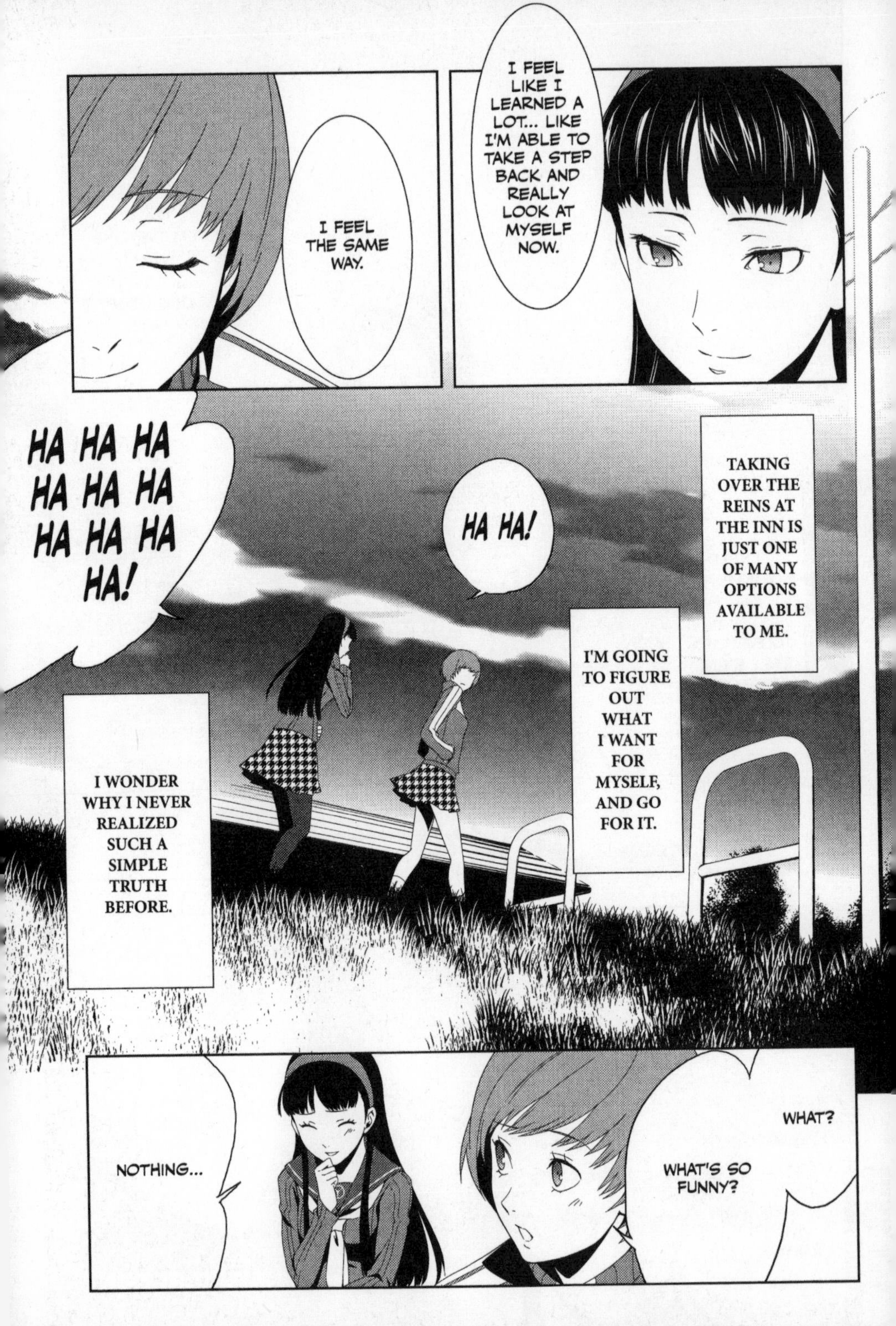
I FEEL LIKE I LEARNED A LOT... LIKE I'M ABLE TO TAKE A STEP BACK AND REALLY LOOK AT MYSELF NOW.
I FEEL THE SAME WAY.
TAKING OVER THE REINS AT THE INN IS JUST ONE OF MANY OPTIONS AVAILABLE TO ME.
I'M GOING TO FIGURE OUT WHAT I WANT FOR MYSELF, AND GO FOR IT.
HA HA!
HA HA HA HA HA HA HA HA HA HA!
I WONDER WHY I NEVER REALIZED SUCH A SIMPLE TRUTH BEFORE.
WHAT?
WHAT'S SO FUNNY?
NOTHING...

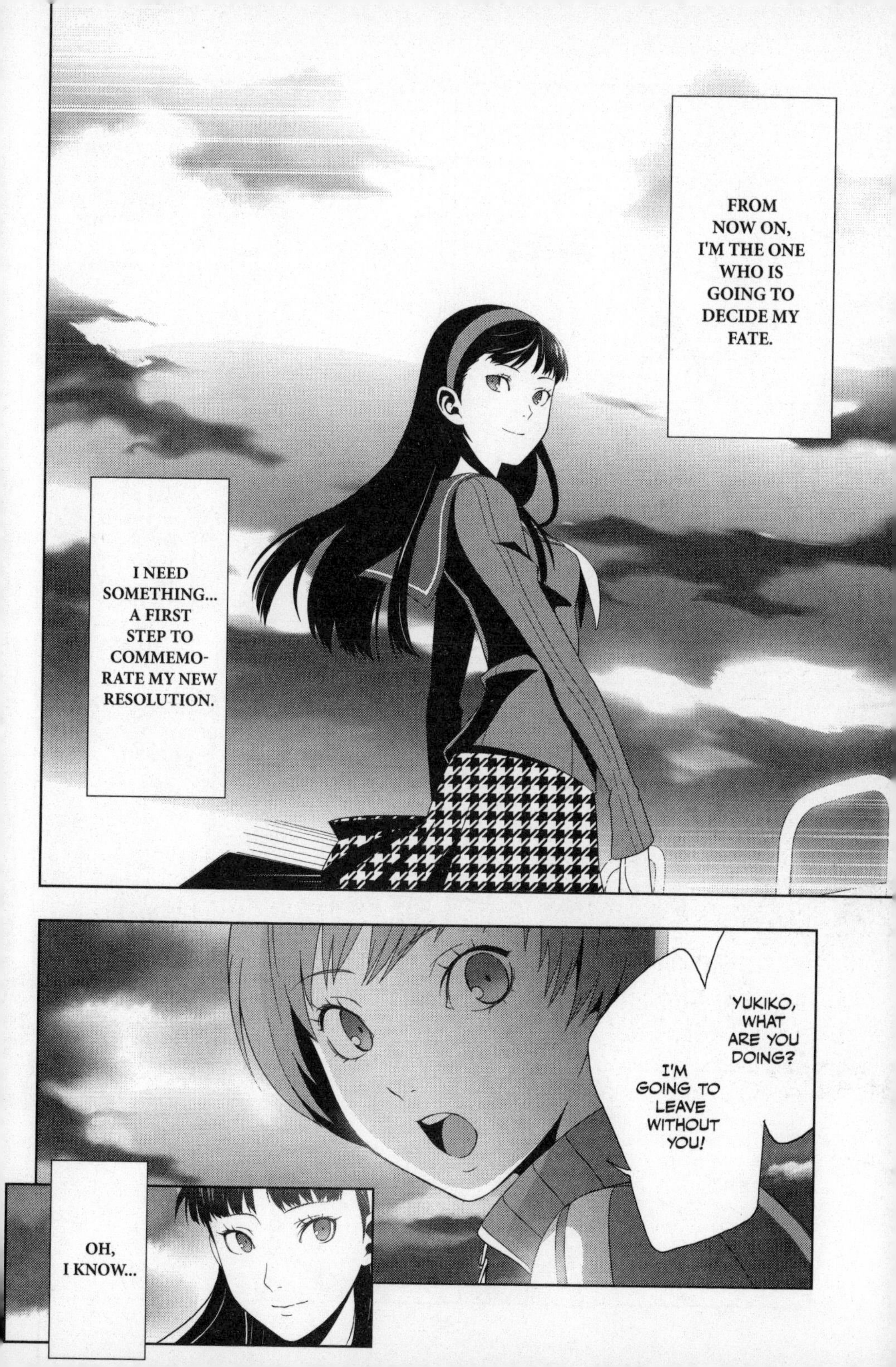
FROM NOW ON, I'M THE ONE WHO IS GOING TO DECIDE MY FATE.
I NEED SOMETHING... A FIRST STEP TO COMMEMO-RATE MY NEW RESOLUTION.
YUKIKO, WHAT ARE YOU DOING?
I'M GOING TO LEAVE WITHOUT YOU!
OH, I KNOW...

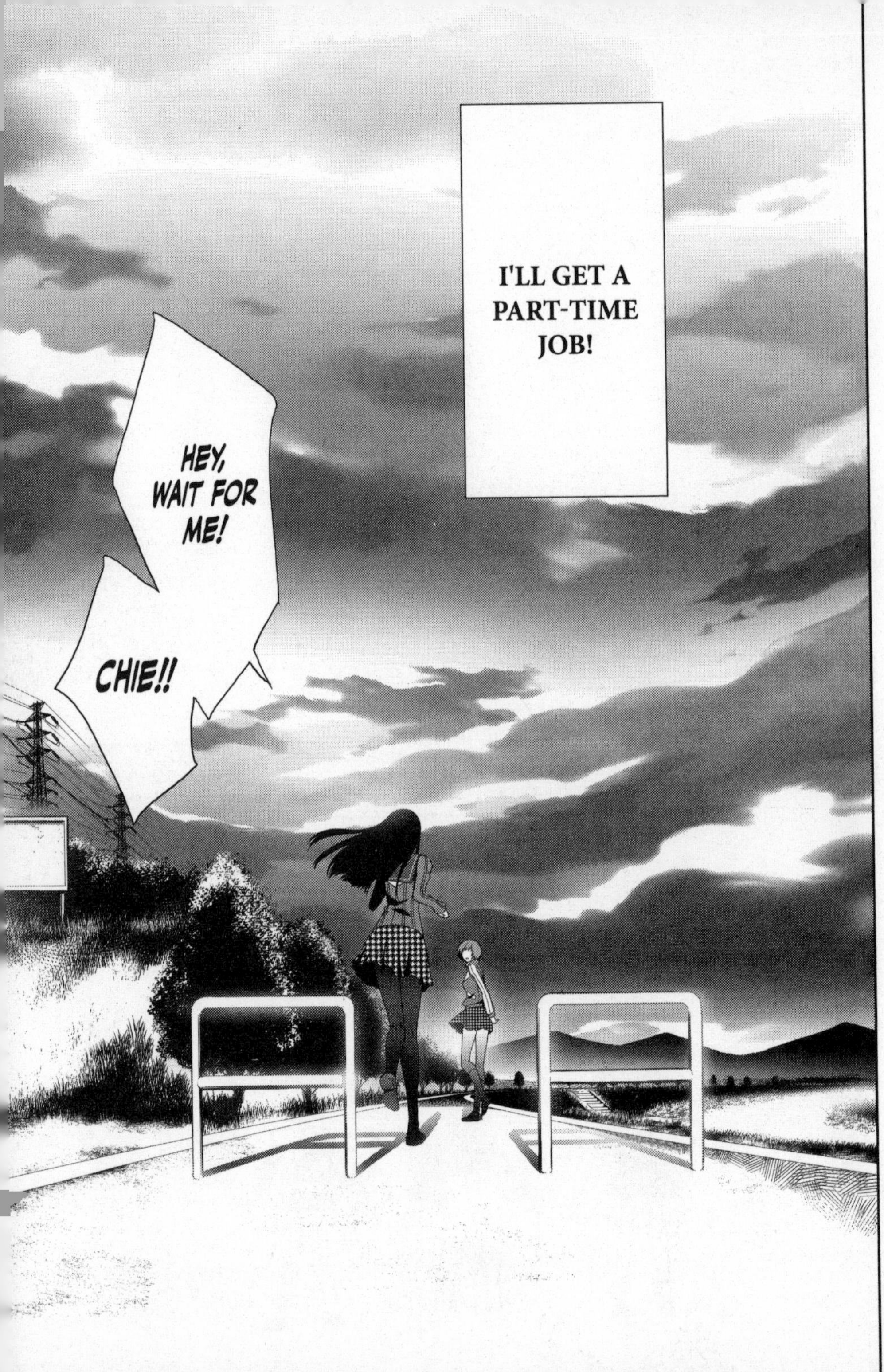
I'LL GET A PART-TIME JOB!
HEY, WAIT FOR ME!
CHIE!!

Design sketch

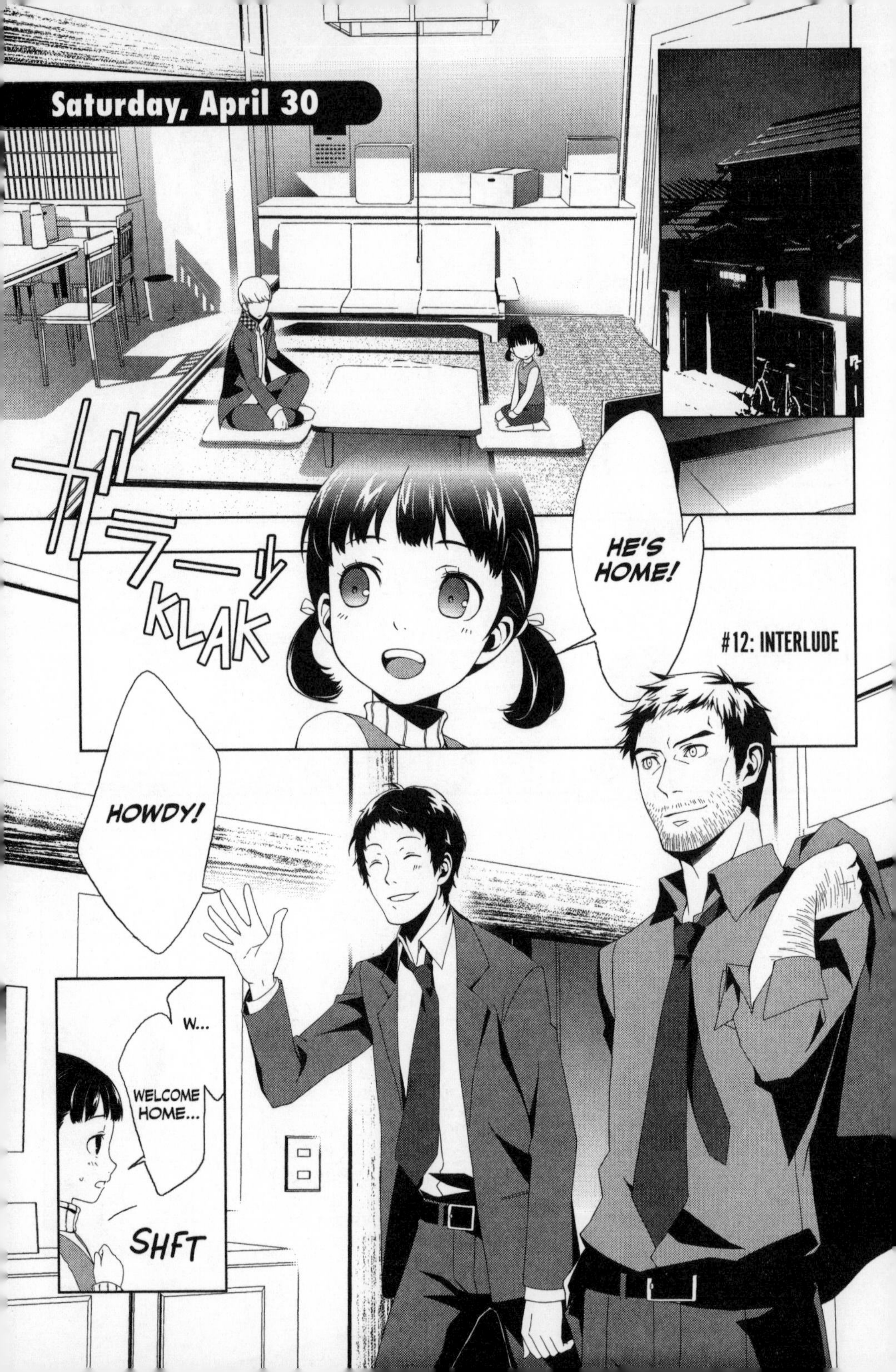
Saturday, April 30
ガラーッ
KLAK
HE'S HOME!
#12: INTERLUDE
HOWDY!
W...
WELCOME HOME...
SHFT

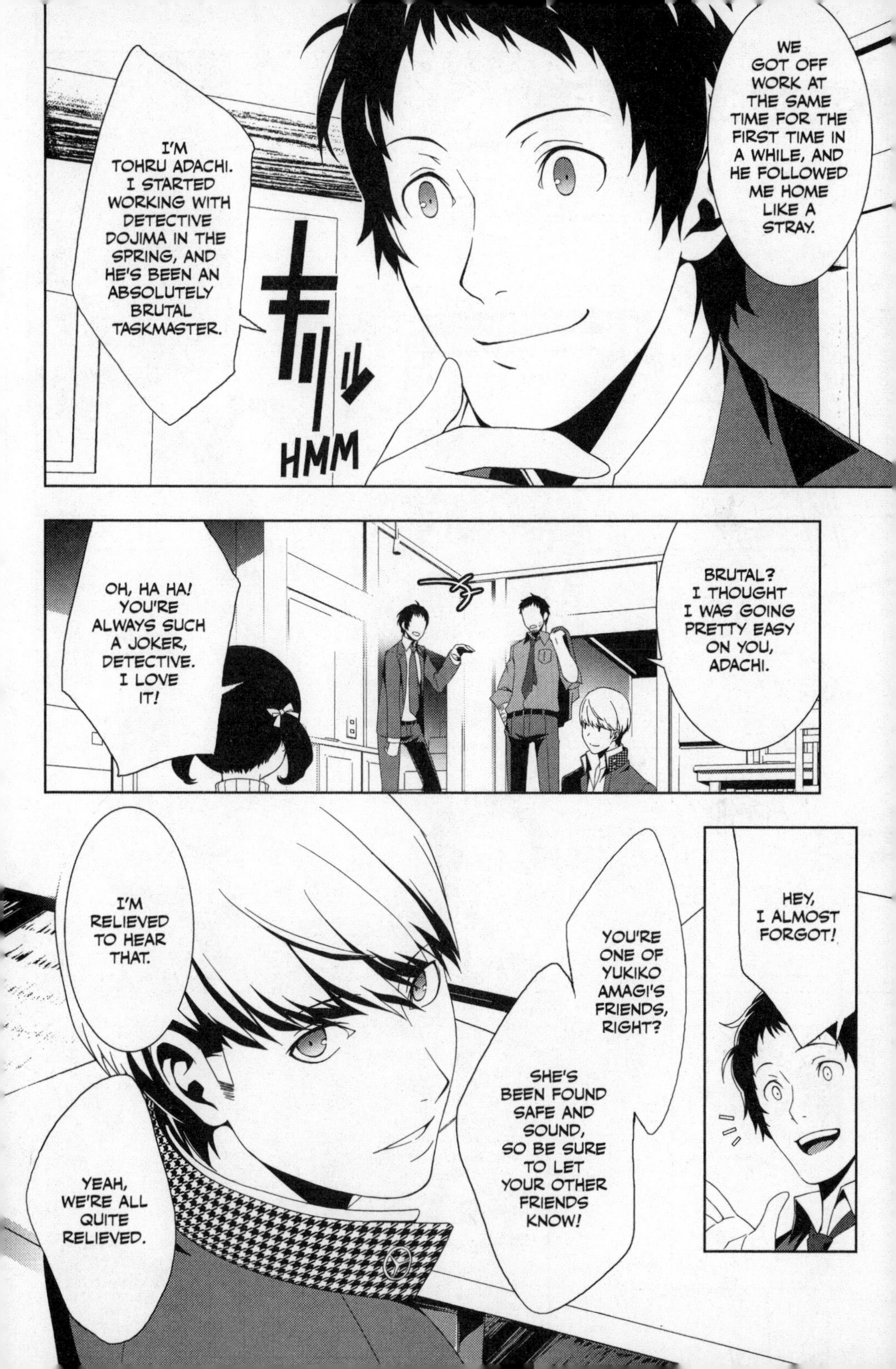
WE GOT OFF WORK AT THE SAME TIME FOR THE FIRST TIME IN A WHILE, AND HE FOLLOWED ME HOME LIKE A STRAY.
I'M TOHRU ADACHI. I STARTED WORKING WITH DETECTIVE DOJIMA IN THE SPRING, AND HE'S BEEN AN ABSOLUTELY BRUTAL TASKMASTER.
HMM
BRUTAL? I THOUGHT I WAS GOING PRETTY EASY ON YOU, ADACHI.
OH, HA HA! YOU'RE ALWAYS SUCH A JOKER, DETECTIVE. I LOVE IT!
HEY, I ALMOST FORGOT!
YOU'RE ONE OF YUKIKO AMAGI'S FRIENDS, RIGHT?
SHE'S BEEN FOUND SAFE AND SOUND, SO BE SURE TO LET YOUR OTHER FRIENDS KNOW!
I'M RELIEVED TO HEAR THAT.
YEAH, WE'RE ALL QUITE RELIEVED.

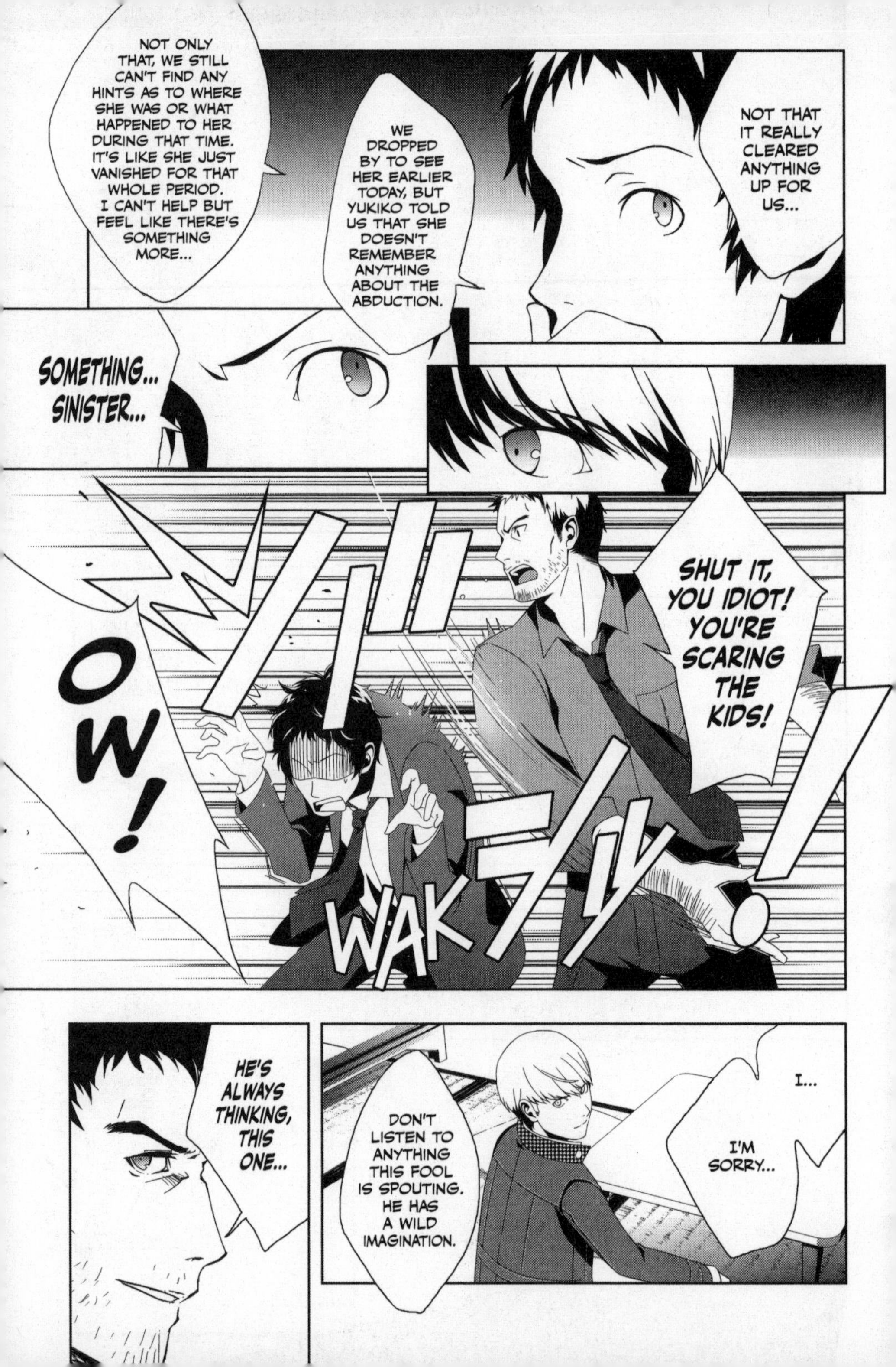
NOT THAT IT REALLY CLEARED ANYTHING UP FOR US...
WE DROPPED BY TO SEE HER EARLIER TODAY, BUT YUKIKO TOLD US THAT SHE DOESN'T REMEMBER ANYTHING ABOUT THE ABDUCTION.
NOT ONLY THAT, WE STILL CAN'T FIND ANY HINTS AS TO WHERE SHE WAS OR WHAT HAPPENED TO HER DURING THAT TIME. IT'S LIKE SHE JUST VANISHED FOR THAT WHOLE PERIOD. I CAN'T HELP BUT FEEL LIKE THERE'S SOMETHING MORE...
SOMETHING... SINISTER...
SHUT IT, YOU IDIOT! YOU'RE SCARING THE KIDS!
WAK
OW!
I...
I'M SORRY...
DON'T LISTEN TO ANYTHING THIS FOOL IS SPOUTING. HE HAS A WILD IMAGINATION.
HE'S ALWAYS THINKING, THIS ONE...

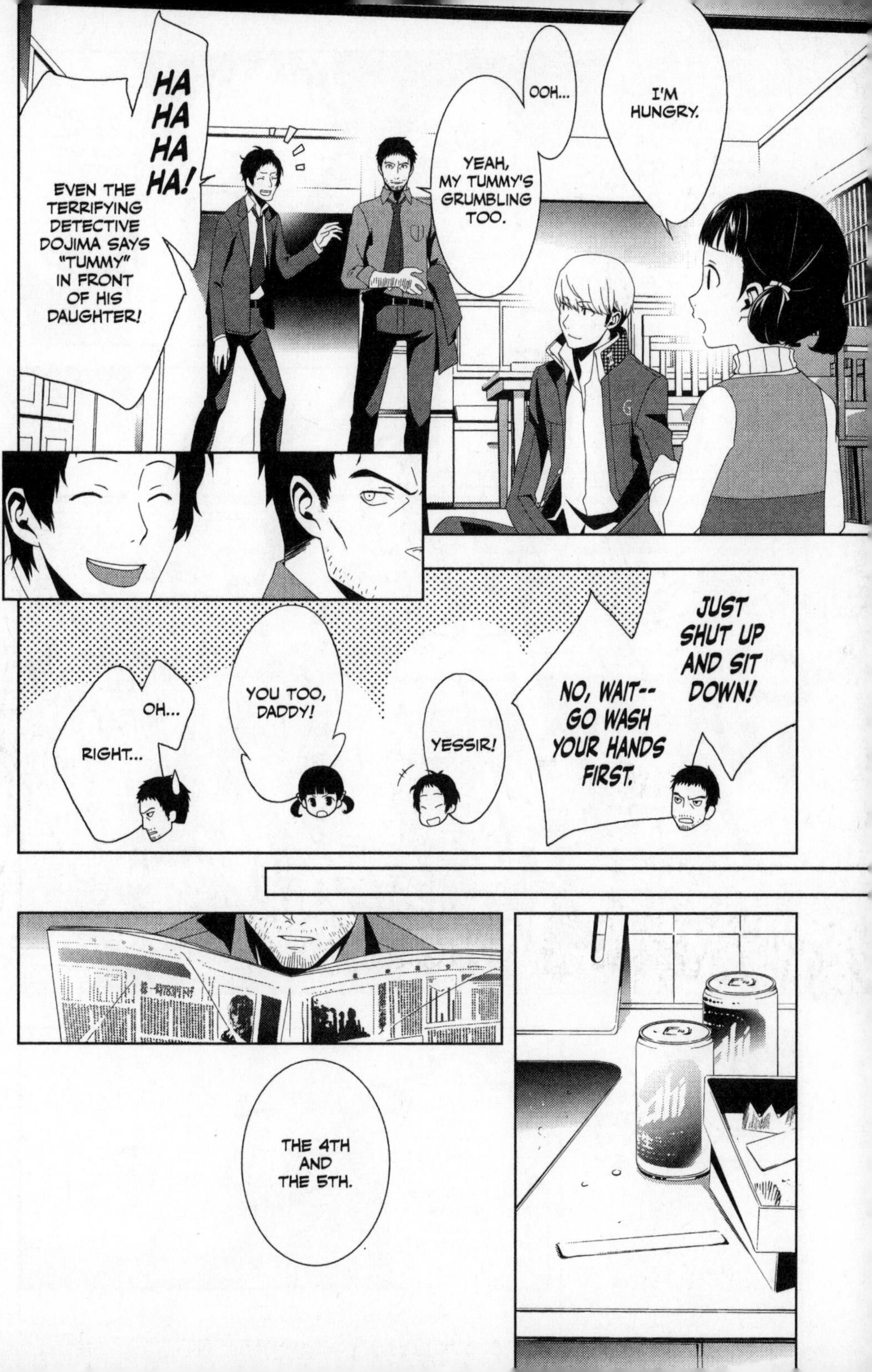
I'M HUNGRY.
OOH...
YEAH, MY TUMMY'S GRUMBLING TOO.
HA HA HA HA!
EVEN THE TERRIFYING DETECTIVE DOJIMA SAYS "TUMMY" IN FRONT OF HIS DAUGHTER!
JUST SHUT UP AND SIT DOWN!
NO, WAIT-- GO WASH YOUR HANDS FIRST.
YESSIR!
YOU TOO, DADDY!
OH...
RIGHT...
THE 4TH AND THE 5TH.

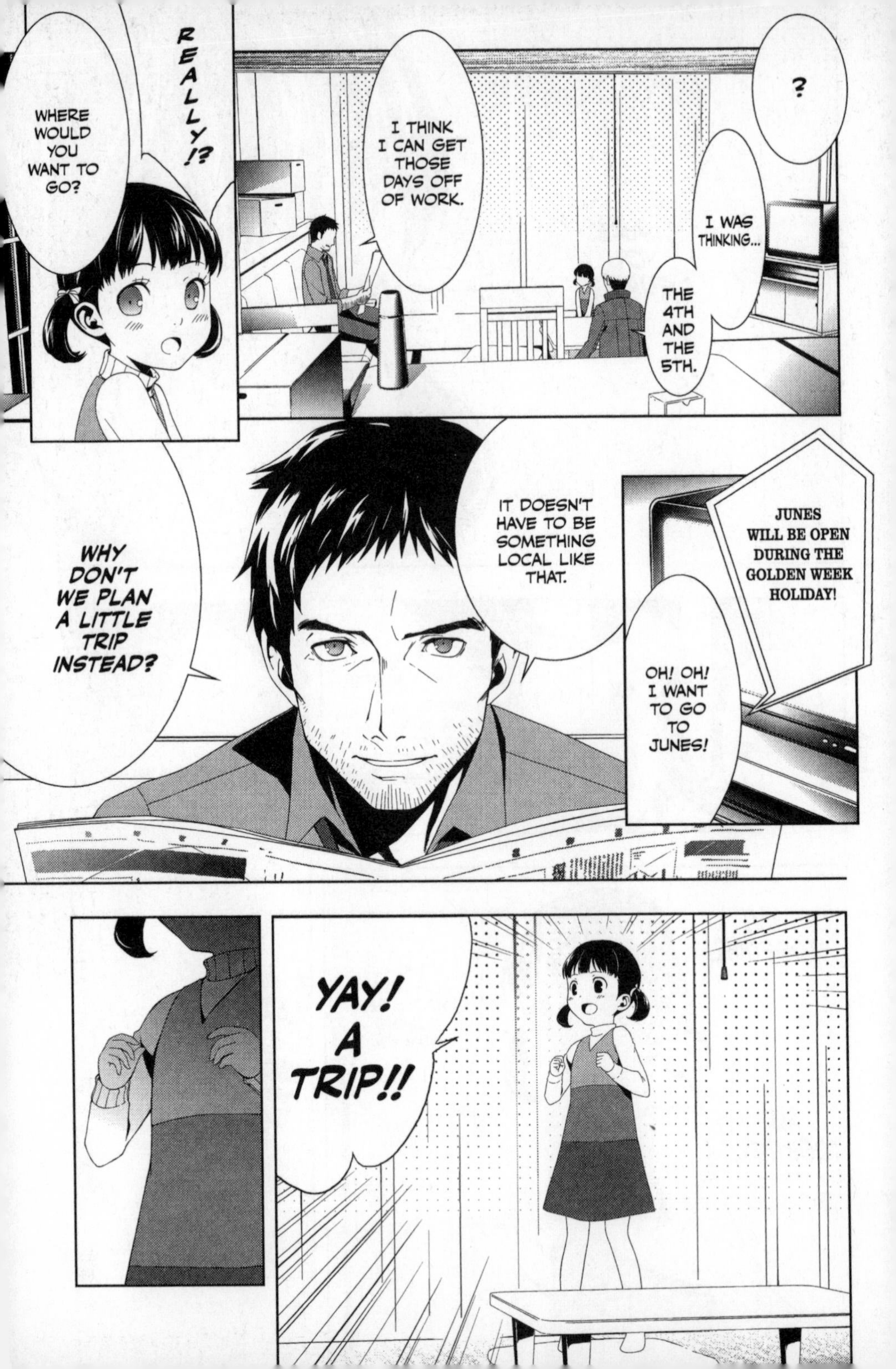
?
I WAS THINKING...
THE 4TH AND THE 5TH.
I THINK I CAN GET THOSE DAYS OFF OF WORK.
REALLY!?
WHERE WOULD YOU WANT TO GO?
JUNES WILL BE OPEN DURING THE GOLDEN WEEK HOLIDAY!
OH! OH! I WANT TO GO TO JUNES!
IT DOESN'T HAVE TO BE SOMETHING LOCAL LIKE THAT.
WHY DON'T WE PLAN A LITTLE TRIP INSTEAD?
YAY! A TRIP!!

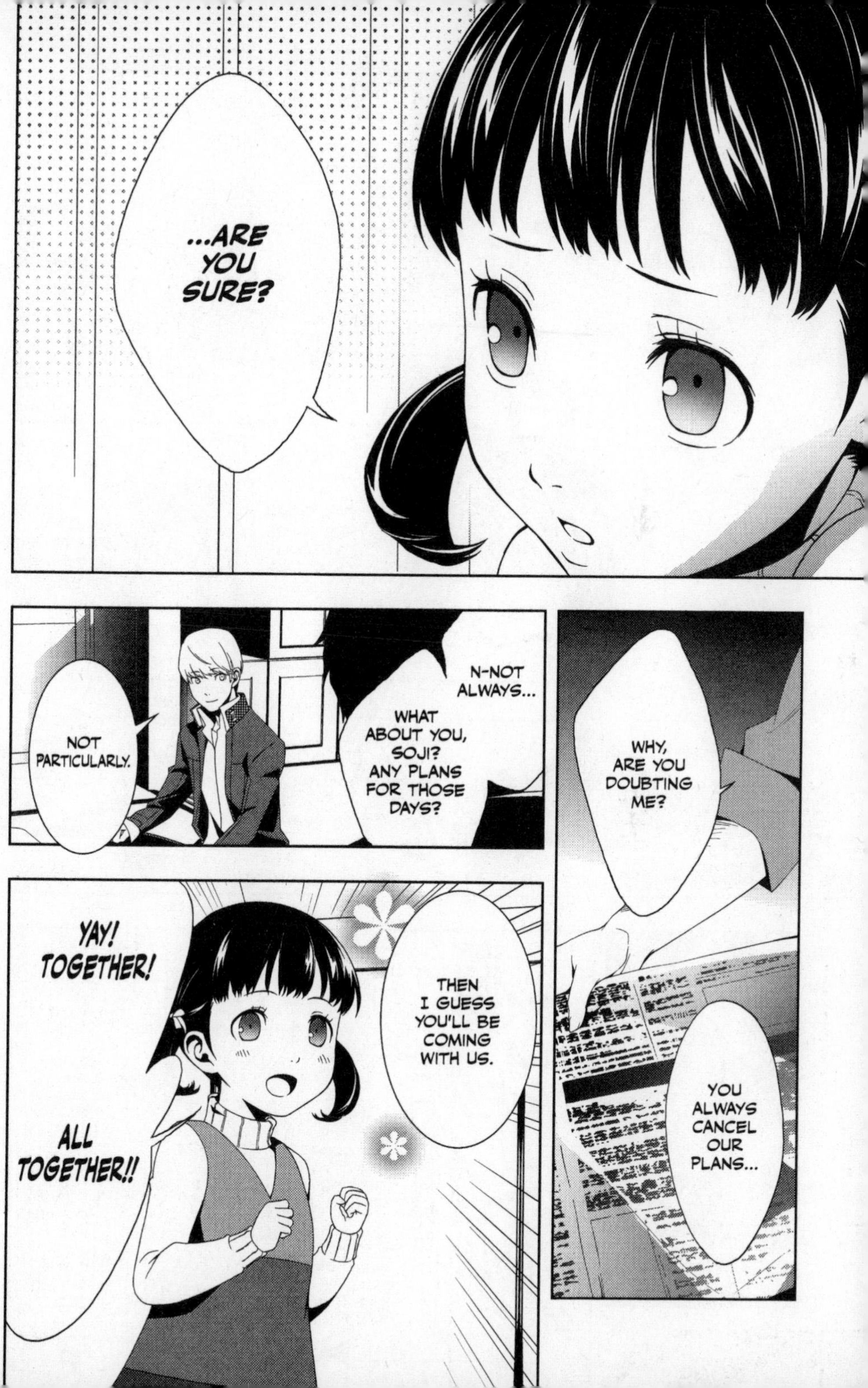
...ARE YOU SURE?
WHY, ARE YOU DOUBTING ME?
YOU ALWAYS CANCEL OUR PLANS...
N-NOT ALWAYS...
WHAT ABOUT YOU, SOJI? ANY PLANS FOR THOSE DAYS?
NOT PARTICULARLY.
THEN I GUESS YOU'LL BE COMING WITH US.
YAY! TOGETHER!
ALL TOGETHER!!

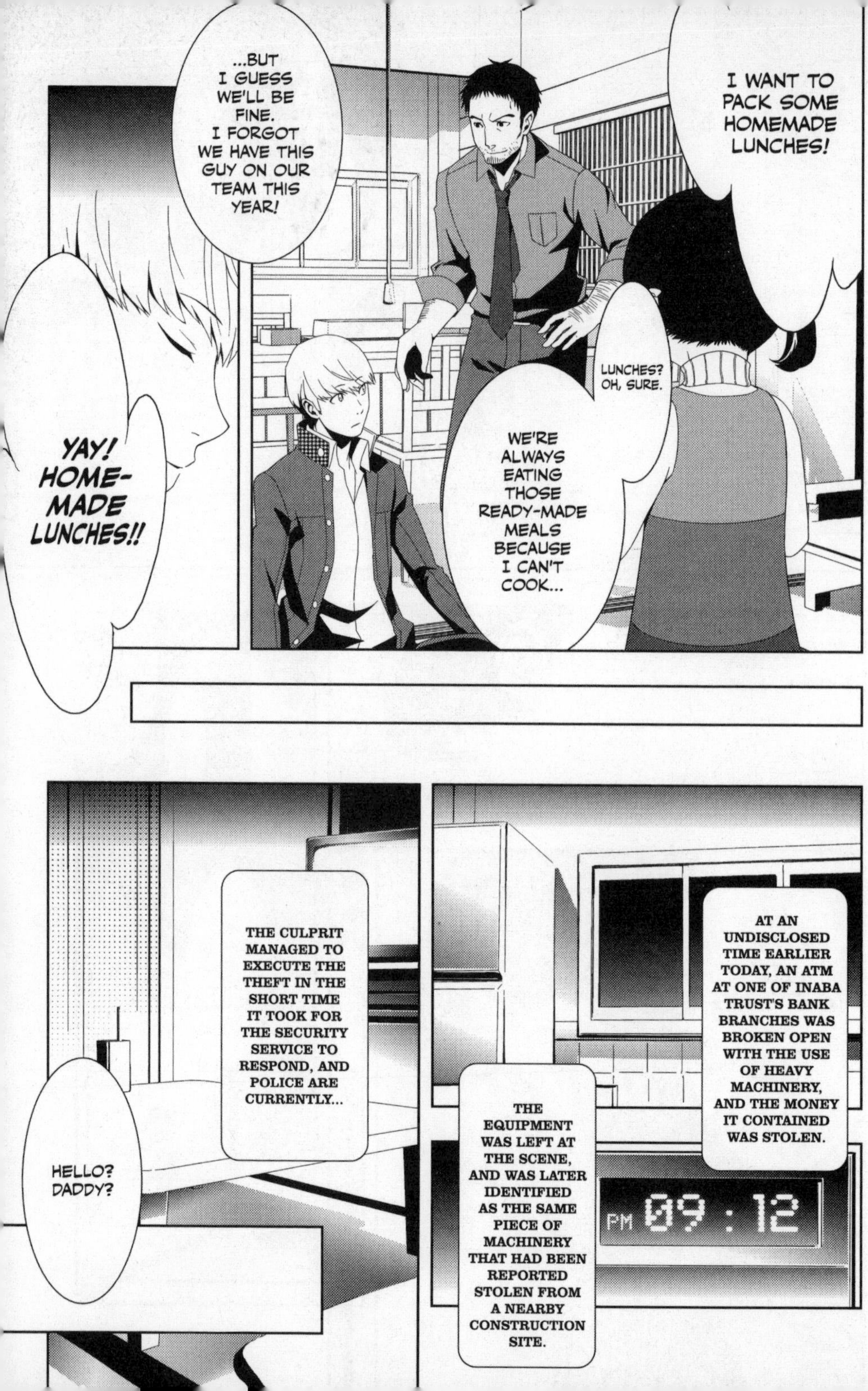

I WANT TO PACK SOME HOMEMADE LUNCHES!
LUNCHES? OH, SURE.
WE'RE ALWAYS EATING THOSE READY-MADE MEALS BECAUSE I CAN'T COOK...
...BUT I GUESS WE'LL BE FINE. I FORGOT WE HAVE THIS GUY ON OUR TEAM THIS YEAR!
YAY! HOME-MADE LUNCHES!!
AT AN UNDISCLOSED TIME EARLIER TODAY, AN ATM AT ONE OF INABA TRUST'S BANK BRANCHES WAS BROKEN OPEN WITH THE USE OF HEAVY MACHINERY, AND THE MONEY IT CONTAINED WAS STOLEN.
THE EQUIPMENT WAS LEFT AT THE SCENE, AND WAS LATER IDENTIFIED AS THE SAME PIECE OF MACHINERY THAT HAD BEEN REPORTED STOLEN FROM A NEARBY CONSTRUCTION SITE.
PM 09 : 12
THE CULPRIT MANAGED TO EXECUTE THE THEFT IN THE SHORT TIME IT TOOK FOR THE SECURITY SERVICE TO RESPOND, AND POLICE ARE CURRENTLY...
HELLO? DADDY?

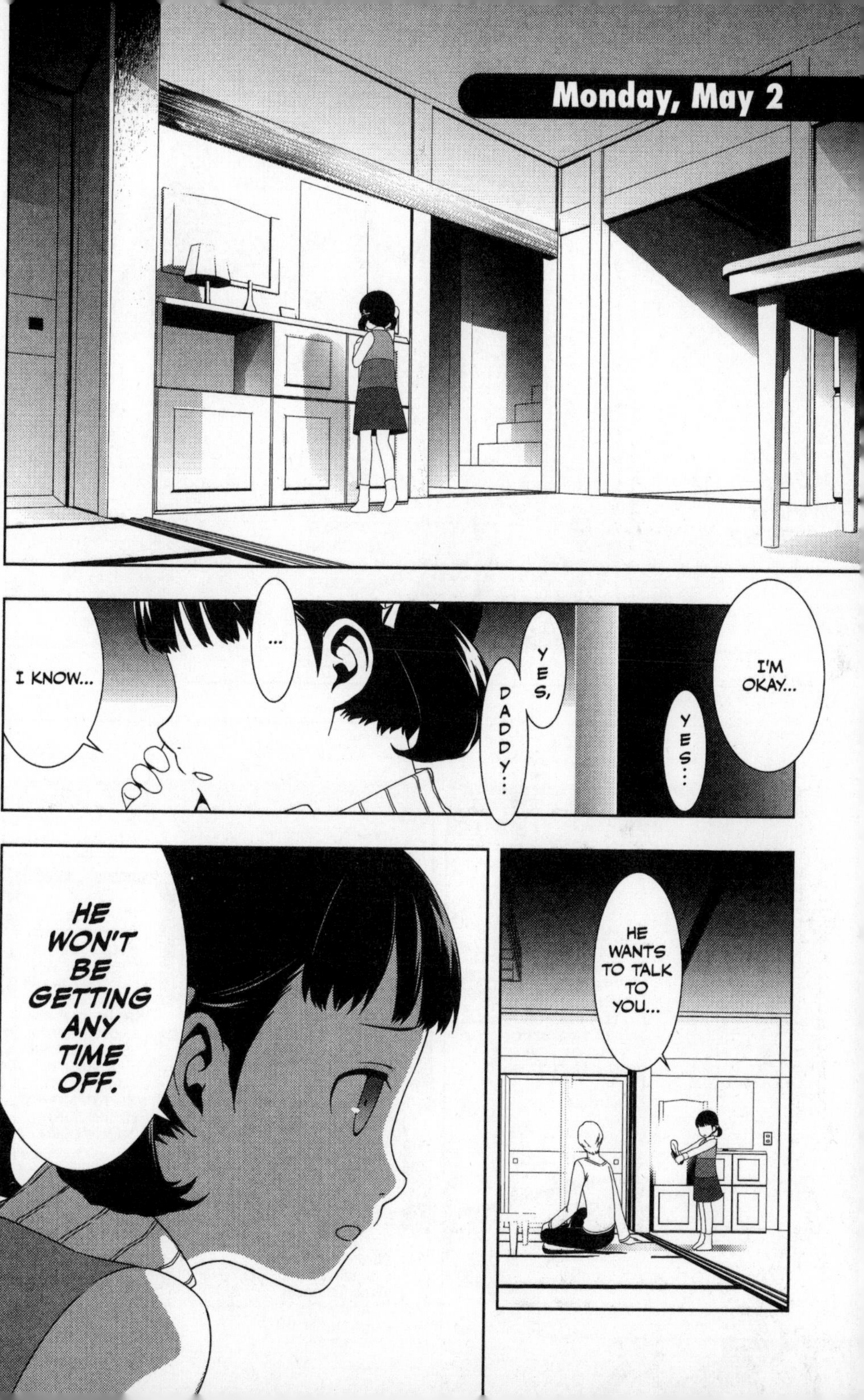
Monday, May 2
I'M OKAY...
YES...
YES, DADDY...
...
I KNOW...
HE WANTS TO TALK TO YOU...
HE WON'T BE GETTING ANY TIME OFF.

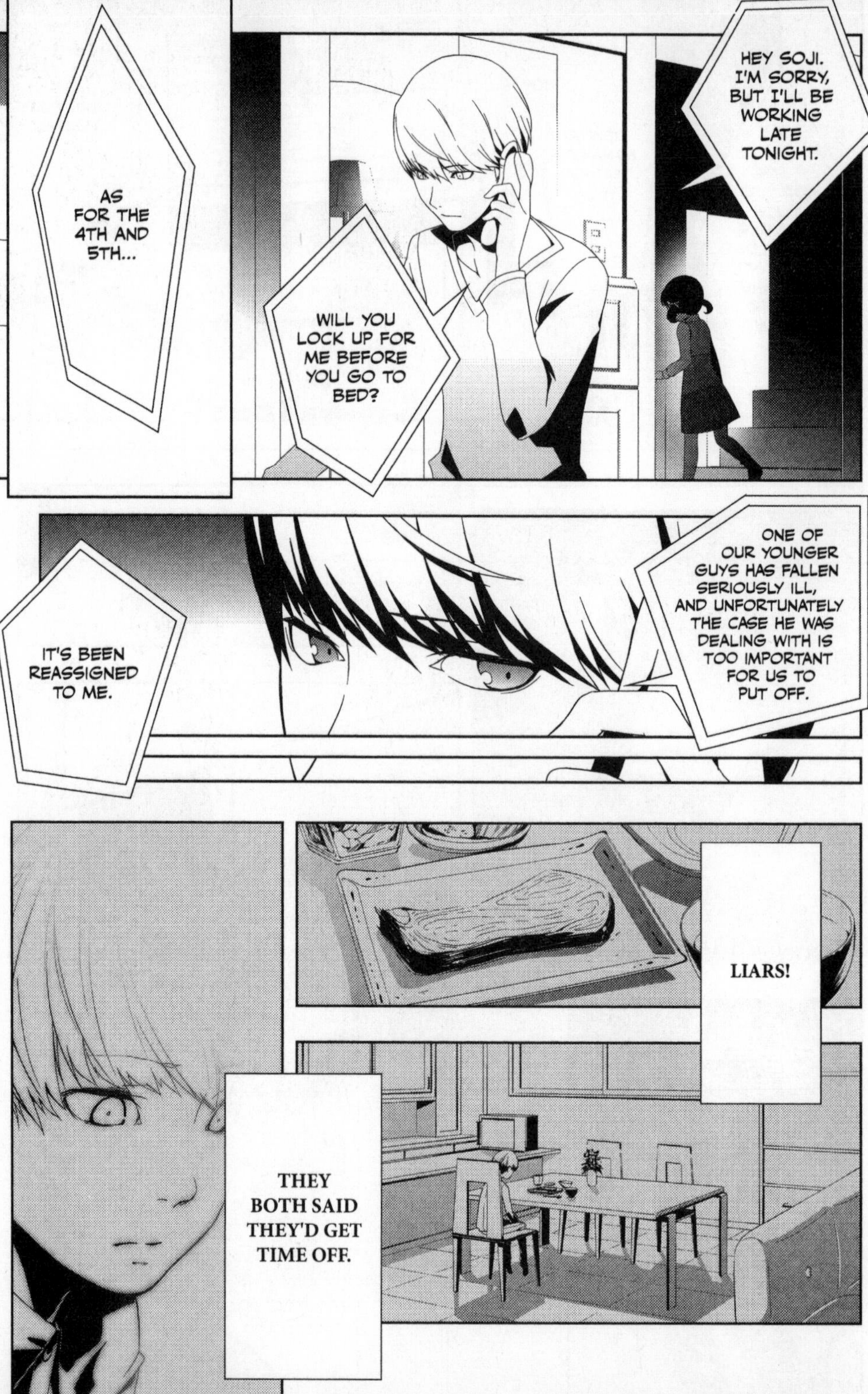
HEY SOJI. I'M SORRY, BUT I'LL BE WORKING LATE TONIGHT.
WILL YOU LOCK UP FOR ME BEFORE YOU GO TO BED?
AS FOR THE 4TH AND 5TH...
ONE OF OUR YOUNGER GUYS HAS FALLEN SERIOUSLY ILL, AND UNFORTUNATELY THE CASE HE WAS DEALING WITH IS TOO IMPORTANT FOR US TO PUT OFF.
IT'S BEEN REASSIGNED TO ME.
LIARS!
THEY BOTH SAID THEY'D GET TIME OFF.

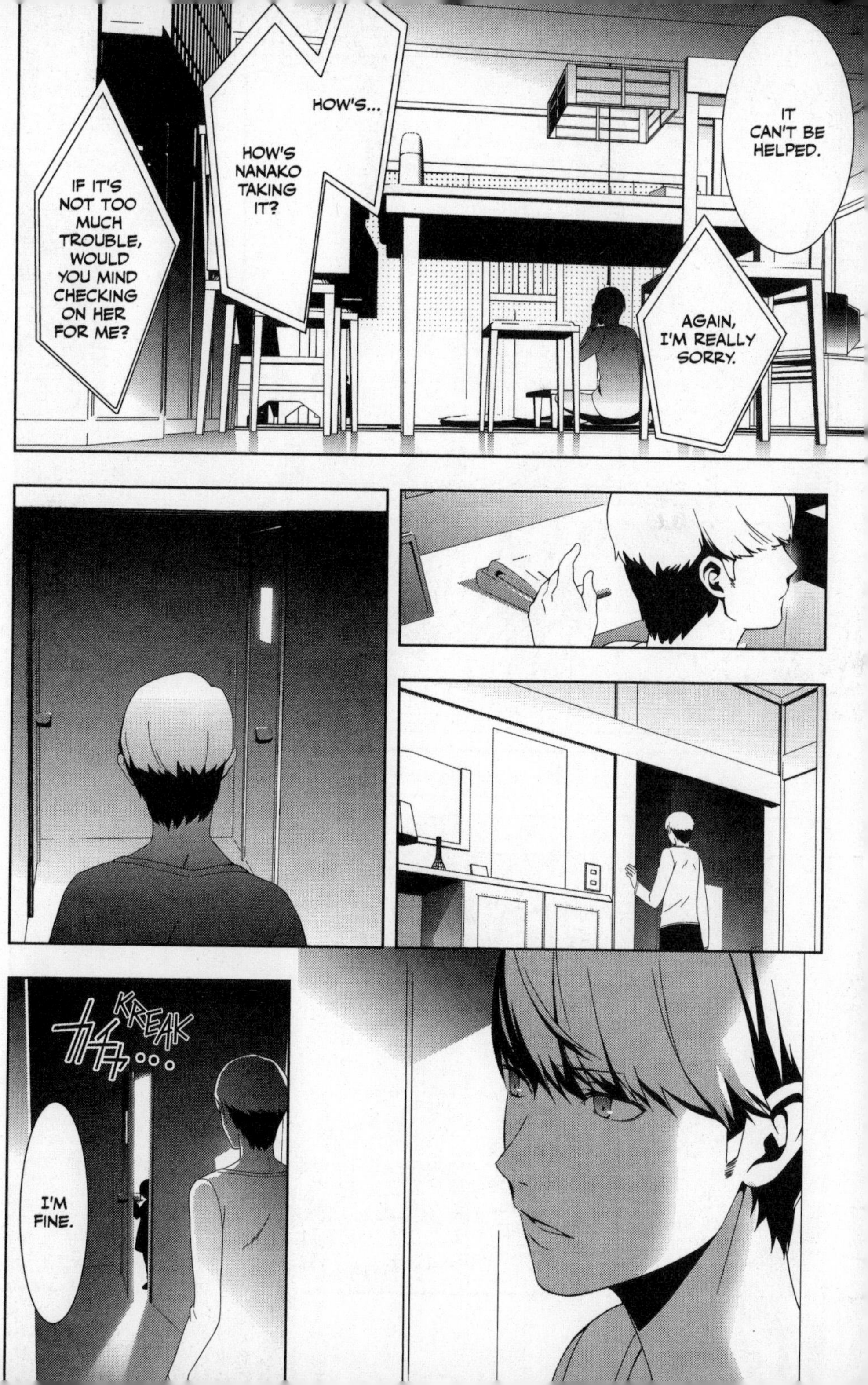
IT CAN'T BE HELPED.
AGAIN, I'M REALLY SORRY.
HOW'S...
HOW'S NANAKO TAKING IT?
IF IT'S NOT TOO MUCH TROUBLE, WOULD YOU MIND CHECKING ON HER FOR ME?
KREAK
カチャ…
I'M FINE.

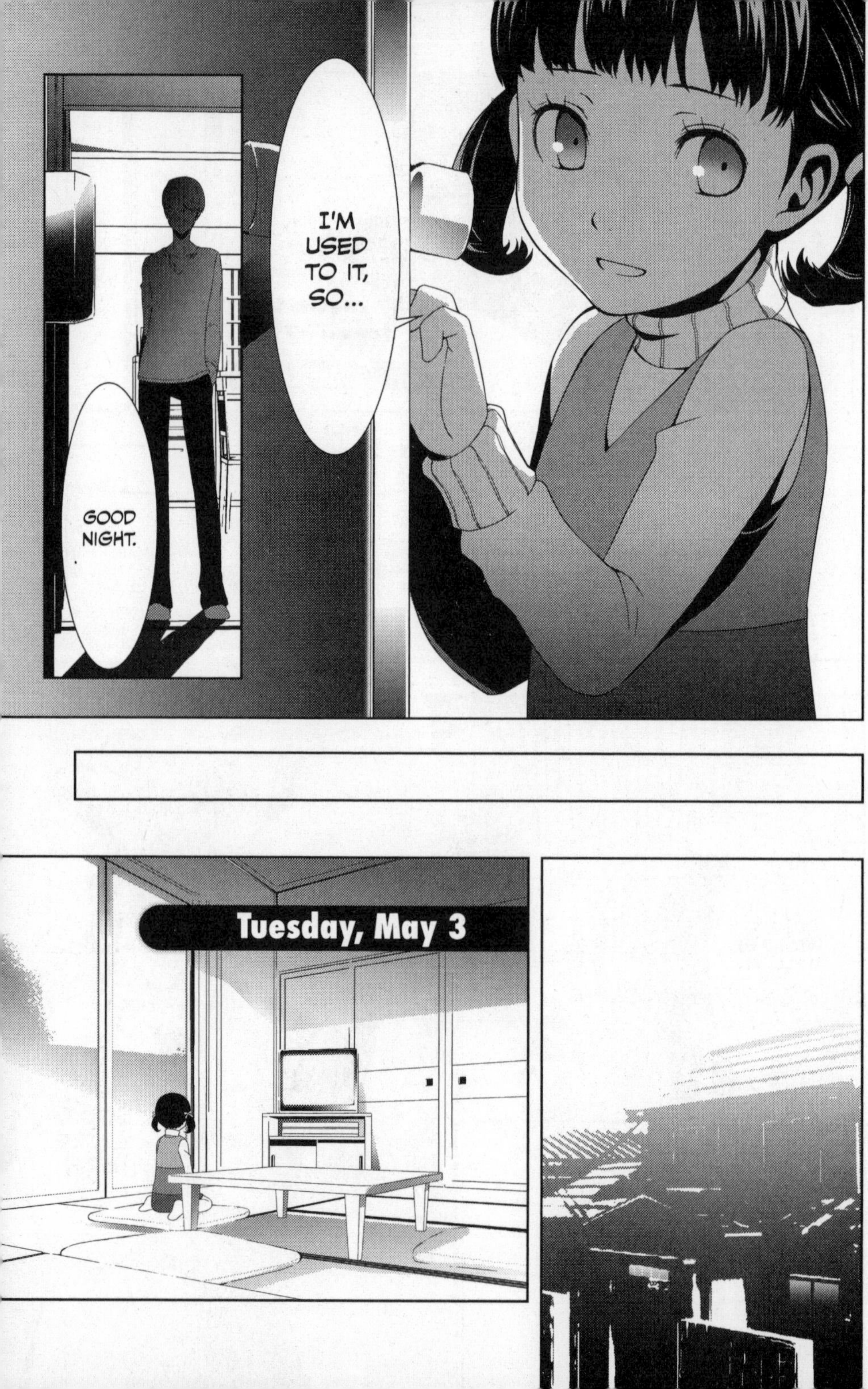
I'M USED TO IT, SO...
GOOD NIGHT.
Tuesday, May 3

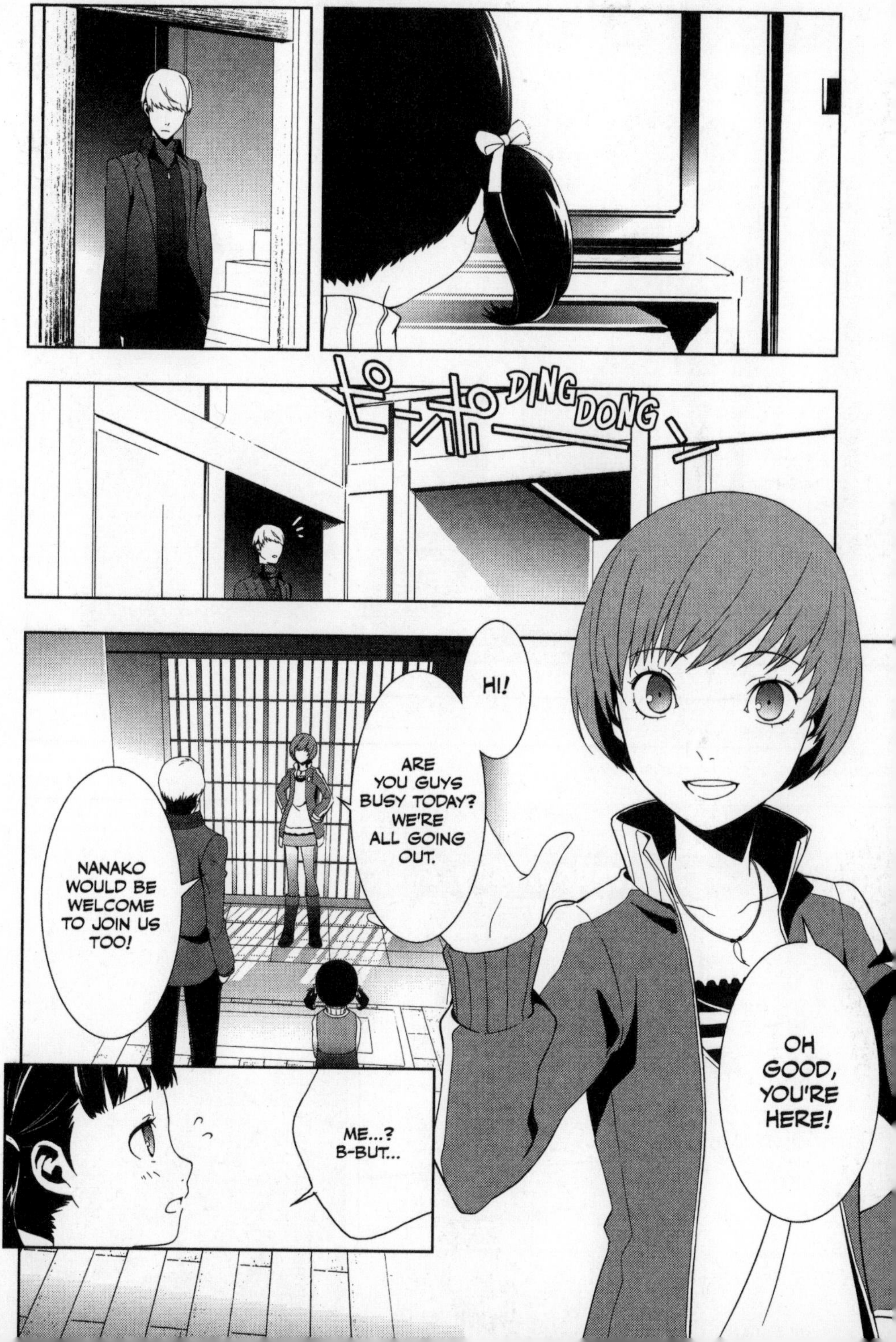
DING DONG
OH GOOD, YOU'RE HERE!
HI!
ARE YOU GUYS BUSY TODAY? WE'RE ALL GOING OUT.
NANAKO WOULD BE WELCOME TO JOIN US TOO!
ME...? B-BUT...

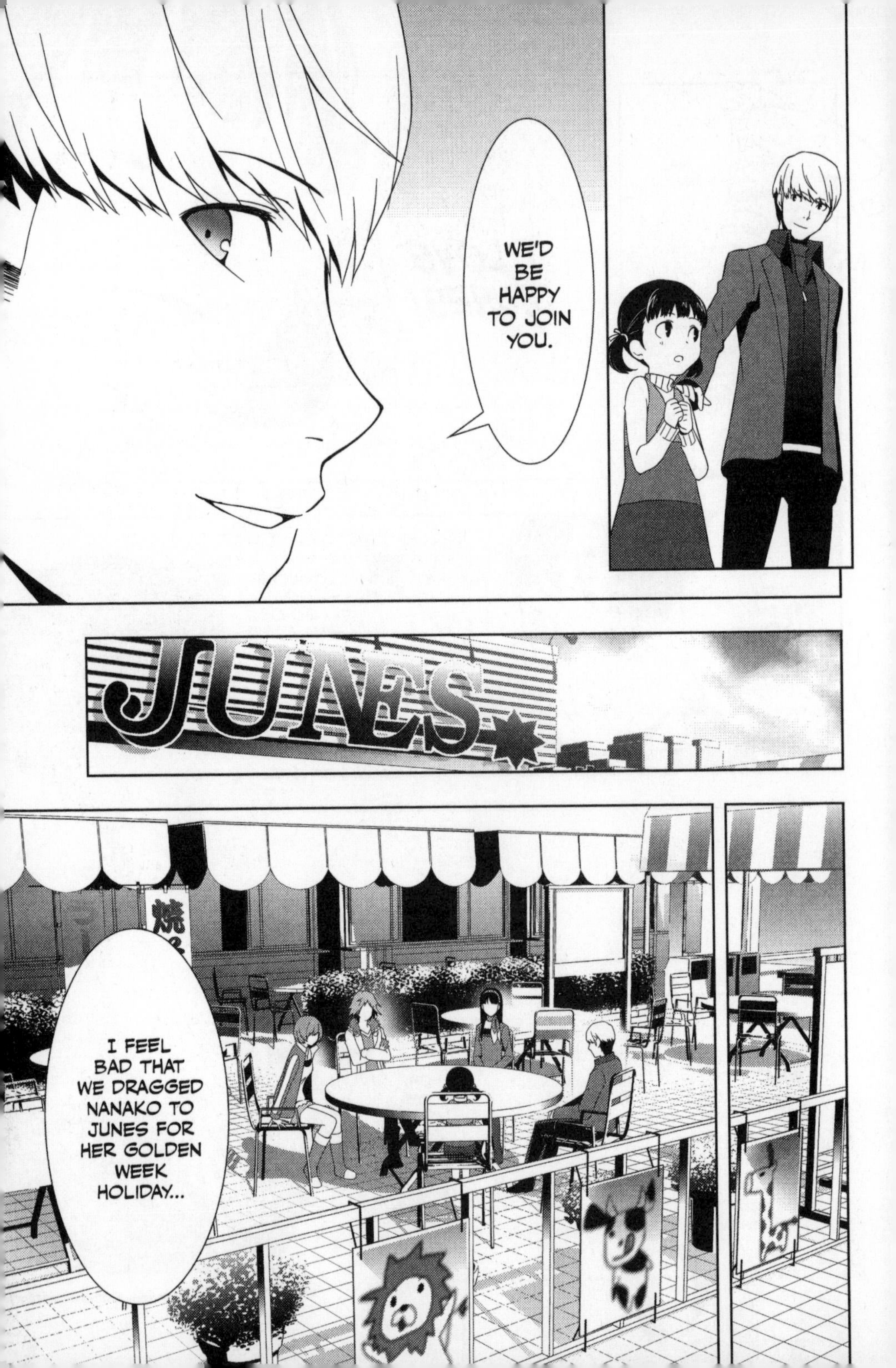
WE'D BE HAPPY TO JOIN YOU.
JUNES
I FEEL BAD THAT WE DRAGGED NANAKO TO JUNES FOR HER GOLDEN WEEK HOLIDAY...

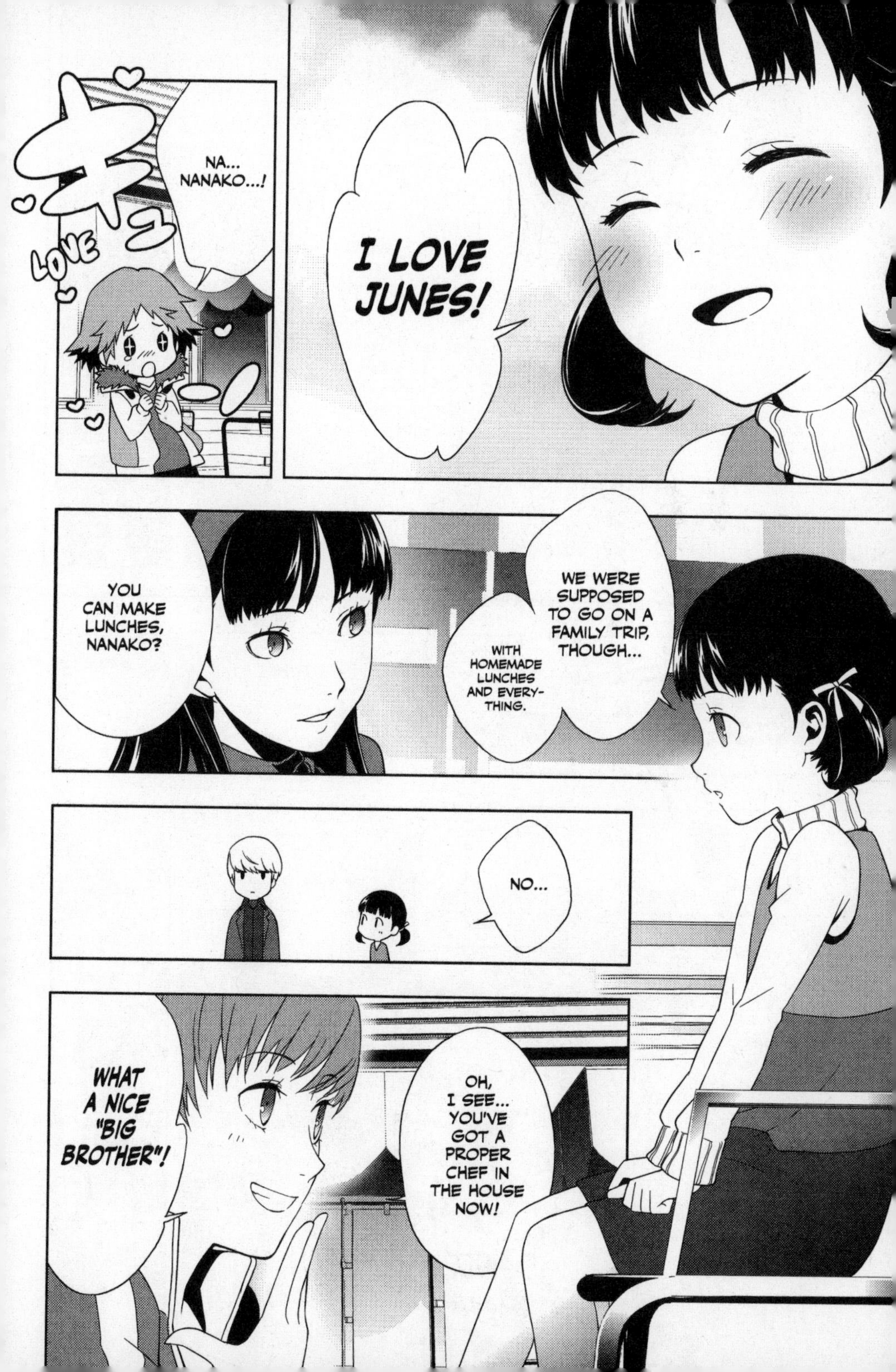
I LOVE JUNES!
LOVE
NA... NANAKO...!
WE WERE SUPPOSED TO GO ON A FAMILY TRIP, THOUGH...
WITH HOMEMADE LUNCHES AND EVERYTHING.
YOU CAN MAKE LUNCHES, NANAKO?
NO...
OH, I SEE... YOU'VE GOT A PROPER CHEF IN THE HOUSE NOW!
WHAT A NICE "BIG BROTHER"!

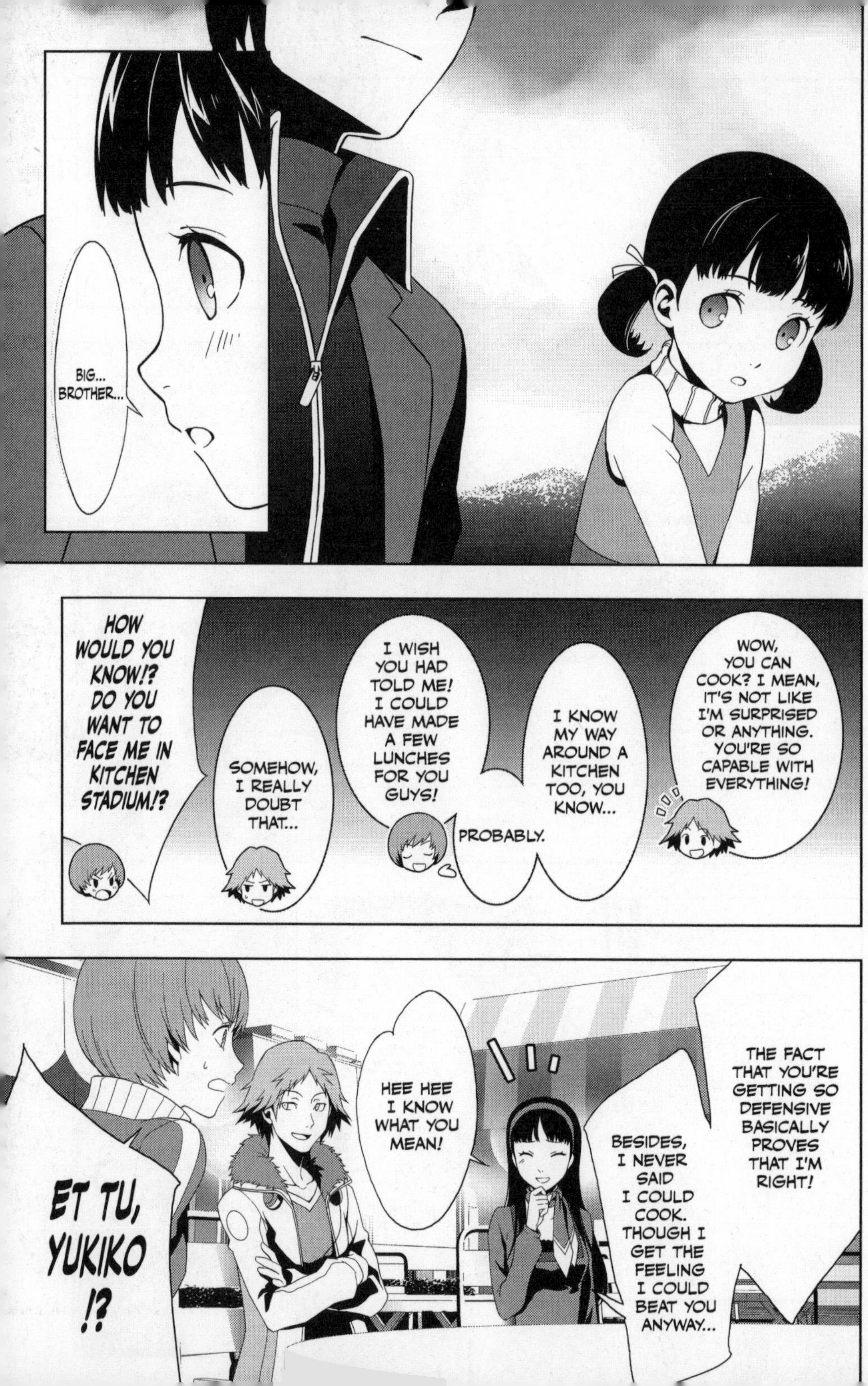
BIG... BROTHER...
WOW, YOU CAN COOK? I MEAN, IT'S NOT LIKE I'M SURPRISED OR ANYTHING. YOU'RE SO CAPABLE WITH EVERYTHING!
I KNOW MY WAY AROUND A KITCHEN TOO, YOU KNOW...
PROBABLY.
I WISH YOU HAD TOLD ME! I COULD HAVE MADE A FEW LUNCHES FOR YOU GUYS!
SOMEHOW, I REALLY DOUBT THAT...
HOW WOULD YOU KNOW!? DO YOU WANT TO FACE ME IN KITCHEN STADIUM!?
THE FACT THAT YOU'RE GETTING SO DEFENSIVE BASICALLY PROVES THAT I'M RIGHT!
BESIDES, I NEVER SAID I COULD COOK. THOUGH I GET THE FEELING I COULD BEAT YOU ANYWAY...
HEE HEE I KNOW WHAT YOU MEAN!
ET TU, YUKIKO !?

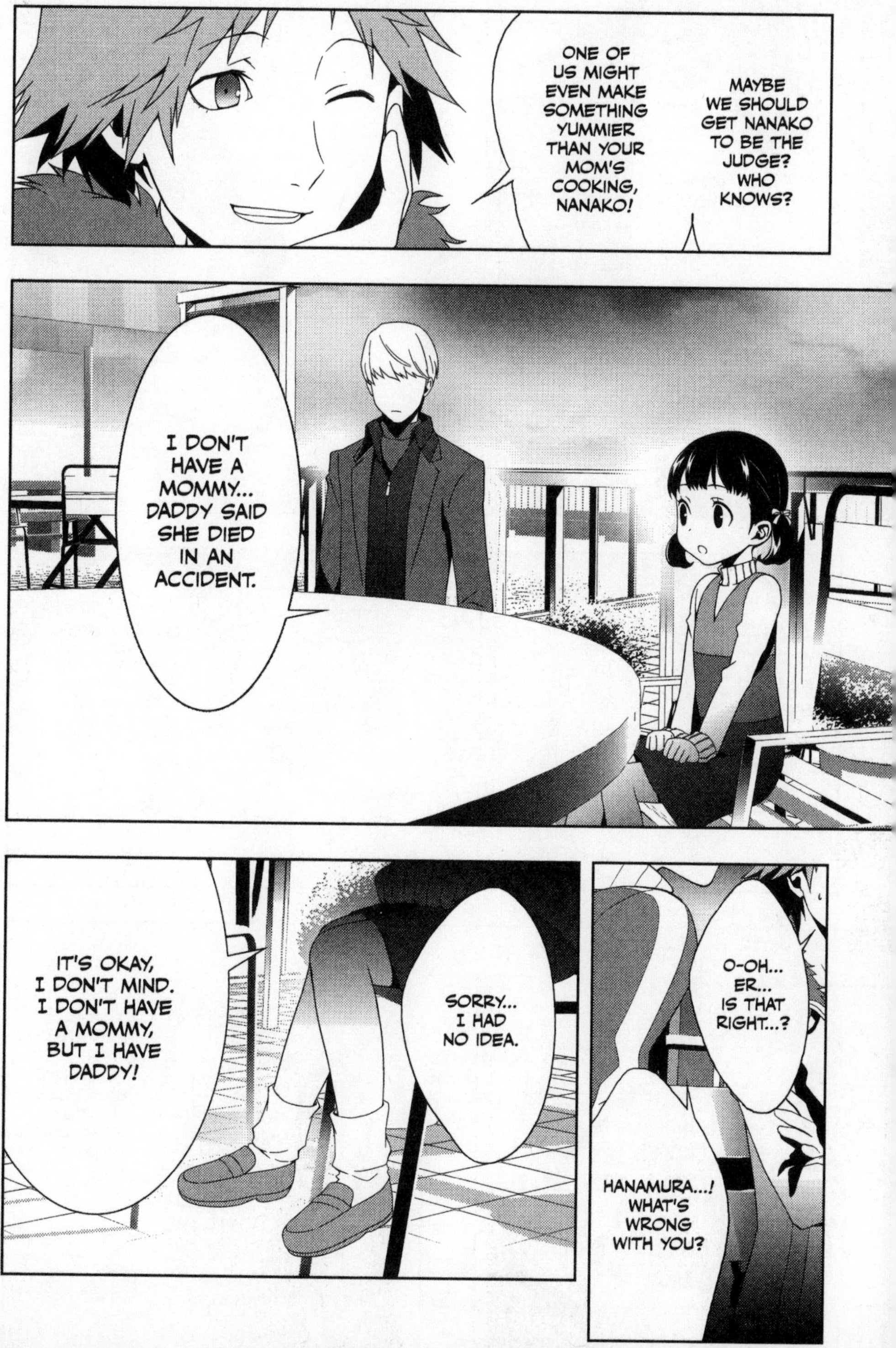
MAYBE WE SHOULD GET NANAKO TO BE THE JUDGE? WHO KNOWS?
ONE OF US MIGHT EVEN MAKE SOMETHING YUMMIER THAN YOUR MOM'S COOKING, NANAKO!
I DON'T HAVE A MOMMY... DADDY SAID SHE DIED IN AN ACCIDENT.
O-OH... ER... IS THAT RIGHT...?
HANAMURA...! WHAT'S WRONG WITH YOU?
SORRY... I HAD NO IDEA.
IT'S OKAY, I DON'T MIND. I DON'T HAVE A MOMMY, BUT I HAVE DADDY!

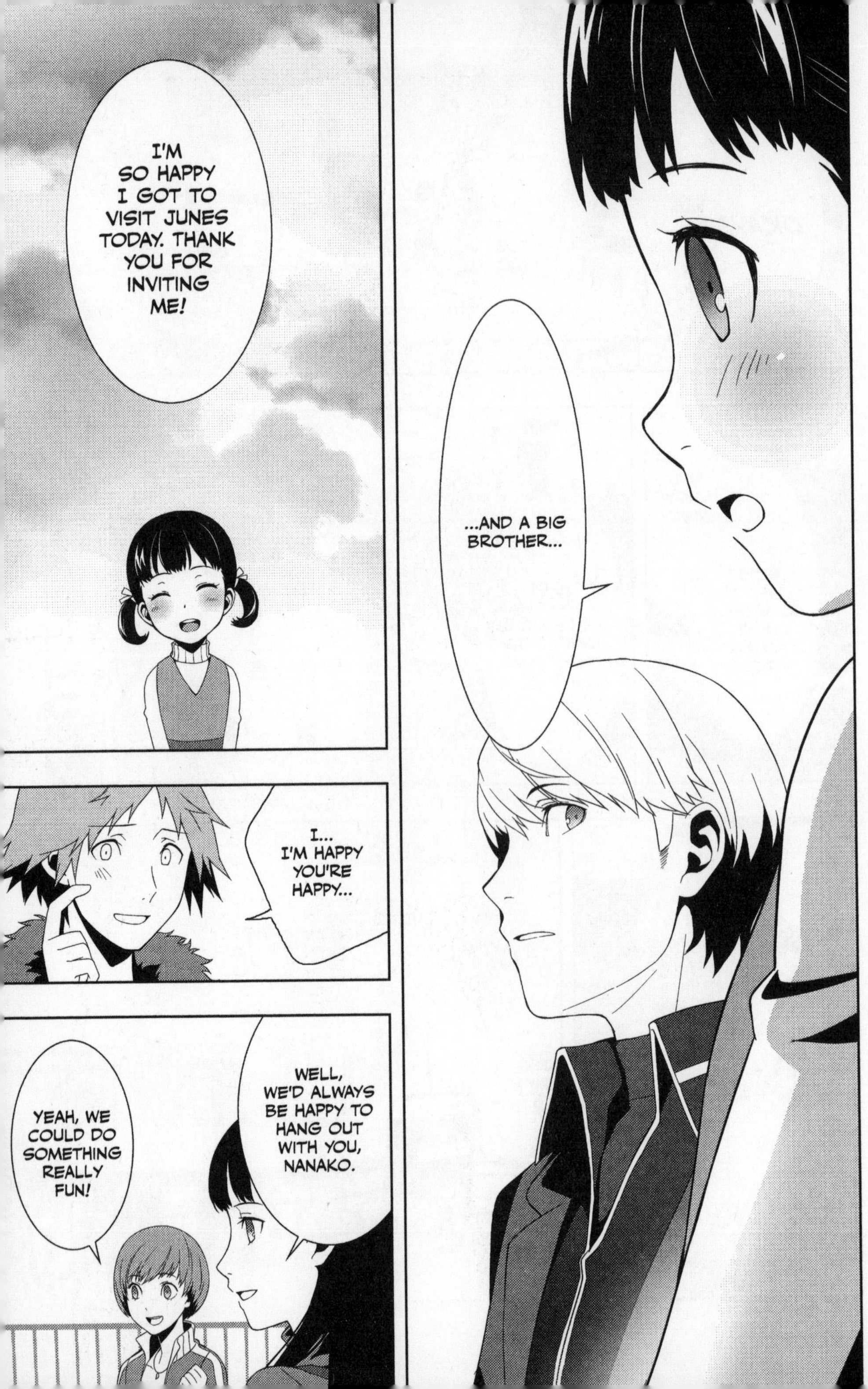
...AND A BIG BROTHER...
I'M SO HAPPY I GOT TO VISIT JUNES TODAY. THANK YOU FOR INVITING ME!
I... I'M HAPPY YOU'RE HAPPY...
WELL, WE'D ALWAYS BE HAPPY TO HANG OUT WITH YOU, NANAKO.
YEAH, WE COULD DO SOMETHING REALLY FUN!

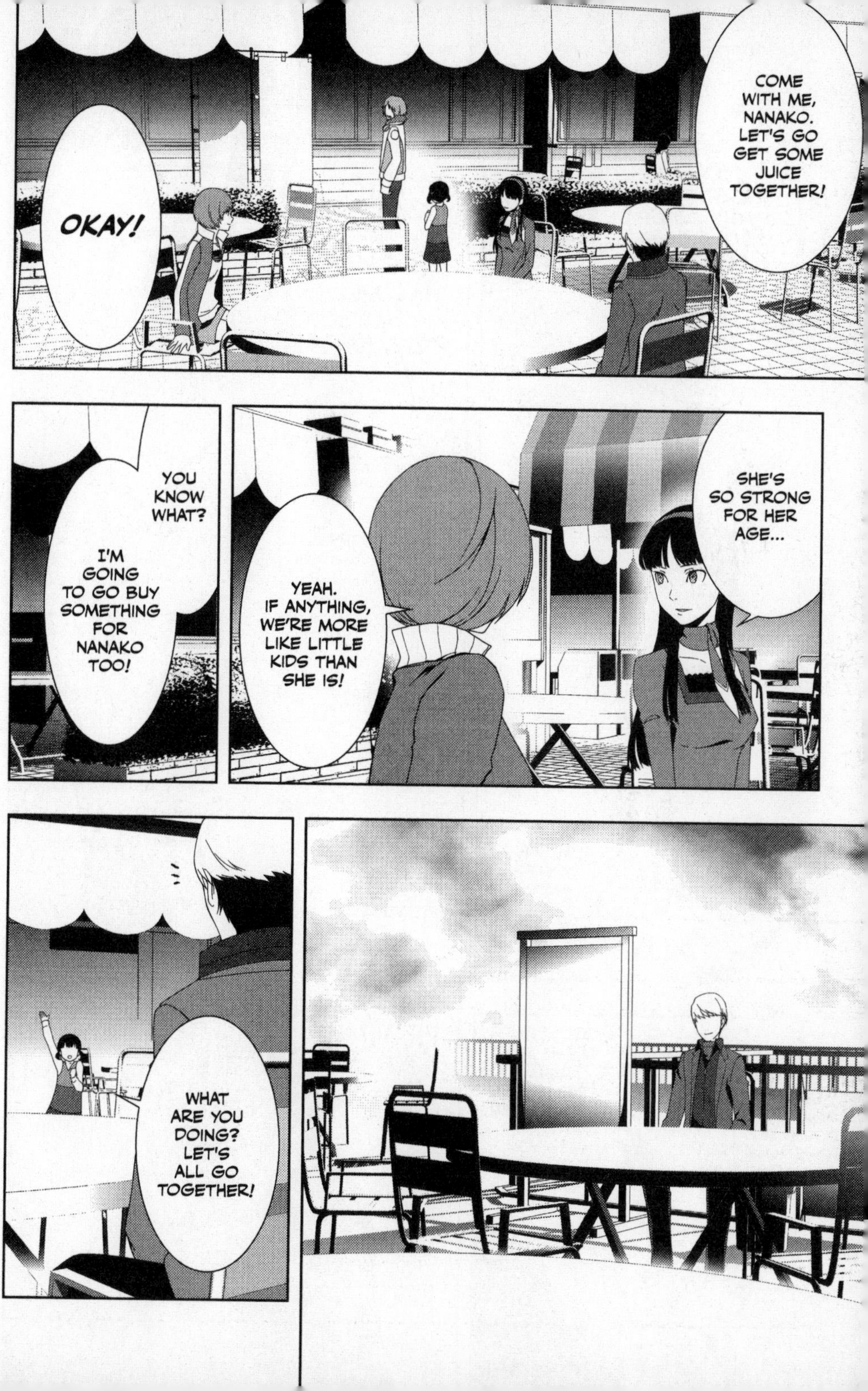
COME WITH ME, NANAKO. LET'S GO GET SOME JUICE TOGETHER!
OKAY!
SHE'S SO STRONG FOR HER AGE...
YEAH. IF ANYTHING, WE'RE MORE LIKE LITTLE KIDS THAN SHE IS!
YOU KNOW WHAT?
I'M GOING TO GO BUY SOMETHING FOR NANAKO TOO!
WHAT ARE YOU DOING? LET'S ALL GO TOGETHER!

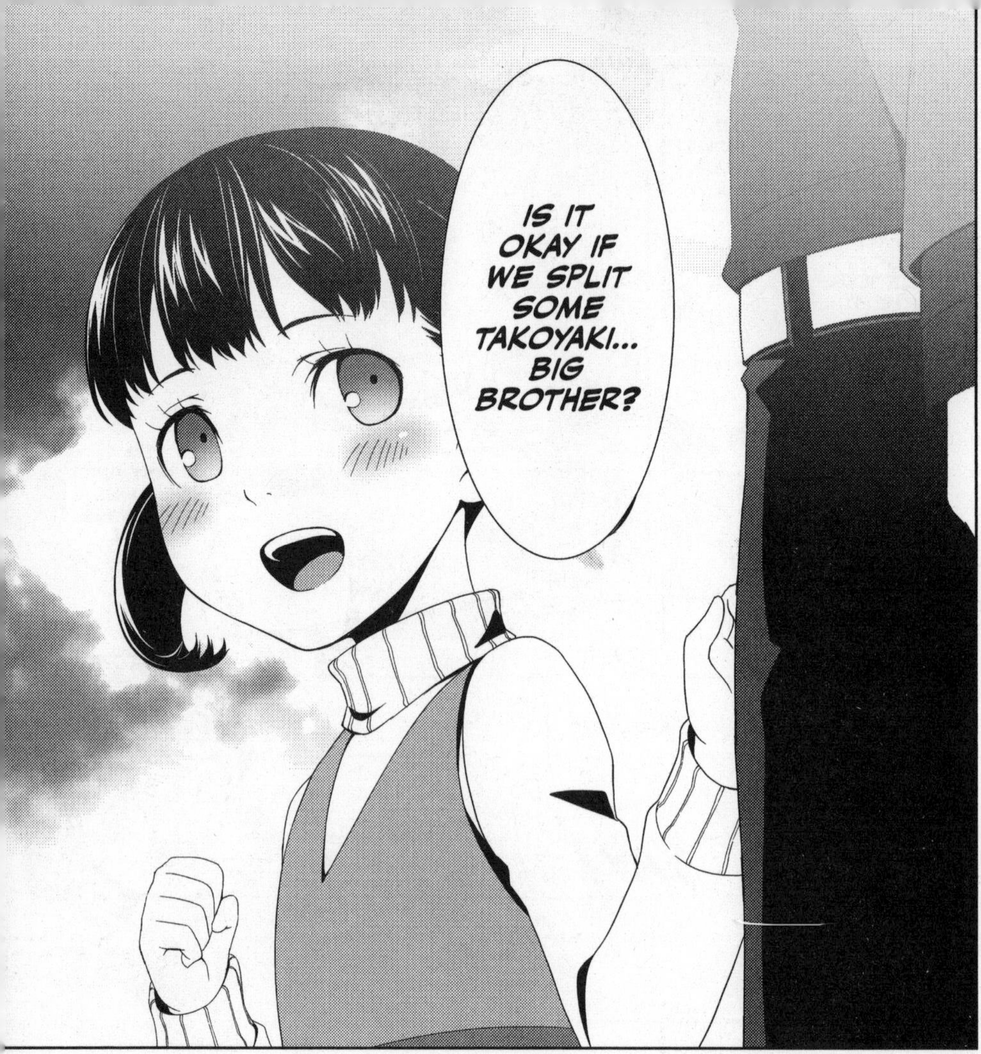
IS IT OKAY IF WE SPLIT SOME TAKOYAKI... BIG BROTHER?

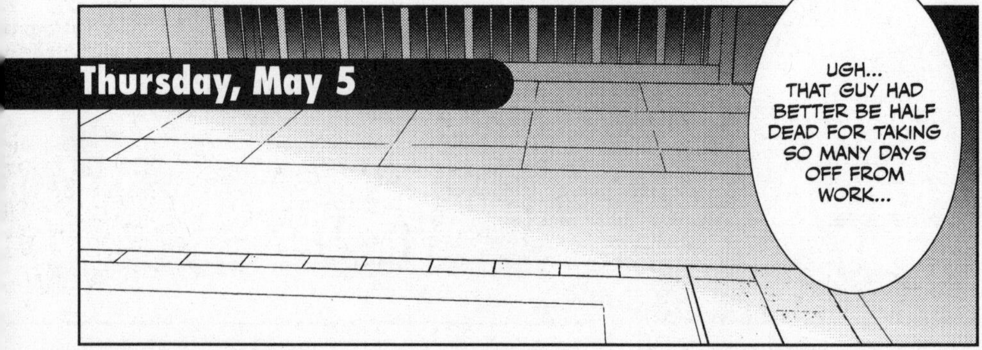
UGH... THAT GUY HAD BETTER BE HALF DEAD FOR TAKING SO MANY DAYS OFF FROM WORK...
Thursday, May 5

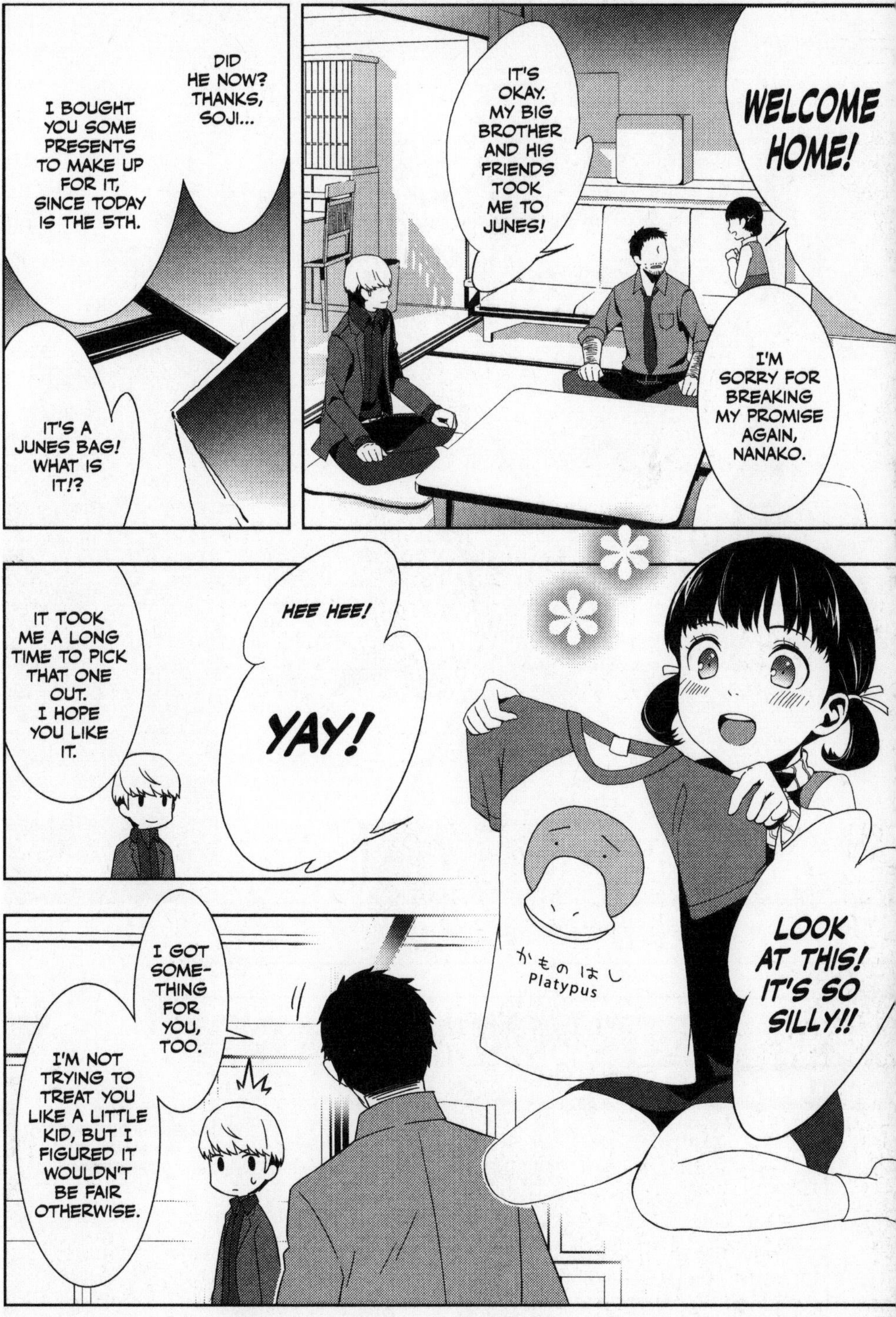
WELCOME HOME!
I'M SORRY FOR BREAKING MY PROMISE AGAIN, NANAKO.
IT'S OKAY. MY BIG BROTHER AND HIS FRIENDS TOOK ME TO JUNES!
DID HE NOW? THANKS, SOJI...
I BOUGHT YOU SOME PRESENTS TO MAKE UP FOR IT, SINCE TODAY IS THE 5TH.
IT'S A JUNES BAG! WHAT IS IT!?
LOOK AT THIS! IT'S SO SILLY!!
かものはし
Platypus
HEE HEE!
YAY!
IT TOOK ME A LONG TIME TO PICK THAT ONE OUT. I HOPE YOU LIKE IT.
I GOT SOME-THING FOR YOU, TOO.
I'M NOT TRYING TO TREAT YOU LIKE A LITTLE KID, BUT I FIGURED IT WOULDN'T BE FAIR OTHERWISE.

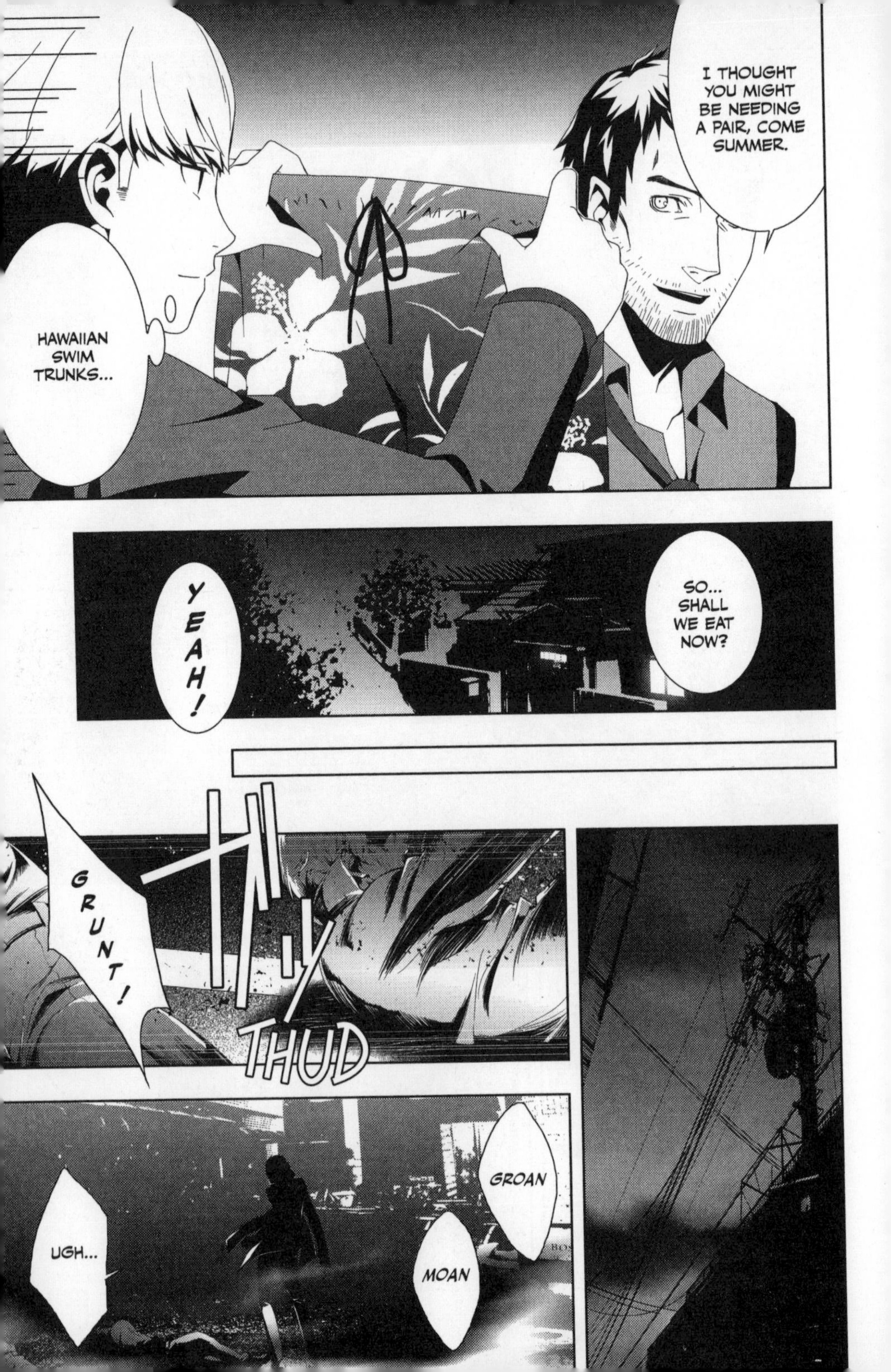
I THOUGHT YOU MIGHT BE NEEDING A PAIR, COME SUMMER.
HAWAIIAN SWIM TRUNKS...
SO... SHALL WE EAT NOW?
YEAH!
GRUNT!
THUD
GROAN
MOAN
UGH...

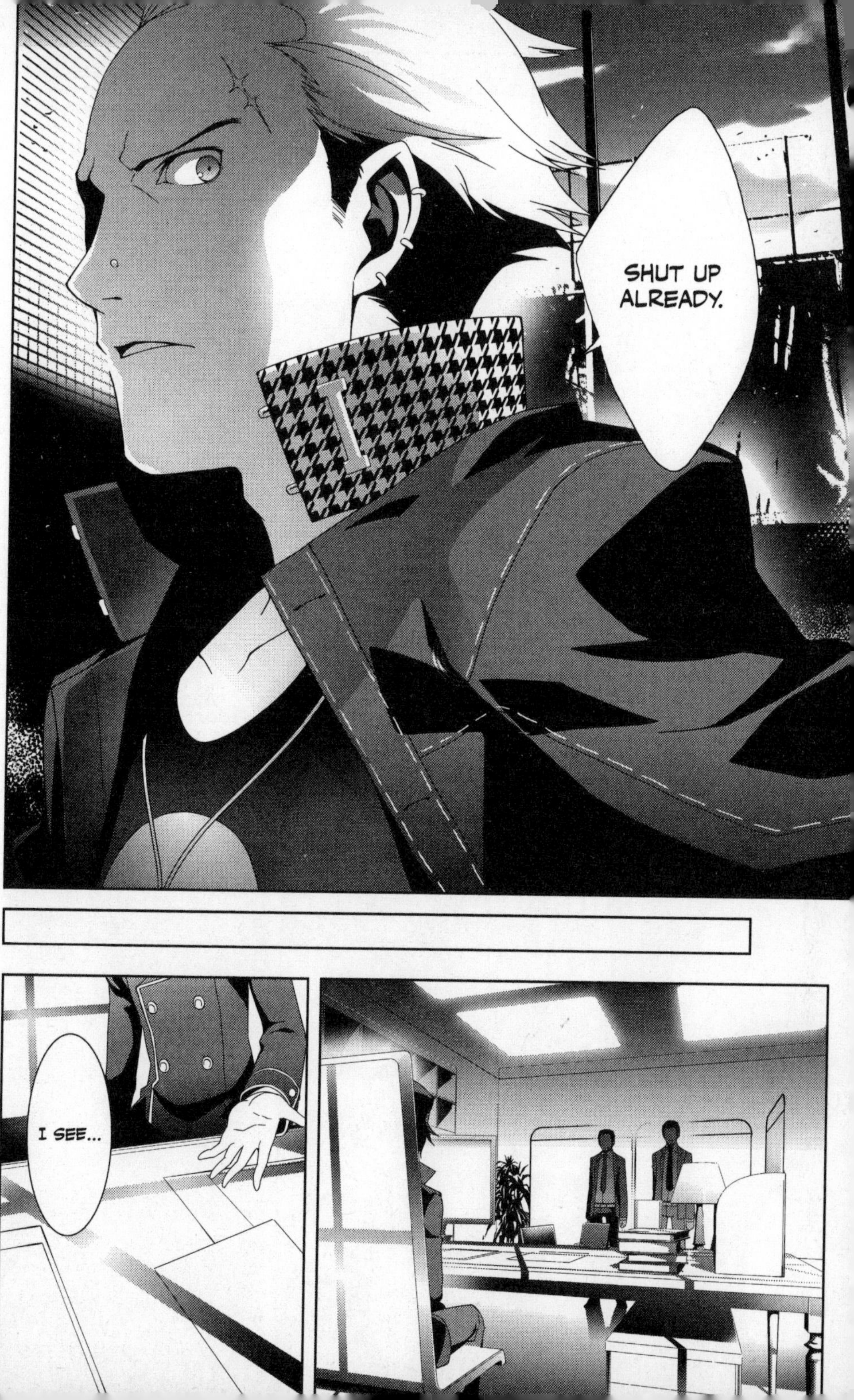
SHUT UP ALREADY.
I SEE...

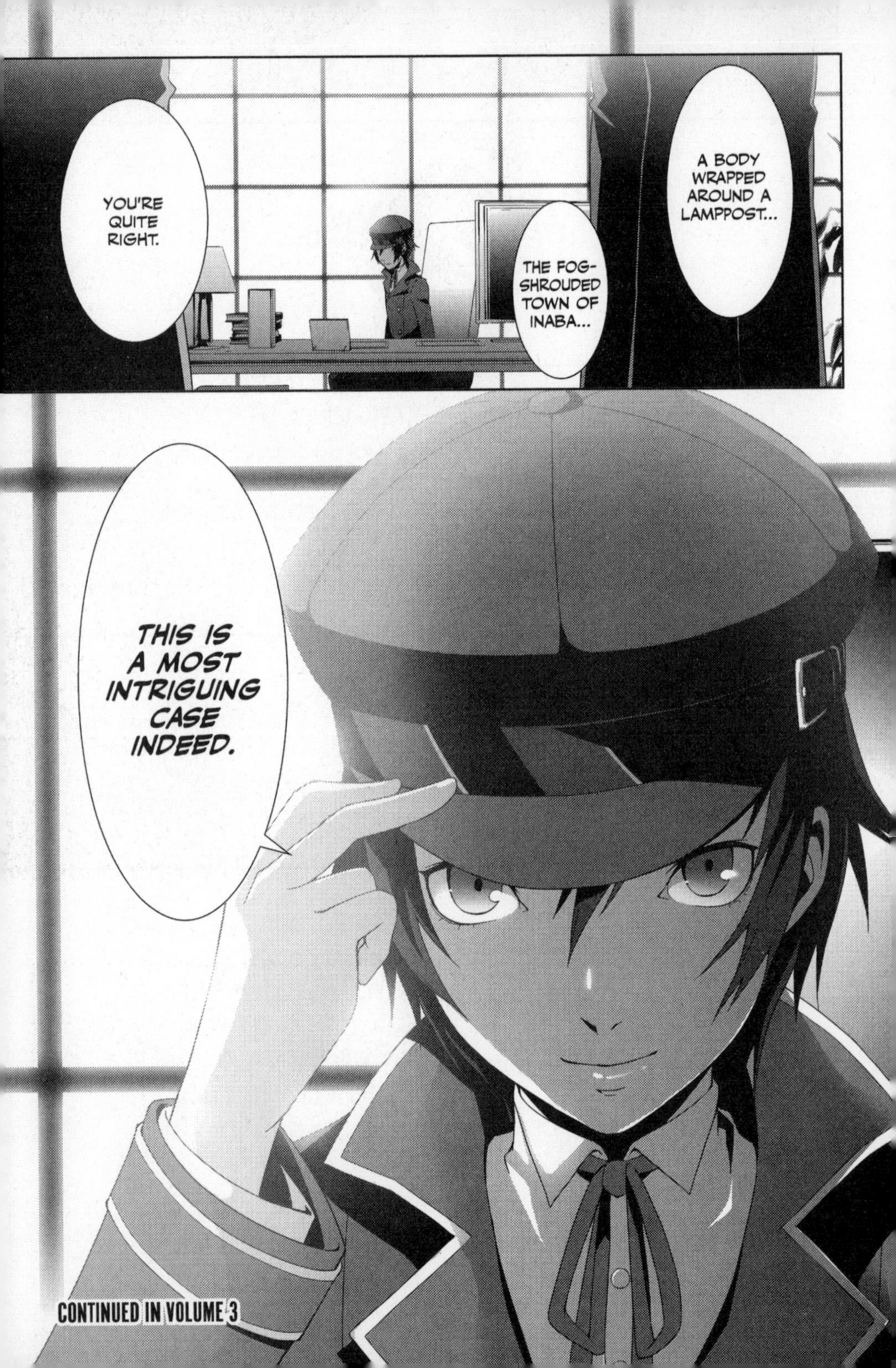
A BODY WRAPPED AROUND A LAMPPOST...
THE FOG-SHROUDED TOWN OF INABA...
YOU'RE QUITE RIGHT.
THIS IS A MOST INTRIGUING CASE INDEED.
CONTINUED IN VOLUME 3

sogabe now vii (seven)

thank you for purchasing volume 2 of the persona 4 manga!

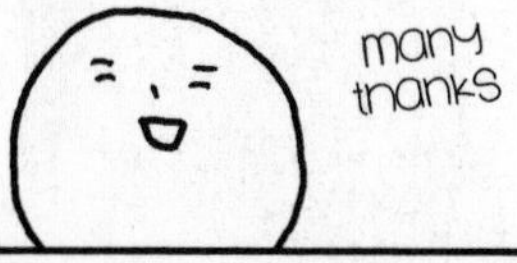
many thanks

lately, I've been spending a lot of time day-dreaming about the places I'd like to visit.

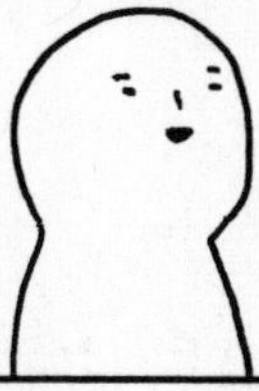

I wish I had gotten my driver's license when I had the chance.

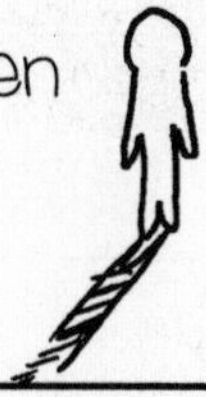

last year, just prior to the release of volume 1, I visited a very rural area. I climbed mountains, got really close to a waterfall, and even saw the ocean. the trip wasn't intended as a location scouting expedition for the persona 4 manga, but it kind of turned out that way.

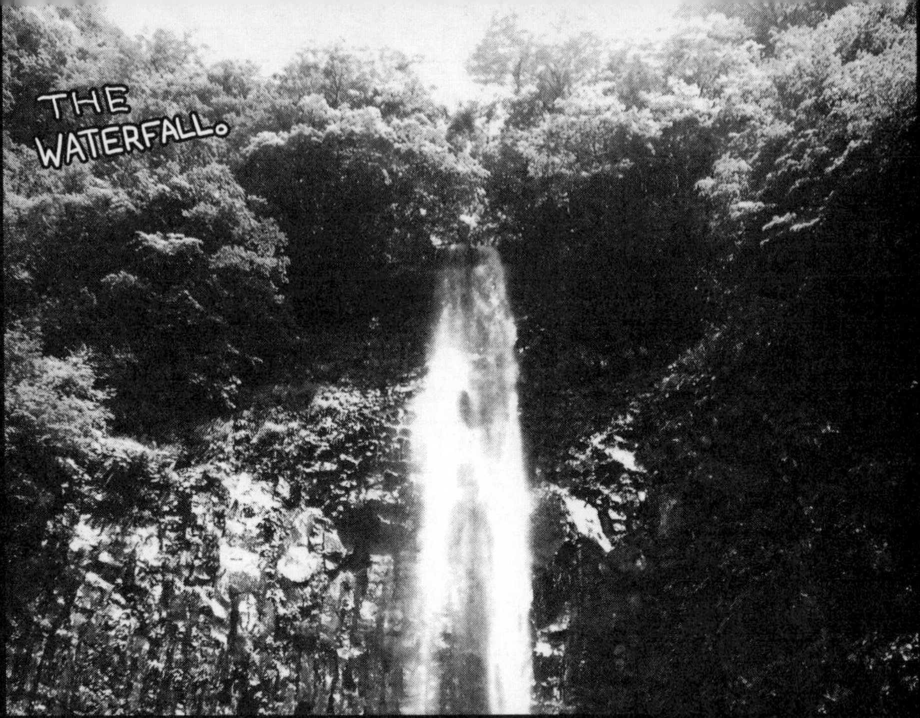
THE WATERFALL.

I took this photo with my cell phone while basking in the negative ions.

But enough of that. Did you enjoy volume 2?

I've been adding a few little things that weren't in the game. I wonder if you noticed...

regardless, I very much appreciate all of the wonderful support I've been getting. a great big thank you to everyone who came out to my autograph session, the people who comment on my blog, and of course all of you who have taken the time to read my mangas. thank you so much, from the bottom of my heart. I hope you enjoy the next volume as well!

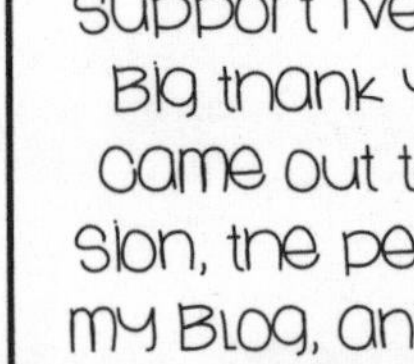

完 -FIN-

(NOT FUNNY ENOUGH?)

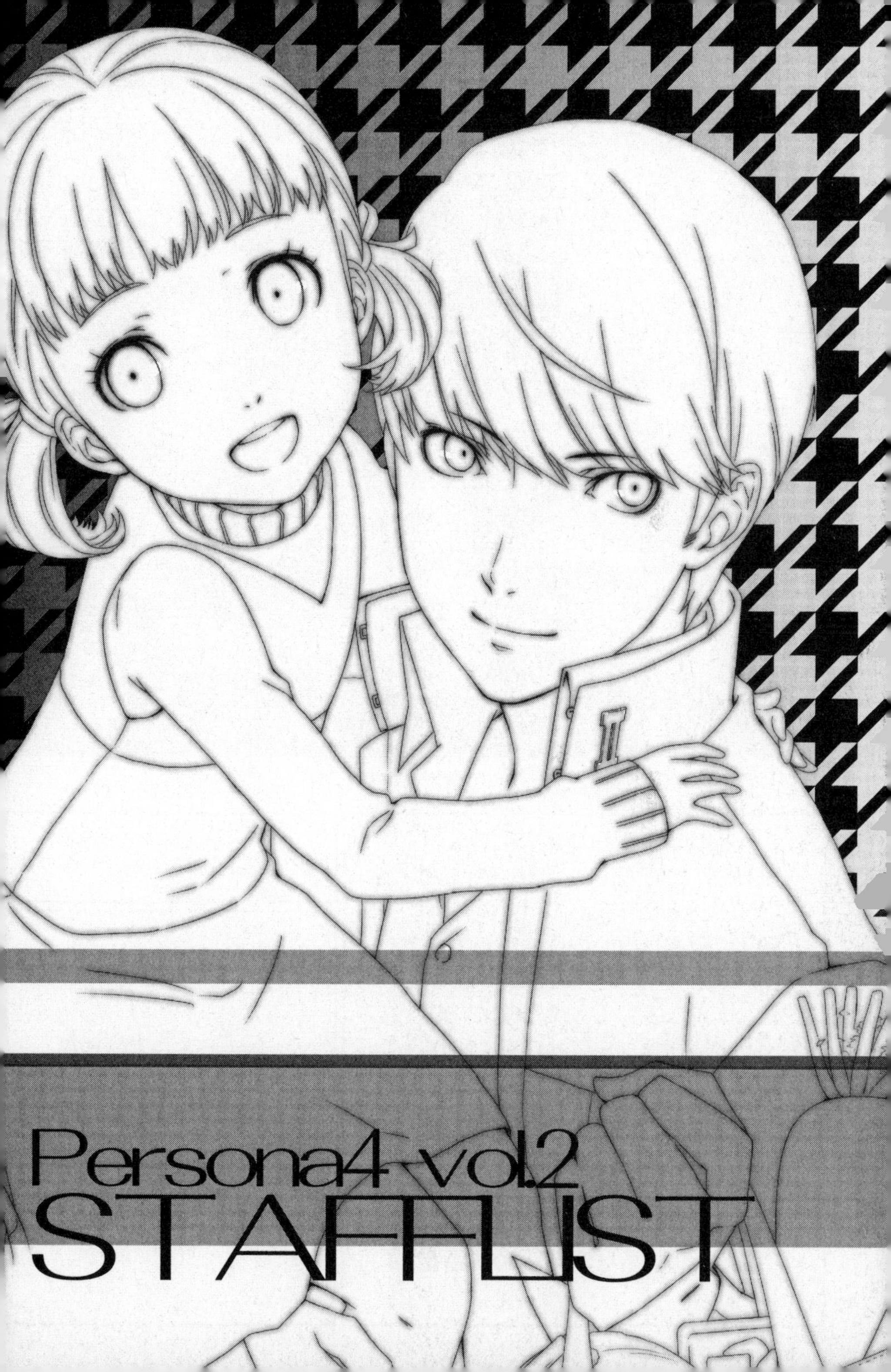
Persona4 vol.2
STAFFLIST

Original Work
ATLUS

Original Art Director
Shigenori SOEJIMA (ATLUS)

Manga / Story
Shuji SOGABE

Production / 3D Modeling & Layout / Art
Ryota HONMA (studioss)

Lead Artist
Haruna AOKI (studioss)

Art Team
Asami SAKUMA (studioss)

Design
Keiko SEKI (SELFISH GENE)
studioss

Editing
Naoki IIJIMA

Special Thanks
Junichi MORI (ATLUS)
Ikuya KOBAYASHI (ATLUS)

PERSONA 4 ORIGINAL STAFF

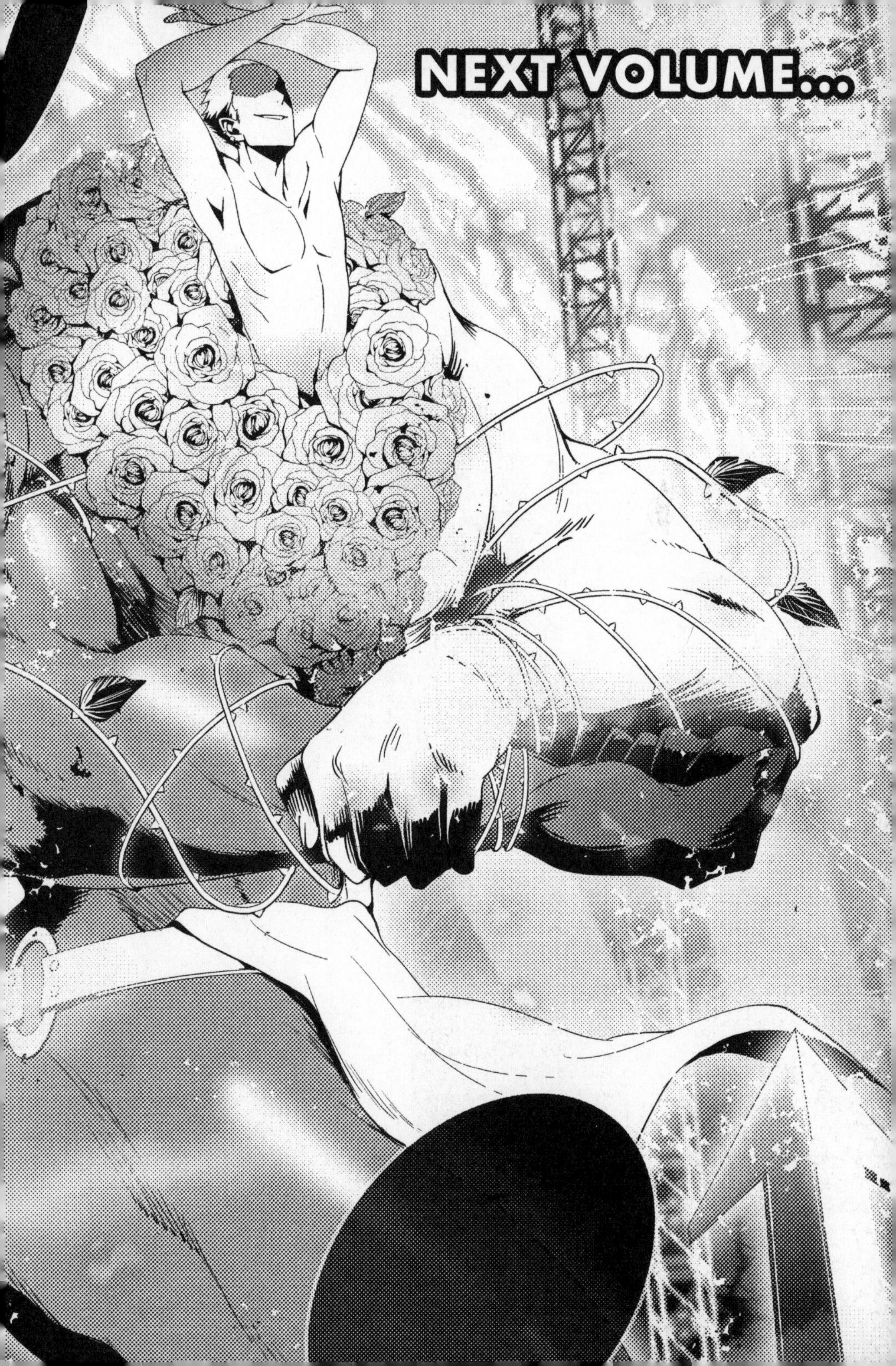
NEXT VOLUME...

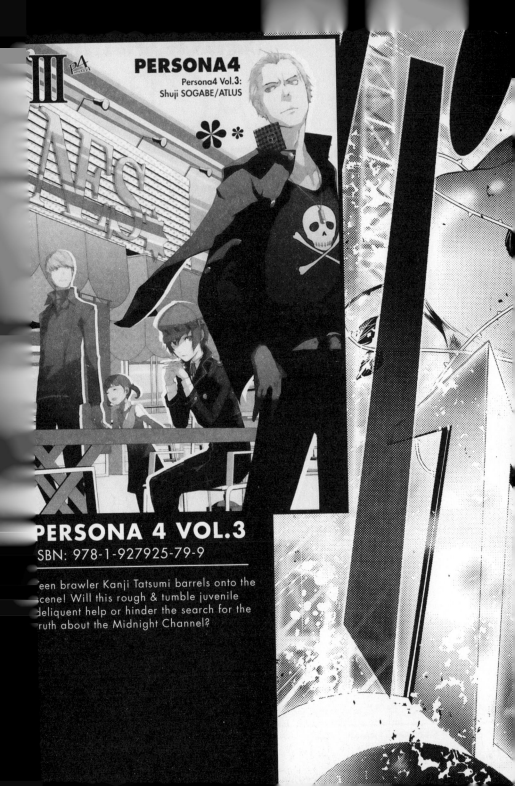

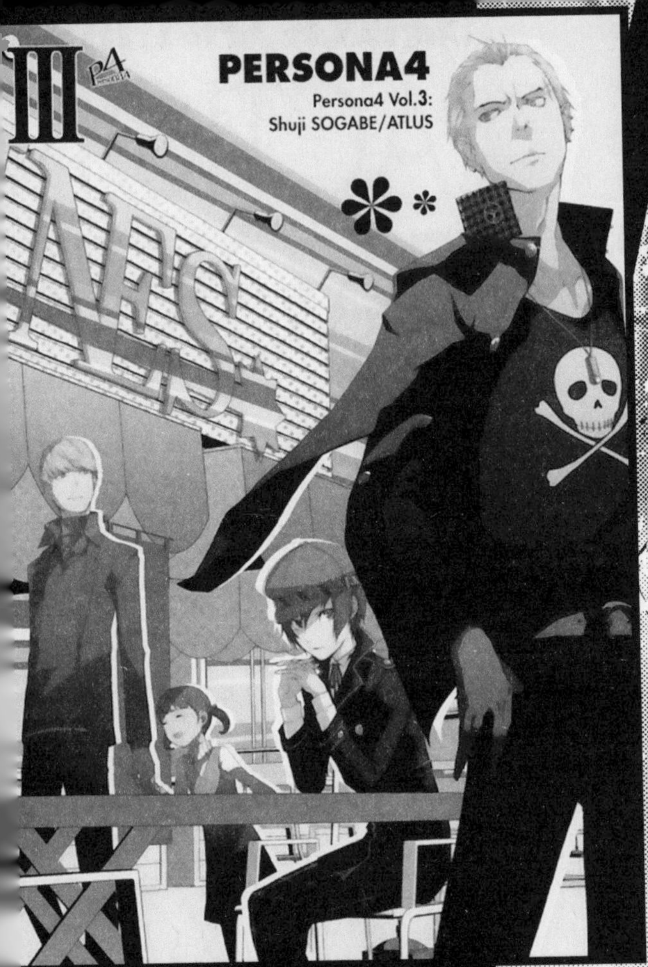
III
P4
PERSONA4
Persona4 Vol.3:
Shuji SOGABE/ATLUS

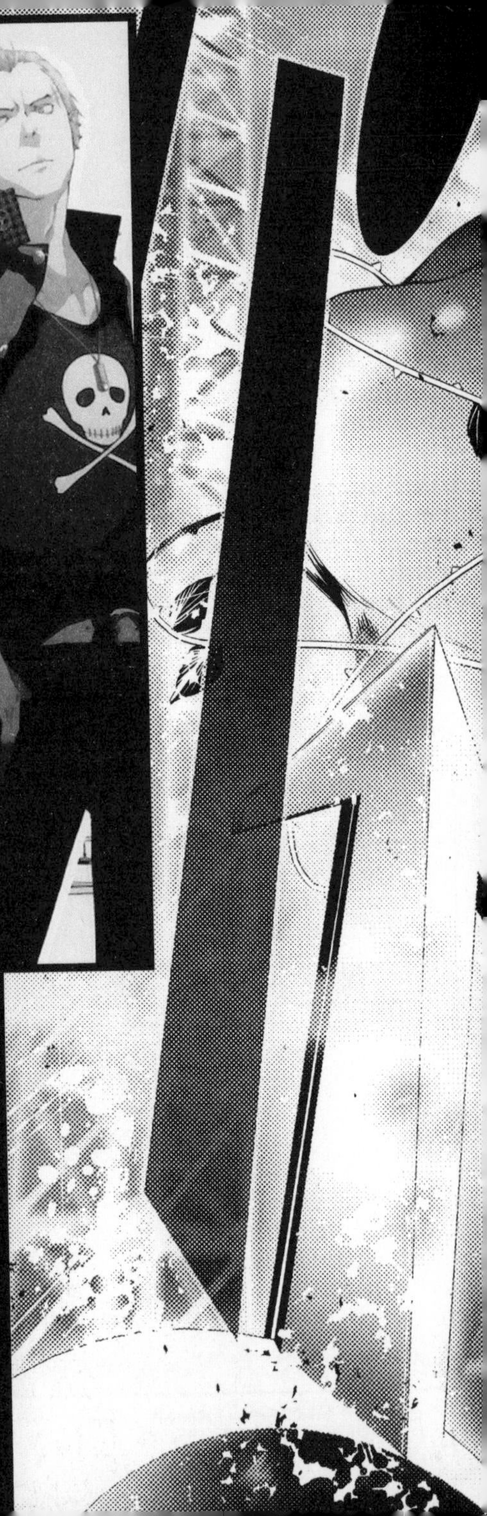

PERSONA 4 VOL.3

ISBN: 978-1-927925-79-9

Teen brawler Kanji Tatsumi barrels onto the scene! Will this rough & tumble juvenile deliquent help or hinder the search for the truth about the Midnight Channel?

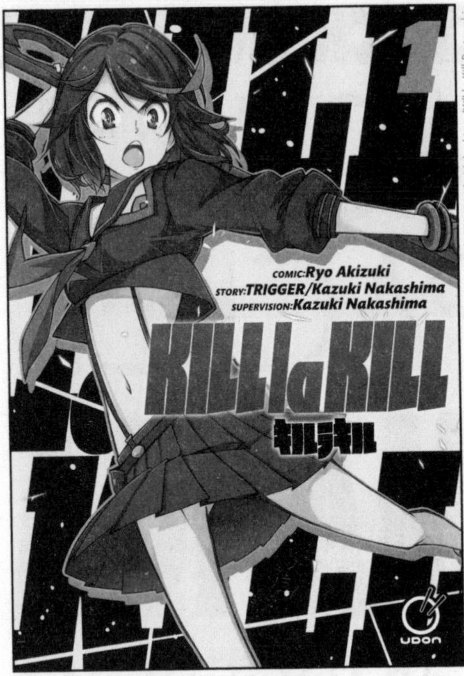
1
COMIC: Ryo Akizuki
STORY: TRIGGER/Kazuki Nakashima
SUPERVISION: Kazuki Nakashima
KILL la KILL
キルラキル
UDON

KILL LA KILL Volume 1

ISBN: 978-1-927925-49-2

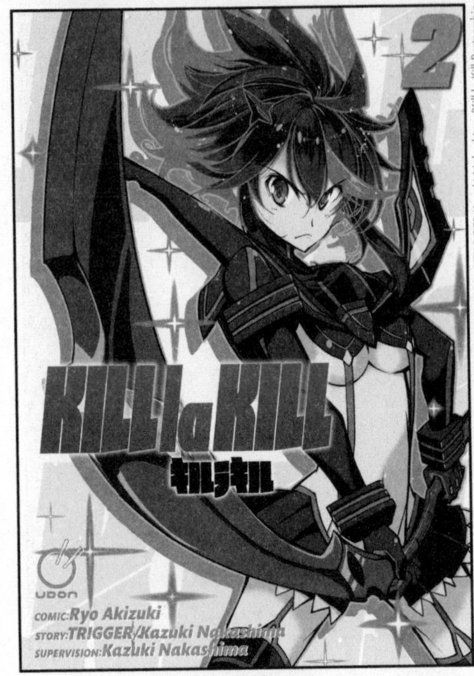
2
KILL la KILL
キルラキル
UDON
COMIC: Ryo Akizuki
STORY: TRIGGER/Kazuki Nakashima
SUPERVISION: Kazuki Nakashima

KILL LA KILL Volume 2

ISBN: 978-1-927925-54-6

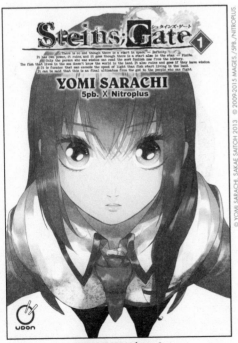

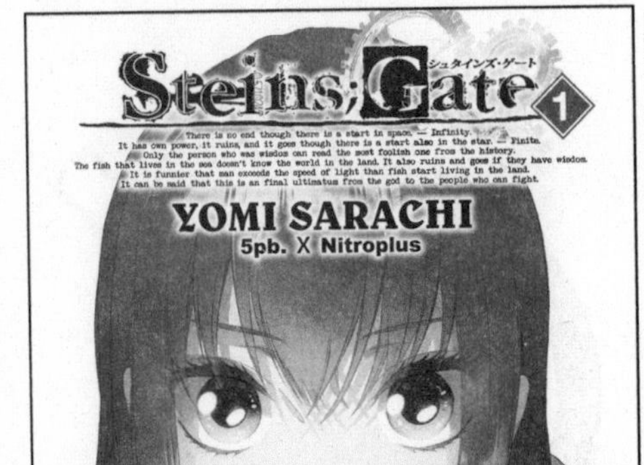
Steins;Gate
シュタインズ・ゲート
1
There is no end though there is a start in space. — Infinity.
It has own power, it ruins, and it goes though there is a start also in the star. — Finite.
Only the person who was wisdom can read the most foolish one from the history.
The fish that lives in the sea doesn't know the world in the land. It also ruins and goes if they have wisdom.
It is funnier that man exceeds the speed of light than fish start living in the land.
It can be said that this is an final ultimatum from the god to the people who can fight.
YOMI SARACHI
5pb. X Nitroplus
UDON

STEINS;GATE Volume 1

ISBN: 978-1-927925-50-8

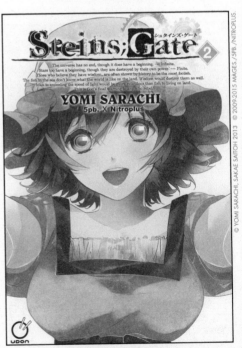

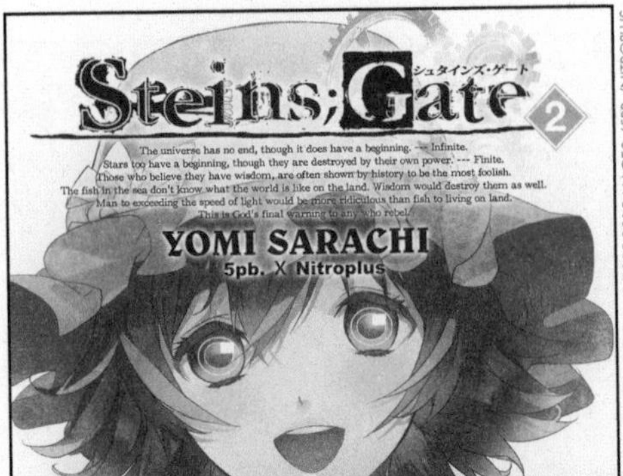
Steins;Gate
シュタインズ・ゲート
2
The universe has no end, though it does have a beginning. --- Infinite.
Stars too have a beginning, though they are destroyed by their own power. --- Finite.
Those who believe they have wisdom, are often shown by history to be the most foolish.
The fish in the sea don't know what the world is like on the land. Wisdom would destroy them as well.
Man to exceeding the speed of light would be more ridiculous than fish to living on land.
This is God's final warning to any who rebel.
YOMI SARACHI
5pb. X Nitroplus
UDON

STEINS;GATE Volume 2

ISBN: 978-1-927925-55-3

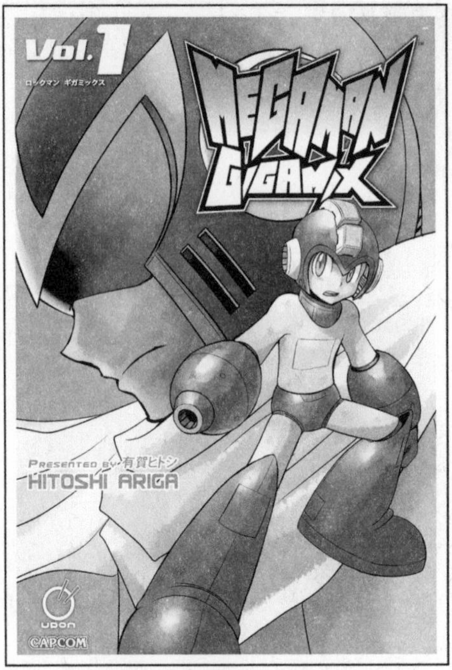
Vol. 1
ロックマン ギガミックス
MEGAMAN GIGAMIX
PRESENTED BY: 有賀ヒトシ
HITOSHI ARIGA
UDON
CAPCOM

MEGA MAN GIGAMIX Volume 1
ISBN: 978-1-926778-23-5

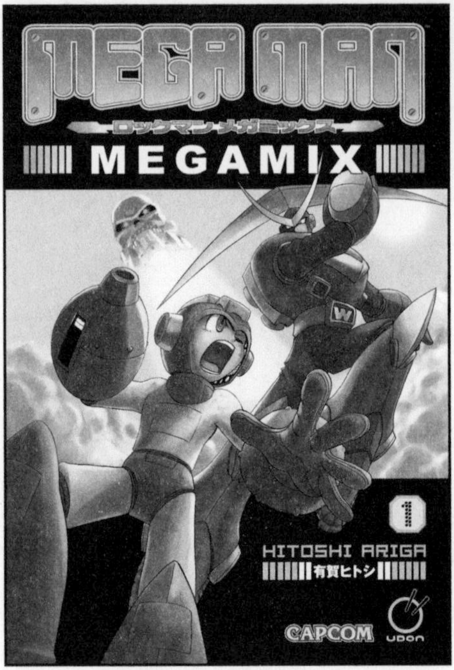
MEGA MAN
ロックマン・メガミックス
MEGAMIX
1
HITOSHI ARIGA
有賀ヒトシ
CAPCOM
UDON

MEGA MAN MEGAMIX Volume 1
ISBN: 978-1-897376-16-4

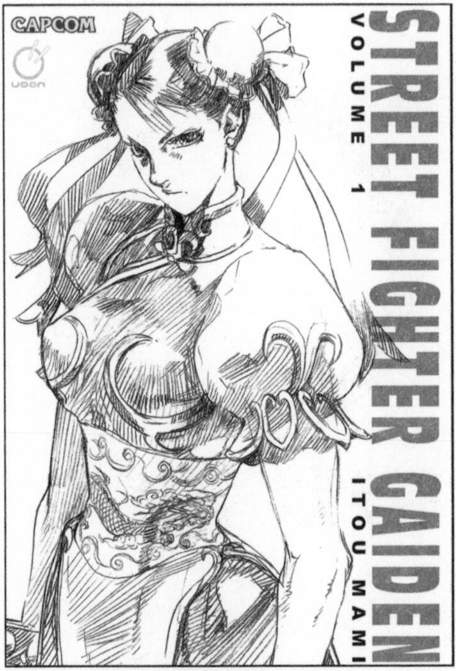
CAPCOM
UDON
STREET FIGHTER GAIDEN
VOLUME 1
ITOU MAMI

STREET FIGHTER GAIDEN Volume 1
ISBN: 978-1-926778-11-2

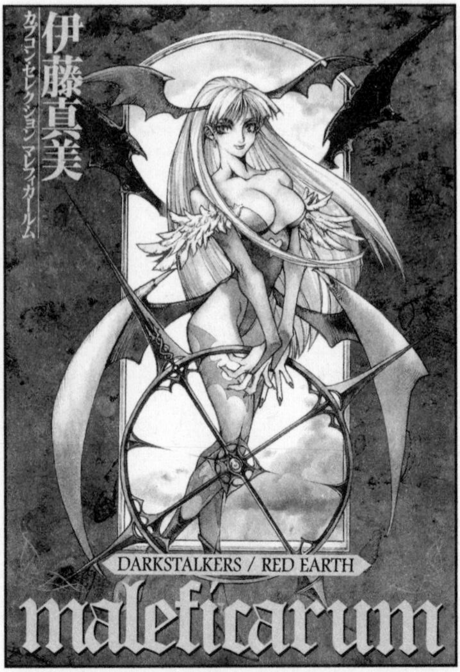
伊藤真美
カプコン・セレクション マレフィカールーム
DARKSTALKERS / RED EARTH
maleficarum

DARKSTALKERS/RED EARTH: MALEFICARUM Volume 1
ISBN: 978-1-926778-08-2